# IFIP Advances in Information and Communication Technology

693

## IFIP Advances in Information and Communication Technology

The IFIP AICT series publishes state-of-the-art results in the sciences and technologies of information and communication. The scope of the series includes: foundations of computer science; software theory and practice; education; computer applications in technology; communication systems; systems modeling and optimization; information systems; ICT and society; computer systems technology; security and protection in information processing systems; artificial intelligence; and human-computer interaction.

Edited volumes and proceedings of refereed international conferences in computer science and interdisciplinary fields are featured. These results often precede journal publication and represent the most current research.

The principal aim of the IFIP AICT series is to encourage education and the dissemination and exchange of information about all aspects of computing.

More information about this series at https://link.springer.com/bookseries/6102

Eunika Mercier-Laurent · Gülgün Kayakutlu ·
Mieczyslaw Lech Owoc · Abdul Wahid ·
Karl Mason
Editors

# Artificial Intelligence for Knowledge Management, Energy and Sustainability

10th IFIP International Workshop on Artificial Intelligence for Knowledge Management, AI4KMES 2023
Krakow, Poland, September 30 – October 1, 2023
Revised Selected Papers

Springer

*Editors*
Eunika Mercier-Laurent
University of Reims Champagne-Ardenne
Reims, France

Gülgün Kayakutlu
Energy Institute
Istanbul Technical University
Istanbul, Istanbul, Türkiye

Mieczyslaw Lech Owoc
Wroclaw University of Economics and Business
Wroclaw, Poland

Abdul Wahid
University of Galway
Galway, Ireland

Karl Mason
University of Galway
Galway, Ireland

ISSN 1868-4238 ISSN 1868-422X (electronic)
IFIP Advances in Information and Communication Technology
ISBN 978-3-031-61071-4 ISBN 978-3-031-61069-1 (eBook)
https://doi.org/10.1007/978-3-031-61069-1



This Springer imprint is published by the registered company Springer Nature Switzerland AG
The registered company address is: Gewerbestrasse 11, 6330 Cham, Switzerland

# Preface

After the initial IFIP TC12.6 AI4KM workshop at ECAI (European Conference on Artificial Intelligence) 2012 held in Montpellier, France, in 2023 our workshop in extended form was back at ECAI 2023. Actually, it brought together in Krakow, Poland, the IFIP TC12.6 and TC12.11 working groups and our colleagues from the University of Galway working on AI for Sustainable Agriculture.

This common workshop was the second AI4KMES after those at IJCAI-21, Montréal, held online. The virtual conference, exposition and social events were amazing, however, they still lacked human exchanges, energy and serendipity.

Combining Knowledge Management, Energy and Sustainability leads to better understanding of the scope of each and of connections between the topics.

Sustainability covers many concerns often addressed separately. The answers of Chat GPT clearly demonstrate this separation. However, all elements influence each other and should be considered from various perspectives. The holistic approach to Knowledge Management provides a deeper understanding of the interconnections between the various domains and their interplay.

During these two days the participants improved their understanding of overall aspects of sustainability through various lenses and their connections with Climate Change.

Some information about the reviewing process:

We received 49 papers, of which 27 papers (10 long and 17 short) were accepted for presentation during these two days. The submitted papers were single-blindly reviewed; the acceptance rate is 55.1%. Number of reviews per paper: two or three in case of conflict. The invited speakers were selected to represent the current trends in the addressed fields and interest of the audience. They provided their abstracts, and their presentations are available on the workshop website.

The accepted papers covered a large scope of topics related to sustainability in various contexts such as smart cities, agriculture, energy and gas production and distribution, industry, management and biodiversity. The authors covered most of the 17 SD UN goals.

The three invited talks by Anne Nowé, Antoni Ligęza and Mieczyslaw Owoc emphasized the growing importance of multi-agent systems (MAS), the need for accurate explanations in neural network-based applications, and possible fake detection or insufficient understanding of sustainability and processing using knowledge-based AI approaches.

Anne Nowé did not find time to write a detailed paper, but she presented her work on the NRGcoin project https://nrgcoin.org/ with emphasis on optimizing energy consumption with Multi-agent Systems, illustrated by control of windmills.

At the end of the second day the present PC members and organizers selected the best papers to be extended for this volume.

This selection focused on new contributions in any research area concerning the use of any AI field for Knowledge Management, Energy and Sustainability. An extended Program Committee then evaluated the last versions of the proposals, leading to this volume. The authors of 7 papers were asked for corrections and they made the corrections according to the reviewers' remarks.

The workshop opened with a tribute to Prof. Danielle Boulanger, who passed away last year. She was among the initiators of the AI4KM series and made a great contribution to the quality of these workshops and related publications.

Eunika Mercier-Laurent introduced the covered fields and their interconnections in the article entitled "**Artificial Intelligence, Sustainability and Climate Change".**

Our first invited speaker Prof. Antoni Ligęza presented the ongoing and innovative research of his team in the area of eXplainable Artificial Intelligence. His paper titled "**In Search for Model-Driven eXplainable Artificial Intelligence**" reports on this research. A traditional XAI task is considered as finding an explanation of the model generated via Machine Learning by identifying the most influential variables for local decision-making. The proposed approach moves the explanatory process to the knowledge-level dimension. It is oriented towards Model Discovery, i.e. the internal structure and functions of the components.

The following article "An intelligent chatbot based on hybrid approach implementing technical knowledge to support maintenance and training activities at Electricity of France (EDF)" relates industrial experience in building a hybrid chatbot to assist technicians in installation and maintenance of an air conditioner in a nuclear plant. This chatbot elaborated by a team of engineers, designers, data scientists, technicians and academics mimics the human expert by combining "design shits", data and experience.

The next paper entitled **"Supporting Food Computing with Ontologies and Artificial Intelligence Methods for Sustainability"** investigates the potential of combining food ontologies and AI in the food sector for enhanced sustainability. This combination can foster sustainable food systems, underscoring how semantic structures and AI can facilitate precision agriculture, sustainable food choices, personalized diets and climate change mitigation. The authors present an overview of food ontologies and knowledge graphs highlighting their structures and focal points, and illustrate the value of ontological reasoning through practical food domain examples, using SPARQL queries and ontological reasoning for insightful knowledge derivation. This article ends by a discussion on how to combine AI and ontologies to create new knowledge resources for improved data integration and management.

The authors of **"The use of semantic networks for the categorization of prosumers"** focus on sustainable business by creating a synergy buyer-seller. A consumer provides opinions, suggests solutions, and tests and evaluates the advantages and disadvantages of the product. This requires an identification of groups of consumers susceptible to cooperation with the organization. The authors experiment with the use of semantic networks for the categorization of consumers and defining the category of prosumers. The results presented in the article were obtained through the application of triangulation of research methods, such as analytical literature review, computer simulation conducted using Protégé software, and a research experiment consisting of simulation of selected problem situations.

The next paper entitled **"Methods for mitigating gender bias in binary classification models – a comparative analysis"** addresses the gender issues of UN SD goals 2 and 10. The growing importance of data requires verifications that the methods used to analyze it do not return unfair results. The purpose of this article is to identify gender bias in the selected dataset and compare which of the selected solutions gives the best result when used to mitigate the impact of this type of unfairness on the model's predictions.

Generative AI influences the education process to the point that teachers have to reconsider their teaching methods. The authors of **"Chat GPT as a Learning Tool in Business Education. Re-search on Students' Motivation"** studied the influence of Chat GPT as a learning tool in business education on the motivation of students and their learning experience. It can vary depending on implementation, context or individual student characteristics. They propose a diagnosis tool to evaluate the use of ChatGPT by Wroclaw University of Economics students considering motivation, scope of questions/tasks, frequency of use, concerns and satisfaction. The related knowledge verification methods need also to evolve.

The next part of this book is devoted to the management of energy systems.

The first article in this part titled **"Integrating Artificial Intelligence into Electric Vehicle Energy Systems: A Survey"** discusses the contribution to planet protection and changes introduced by electric vehicles. Integrating electric vehicles into existing electricity grids, refuelling stations and supply chains presents significant challenges that can be effectively addressed through the implementation of artificial intelligence solutions. After investigation of the challenges associated with the widespread adoption of electric vehicles in society the authors analyse in detail how artificial intelligence can facilitate the smooth integration of electric vehicles. The paper provides also a detailed investigation of the life-cycle emissions of electric vehicles and examines the limitations of existing research in this area and suggests potential avenues for future research.

The following article **"Towards sustainable power systems: exploring the opportunities of multi-task learning for battery degradation forecasting"** focuses on the battery for electric vehicles.

The task of developing a reliable and long-lasting battery system remains a major obstacle to the expansion of the electric vehicle fleet and the improvement of storage systems in renewable energy plants. To overcome this challenge, improving battery ageing models to accurately forecast the battery degradation trajectory is a complex but critical step. The authors propose to address these challenges using a sequence-to-sequence multi-task learning (MTL) method. Empirical results on battery ageing datasets show that the proposed model enhances the data efficiency and precision of capacity and power degradation forecasts for lithium-ion battery cells. Furthermore, it generates new insights into the trade-offs and key decisions for incorporating battery ageing models into the MTL paradigm.

The next article titled **"The Influence of Neural Networks on Hydropower Plant Management in Agriculture: Addressing Challenges and Exploring Untapped Opportunities"** points out the importance of stable renewable energy and water management for sustainable agriculture, especially in drought areas.

A key concern is the potential conflict between electricity generation and agricultural water needs. Prioritizing water for electricity generation can reduce irrigation availability in agriculture during crucial periods like droughts, impacting crop yields and regional food security. Coordination between electricity and agricultural water allocation is necessary to ensure optimal and environmentally sound practices. This work is a call for attention and highlights the potential risks of deploying neural network-based hydropower plant management software without proper scrutiny and control. To address these concerns, the authors propose the adoption of the Agriculture Conscious Hydropower Plant Management framework, aiming to maximise electricity production while prioritizing stable irrigation for agriculture. They also suggest a set of regulatory measures to promote model transparency and robustness, certifying software that makes conscious and intelligent water allocation decisions.

The authors of **"Classification Tree Based AI System for Short Term Prediction for Heat and Power Plants"** note that companies supplying electrical energy rely mainly on long-term agreements with electricity producers. In reality, the daily demand should be precisely predicted for 48 hours considering current weather conditions. A similar analysis applies also for heat and power plants, but the temperature of returning water is most important. Time series models can be used for forecasting. The authors propose to build an AI system to choose the future profile from historical data with time series of 24 hours. Then, these empirical profiles are clustered with hierarchic and non-hierarchic clustering procedures to form homogeneous groups (types of profiles). Finally, the classification methods are applied using weather data and observed demand from previous days (up to one week backwards). The authors propose a measure for the forecasting evaluation.

The article by our invited speaker Mieczyslaw Owoc fits perfectly into the next part devoted to some sustainability aspects.

His paper on **"Usability of Honeybee Algorithms in Practice. Towards Nature-inspired Sustainable Development"**, inspired also by his beekeeping activities, describes the usefulness of Honeybee algorithms (HBAs) for complex problem solving with the focus on optimization and practical usability of these algorithms, exploring their strengths and limitations in real-world applications, particularly within the context of sustainable development. HBAs demonstrate impressive performance in finding optimal solutions, particularly for large-scale and dynamic problems, adaptability (their decentralized nature allows them to handle changes in the environment effectively) and sustainability (they often require fewer resources compared to traditional optimization methods, contributing to a more sustainable approach). Prof. Owoc presents some examples of resource optimization in energy usage in buildings, transportation networks and industrial processes, and in efficient waste management and optimized renewable energy integration.

The next article is **"Automatic Coral Morphotypes Detection with YOLO: A Deep Learning Approach for Efficient and Accurate Coral Reef Monitoring".**

The protection and preservation of marine biodiversity includes the care of coral reefs, which are declining rapidly mostly as a consequence of human activity. Conservation efforts rely on monitoring of coral abundance and composition as predominant indicators of ecosystem health and management success. While manual monitoring of coral abundance is not trivial, artificial intelligence-based automatization can help to improve efficiency and accuracy. The authors experiment with a methodology using YOLOv5-based deep learning for automatic detection of corals and classification by morphotype, representing an important step toward streamlining machine-assisted coral reef monitoring.

The authors of **"Answering Key Questions about Air Pollution Dynamics in Ho Chi Minh City: A Spatiotemporal Analysis Using the XAI-SHAP Clustering Approach"** focus on fresh air preservation in big cities. Their study investigates the impact of various air pollutants in Ho Chi Minh City (HCMC), Vietnam, employing a supervised clustering approach that integrates Shapley Additive exPlanations (SHAP) values with a publicly available outdoor air quality dataset. The research focuses on identifying influential pollutant factors, affected city regions, their impact on surrounding areas, and the effectiveness of supervised clustering using SHAP values in pinpointing intersections between impacted stations. Key findings indicate a pronounced influence of Nitrogen Dioxide (NO2) and Temperature on morning air quality, largely attributed to traffic congestion. Conversely, Carbon Monoxide (CO) and Ozone (O3) significantly affect the afternoon air quality, influenced by solar radiation and industrial activities.

The authors of the article titled **"Crowdsourcing as a tool for Smart City within Sustainable Development"** study innovations in management methods for effective urban resources management. The Smart City (SC) concept, increasingly adopted in various global metropolises, significantly enhances residents' quality of life, safety, social participation, and operational efficiency of urban areas, aligning with the crucial paradigm of Sustainable Development (SD). A key initiative underpinning the SC model is crowdsourcing, a method whereby urban administrations gather knowledge and feedback from their citizens.

This paper presents findings from an examination of scientific literature indexed in the Scopus database, using keywords: 'crowdsourcing', 'smart cities', and 'sustainable development'. Employing Classical Literature Review (CLR) and Systematic Literature Review (SLR) methodologies, supplemented by bibliometric analysis with VOSviewer software, this study conducts an in-depth investigation of keywords and research themes closely linked to the development of crowdsourcing within the SC framework, specifically in the context of SD.

The next article is devoted to the **"Model of Relationship between Circular Economy and Industry 5.0".** The author studies the interactions between Industry 5.0 and Circular Economy in the European Union countries. The primary goal of this research is to develop an econometric model demonstrating the impact of CE activities on the advancement toward Industry 5.0. The integration of Sustainable Development (SD) principles across various sectors of industry is also considered. To conduct this research the author uses the selected indicators and data from Eurostat, analyzed using taxonomic method and a regression algorithm.

Information technology (IT) generates also a huge amount of CO2 and waste. While we can find some works on carbon emission by software, the authors of **"Reduction of carbon dioxide emissions of IT hardware"** focus on hardware, vital for running the software. The greening of hardware is also mandatory for achieving sustainable and environmentally friendly technological advancements. The authors study factors such as hardware infrastructure, energy consumption and the carbon footprint of data centers and communication networks. They study the various strategies and technologies that have been developed to reduce CO2 emissions during computations. These include energy efficient designs, advanced cooling techniques, renewable energy integration, audits and controls, and optimization algorithms such as modern AI tools. The advantages and limitations of each approach are discussed, with a focus on their potential for widespread adoption and scalability. The authors point out the need for continuous research and innovation to overcome existing barriers and accelerate the adoption of environmentally friendly hardware systems on a global scale.

We would like to thank the members of the Program Committee for reviewing the submitted papers and helping put together an interesting program. We would also like to thank all authors and our invited speakers Ann Nowé, Antoni Ligęza and Mieczyslaw Owoc for their inspiring presentations.

Finally, our thanks go to the local Organizing Committee and all the supporting institutions and organizations.

We hope that you enjoy reading these papers.

March 2024

Eunika Mercier-Laurent
Gülgün Kayakutlu
Mieczyslaw Lech Owoc
Karl Mason
Abdul Wahid

# Organization

## Program Chairs and Volume Editors

| | |
|---|---|
| Eunika Mercier-Laurent | University of Reims Champagne Ardenne, France |
| Gülgün Kayakutlu | Technical University of Istanbul, Turkey |
| Mieczyslaw L. Owoc | Wroclaw University of Economics and Business, Poland |
| Karl Mason | University of Galway, Ireland |
| Abdul Wahid | University of Galway, Ireland |

## Program Committee

| | |
|---|---|
| Weronika Adrian | AGH University of Science and Technology, Poland |
| Imene Brigui | Emlyon Business School, France |
| Noël Conruyt | University of Reunion, France |
| Anne Dourgnon | EDF Research Center, France |
| Helena Dudycz | Wroclaw University of Economics and Business, Poland |
| Konstantin M. Golubev | General Knowledge Machine Research Group, Ukraine |
| Marco Haimann | IAE Lyon School of Management, France |
| Marcin Hernes | Wroclaw University of Economics and Business, Poland |
| Otthein Hertzog | Jacobs University, Germany |
| Knut Hinkelmann | University of Applied Sciences and Arts, Switzerland |
| Gülgün Kayakutlu | Istanbul Technical University, Turkey |
| M. Ozgur Kayalica | Istanbul Technical University, Turkey |
| Krzysztof Kluza | AGH University of Science and Technology, Poland |
| Mario Lezoche | University of Lorraine, France |
| Antoni Ligęza | AGH University of Science and Technology, Poland |
| Vítězslav Máša | Brno University of Technology, Czech Republic |
| Nada Matta | Troyes Technical University, France |
| Eunika Mercier-Laurent | University of Reims Champagne Ardenne, France |
| Cristina Monsone | University of Gyor, Hungary |
| Mieczyslaw Lech Owoc | Wroclaw University of Economics and Business, Poland |
| Maciej Pondel | Wroclaw University of Economics and Business, Poland |
| Vincent Ribiere | IKI, Thailand |
| Michael Stankosky | George Washington University, USA |
| Abdul Sattar | Griffith University, Australia |
| Frederique Segond | Inria, France |
| Guillermo Simari | Universidad Nacional del Sur, Argentina |

| | |
|---|---|
| Guilaine Talens | University Lyon 3, France |
| Eric Thivant | University Lyon 3, France |
| Abdul Wahid | University of Galway, Ireland |
| Krystian Wojtkiewicz | Wroclaw University of Science and Technology, Poland |
| Janusz Wojtusiak | George Mason University, USA |

## Local Organizing Committee

| | |
|---|---|
| Grzegorz Nalepa | Jagiellonian University, Poland |
| Krzysztof Kluza | AGH University of Science and Technology, Poland |

# Contents

# Artificial Intelligence, Sustainability and Climate Change

Eunika Mercier-Laurent(✉)

CReSTIC Centre de Recherche en Sciences et Technologies de l'Information et de la Communication - UR 3804, University of Reims Champagne Ardenne, Reims, France
eunika.mercier-laurent@univ-reims.fr

**Abstract.** This paper presents a short introduction to the AI4S workshop aiming in painting a "big picture" of various interrelated aspects of Sustainability and Climate Change. The connections between energy, agriculture, water and technology, usually addressed separately, are vital to properly address the given challenges.

The concern about the sustainability and climate change weakly considers in the debates the pollution induced by technology and innovation. While technology produces twofold effect – benefits and waste, the capacity of available technology and in particular Artificial Intelligence for related complex problems solving is still underexplored.

The knowledge-based AI and connectionist approaches and techniques combined with adequate thinking may innovate the way of managing industry, administration and in other contexts and improve the effectiveness of efforts in sustaining the Planet. Knowledge-based AI help improving the explanation of the results got from Deep learning.

After the introduction aiming in connecting the "dots" between AI, sustainability and Climate actions, this paper presents shortly some contribution of AI to Climate actions and comments the conditions for minimizing the footprint.

**Keywords:** Artificial Intelligence · Digital Transformation · Method · Sustainability · Sustainable Development · Planet Crisis · Climate Change · Data Obesity

## 1 Introduction – Sustainability and Climate Change

Sustainability is a broad concept and one of the least understood. There are many ways to define and address these issues depending on various perspectives and motivations.

The concern is not new. Antoine de Saint Exupéry, the pioneering French aviator, journalist and writer emphasizes the beauty of our planet Earth (Terre des hommes) and necessity to protect it [1].

Since the early days of intensive industrialization, a number of authors have tried to warn of the consequences of such rapid development for our environment [2–4]. Nobody paid attention to these voices. Globalization and the growing intensity of business, amplified by the internet, Covid pandemics and intensive agriculture accelerated the decline


Published by Springer Nature Switzerland AG 2024
E. Mercier-Laurent et al. (Eds.): AI4KMES 2023, IFIP AICT 693, pp. 1–10, 2024.
https://doi.org/10.1007/978-3-031-61069-1_1

of our environment. Introduced by Google the advertisement-based business model as well as new practices of marketing amplified by AI are pushing people to buy more and throw out. The business trends such as planned obsolescence [5] and shrinkflation [6] produces more waste. Many seems to ignore that recycling needs the energy and generates pollution affecting also our health [7, 8].

The second consciousness awakening have seen various approaches defined and introduced in companies and organizations. Among them Corporate Social Responsibility (CSR) defines sustainability as an intersection of social, economic and environmental aspects. Actually this initial definition evolved in various context, from company to for example community [9]. Another definition of CSR proposes "balancing people, profit and planet" [10]. However, some large companies still practice intensive business and preach "sustainable development". Despite all these actions the planet decline accelerates [7, 11 and 12].

Following the debates on governmental levels that begun in 1992 in Rio, the UN defined 17 Sustainable Development goals [13] that many try to achieve with separate actions such as replacement of all cars by electric ones without considering the battery lifecycle, installing wind farm on the sea or on land, solar panels on the roofs and on lands that can be cultivated. Such actions in one area can have ripple effects across others [14].

Despite all these single actions the natural catastrophes as earthquakes, drought, flooding, melting ice, species extinction due to pollution or poachers are more and more frequent leading to planet decline.

The COP28 just ended. This event brought registered 97 372 registered participants [15]. Many come here just to be visible and to talk. The majority of sponsors called "climate innovators (!) is more concerned by sustainable business [16].

I wonder who among the advisory committee (mainly politicians) has a real practice in managing such a complex actions, what conclusion, how far technology is considered. At least the carbon emission of such event has to be evaluated.

The scientific works on various aspects such as climate modeling. Among them Caltech founded CLiMA, Climate Modeling Alliance [17]. They are developing a Climate Machine, probably the first Earth system model able to learn automatically from diverse data sources. Their model uses machine learning and data assimilation to learn from observations and from data generated on demand in targeted high-resolution simulations, for example, of clouds or ocean turbulence. They expect that this work will allow reducing and quantify uncertainties in climate predictions.

The modelling of such complex systems requires a huge amount of data and the use of this data for prediction with AI considers mostly linear approximation while there are not. How such models can lead to relevant actions?

French research center BRGM [18] works on various aspects related to water ecosystems.

Despite the adoption of the Paris Agreement on climate change and the establishment of the 2030 United Nations Sustainable Development Goals, significant gaps remain between the scientific and political communities when it comes to understanding how climate change risks cascade through environmental, social, and economic systems.

The World Meteorological Organization has established seven climate indicators shown in Fig. 1.

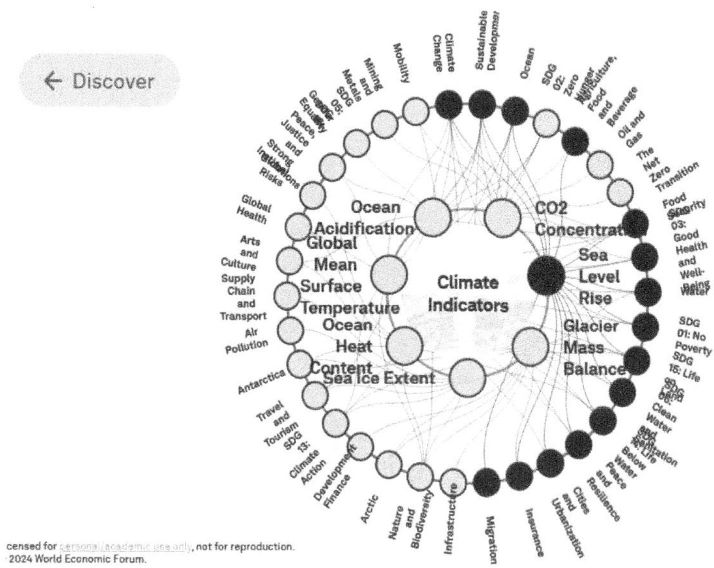


**Fig. 1.** WEF Climate indicators [19], credit https://intelligence.weforum.org

Among them the CO2 concentration, sea level rise, glacier mass balance, sea ice extend, ocean heat content, global mean surface temperature and ocean acidification. This interactive representation helps understanding partially some connections between items, for example clicking on "sea level rise" displays the connections shown in black.

Among the last trends is the "zero net transition". Achieving this objective seems rather utopic. Some elements and their impacts are also represented on interactive drawing [20]. We find here advanced manufacturing but not IT, neither AI.

The AI impact is represented in another graphic but does not include environmental impact [21].

All representations available on weforum.org website are very useful in elaborating a "big picture" with a system view.

The organizations involved in various aspects of Sustainability and Climate Change still did not elaborated an adequate assessment to measure the progress.

Our recent article [22] proposes an assessment to evaluate the progress in Planet protection. The small surface represents the current situation and the external curve represents the objectives. Of course the axes can be defined in function of a given context. Such assessment should be conduct on regular basis to see the progress.

Hoping more interest for it (Fig. 2).

Artificial Intelligence (both Knowledge-based and connectionist) has a great potential in effective addressing of those challenges. Some examples how are mentioned in [23].

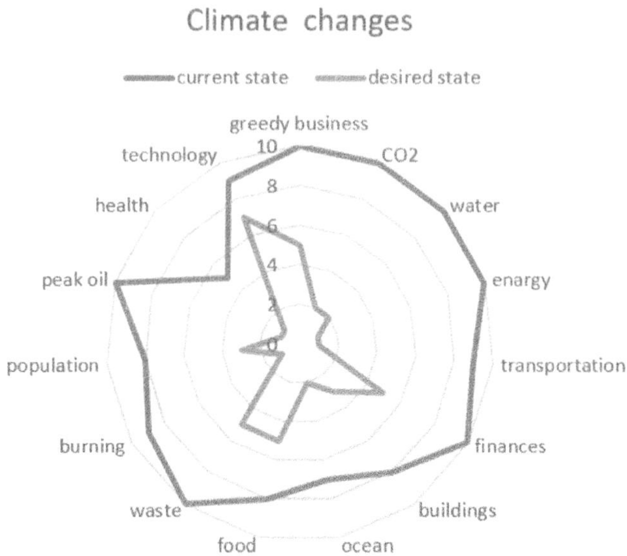


**Fig. 2.** Initial assessment for Climate Change, own drawing [22]

## 2 Contribution of AI to Climate Action

Climate actions shown in another weforum drawing [24] do not include smarting and greening IT and AI, neither data sliming, the raw material for connectionist Machine Learning and Deep Learning.

Actually, many collect data, but nobody manage them at the global level. Among the recent initiatives those of https://handprint.tech/calculator/ a smart way of collecting data by evaluation of a company alignment with Paris Agreement goals. The quality and relevance of the results obtained from ML or DL systems strongly depends on the quality of data used for training.

The data-wore Chat GPT in answer to "How AI helps addressing the sustainability challenges" provides the list of traditional items:

"Artificial Intelligence (AI) plays a crucial role in addressing sustainability challenges across various sectors. However, such way of considering it is not effective. This extremely complex and full of contradictions topic requires a different approach.

Here are several ways in which AI is contributing to sustainability efforts:

- Energy Efficiency:
  - Smart Grids: AI helps in optimizing energy distribution in smart grids, reducing energy waste, and enhancing overall grid efficiency.
  - Predictive Maintenance: AI algorithms can predict equipment failures, allowing for timely maintenance and preventing energy inefficiencies.

- Renewable Energy:
  - Optimized Resource Allocation: AI is used to optimize the placement and operation of renewable energy sources like solar panels and wind turbines, maximizing energy production.
  - Energy Forecasting: AI models can predict energy production from renewable sources, aiding in better grid management.
- Climate Modeling and Prediction:
  - Data Analysis: AI processes vast amounts of data for climate modeling, helping scientists understand and predict climate patterns and changes.
  - Risk Assessment: AI is used for risk assessment related to natural disasters, allowing for better preparedness and response planning.
- Supply Chain Optimization:
  - Reducing Waste: AI helps optimize supply chain processes, reducing waste and improving efficiency in manufacturing and distribution.
  - Predictive Analytics: AI enables better forecasting, reducing overproduction and minimizing environmental impact.
- Conservation and Biodiversity:
  - Monitoring Ecosystems: AI assists in monitoring and analyzing ecosystems, helping in the conservation of biodiversity.
  - Wildlife Protection: AI-powered cameras and sensors are used for wildlife monitoring and protection against poaching.
- Waste Management:
  - Sorting and Recycling: AI is used in automated sorting systems for recycling, improving the efficiency of waste management processes.
  - Optimizing Collection Routes: AI helps optimize waste collection routes, reducing fuel consumption and emissions.
- Water Management:
  - Leak Detection: AI can identify water leaks in real-time, helping in the efficient management of water resources.
  - Water Quality Monitoring: AI is used for analyzing water quality data, ensuring safe and sustainable water sources.
- Smart Cities:
  - Traffic Management: AI optimizes traffic flow, reducing congestion and emissions in urban areas.

  - Public Transportation Optimization: AI can improve the efficiency and sustainability of public transportation systems.

- Agriculture:

  - Precision Farming: AI helps optimize farming practices, reducing resource use and environmental impact.
  - Crop Monitoring: AI assists in monitoring crop health and predicting potential issues.

- Carbon Footprint Reduction:

  - Green Computing: AI contributes to energy-efficient computing, reducing the carbon footprint of data centers.
  - Optimizing Industrial Processes: AI helps industries optimize processes to reduce energy consumption and emissions.

Asked on interconnections between the items Chat GPT answers: "In conclusion, AI has the potential to drive significant positive impacts on sustainability by optimizing resource use, improving efficiency, and contributing to informed decision-making in various sectors. However, it's essential to consider ethical and responsible AI practices to ensure that AI solutions align with sustainable development goals." This answer demonstrates a lack of reasoning.

In the initial answer we notice some important keywords such as "optimization, forecasting, preventive, prediction and risk assessment" without mentioning the adequate AI technics to effectively address the related challenges. Very important keyword "knowledge" is missing as well as a comment on combination of knowledge (human and AI with connectionist AI implemented in hybrid systems).

The implementation and acceptation of some mentioned items requires the radical change in human behaviors.

Some of the cited items were discussed in the workshop, however, we also exchanged on interinfluences between them and carbon footprint of generative AI. Only one paper presented the impact of hardware and data centers on sustainability.

### 2.1 Environmental Impact of Generative AI

The recent Stanford study published by the Human-Centered AI lab [26] confirms that that "AI is both helping and harming the environment". According to Luccioni et al., 2022, BLOOM's training run emitted 25 times more carbon than a single air traveler on a one-way trip from New York to San Francisco [27]. Still, new reinforcement learning models like BCOOLER show that AI systems can be used to optimize energy usage.

The Fig. 3 presents the studied impacts.

The European Union emphasis is also on innovation in digital transformation [28] as well as on "twin digital and green transition" [29]. While the role of AI is considered here, the carbon footprint of AI is not.

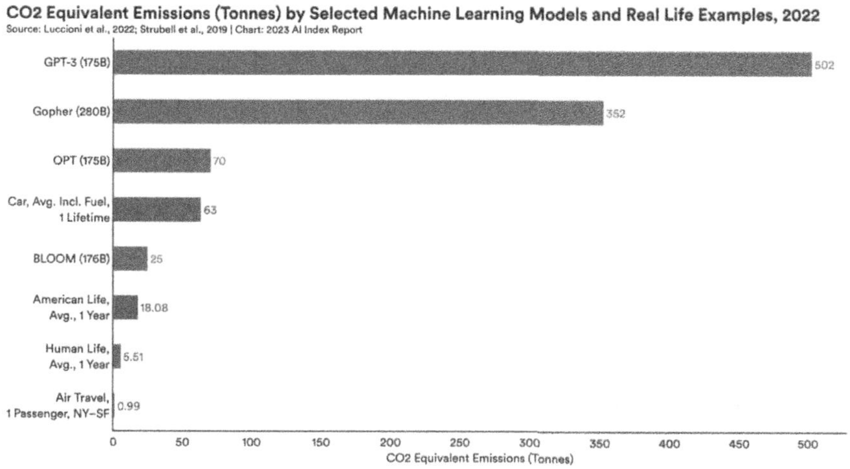


**Fig. 3.** Carbon footprint of selected genAI compared with plane travel, source https://aiindex.stanford.edu/report/

Since years the AI researchers and practitioners have been invented and practiced various AI techniques. We can consider them as AI toolbox to use in function of problem to solve with the aim of selecting "smarter and greener". The art of using the available AI approaches (problem solving, modularity, genericity, reusability) and techniques must be shared and taught.

The fields AI can help us are among others:

- Education (with Chat GPT)
- Deep-understanding of complex problems to solve them "smart & green"
- Decision Support Systems
- Resource allocation
- Simulation before doing, evaluation of impacts
- Eco-design [31]
- Optimization using for ex. Constraint programming for scheduling, resource allocation, frequency, networks, timetable, transportation, logistics…
- Industry 5.0 at the condition "human in the loop" [30]
- Natural resources management
- Agriculture (agroecology)
- Health – diagnosis and prevention
- Short term challenges:
  - Detection of fakes
  - Prevention of crimes - Cybersecurity and global security (TC12.13)
  - Personal intelligent assistant learning RT with its user
  - Twin transformation – digital & green [29]
  - Understanding the climate change for impactful actions

The whole life-cycle of IT should use eco-design and reusable components, be free of planned obsolescence, smartly manufactured, easy to update and recycling [31].

The future depends on how we use adequate AI combined with human knowledge to balance the system components presented in Fig. 4.

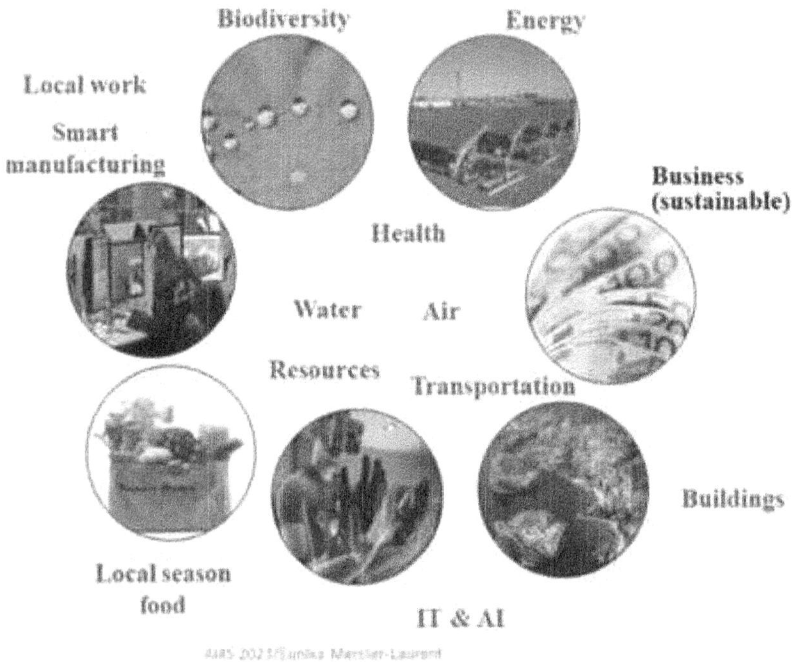


**Fig. 4.** A condition for sustainable Future, own drawing

Preserving our Planet requires the global awakening about the current situation that should be assessed to facilitate the progress, the global "wisening" and the art of combining human knowledge and adequate AI systems.

## 3 Conclusion and Future Work

In the context of Planet Emergency, sustainability is still a big challenge for humanity. Before applying the various AI techniques to solve separate problems, the understanding of the overall picture is required. It comes with the awareness about our impact and evolution of individual and companies behaviors, radical change of focus from having more to living better in harmony with nature.

To remain sustainable, the IT development requires a smart use of available AI techniques, not only trendy ones but also those effective for a given case. Combined with intensive use of available knowledge – individual and collective, from related domains, from the past and currently gained from experience such systems can really help minimizing the impact of human activity.

AI can help managing many aspects when used appropriately, but we still need to define the right metrics for correct evaluation of the effects of our actions – individual and collective. Simulators can help understanding the impacts, evaluating the situation, testing effect of influencing factors and consequence of decisions to take before doing. It applies in industry, city and in our lives.

The balance between the use of technology and human capacity should be preserved. Technology producers have tendency to produce software and devices that think instead of the human and take decisions for him/her. This kind of applications may replace human at the long run and reduce his cognitive capacity. That is why we have to design applications able to enhance human intelligence without switching it off.

Technology alone cannot save Planet, but can help us to be smarter. It is a lot to do and it is the reason we will continue to run this workshop hoping including more concerned fields and also influence more human-AI synergy.

## References

1. Antoine de Saint Exupéry: Terre des hommes, Galimard (1939). https://www.antoinedesaintexupery.com/ouvrage/terre-des-hommes-1939/
2. Lenkowa A.: Oskalpowana ziemia, Omega (1961)
3. Eckholm, E.P.: Loosing Losing Ground: Environmental Stress and World Food Prospect. W.W. Norton, New York (1976)
4. Aleksandrowicz, J.: Sumienie ekologiczne, WP (1979)
5. Cueto J.: Planned Obsolescence – An Economic and Cultural Anxiety, July 2009. Source researchgate.net
6. https://www.businessinsider.com/shrinkflation-grocery-stores-pringles-cereal-candy-bars-chocolate-toilet-paper-cadbury-2021-7?op=1&r=US&IR=T. Accessed 5 Mar 2024
7. Mercier-Laurent, E.: The Innovation Biosphere –Planet and Brains in Digital Era. Wiley, New York (2015)
8. WHO: Environment and Health. https://www.euro.who.int/en/health-topics/environment-and-health/Climate-change/data-and-statistics. Accessed Dec 2021
9. Tata CSR. https://www.tatasteelthailand.com/en/sustainability/corporate-social-responsibility/. Accessed 5 Mar 2024
10. ISO 26000. https://www.iso.org/iso-26000-social-responsibility.html. Accessed 5 Mar 2024
11. OECD: Work in support of Climate actions, December 2019. https://www.oecd.org/environment/cc/OECD-work-in-support-of-climate-action.pdf
12. Changements climatiques: les éléments scientifiques du GIEC, August 2021. https://www.ecologie.gouv.fr/sites/default/files/21144_GIEC-2.pdf
13. https://www.un.org/sustainabledevelopment/sustainable-development-goals/. Accessed 5 Mar 2024
14. Impact of wind farms in Brazil. https://www.lemonde.fr/planete/article/2024/03/04/au-bresil-les-ravages-de-la-ruee-vers-le-vent_6219968_3244.html
15. https://unfccc.int/sites/default/files/resource/COP28.PLOP_.pdf. Accessed 5 Mar 2024
16. https://www.cop28.com/en/climate-innovators. Accessed 5 Mar 2024
17. https://clima.caltech.edu/. Accessed 5 Mar 2024
18. BRGM. https://www.brgm.fr. Accessed 5 Mar 2024
19. https://intelligence.weforum.org/topics/a1G680000004Cv2EAE. Accessed 5 Mar 2024
20. Zero-net-transition. https://intelligence.weforum.org/topics/a1G680000004C93EAE?tab=publications. Accessed 5 Mar 2024

21. Artificial Intelligence. https://intelligence.weforum.org/topics/a1Gb0000000pTDREA2. Accessed 5 Mar 2024
22. Mercier-Laurent, E.: Climate change – can AI help understanding and more effective facing of various interrelated impacts? In: Kayakutlu, G., Kayalica, M.Ö. (eds.) Decision Making Using AI in Energy and Sustainability. Applied Innovation and Technology Management. Springer, Cham (2023). https://doi.org/10.1007/978-3-031-38387-8_1
23. Mercier-Laurent, E.: Can artificial intelligence effectively support sustainable development? In: Mercier-Laurent, E., Kayalica, M.Ö., Owoc, M.L. (eds.) AI4KM 2021. IAICT, vol. 614, pp. 144–159. Springer, Cham (2021). https://doi.org/10.1007/978-3-030-80847-1_10
24. Climate actions. https://intelligence.weforum.org/topics/a1G0X0000057N0oUAE. Accessed 5 Mar 2024
25. Mercier-Laurent, E.: Greening and smarting IT – case of digital transformation. In: Mercier-Laurent, E., Kayakutlu, G. (eds.) AI4KMES 2021, vol. 637, pp. 1–18. Springer, Cham (2022). https://doi.org/10.1007/978-3-030-96592-1_1
26. https://aiindex.stanford.edu/report/. Accessed 6 Mar 2024
27. Luccioni, A.S., Viguier, S., Ligozat, A.-L.: Estimating the Carbon Footprint of BLOOM, a 176B Parameter Language Model, November 2022. https://arxiv.org/pdf/2211.02001v1.pdf
28. Shaping the Digital transformation. https://www.europarl.europa.eu/topics/en/article/20210414STO02010/shaping-the-digital-transformation-eu-strategy-explained. Accessed 6 Mar 2024
29. The twin green and digital transition. https://joint-research-centre.ec.europa.eu/jrc-news-and-updates/twin-green-digital-transition-how-sustainable-digital-technologies-could-enable-carbon-neutral-eu-2022-06-29_en. Accessed 6 Mar 2024
30. Schneider 2018-2019 Sustainability Report. https://www.schneider-electric.com/en/about-us/sustainability/
31. Feng, Z., et al.: Toward a systemic navigation framework to integrate sustainable development into the company. J. Clean. Prod. **54**, 199–214 (2013)
32. Monsone, C., Mercier-Laurent, E., Janos, J.: The overview of digital twins in Industry 4.0: managing the whole ecosystem. In: Kamis 2018 (2018)

# In Search for Model-Driven eXplainable Artificial Intelligence

Antoni Ligęza(✉) and Dominik Sepioło

Faculty of Electrical Engineering, Automatics, Computer Science and Biomedical Engineering, Department of Applied Computer Science, AGH University of Krakow, al. Mickiewicza 30, 30-059 Krakow, Poland
{ligeza,sepiolo}@agh.edu.pl

**Abstract.** This paper reports on ongoing and innovative research in the area of *eXplainable Artificial Intelligence* (XAI). A classical XAI task is considered as finding an explanation of the model generated via Machine Learning by identifying the most influential variables for local decision-making. Such an approach suffers from severe limitations. The proposed approach moves the explanatory process to a new, knowledge-level dimension. It is oriented towards Model Discovery, i.e. the internal structure and functions of the components. The concept of Model-Driven XAI is put forward and explained with examples. An experiment on Function Discovery via Grammatical Evolution is reported in brief.

**Keywords:** explainable artificial intelligence · grammatical evolution · structural regression · model-driven explainable artificial intelligence

## 1 Introduction

Classical *Artificial Intelligence* (AI) is often described as *the study of agents that receive percepts from the environment and perform actions* [11] or *the field that studies the synthesis and analysis of computational agents that act intelligently* [9]. Whatever the definition is, an intelligent entity should have the ability to perceive the environment, *build an internal knowledge-based model of it*, perform reasoning and present its decisions, as some widely-accepted minimum.

Two distinctive paradigms are prevailing in AI. The first consists in developing a model and algorithms for reasoning within a specific domain of application. This is the case of specialized algorithms developed for automated reasoning and theorem proving, graph search, game playing, automated planning, constrained programming and many others. Note that in this case the way of inference can be traced by human, and hence, the results can be always comprehended, explained, trusted and proved. The resulting knowledge and solutions remain open, readable, and so-to-say declarative by nature. The second approach is based on providing the agent with example inputs and corresponding outputs, and making it


Published by Springer Nature Switzerland AG 2024
E. Mercier-Laurent et al. (Eds.): AI4KMES 2023, IFIP AICT 693, pp. 11–26, 2024.
https://doi.org/10.1007/978-3-031-61069-1_2

learn some desired behavior. This seems much more attractive, and saves much human effort, since hand-crafted knowledge edition is a tedious and error-prone activity. However, in this case the way of inference typically cannot be traced by human, and hence, the results are hard to comprehend, explain, trust and prove. The resulting knowledge and solutions remain closed, unreadable, and so-to-say procedural, ones of black-box type by nature.

Despite the unquestionable successes and advantages of the first approach, spectacular progress has been observed in the area of Machine Learning (ML), with impressive progress in subdomains of ML such as Deep Learning (DL) and Large Language Models (LLM).

Some of the most challenging and complex AI issues of today, concern real understanding of how systems, including intelligent systems work; these include the study of Causality [8], Model-Discovery for Model-Based Reasoning [7], eXplainable Artificial Intelligence (XAI) [1,2], Trustworthy and Responsible Decision-Making, Interpretable and Explainable AI[1] and others. In order to make a step towards building Model-Driven XAI, the incorporation of Knowledge-Based components and more advanced function identification methods (e.g. symbolic regression, grammatical evolution) seems to be necessary and promising.

This paper[2] is based on the invited presentation delivered at the *Artificial Intelligence for Sustainability Workshop of ECAI'2023 Conference.* It puts forward some relatively new approach for combining ML with integration of knowledge-based components. The classical XAI task is considered as finding an explanation of the model generated via ML tools by post-hoc identification of the most influential variables for local decision-making. Such an approach suffers from severe limitations. The proposed approach moves the explanatory process to a new, knowledge-level dimension. It is oriented towards Model Discovery, i.e. the internal structure and functions of the components. The concept of Model-Driven XAI is put forward. The ultimate goal is to contribute towards eXplainable Artificial Intelligence based on direct Model Discovery rather than attempts at black-box model explanation.

The paper is structured as follows: Sect. 2 describes the state-of-the-art in XAI. Section 3 comments on critical evaluation of current XAI. In Sect. 4 we provide some further motivation for the proposed approach. In Sect. 5 we put forward the idea of Singular Case Analysis, some core problem formulation. Theoretical aspects of Grammatical Evolution are described in Sect. 6. This is followed by a description of an experiment with function identification in Sect. 7. Concluding remarks are presented in Sect. 8.

## 2 XAI: State-of-the-Art

*Explainable Artificial Intelligence* is focused on assuring transparency of solutions worked out with AI and ML methods and tools. An ultimate goal is that

[1] https://www.bmc.com/blogs/machine-learning-interpretability-vs-explainability/.

[2] A former, shorter version of this research were presented at PP-RAI 2023 [15], a Polish AI conference and Hydra'2003 [16] - an ECAI'2023 Workshop.

suggested decisions, provided predictions or generated output should be understood by humans. However, the majority of current ML techniques (e.g. Deep Learning) are based on *black-box* models. In order to assure an appropriate level of transparency, and further *justifiability* and *trustability*, man must be aware of the underlying *rules of the game*, i.e. some *Deep Knowledge* describing the work of the considered system.

In fact, the need and implementation of eXplainability have been present in AI for quite a couple of decades. Many of the classical AI approaches were based on the concept of *white-box models*, and open, declarative knowledge representations. Some most common direct approaches to *eXplainable in Artificial Intelligence* may include knowledge representation and reasoning with logic, declarative programming; e.g. with PROLOG, rule-based systems (with the Why, How, and What-is explanations), automated planning systems, especially ones using the STRIPS paradigm, and then PDDL, causal graphs and Bayes Networks, Model-Based Reasoning (MBR), *Explainability by Design*, e.g. when designing circuits and systems so that they satisfy required functionalities, Constraint Programming, etc. Many such approaches, their underlying theory and algorithms are described in [7–9,11]; also [5,6].

In general, the approaches to make AI and AI tools can be classified into white-box vs. black-box ones, with a wide spectrum of somewhat in-between models. A very rough, but symptomatic classification can be as follows (we list only the most representative ones):

- **White-box models:**
  - Logical Models; declarative KRR,
  - Rule-Based Models/Learners, Rule Induction,
  - Model-Based Reasoning, Causal Modelling, Structure Discovery, Qualitative Physics, ...
- **Semi-White-box models:** (Models featuring interpretable components constructed solely from data, lacking semantic understanding)
  - Linear/Logistic Regression,
  - Decision Trees,
  - Decision Graphs (including BPMN),
- **Black-box models:**
  - Tree Ensembles,
  - Computational Intelligence and Bio-Inspired Models,
  - Neural Networks, Convolutional Neural Network, Deep Learning.

Modern approaches to XAI have been developed as a consequence of the rapid developments in the area of *Computational Intelligence* (CI) and in fact they attempt to provide post-hoc explanations to the decisions generated by ML/Deep Learning models. Such approaches to develop XAI often lean towards using *shallow models*. By sacrificing an in-depth understanding, a simple but easily interpretable model is built upon the one generated with ML technologies. Its work is demonstrated on a subset of the original input data, and there is no way to incorporate auxiliary domain expert knowledge. In [1,2] a vast, representative selection of the proposed shallow approaches and tools is presented.

A simple tree-like taxonomy summarizing the above discussion can be presented below (Fig. 1):

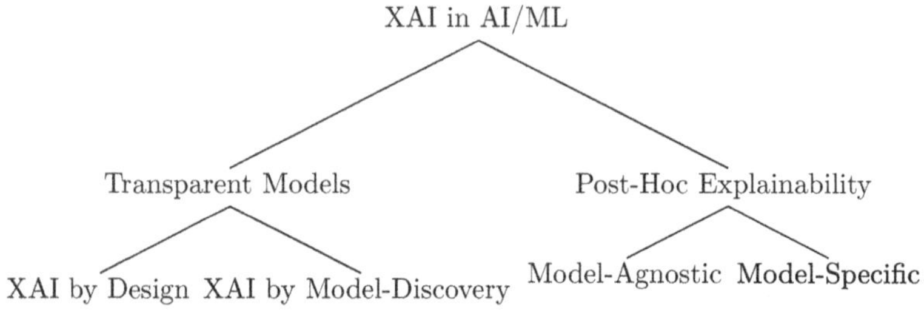


**Fig. 1.** A simple taxonomy of XAI

Some of the best-known post-hoc XAI tools are the LIME and SHAP [1]. Local Interpretable Model-Agnostic Explanations (LIME) are the most eminent example of explanations by simplification. LIME algorithm constructs an explanation for a specific prediction by formulating a straightforward, interpretable, linear model that approximates the behavior of the complex model in the vicinity of the given prediction. SHapley Additive exPlanations (SHAP) are another benchmark technique of explainability. SHAP utilizes a game theoretic approach (the *Shapley values*) to create an explanation that shows feature importance for each prediction. Other methods include e.g. visualization techniques and explanations by example. In [14] we provided a comprehensive, critical overview of the current shallow approaches to XAI.

## 3 XAI: Critical Evaluation

The observed recently development for building post-hoc explanations for black-box models [1] proves that indeed, there is a need to focus on in-depth understanding of the nature, semantics and work of the generated models [12]. Unfortunately, the aforementioned approaches are considered *shallow* since they furnish explanations characterized by a high level of abstraction, lacking a comprehensive grasp of the fundamental principles of the underlying model and external declarative knowledge. An inherent limitation of these shallow methods is the inability to capture the full underlying complexity of the model. It is important that they should be applied only together with other, deep and more transparent, techniques for a more complete understanding of the behavior and structure of the model.

When considering the rapid development of Deep Learning ML technology and observing its unquestionable success, in the context of XAI, one must be aware that AI is not limited to ML (although there is a significant intersection) and ML is not the whole AI (there are many technologies that go far beyond straightforward applications of ML). There are also at least the following born-in, intrinsic limitations to the post-hoc explanations approach, such as presented in [1]:

- no holistic, general framework is provided; only local, a *peep-hole view*,
- no Causal Models are in play; lack of structural approach is visible,
- no background/commonsense/domain knowledge is taken into account,
- explanations created *a posteriori* are based *on the base of the same data* as being used for learning.

Local explanation models are typically unstable and not well fixed in reality. On the other hand, holistic system thinking is the way a human develops meaningful theories in sciences such as physics or astronomy. Building structural frameworks is often based on capturing the phenomenon of causality and functional dependencies.

External knowledge components play a crucial role in enriching ML models. One such approach is through the use of Ontologies and Knowledge Graphs, which provide structured and organized knowledge that can enhance the model understanding and reasoning. Another idea consists in using Causal Graphs and Functional Components describing the behavior of the system. Context-free grammars are yet another powerful tool to formalize this external knowledge, enabling the creation of well-defined explanation models. By applying these grammars, the structure of the explanation model can be constrained, leading to more interpretable and coherent explanations.

By combining various methods and external knowledge, a more hybrid, more complete and nuanced interpretation of the AI decision-making process can be achieved. This integration of different techniques enables to bridge the gap between interpretability and complexity, in hope of leading to a more efficient, reliable and trustworthy AI system.

## 4 Motivation for Model-Driven XAI

In this section, we briefly present the motivation for research on direct model generation rather than attempts at ex-post explanation of some Black-Box models obtained by today's Machine Learning methods. First, we focus on the skills necessary for any intelligent agent. Then, in the provided context we simply provide a list of born-in limitations of the ex-post approaches, such as ones carefully revised in [1] and in consequence, we put forward a bunch of postulates concerning the novel approach.

As it was mentioned in Sect. 1, an intelligent entity, often named an Intelligent Agent, should have the ability to perceive the environment, build an internal knowledge-based model of it, perform reasoning and output its decisions. Having a model of the external environment seems to be crucial for understanding the world, analyzing it, planning and decision-making. Manipulating the world – at the level of the model – means in fact reasoning about the world.

Reasoning can take various forms, but the three basic paradigms coming from logic are: (i) deduction, (ii) abduction, and (iii) induction. Deduction is a kind of feed-forward inference where, having some facts and inference rules, new facts can be produced as logical consequences. Abduction is a kind of backward reasoning, where potential hypotheses are generated to explain observed manifestations. Operationally, abduction can be considered as a search for potential solutions being given a set of constraints. Induction means generalization and learning from examples, including past experience.

The last point – i.e. induction – is covered by ML algorithms (well, performed in some specific forms). However, discovering and understanding the real meaning, and further on – ability to perform deductive and abductive reasoning require some extra features and skills. Such skills should include open, readable, interpretable knowledge representation, transparent and flexible manipulation of the knowledge, incorporation of new knowledge and knowledge sharing via explanation, justification and proving the generated results or decisions.

In this context, we provide a short list of intrinsic limitations of current ML technologies: (i) majority of ML models cover *shallow* knowledge only, (ii) the learning process is only data-driven, i.e. learning is limited to analysis of the input-output data typically restricted to a large data table, (iii) most of them are of decision/classification type; there is no meaningful *functional* output, etc. Finally, the eternal question: 'How does it work?' is left with no answer.

In consequence, the induced decision models are operational, and there is no place for a deeper insight into understanding the system or process under analysis. Post-hoc or a posteriori approaches to provide explanations, as presented in [1], do not remove the stated-above limitations. It is visible that they are based on the same data as the learning input, no existing background knowledge can be incorporated, and no causal/functional scheme is searched for.

Hence, the motivation for a deeper Model-Driven approach to explainability takes into account that:

- the obtained models should be *readable* and *interpretable models*; easy to read by human,
- as knowledge is more concise than just data, the focus should be on discovering causal and functional dependencies,
- if available, existing knowledge should be incorporated,
- the focus should be on an in-depth analysis, leading to multi-level models representing knowledge at various levels of abstraction.

In this paper, we put forward the idea of Model-Driven Explainability, which is assumed to be achieved by *Model Discovery*. It is proposed that the model should be defined by specification of variables defining the input, the output and the internal state of the system, according to the following principles:

- direct specification of system *Components* – and the functions performed by them,
- direct specification of *Causal* links, e.g. defining the influence of certain variables over the other,

- direct specification of *Connections* - the internal struCture,

The 3 points above will be referred to as the *3C Principle*; in fact, for understanding the work of a system we need to know its Components, Causal dependencies and the overall struCture of signal flow.

## 5 A Generic Scenario: Singular Case Analysis

In this section, we briefly introduce the SiCA concept. SiCA stays for *Singular Case Analysis*, and it seems to be a generic Artificial Intelligence-based problem-solving case, staying in some opposition to massive tabular data analysis and the current so mechanical Machine Learning. In fact, SiCA is a basic case pattern, frequently encountered in reality and omnipresent in problem-solving. The main characteristics of SiCA are as follows:

- a *new* problem is encountered and must be solved; there are no standard AI algorithms that can be applied, and the problem does not belong to any specialized/narrow class of classical AI, such as graph search, planning, constraint programming, etc.
- both domain knowledge and commonsense knowledge are available, and they must be used and combined in a way so characteristic for intelligent human investigation,
- some inspection and analysis of the system under consideration is possible, and selected further data can be obtained on demand.

In order to provide some intuitions, below we list a set of such example problems, for which the generic eternal question is: How does it work? And also: what did happen? What was the cause of the observed behavior? What is the fault?

- The famous diagnostic circuit introduced in by R. Reiter [10]; example non-standard AI-based analyses were presented in [4] by constructive abduction, [5] by causal structure discovery, and in [3] with constraint programming;
- The famous Antikythera mechanism; recovered on May 17, 1901. The instrument has been variously dated to about 87 BC, or between 150 and 100 BC, or in 205 BC[3];
- The Boeing 737 Max 8 case. The plane was introduced into exploitation in 2017 shortly after that, two serious crashes happened:
  1. Crash: October 2018, Lion Air (Malaysia)
  2. Crash: March 2019, Ethiopian Airlines
  
  Explanation: MCAS System (Maneuvering Characteristics Augmentation System)[4];
- The case of Morandi Bridge. The viaduct was built between 1963 and 1967 costing 3.8 billion Italian lire and opened on 4 September 1967. It had a length of 1,182 m (3,878 ft), a height above the valley of 45 m (148 ft) at road

[3] See: https://en.wikipedia.org/wiki/Antikythera_mechanism.

[4] https://en.wikipedia.org/wiki/Boeing_737_MAX.

level, and three reinforced concrete pylons reaching 90 m (300 ft) in height; the maximum span was 210 m (690 ft).
On 14 August 2018, a 210-m (690 ft) section of the viaduct collapsed during a rainstorm, killing forty-three people[5].
- The case of diagnosis and repair of a number of everyday use technical systems, with the automatic washing machine being a primary example. The system combines mechanical, hydraulic, pneumatic, electric, and electromechanical subsystems, interconnected in a number of ways.

In any of the cases above, an intelligent analysis and investigation of the problem requires flexible use of domain knowledge, as well as combined inference modes. As the ultimate goal is to discover the real causes of the problem, the notion of *Explainability in Artificial Intelligence* plays a crucial role.

Note that contrary to situations where standard AI methods are applied in case of well-standardized classes of problem, and further, contrary to so modern Machine Learning/Deep Learning, the issue of generating an explainable solution must take into account the following border conditions:

- only limited, and incomplete data is available (no big dataset of examples),
- on the other hand, some (partial) domain knowledge is present:
  - on *Components*,
  - on *Connections*,
  - on *Causal Dependencies*;
- *partial inspection* of the system is possible,
- abductive reasoning is used instead of induction,
- flexible, smart, creative reasoning seems to be the key to success,
- commonsense knowledge may play a crucial role.

In such a case, pure, classical AI or ML paradigms alone are out of play. Such cases will be referred to as SiCA: *Singular Case Analysis*, with the eternal question: *How does it work?*. And a key technique to approach such problems is the *Model-Based Reasoning* [7].

## 6 A Note on Grammatical Evolution, Ongoing Research and Tools

Grammatical evolution (GE) is a type of Evolutionary Algorithm (EA) that takes inspiration from the biological evolutionary process to search for solutions to problems [13]. In contrast to traditional EA, GE stands out by seamlessly integrating genetic algorithms with formal language theory. This approach involves the use of user-defined context-free grammars, which impose specific constraints on the structure and syntax of the genome. This constraint-driven mechanism ensures the generation of solutions with precise and well-defined configurations, enhancing the interpretability of the evolved solutions.

[5] https://en.wikipedia.org/wiki/Ponte_Morandi.

The evaluation of each generated solution is accomplished through the assignment of a fitness value, determined by a predefined objective function. This fitness value serves as a measure of the solution effectiveness in addressing the given problem, guiding the evolutionary process toward more favorable outcomes.

According to [17] GE system comprises three primary elements:

- Problem Instance: in order to apply the proposed solution, with the problem instances, is necessary to use a fitness function to perform the optimization process.
- Grammar: it serves to establish a mapping between the genotype and the phenotype. The design of this grammar is designed based on the specifics of the given problem instance.
- Search Engine: responsible for managing the optimization process, the search engine introduces modifications to the genotype based on the quality of the phenotype applied to the problem instances.

One of the notable applications of GE lies in the creation of variable-length linear genome encodings for computer programs. This capability makes GE particularly well-suited for evolving solutions in scenarios where the structure of the desired solution is not fixed and may vary in length or complexity.

Beyond its primary application in program synthesis, GE exhibits versatility by extending its utility to tasks such as *symbolic regression* (in order to derive an indicative expression from the provided data) and the identification of functional dependencies. This adaptability underscores the broad range of problems that Grammatical Evolution can effectively solve, making it a valuable tool in the domain of evolutionary computation and problem-solving.

There are numerous implementations of GE algorithms; including PyNeurGen, PonyGE and PonyGE2 for Python, GEVA and ECJ for Java, and GELab for Matlab, gramEvol for R and others[6].

## 7 An Experiment with Different Explainability Methods

Body Mass Index (BMI) is a simple numeric medical parameter that provides an assessment of whether the body weight of a person of a given height falls within the healthy range. Calculated by dividing a person's weight in kilograms by the square of their height in meters, BMI provides a quick and standardized indicator of body weight status.

A series of experiments, executed using the R language (i.e. gramEvol and caret packages), was carried out to develop models that attempt to discover the BMI function from provided sample data. Besides standard ML methods such as Decision Trees and Random Forest models, Grammatical Evolution was applied. The experiments were conducted with varying amounts of training data. Initially, the models were trained using 10 observations, and subsequently, this was augmented to 50 observations. Finally, the models underwent training with a dataset comprising 100 observations.

[6] https://en.wikipedia.org/wiki/Grammatical_evolution#Implementations.

The first technique applied was Decision Tree. With only 10 observations, the resulting tree had only one node: the root, which returned the mean BMI value derived from the input data. The model had 85% accuracy, however, it was overfitted and significantly underperformed when applied to test data. Scaling up the training data to 50 observations did not lead to an improvement in accuracy; instead, it exacerbated the overfitting issue. Decision Tree generated with 100 observations performed at around 90% accuracy. Although the model boasted a simple, interpretable structure, as illustrated in Fig. 2, the overall prediction accuracy proved to be less impressive.

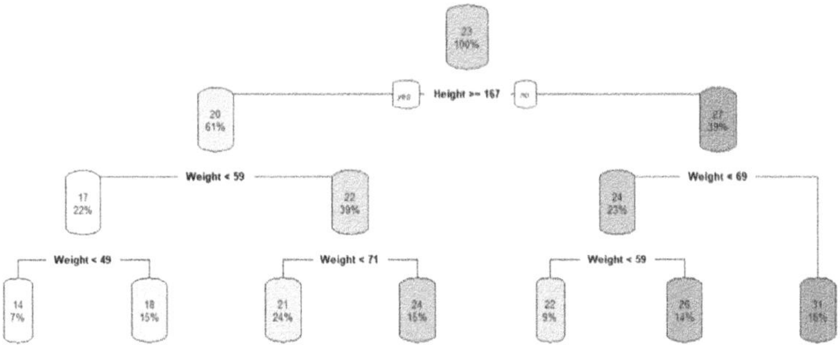


**Fig. 2.** Resulting decision tree.

Secondly, the Random Forest algorithm was employed for BMI computation. With both 10 and 50 observations, the model exhibited an accuracy of approximately 95%, yet both models were overfitted. For 100 training instances, the training accuracy was 97.5% and 93% for test data. Given the black-box nature of the Random Forest model, LIME and SHAP methods were implemented to generate explanations. Notably, for certain predictions, the explanations provided by these techniques showed significant disparities. An illustration of such a discrepancy is depicted in Fig. 3. LIME explanation for a given instance indicates that an individual's height in the range of 160–169 cm contributes to an increased BMI value, whereas the person's weight in the range of 61.5–74.6 kg has a decreasing effect. Notably, the Height variable exerts a seven times stronger influence on the predicted value compared to the Weight variable. In contrast, the SHAP explanation for the same instance reveals that both Weight and Height have a negative contribution to the predicted BMI value. Furthermore, the Weight variable makes a more substantial contribution to the result compared to the Height variable. Potential reasons for this discrepancy include different theoretical assumptions of the mentioned explanation techniques, as well as potential model instability. Another disadvantage of local explanations' technique for BMI prediction is that it assumes that for each prediction BMI coefficient was generated using another formula, while all predictions can be calculated using a single, more straightforward function.

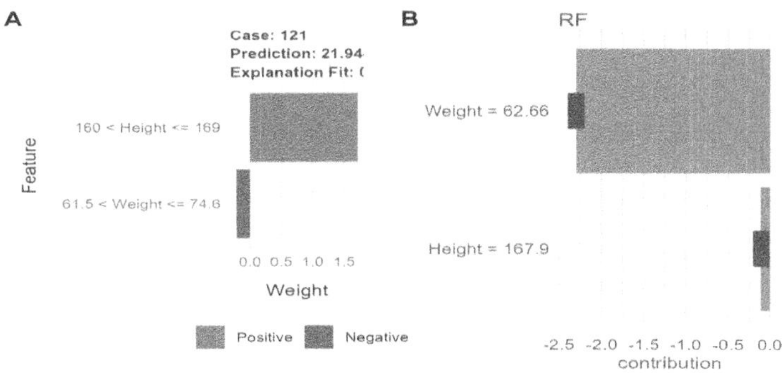


**Fig. 3.** LIME (A) and SHAP (B) explanation.

Given the critical differences in explanations of the model behavior provided by LIME and SHAP techniques for a given prediction, the necessity for a more profound understanding of the problem structure becomes visible. For this reason, we decided to implement the grammatical evolution approach. The aim was to uncover causality and functional dependencies within the data, ultimately creating a deep and transparent model that could offer more comprehensive insights into the underlying relationships.

The definition of the proposed context-free grammar for the identification of the BMI function, incorporating external domain knowledge, is outlined as follows:

```
<expr>  ::= <op>(<expr>, <expr>) | <func>(<expr>) | <var>
<func>  ::= 'log' | 'sqrt'
<op>    ::= "+" | "-" | "*" | "/" | "^"
<var>   ::= Weight | Height | <n>
<n>     ::= -3 | -2 | -1 | 0 | 1 | 2 | 3
```

We allowed basic functions and arithmetic operations and variables: Weight, Height and $n \in \mathbb{Z}$ from $\langle -3, 3 \rangle$ interval as structural elements in the final expression. A mere 10 observations proved sufficient to accurately discern the formula for the BMI coefficient through grammatical evolution operations. The outcome of these operations is shown below:

```
Best Expression:  Weight * Height^-2
```

The resulting expression (function) is coherent with the BMI formula. The discovered functional model ensures 100% accuracy for each instance of input data and outperforms ML solutions. Furthermore, it provides information that enables understanding of the model behavior and structure.

### 7.1 Introduction of Meaningful Intermediate Variables

We executed the same experimental steps for a more complex problem. Let us consider the following data table (Table 1); it will serve as the input for ML algorithms.

**Table 1.** A schematic presentation of the input data. The table contains a sample of the data used for experiments.

| a | b | c | decision |
|---|---|---|---|
| 3 | 9 | 7 | 0 |
| 1 | 4 | 4 | 1 |
| 5 | 9 | 4 | 2 |
| ⋮ | ⋮ | ⋮ | ⋮ |

The structure of the data is as follows: there are three independent *input columns* (named $a$, $b$, and $c$) and one *output* or *decision column* (named *decision*). The input values are in general real numbers, while the output is specified by an integer taking the values 0, 1 or 2. Hence, the input triples are classified into three separate classes in a deterministic way. The task of ML is to learn a *prediction model* of the output value (decision) for an arbitrary input value. As in the previous experiment, we generated LR, DT and RF models with 10, 50 and 100 observations. None of the models performed at acceptable accuracy.

Due to this reason, we redefined the experiment with the same input data table, but according to the improved and extended proposed methodology oriented towards *Model Driven XAI* (MD-XAI). The main idea of the proposed MD-XAI approach consists in incorporating a Knowledge Component (KC). The KC consists of a set of definitions of (local) *functional dependencies* among the input variables[7]. For intuition, a variable $Y$ is functionally dependent from variables $X_1, X_2, \ldots X_n$ if having the values of the $X = \{X_1, X_2, \ldots X_n\}$ the value of variable $Y$ is determined in a unique way. This will be denoted as $X \longrightarrow Y$. For obvious reasons, we are taking into account only *minimal functional dependencies*, i.e. such that none of the $X_i$ can be deleted from $X$ (in a way such that the functional dependency is preserved).

The functional dependencies are provided (suggested) by domain experts; they can be ones well-known in the domain or hypothetical ones (to be confirmed). The functional dependencies can also be ones discovered by specialized algorithms, e.g. ones for *Causal Structure Discovery* [18].

[7] The notion of a functional dependency comes from the Relational Databases.

The functional dependencies can be:

- internal ones, i.e. among the variables of the original input data,
- external or extended ones, i.e. allowing to incorporate new, externally introduces variables.

As the variables $a$, $b$ and $c$ are independent ones, there exists no functional dependency among them (expert knowledge). But let us propose to introduce an external *Knowledge Aggregation Variable* $d$, such that $a, b, c \longrightarrow d$. Let the value of $d$ is calculated by an expert-provided formula $d = b^2 - 4ac$. And now, this a bit mysterious example becomes obvious...

Let us rearrange the initial example, modified by adding the KC. As a first step, let us complete the input data table. Table 2 represents the new, enriched set of data (again, this is a sample only).

**Table 2.** A Meaningful Intermediate Variable (MIV) added.

| a | b | c | d | decision |
|---|---|---|---|---|
| 3 | 9 | 7 | −3 | 0 |
| 1 | 4 | 4 | 0 | 1 |
| 5 | 9 | 4 | 16 | 2 |
| ⋮ | ⋮ | ⋮ | ⋮ | ⋮ |

The meaning of the $d$ parameter is obvious. Note that the classification rule becomes obvious as well, and it can be reproduced with a three-level relay-type function by hand. The introduction of the $d$ parameter significantly improved the prediction accuracy of all methods (e.g. DT performed 100% accurately).

Once more, let us redefine the experiment again and assume that the domain expert provided us only with numerical values of the variable $d$ as a column with experimental results. However, basing on domain-specific knowledge, the expert can provide insights into how the variable $d$ may depend on other variables. External knowledge can be then formalized as context-free grammar and taken as input for GE process. An example of such grammar is presented below:

```
<expr> ::= <var> | <op>(<n>, <var>) | <op>(<var>, <n>)
         | <op>(<expr>, <expr>)
<op>   ::= "-" | "*" | "^"
<var>  ::= a | 'c' | b
<n>    ::= 1 | 2 | 3 | 4
```

As GE can perform symbolic regression tasks, functional dependencies can be found in data. The following expression for $d$ variable can be obtained or checked using grammatical evolution:

```
Best Expression:  b^2 - c * 4 * a
```

Based on the presented formula for $d$, another component of the model was introduced. The problem of three-class classification was simplified into 3 cases of binary classification. The following rules defining the number of roots of a quadratic equation were generated for each case:

```
ifelse(d > 0, "two", "other no. of roots")
ifelse(d == 0, "one", "other no. of roots")
ifelse(d < 0, "zero", "other no. of roots")
```

Note that, although `d > 0`, `d == 0` or `d < 0` was always present in the result of GE process, sometimes more complex rules e.g. `ifelse((b > min(b)) & (d == 0), "one", "other no. of solutions")` were presented as final solution. The result of combined rules is a simple and human-interpretable classification rule:

```
ifelse(d > 0, "two", ifelse ( d == 0 , "one", "zero"))
```

As it might be expected, we obtained a meaningful classification model that performs at 100% accuracy.

Finally, the explanation for the classification is provided by a functional structural diagram presented in Fig. 4 below. The diagram is composed of two functional boxes, the first one for calculating the value of $d$ and the second one for determining the actual class being given the value of $d$.

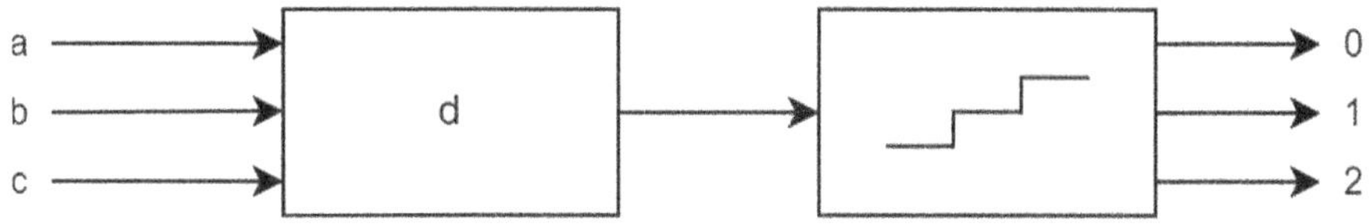


**Fig. 4.** Functional model

In many cases, incorporating external knowledge components can contribute to building more trustworthy AI models. KC can enhance interpretability, mitigate ethical concerns, add context and improve model performance. By aligning the model's decision-making process with known principles or rules, it becomes easier to understand and explain its predictions. By incorporating domain rules, logical constraints, or expert guidelines, models can generate explanations that align with human understanding. What is more, with domain expertise the model can capture underlying patterns and relationships that may not be evident in the training data alone, which leads to a better generalization for previously unseen data.

While incorporating external knowledge can be beneficial, it is important to check the reliability and quality of the external knowledge source and consideration should be given to potential biases or limitations in the external information.

## 8 Conclusions

The presented experiment shows that relying solely on shallow explainability techniques may result in inconsistent and misleading or even inconsistent explanations for the same prediction. Explanation discrepancies highlight the limitations of the shallow, model-agnostic approach. Preferably, one should opt for simple models and explanation techniques that facilitate a *deep understanding* of the model behavior and structure, as they ensure responsible application of AI solutions. Some early proposal of such approach incorporating Constraint Programming we presented in [5,6].

Grammatical Evolution emerges as a promising technology for extension and further developments in identifying interpretable functional structure. It can be successfully applied to the identification of functional dependencies in data. The reported experiment shows advantages of an accurate model generated with a very limited amount of training data over other shallow methods.

External Knowledge can help to create models that are more robust against uncertainties, missing information or noisy data. Additionally, expert knowledge can support building robust, general solutions, open to new data and scenarios.

Although context-free grammars can be utilized in order to restrict the structure of an explanation model, there is emerging need of penalization of complexity and redundancy of the model. At the moment there are no checks if the proposed genome contains redundant information, so there is no simple way to exclude redundant components. Moreover, it is not straightforward to estimate *a priori* number of building-blocks of a functional model.

Incorporating external knowledge is essential for ensuring ethical and legal compliance. Models must adhere to regulations, privacy standards, and ethical guidelines. By integrating external knowledge that covers these aspects, models can be developed with reliability and responsible decision-making in mind.

## References


1. Arrieta, A.B., et al.: Explainable artificial intelligence (XAI): concepts, taxonomies, opportunities and challenges toward responsible AI. Inf. Fusion **58**, 82–115 (2019)
2. Guidotti, R., Monreale, A., Ruggieri, S., Turini, F., Giannotti, F., Pedreschi, D.: A survey of methods for explaining black box models. ACM Comput. Surv. **51**(5), 1–42 (2019). https://doi.org/10.1145/3236009. http://dx.doi.org/10.1145/3236009
3. Ligęza, A.: Constraint programming for constructive abduction. A case study in diagnostic model-based reasoning. In: Kościelny, J.M., Syfert, M., Sztyber, A. (eds.) DPS 2017. AISC, vol. 635, pp. 94–105. Springer, Cham (2018). https://doi.org/10.1007/978-3-319-64474-5_8
4. Ligęza, A.: Towards constructive abduction: solving abductive problems with constraint programming. In: Fred, A.L.N., Dietz, J.L.G., Aveiro, D., Liu, K., Filipe, J. (eds.) KEOD 2015 - Proceedings of the International Conference on Knowledge Engineering and Ontology Development, part of the 7th International Joint Conference on Knowledge Discovery, Knowledge Engineering and Knowledge Management (IC3K 2015), Lisbon, Portugal, 12–14 November 2015, vol. 2, pp. 352–357. SciTePress (2015). https://doi.org/10.5220/0005625603520357

5. Ligęza, A.: An experiment in causal structure discovery. A constraint programming approach. In: Kryszkiewicz, M., Appice, A., Ślęzak, D., Rybinski, H., Skowron, A., Raś, Z.W. (eds.) ISMIS 2017. LNCS (LNAI), vol. 10352, pp. 261–268. Springer, Cham (2017). https://doi.org/10.1007/978-3-319-60438-1_26
6. Ligęza, A., et al.: Explainable artificial intelligence. Model discovery with constraint programming. In: Stettinger, M., Leitner, G., Felfernig, A., Ras, Z.W. (eds.) ISMIS 2020. SCI, vol. 949, pp. 171–191. Springer, Cham (2021). https://doi.org/10.1007/978-3-030-67148-8_13
7. Magnani, L., Bertolotti, T.: Springer Handbook of Model-Based Science. Springer, Cham (2017)
8. Pearl, J.: Causality, 2nd edn. Cambridge University Press, Cambridge (2009)
9. Poole, D.L., Macworth, A.K.: Artificial Intelligence 3E: Foundations of Computational Agents, 3th edn. Cambridge University Press (2023). https://artint.info/3e/html/ArtInt3e.html
10. Reiter, R.: A theory of diagnosis from first principles. Artif. Intell. **32**(1), 57–95 (1987). https://doi.org/10.1016/0004-3702(87)90062-2
11. Roussell, S., Norwig, P.: Artificial Intelligence: A Modern Approach, 4th edn. Pearson, Hoboken (2020)
12. Rudin, C.: Stop explaining black box machine learning models for high stakes decisions and use interpretable models instead. Nat. Mach. Intell. **1**(5), 206–215 (2019). https://doi.org/10.1038/S42256-019-0048-X
13. Ryan, C., O'Neill, M., Collins, J.J. (eds.): Handbook of Grammatical Evolution. Springer, Cham (2018). https://doi.org/10.1007/978-3-319-78717-6
14. Sepiolo, D., Ligęza, A.: Towards explainability of tree-based ensemble models. a critical overview. In: Zamojski, W., Mazurkiewicz, J., Sugier, J., Walkowiak, T., Kacprzyk, J. (eds.) New Advances in Dependability of Networks and Systems, pp. 287–296. Springer, Cham (2022). https://doi.org/10.1007/978-3-031-06746-4_28
15. Sepioło, D., Ligęza, A.: A comparison of shallow explainable artificial intelligence methods against grammatical evolution approach. In: Progress in Polish Artificial Intelligence Research, vol 4, pp. 89–94. Lodz University of Technology Press (2023). https://doi.org/10.34658/9788366741928.12
16. Sepioło, D., Ligęza, A.: Towards model-driven explainable artificial intelligence. An experiment with shallow methods versus grammatical evolution. In: Nowaczyk, S., et al. (eds.) ECAI 2023, vol. 1948, pp. 360–36. Springer, Cham (2024). https://doi.org/10.1007/978-3-031-50485-3_36
17. Sotelo-Figueroa, M.A., Aguirre, A.H., Espinal, A., Soria-Alcaraz, J.A., Ortíz-López, J.: Symbolic regression by means of grammatical evolution with estimation distribution algorithms as search engine. In: Fuzzy Logic Augmentation of Neural and Optimization Algorithms (2018)
18. Yu, K., Li, J., Liu, L.: A review on algorithms for constraint-based causal discovery. arXiv preprint arXiv:1611.03977 (2016)

# An Intelligent Chatbot Based on Hybrid Approach Implementing Technical Knowledge to Support Maintenance and Training Activities at Electricity of France (EDF)

Anne Dourgnon[1](✉), Alain Antoine[2], Pascal Albaladejo[3], and Fabrice Vinet[1]

[1] EDF R&D, Chatou, France
anne.dourgnon@edf.fr
[2] University of Lorraine, Nancy, France
[3] EDF DIPDE, Marseille, France

**Abstract.** From a practical point of view, Knowledge Management (KM) is both a mix of well-established corporate procedures and an emerging field of academic research. The opposition might be strong between these different points of view. To go a step forward, we had a pragmatic approach (Lorino 2016; Thievenaz 2019), including theory and practice, engineers, and academics. We will see how an innovation can germinate at low noise level, with a classical KM problem: experts are retiring soon, how could we "transfer" their experience?

Therefore, we followed a *Data Sliming* methodology (Kayakutlu & Mercier-Laurent 2016), combining Technical Expertise and Contextual Data. In this paper, we focus on an air conditioner: how and where to install it? The discussions in the team (made up of engineers, technicians, and schematic designers, then computer scientists and, to a lesser extent, academics) set up an innovation: a "conversationalist", i.e., a chatbot whose dialog is that of an expert.

In the first part, we will present the air conditioner problem and the problem of semantic shift. In power plants, "long term Knowledge" (Dourgnon; Mercier-Laurent; Roche 2005) has been alive for decades! In the second part, we will see how the team built "design sheets" for the air conditioner. We will follow the discussions and see how we made a living chatbot.

This innovation was made possible by a favourable environment, with the help of the Open Innovation Team, and has been hailed as such.

**Keywords:** Knowledge Management · Chatbot · Dialoguer · Abductive Reasoning · Data Sliming

## 1 Introduction

Knowledge Management (KM) is both a practice with a set of processes implemented in organisations (companies, institutions, etc.) and an emerging academic field. The oppositions between different conceptions of KM remain strong (Hislop, Bosua & Helms


Published by Springer Nature Switzerland AG 2024
E. Mercier-Laurent et al. (Eds.): AI4KMES 2023, IFIP AICT 693, pp. 27–37, 2024.
https://doi.org/10.1007/978-3-031-61069-1_3

2018; Holford 2020; Amidon, D. 2009). Anyway, KM is a reference discipline used in other fields (Organisational theory, information systems and ICT (Antoine & Blum 2013; Serenko & Bontis 2013; Syed, Murray, Hislop & Mouzugui 2018). The publication of the ISO 30401 km Standard will not put an end to the wide diversity of practices in organizations and businesses.

To move forward to new stages in KM, we are adopting a pragmatic approach that combines theory and practice, professionals, and academics, in a single development process (Lorino 2016; Thievenaz 2019). We will pay particular attention to the notion of Open Innovation (Chesbrough 2006; Rampa & Agogué 2020).

Our aim in this paper is to show that in a large company (EDF), an innovation can germinate little by little. The starting point is very traditional in KM field: how to preserve and disseminate practical knowledge from the field in specific contexts such as the leaving in retirement of an expert? His or her experiential knowledge is all the more important given the long lifespan of a power plant - several decades. What's more, during that period, design semantics lose their strength in favour of operational semantics. This semantic shift poses a problem in terms of capitalising knowledge and transferring it to newcomers.

This innovation, which follows on from our work on the classification of knowledge, was hailed as such by the EDF company (participation in the R&D 2020 Trophy). It is part of the evolution of engineering professions.

It is based on the *Data Sliming* concept (Kayakutlu & Mercier-Laurent 2016): how to obtain good results based on a combination of targeted data and business knowledge. The reduction in the volume of data is made possible by expertise, capable of interpreting the data and inferring the applicable resolutions.

To present it, we will examine the process by which the problem was posed and, ultimately, in our case study, to incriminate the air conditioner. There were several possible solutions but the team (made up of engineers, technicians and schematists, then computer scientists and, to a lesser extent, academics) gradually decided to make a chatbot.

As the name suggests, a chatbot involves dialogue and conversation. We consider them in their performative dimensions. They generate new knowledge for the company and enable achievements that were not initially anticipated. Building a demonstrator in a context that encourages innovation was an important step.

In the first part, we present the "air conditioner" case in its context. It is presented here for its essentially didactic aspect, as shown in the film "The Clic & Connect of the EO". The second, a very concrete point, will show the background to the "Application Sheets", in relation to the "design prescriptions". The following point is an abductive one (Lorino 2018) and of type of problem setting: "how do you decide on an air conditioner?". Points 4 and 5 show how the discussions led to the production of new data that make the chatbot a living being. This innovation has been quietly working to meet its main objective: transforms the traditional uses of chatbots.

## 2 An Air-Conditioner in the Electrical Room?

How to install an air conditioner in a power unit electrical room? This question was put very specifically to the Engineering Office (EO). The EO is studying modifications to first-generation power plants (about 30 in France) following the National Heatwave Plan and its regular updates since the 2003 alert.

The electrical room is a vast room with rows of electrical cabinets, monitored by sensors. It is essential that the air conditioner does not interfere with the operation of these sensors, which were installed when the power station was commissioned.

Half a dozen of Schematists is working in the EO. These experts translate the plant's design data into diagrams on long, wide sheets called "bed sheets" in business language. The diagrams show the physical nature of the installations, for example a particular electromagnetic relay at a particular location. They are used by the service providers responsible for carrying out the work.

This schema language is particularly rigorous. Schematists have a very specific professional skill that can be found in other industries, such as metallurgy. This skill is acquired through in-house training and, above all, through intergenerational experience. This enables the EO to play a major role in preserving and updating knowledge. Operating a power plant is a long-term process. With the renewal of equipment (electromagnetic relays, for example), design terms lose their effectiveness. The semantic shift is inevitable: the terminology in use tends to erase the design terminology. The expert knowledge of Schematists is essential. The leaving in retirement of the head of the EO and his replacement by Mr P gave rise to a new dynamic: how to capitalise on this knowledge?

To answer this question, one engineer (Mrs A) has capitalised on the knowledge of the EO for the EO. Documenting this knowledge requires writing skills and, above all, skills inspired by ethnomethodology. To be successful, this dual skill requires a propitious context: capitalising knowledge requires teamwork within a professional community led by a coordinating manager (Mr P).

In this paper, we will show how the initial objective of capitalising the EO's knowledge has evolved to become a conversational assistant or chatbot. In French, we use the term "Dialogueur" (dialoguer): it underlines the value of dialogue as an input to the IT application. It's not only a discussion between a human actant and a non-human actant, or between a human and a machine or robot. Basically, the question is that the dialogue generator has been, and is, and will be fed with data. These data were produced by conversations that have taken place within the EO. A dialoguer should be remained up to date.

The example of the air conditioning unit to be installed in a PWR (Pressurised Water Reactor) power unit's electrical room is our guideline for explaining the importance of discursive processes. In practice, through successive tests and errors, they make it possible to address the digital world of new generations of design engineers. Mrs A discreet sense of observation in situ revealed a self-evident and unquestioned practice.

First, we'll show how this engineer, her colleague (Mr F) and the head of the EO (Mr P) were able to develop the Knowledge Base (Instruction Documents), by moving away from the requirement of expert systems, which presupposed the modeling of a knowledge domain.

## 3 Produce New Documentation with Notes and Instructions to Capitalize on Knowledge

Design instructions - or more precisely, prescriptions - are set out in a succession of documents, ranging from general instructions to practical, case-by-case instructions. For easy consultation, these are set out in sheets called "Principle Sheets" or "Application Sheets" (instructions are applied without discussion). When a new case arises, the designers draw up a new sheet, so that a sheet remains in its original version. The application sheet below, applicable to level 1 (electrotechnical equipment), dates from 1992. It is the definitive version (Fig. 1).

FICHE D'APPLICATION 1.2.4

NIVEAU 1

| *Indice de la note* | *Rédacteur* | | *Vérificateur* | | *Contrôle hiérarchique* | | *Approbateur* | |
|---|---|---|---|---|---|---|---|---|
| | *Nom/Visa* | *Date* | *Nom/Visa* | *Date* | *Nom/Visa* | *Date* | *Nom/Visa* | *Date* |
| *Prov.* | D. C | | | | | | | |
| *Indice A* | D. C | 06/10/92 | J.M. P | 08/10/92 | H. H | 09/10/92 | B. A | 12/10/92 |
| *Indice B* | | | | | | | | |
| *Indice C* | | | | | | | | |
| *Indice D* | | | | | | | | |
| *Indice E* | | | | | | | | |

**Fig. 1.** Cover page of an application sheet (anonymized)

Originally, this "freezing" of the index sheets was not imagined: it was expected that the indexes would progress. However, it depends on the technological context. The automation systems in the oldest power plants are not based on software but made up of an assembly of electromagnetic equipment; the door stays open to further improvements via new data sheets. Highly structured and proprietary Control Systems were used for the next generation of Power Plants. It has made practices more rigid, and thereby limited the possibilities for new sheets. A few changes may nevertheless be made at the margin and give rise to new indexes.

The sheets are written according to a standard framework, in line with a traditional culture of writing, where stylistic formulas are banished, and the focus is on the essential, formalized in a precise, rigorous way. Here's a simplified outline of an Application Sheet (Fig. 2).

The title gives a summary of the instructions, followed by the asset, the (electrical) diagram and the room (usually the electrical room). This elementary data gives context to the design instruction. The next part concerns instructions.

- How are the instructions motivated?
- What are the design principles behind it?
- What are the explanations for this principle?

Sheet title

***Asset:***
***Schema:***
***Room:***
***Justification (motivation):***
***Principles:***
***Explanations:***
***Documentation:***

**Fig. 2.** Sheet Framework

- Additional documents are also listed.

As instructions are nearly fixed from the design stage, they are rarely updated. They reflect decades of experience that must now be shared with new hands. But these newcomers don't have the same written culture as their elders. In addition, they sometimes have difficulty in understanding the sheets because of a lack of knowledge, that is the famous tacit knowledge, so obvious to the older generation that they often fail to mention it. Experts rarely talk about it, and younger people are sometimes reluctant to ask.... Yet questioning them is where the implicit is expressed.

Our approach was based on observation, questioning and dialogue. It's a long-term project; a "sprint" operation is not possible.

## 4 How Did the Air Conditioner Come About?

A design engineer comes to the EO with a problem concerning a fire alarm that triggers unexpectedly on a power plant. The discussion then begins with all the members of the EO.

The EO first translates this question into its own technical language. The fire detector is called JDT. Everyone can see what it means, as this acronym has been used since the 1970s. In fact, JDT is a "trigram", which means, in "EDF language": 3-character code for one of the 250 main functions (called Elementary Systems, as we might say elementary blocks, basic blocks) (Fig. 3).

| CP1 CP2 | J : INCENDIE |
|---|---|
| JDT | DETECTION INCENDIE |
| JPD | DISTRIBUTION EAU INCENDIE |
| JPF | PROTECTION INCENDIE FACADES |
| JPH | PROTECTION CUVES A HUILE SALLE DES MACHINES |

**Fig. 3.** Some trigrams "Fire" PWR 900 MW

The EO is investigating these unexpected JDT triggers and has put forward several hypotheses:

- Hypothesis #1: The EO suspects a change in the electronic circuits. First, it checks whether any modifications have been made to these detectors that could have altered their behaviour. The electronic cards have recently been replaced, they're from a new manufacturer. Taking a closer look (that's the role of the EO, not the Design Office), the EO concludes that there has been no change of functionality on these cards.
- Hypothesis #2: This may involve a change to the power supplies. The EO checks the power supplies for the entire fire detection system. Here again, no changes have been made.
- Hypothesis #3: The EO then suspects that changes have been made around the fire detector. The EO asks his colleagues in the Installations Office (IO) for a list of everything that has recently been installed there. The EO then learns that an air conditioner has been installed in the electrical rooms. After discussions with the production site, the EO quickly concluded that it was this new air conditioner that was interfering with the detector.

How are the areas of expertise divided between the EO and the IO? The photo below gives a good idea of the distribution of skills between these professions: the circuits installed in the hundreds of chassis lined up along the bays of the electrical rooms are designed by the control engineers, translated into diagrams by the EO and installed by… The fitters. The installers are responsible for the entire installation, including what is needed for it to work properly: the air conditioner (Fig. 4).

**Fig. 4.** A bay in the electrical room of a 900MW PWR power plant

Air conditioners are not strictly speaking part of circuit design skills. But in this "job for insiders", as Mr P puts it, it is invaluable to be able to spot the presence of the air conditioner on the plan. And, indeed, reading a plan is not self-evident: only insiders "see" an air conditioner on the plan below (Fig. 5).

Once this third hypothesis had been chosen, the questions came fast at the EO to find a robust and rapid solution. The whole EO took part in the discussion, and the debates were lively, with some solutions being considered and then abandoned.

- Can the air conditioner be installed in the lower section?
- Is there another place in the room to move the air conditioner?

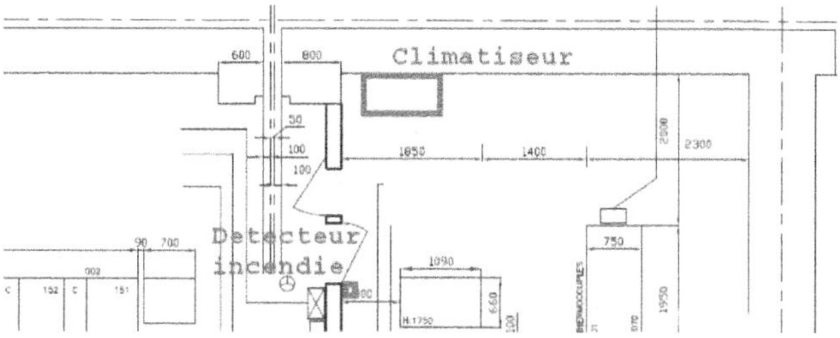


**Fig. 5.** Plan of the electrical room with the air conditioner and fire detector

- Are the cables long enough?
- What type of room are we in (protected or unprotected work)?
- What equipment could be affected in the new location?

A great deal of knowledge and know-how is required: about the equipment and installations (the location and nature of the sensors, the types of signals, changes, and behaviour over time) but also about life in the room (the comings and goings of the operators and maintenance staff).

Following this questioning, solutions emerge. Each question calls into question certain solutions, ultimately leading to a permanent solution. The plans are updated.

As the discussion progressed, Mrs A drew up a note summarising the list of questions asked and the solution chosen, with its justifications and explanations. At the end of the discussion, Mr P and Mrs A reread the note together and amend it if necessary.

This applies to virtually all discussions at the design office. Every request leads to questioning and dialogue to clarify and complete it so that the most appropriate electrical diagram can be produced.

## 5 How Do Discussions Feed the Dialoguer?

To avoid a new disruption, a sheet is initiated with this note. It is based on those already in existence, which record all the design principles, but so as not to confuse them, it is called a "Design Sheet".

A traditional sheet is "passive": it is not possible to interact with it. To make it "active", we must give it a part of the life that took place at the EO.

The initial question is noted, followed by the progression of the questions and the answers given according to the cases encountered. The lexicon (fire detector = JDT) is also included. To maximise the success rate for the answers, the different wording of the questions is entered:

- I need to install an air conditioner, what should I do?
- How do I install an air conditioner?
- Where should I position an air conditioner?

The problem is then capitalised on to make it available to as many people as possible:

- *How are the instructions justified?* Air conditioner must be installed in an area protected from the risk of disturbance.

- *What principles should underlie this installation?* The air conditioner must be installed on the floor, in a defined area, according to the plans given.
- *What explanations are given for this principle?* The air conditioner must be kept away from certain overly sensitive sensors that it could interfere with.

The conclusion is a warning about this phenomenon of disturbance, as well as a suggestion to get in touch with the IO before each installation of an air conditioner to check the surrounding equipment.

It is important to explain the disadvantages of air conditioner too close to the sensors, with a clear explanation of the consequences of any erroneous action. Contrary to what some KM theorists claim, the pseudo-taboo of Judeo-Christian culture does not exist in industrial practice: *we say and write what not to do.*

# 6 The Dialoguer and AI

## 6.1 AI Enables Dialogue

An instruction does not follow a straight line, and there are many design variants. The expert knows them well, but this is not the case for novices. To help them, Mr P draws and diagrams the different possibilities as he sees them (the different cases are rarely verbalised, they are drawn).

Each case, each situation, is associated with a design principle:

IF (Case #i) THEN (Principle #j)

This rule of deduction is well known in artificial intelligence, used in forward chaining or backward chaining. In forward chaining, we start from the data, for example we recognise Case #i and deduce the application of Principle #j (deductive reasoning, based on the data). In backward chaining, when we want to know if Principle #j is applicable, we look to see if Case #i arises (hypothetical reasoning, based on the goals).

The knowledge contained in these sheets is used by an AI system, which reasons according to the situations encountered. The expert's knowledge, his or her ability to recognise situations to which a novice would not necessarily pay attention, is apparent at every step. The transmission of knowledge through dialogue has thus made headway. The dialogue is provided by an intelligent system, according to the situations encountered in the field.

The Design Sheets are adapted to the dialogue:

- Addition of a § Questions. Questions from another context (Where to install a conditioner? How to control a conditioner?).
- Addition of a § Verb/Action. Verbs also have synonyms (install, set up).
- Addition of a § Comment by the users.

Mrs A reworked the sheets with her colleague Mr. F, who is very familiar with the field of electricity and the logic of wiring. EDF R&D Open Innovation Team introduced them to voice solutions. They decided to try out to better test the sequence of questions. The dialogue was refined over time.

- The user: "How do I install an air conditioner?"
- The application: "What room are you in?"
- The user: "In the Control Room".
- The application: "You need to install the air conditioner in an area that is sheltered from the risk of disturbance" (justification).
- The user: "How?"
- The application: "In which case are you?"
- The user: "Case #1".
- Application: "The air conditioner must be installed on the floor, in a defined area, according to the plans given" (principle).
- The user: "Why?"
- The application: "The air-conditioner must be located away from certain sensors that are too sensitive and could interfere with them" (explanation).

All the sheets are reviewed with this dialogue in mind, which helps to solidify them (they tended to drift over time: the principle slipped partly into the justification and the justification into the explanation).

The principle now lists all possible cases (the application sheet only lists one case at a time). The Design Sheets will be updated as situations evolve (a slow and rare process).

### 6.2 The Life of the Dialoguer

The Open Innovation Team supports this innovation approach and gives it a breath of fresh air with Lean Startup. Iterative experimentation is authorised and even encouraged!

The team had the idea of using these sheets in a chatbot, a tool traditionally designed for simple, recurring questions rather than complex technical ones. Unlike a voice server, a chatbot is mute, with a text-only or graphical interface. The advantage of a chatbot is that it is easy to use: a question leads to an answer, or even a more detailed explanation, illustrated by diagrams. The user can give feedback on the answer, which helps to improve the tool and keep it alive.

Knowledge is not structured in the same way as it is in Expert Systems. There is no modelling of the knowledge domain: there is no way of describing the variety of knowledge involved, in the form of a semantic network, an ontology or even a hierarchy of concepts. It is the dialogue, with its succession of questions and answers, that organises the knowledge, taking account of "semantic shifts". In other words, the Data Model - or rather, the Knowledge Model - is dictated by the dialogue modes. This optimisation requires a great deal of rigour, from design to implementation. It is the price to pay for the tool to operate in a contextualised and relevant way. Especially as the application is rich in documents, diagrams, plans and links with other applications, references that need to be carefully managed.

The AI Team at EDF Solution Lab took matters into their own hands, producing a very convincing demonstrator and prototype. The prototype is systematically tested before being put into service to ensure that it complies with the dialogue set out in the Design Sheets. The tests are exhaustive and recorded in a thick test book, bugs are corrected, and the application is tested again.

Once installed on workstations, the dialoguer is directly accessible to engineers and technicians. It reaches its target audience straight away! Its commissioning is satisfactory: thanks to the completeness of its knowledge base, 94% of the themes are recognized. Unrecognized themes and user comments are reviewed weekly by the expert, who improves the tool and brings it to life. In fact, the life of the dialoguer can only be sustained by the questioning of users (assisted, in the future, by chatbot suggestions?).

## 7 Conclusions

The installation of the air-conditioner has shown us that the design and production of a dialoguer leads to an innovative practice, which can be disseminated through the production of a short film: "The Clic & Connect of the EO". This new practice makes it possible to capitalise on experiential knowledge following, for example, a leaving in retirement. It adapts to very specific and localised cases.

This innovation is the result of the performance of inter-professional discussions within an informal group driven largely by a team spirit and a community of "common concern" views.

It saves on data and knowledge. In this sense, it contributes to the sustainable development of the company's digital economy.

The chatbot has acquired a certain notoriety: it knows how to provide relevant information in response to a clearly formulated question, in the terms envisaged beforehand by its designer. The dialoguer uses the chatbot's technology but incorporates the questions as formulated by the agents involved in the EO. Cognitive AI enables them to be translated into an application (Dourgnon, Antoine & Samba 2020). Our Chatbot-Dialoguer is able to answer questions formulated in natural language and avoids the time wasted searching through the mass of documents recording experiential knowledge in the field.

The codification of explicit and implicit knowledge cannot be reduced to a process of Knowledge Extraction; it is a socialised process, in which discursive exchanges within different communities play a central role. Wenger's work (Thievenaz 2019) has stimulated a great deal of academic research on Communities of Practice (CoP).

Today, many informal communities, with various names, have developed in companies and organisations (Mabey & Zhao 2017; Lorino, 2016; APQC 2021). A new open question arises: how can these communities be managed effectively for the company and for each of the members of the community? A new challenge for managerial practices?

**Acknowledgments.** We would like to thank our EDF colleagues: Matthieu André, Marie-Astrid De Muynck, Idriss El Asry, Anne-Cécile Ladrange, Thibault Lemattre, Aleksandra Lewicka and Alain Ourghanlian.

## References

Amidon, D.: Innovation Strategy for the Knowledge Economy. Routledge, London (2009)

Antoine, A., Blum, G.: La gestion des connaissances ou le Knowledge Management (KM). Revue internationale de psychosociologie et de gestion des comportements organisationnels, vol. XX, pp. 23–31 (2013)

APQC American Productivity & Quality Center: Atteindre l'excellence avec les Communautés de pratique (2021)

Chesbrough, H.W.: Open Innovation: The New Imperative for Creating and Profiting from Technology. First Trade Paper edn. Harvard Business Review Press, Boston (2006)

Depecker, L.: L'invention de la langue: le choix des mots nouveaux. Armand Colin, Larousse (2001)

Dourgnon, A., Dang T.: High level ontology for "The Internet of Things" adapted to industry - a case study in Electrical Engineering. In: KM Workshop, IJCAI, Stockholm, Suède (2018)

Dourgnon, A., Antoine, A., Samba, M.: Ontologies Combining Design Semantics and Semantics Used in Operation and Maintenance: Feedback from EDF Power Plants Case Studies. I-ESA, Tarbes, France (2020)

Héritier, F.: Une pensée en mouvement. Poches, Odile Jacob, Paris (2013)

Hislop, D., Bosua, R., Helms, R.: Knowledge Management in Organizations: A Critical Introduction. 4th edn. OUP Oxford, Oxford (2018)

Holford, W.D.: Managing Knowledge in Organizations: A Critical Pragmatic Perspective. Palgrave Macmillan, New York (2020)

Kayakutlu, G., Mercier-Laurent, E.: Intelligence in Energy, ISTE Editions, Londres (2016)

Lorino, P.: Pragmatisme et Etude des Organisations. Economica (2018)

Lorino, P.: De Skerlock Holmes au lean management: théorie et pratique, deux dimensions insé-parables de l'enquête. Dans: A La Pointe Du Management. Ce Que La Recherche Apporte Au Manager. Dunod (2016)

Mercier-Laurent E., Kayalica O., Owoc M.L.: Artificial intelligence for knowledge management. In: 8th IFIP WG 12.6 International Workshop, AI4KM 2021, Held at IJCAI 2020, Yokohama, Japan, 7–8 January. Technology Book 614 (2020)

Mabey, C., Zhao, S.: Managing five paradoxes of knowledge exchange in networked organizations: new priorities for HRM? Hum. Resour. Manag. J. **27**, 39–57 (2017). https://doi.org/10.1111/1748-8583.12106

Rampa, R., Agogué, M.: Lorsque les démarches d'exploration nécessitent de l'innovation collective. Rev. Francaise Gest. N° **291**, 53–71 (2020)

Serenko, A., Bontis, N.: The intellectual core and impact of the knowledge management academic discipline. J. Knowl. Manag. **17** (2013). https://doi.org/10.1108/13673271311300840

Syed, J., Murray, P.A., Hislop, D., Mouzugui, Y.: The Palgrave Handbook of Knowledge Management. Palgrave Macmillan, Cham (2018)

Tamba, I.: La sémantique. Que sais-je? PUF, Paris (2007)

Thievenaz, J.: Enquêter et apprendre au travail: Approcher l'expérience avec John Dewey. Editions Raison et Passions (2019)

Wenger, E.: Communities of Practice: Learning, Meaning, and Identity. Cambridge University Press, Cambridge (1998)

# Supporting Food Computing with Ontologies and Artificial Intelligence Methods for Sustainability

Weronika T. Adrian[1(✉)], Julia Ignacyk[1], Katarzyna Pyrczak[2], Krzysztof Kluza[1], Piotr Wiśniewski[1,3], and Antoni Ligęza[1]

[1] AGH University of Krakow, al. A. Mickiewicza 30, 30-059 Krakow, Poland
{wta,kluza,ligeza}@agh.edu.pl

[2] Jagiellonian University Medical College, Montelupich 4, 30-155 Kraków, Poland
katarzyna.pyrczak@student.uj.edu.pl

[3] University of St. Gallen, 9000 St. Gallen, Switzerland
piotr.wisniewski@student.unisg.ch

**Abstract.** This paper investigates the potential of combining food ontologies and AI in the food sector for enhanced sustainability. We argue that this combination can foster sustainable food systems, underscoring how semantic structures and AI can facilitate precision agriculture, sustainable food choices, personalized diets, and climate change mitigation. Our goal is to discuss how these innovative technologies can be harnessed to better understand, manage, and ultimately transform the food domain for a sustainable future. As a first step towards achieving this goal, we provide an overview of prominent food ontologies and knowledge graphs in the food domain highlighting their structures and focal points, and we illustrate the value of ontological reasoning through practical food domain examples, using SPARQL queries and ontological reasoning for insightful knowledge derivation. We also discuss how to combine AI and ontologies to create new knowledge resources for improved data integration and management.

**Keywords:** Food Ontologies · Ontological Reasoning in Food Systems · Sustainability in Food Systems · Knowledge graphs

## 1 Introduction

The concept of sustainability is neither new nor revolutionary. This notion has been prevalent since the late '80s, marked by the publication of the UN report titled "Our Common Future" [8]. Education in sustainability often begins outside university classrooms. However, with the emergence of new environmental risks and the formulation of countermeasures, one should continually expand their knowledge in this domain. This is not only to safeguard the future for upcoming generations but also to enhance the efficiency of our daily lives.


Published by Springer Nature Switzerland AG 2024
E. Mercier-Laurent et al. (Eds.): AI4KMES 2023, IFIP AICT 693, pp. 38–54, 2024.
https://doi.org/10.1007/978-3-031-61069-1_4

While specific objectives such as the 17 Sustainable Development Goals (SDGs) are established by the United Nations [23], there are still different insights on how far we are from achieving them. Divergent views exist e.g. regarding palm oil production, which is implicated in deforestation yet requires less land compared to other vegetable alternatives[1].

There are several of the SDGs directly or indirectly concerned with food and the food industry [23]:

- **Zero Hunger (Goal 2)**: This goal directly targets ending world hunger, achieving food security, improving nutrition, and promoting sustainable agriculture.
- **Good Health and Well-being (Goal 3)**: Although this goal is about health, it is related to food in terms of ending malnutrition and ensuring healthy lifestyles, which is related to diet and nutrition, that might be a product of the food industry.
- **Responsible Consumption and Production (Goal 12)**: This goal encourages sustainable consumption and production patterns, which include how food is produced, processed, and consumed.

As managing complex data is crucial, especially in the multifaceted food industry, ontologies that constitute a key component of semantic web technologies, can effectively model connections between dietary choices, recipes, and ingredients, as well as environmental impacts, facilitating the extraction of valuable insights. Advances in Artificial Intelligence (AI) have shown transformative potential across a wide range of domains. When AI is combined with the structure provided by ontologies, we can achieve superior results in understanding and managing food-related data.

The motivation for integrating food ontologies and AI in the food sector aligns closely with the abovementioned three objectives. We advocate for using smart technology to grow more food, help people make healthier eating choices, and reduce food waste. Addressing Zero Hunger (Goal 2) is pivotal; by utilizing ontology-driven AI, it is possible to enhance agricultural productivity and food security through precision agriculture. Secondly, for Good Health and Well-being (Goal 3), we underscore the role of personalized diets and sustainable food choices facilitated by AI and ontologies, which can lead to better health outcomes and nutritional awareness among populations. Lastly, by leveraging ontological reasoning and AI, it is possible to use these methods to optimize food production, minimize waste, and promote sustainability in the food chain which is essential for Responsible Consumption and Production (Goal 12). This trio of goals forms the bedrock of the paper's motivation, guiding a vision where technology significantly contributes to a more sustainable world.

In this paper, we extend our previous workshop work [2] and discuss how AI and food ontologies can enhance sustainability. We give a brief overview on such issues as biodiversity protection, precision agriculture, food waste reduction, sustainable supply chains, individualized diets, and climate change abatement,

[1] See https://ourworldindata.org/grapher/area-land-needed-to-global-oil.

emphasizing the potential of converging ontologies and AI in the food industry. We also explore the intersection of ontologies and AI in the food domain, focusing on how this combination can be utilized to enhance sustainability. We present an overview of ontologies in the food domain, discussing how they can capture the complexity of food-related data and provide a structured framework for data representation. We delve into ontological reasoning, demonstrating how it allows the extraction of implicit knowledge from food ontologies.

The paper is structured as follows. In Sect. 2, we give an overview how the combination of AI and food ontologies can be harnessed to promote sustainability. Section 3 elaborates on ontologies and their application in the food domain. Section 4 delves into the concept of ontological reasoning and illustrates how reasoning can be used to extract implicit knowledge from food ontologies. In Sect. 5, we discuss how to develop a knowledge base that links existing ontologies with entities automatically learned from recipes. The paper is summarized in Sect. 6.

## 2 Combining AI with Food Ontologies for Sustainability

Ontologies are commonly used in creating knowledge bases. They provide a formal way to represent knowledge. An ontology defines a set of concepts and the relationships between them, which allows for consistent and accurate categorization of information. By using ontologies, knowledge bases can be more easily searched, queried, and updated. [20]. In the field of food computing, ontologies can be used to create knowledge bases that represent and organize food-related information. Domain experts and ontology engineers are responsible for identifying the key concepts and relationships within a particular domain and creating an ontology that accurately reflects them. Once an ontology is developed, it can be used to build a knowledge base populated with instance data of recipes that in turn refer to ingredients, cooking techniques, nutrition information, and other food-related concepts. The created knowledge base can be used for a variety of purposes, such as food recommendation, personalized nutrition planning, or recipe retrieval. There are multiple areas in which food ontologies and AI methods can contribute to improving sustainability [12], such as [2]:

- Biodiversity – Food ontologies can provide a structured knowledge framework about the dependencies in food production.
- Precision Agriculture – Ontologies may offer a framework for structuring and correctly interpreting data from soil sensors, weather reports, and other variables, guiding farmers towards timely planting, irrigation, etc., and therefore minimizing waste and diminishing agriculture's environmental footprint [19].
- Reducing Food Waste – Leveraging food ontologies and AI can enhance demand prediction, and mitigate overproduction, but also minimize food waste [25] in homes by identifying available food items and suggesting recipes to use up ingredients before they spoil.
- Sustainable Supply Chains – Food ontologies might help ensure that the analyzed data is relevant and accurately represents the various elements of the supply chain [13].

- Sustainable Food Choices and Personalized Diets – While AI facilitates personalized diets, tailored to individual health needs and preferences [3,14,18], which enables more sustainable eating decisions [16], ontologies constitute an important element organizing food-related data.
- Climate Change Mitigation – Food ontologies can provide a detailed and organized insight into how different farming methods are linked to their effects on the environment [4].

By using AI to understand food production needs and data from soil and weather, farmers can make better choices about planting and watering. This helps reduce waste and is good for the environment, therefore it could help achieve the goal of ending hunger (SDG 2).

Organizing information about food can also help create diets that meet individual health needs and preferences, leading to better health and awareness about nutrition. This approach is important for making healthier food choices, reducing waste, and improving overall health, contributing to the goal of good health and well-being (SDG 3).

Using ontologies, which help to ensure data is relevant and accurate, can improve predictions about what people need and reduce overproduction. This is key to supporting responsible consumption and production (SDG 12).

## 3 Selected Ontological Knowledge Sources

There exists a variety of ontologies and knowledge graphs in the field of food, each targeting different aspects due to the broad scope of the subject. These ontologies differ in their size and function, some containing detailed instances while others act as more generic frameworks. Our paper primarily explores the ontologies in the nutrition sector, examining their specific characteristics and structural elements.

### 3.1 FoodOn

The FoodOn ontology [10] is the most extensive source of structured information on food. It encompasses 9,600 categories covering various food products like animal, plant, mushroom, and processed foods, along with their processing methods. Beyond food items, FoodOn's scope extends to include ontologies related to harvesting, features, and production of food, which can be explored further at FoodOn's website[2]. This open-source ontology is maintained by the OBO Foundry, a consortium that offers interoperable ontologies for life sciences.

One of the key advantages of FoodOn is its ability to capture the complex relationships between different types of food. The ontology includes relationships between ingredients and recipes, as well as between recipes and the food products they require. This makes it possible to analyze and compare different

[2] See: https://foodon.org/.

types of food in new and innovative ways, and to develop new insights into the relationships between food and health.

The food products described by FoodOn can be classified into four categories.

1. The first is agricultural, unprocessed products derived from ontologies such as ENVO (environment), AGRO (agronomy), NCVBITaxon (taxonomy), and CheBI (chemical units of biological importance).
2. The second type is harvested material, known as crops, which includes plants, animals, and fungi. Ontologies such as PO (plant anatomy), UBERON (animal anatomy), FAO (fungal anatomy), and PATO (Phenotype and trait) comprise this type of product.
3. Processed products are another group. They are described by the ontologies PO2 (processes and observations), FOBI (food biomarkers), FIDEO (food-drug interactions), GenEpiO (genomic epidemiology), DOID (diseases), and ONS (nutritional research).
4. FoodOn also refers to the consumer category, which pulls on the previously stated ontologies - FIDEO, FOBI, DOID, GenEpiO - as well as the ONE (food epidemiology) ontology.

FoodOn's information is universally applicable. They are mentioned in economic, food science, epidemiological, and nutrient content study areas [6]. It is being used to develop new algorithms for recipe recommendation and meal planning, as well as to create new tools for food safety and traceability [1].

### 3.2 Wikidata

Wikidata is a free and open knowledge base that serves as a central repository for structured data and information. It is a collaborative project that was created by the Wikimedia Foundation and launched in 2012. Wikidata's purpose is to provide a common data source that can be used by Wikimedia projects such as Wikipedia, as well as by external applications and organizations. Wikidata uses entities, properties, and statements to structurally arrange information. Real-world items like people, places, events, or concepts are represented by entities identified with "QID"s. Properties describe the connections between entities and determine the traits or properties of those entities. Statements are triples of subject, predicate, and object that are formed by the exact values supplied to properties for a particular entity. Wikidata offers a sizable source of ingredient data and can be used to get comprehensive descriptions, nutrient information, and relationships between items [27]. A huge amount of food information available in Wikidata, enables advancements in food-related applications and technologies.

### 3.3 Other Ontologies and Knowledge Graphs

Food KG [11] is an ontology developed by aggregating data on recipes, nutrients, and preparation times for given meals to be able to recommend recipes to users that fit their preferences. Its purpose is to recommend recipes tailored to individual user preferences, targeting customers and practical uses.

This data is unified into a single knowledge graph and draws from three primary sources:

1. Recipe data, which includes recipes sourced from books, blogs, or structured datasets, primarily derived from the dataset created by the Im2Recipe project.
2. Nutritional information provided by the United States Department of Agriculture (USDA).
3. General food knowledge, where FoodOn is utilized for structuring data regarding the origin, preparation, and processing of food.

Food KG comprises three key components:

1. 'Food' with new classes,
2. 'FoodOn' featuring imported classes from FoodOn,
3. 'Ingredient' containing instances related to recipes and ingredients.

Another ontology that focuses on structuring food products is the SPO [7]. It comprises three distinct modules: external, generic, and application-specific, each further subdivided into various sub-modules. There are two key links between the generic and application-specific modules in the SPO ontology. The 'food' module has relationships with both the 'process' and 'product' modules.

On the other hand, the Ingredients Ontology[3] aims to establish connections between ingredients, their respective categories, and the products derived from them. The notation convention used there is "language:ingredient name". This ontology is under continuous development to keep its data relevant and comprehensive. Within this framework, ingredient names are in the 'Named_ingredient' class, while products that are produced from other ingredients fall into the 'OFF_ingredient' class. Additionally, the 'FoodSource' class is a crucial component of the ontology. It encompasses all potential food sources that serve as the foundation for ingredients, encompassing natural elements, animals, plants, minerals, or fluids.

The Ontology for Nutritional Studies (ONS) formally organizes the body of knowledge surrounding food studies. It encompasses a total of 6,056 distinct classes [26]. ONS was developed by integrating information about food and its processing, derived both from existing ontologies and through the creation of a new classification system for food terminology. A significant part of ONS, specifically 2,809 classes, were directly imported from FoodOn, accounting for nearly half of ONS's total classes. Other contributing sources to ONS include the Ontology for Biomedical Investigations, the Semanticscience Integrated Ontology, and The Information Artifact Ontology.

### 3.4 Comparison of ONS, FoodKG, SPO and FoodOn Ontologies

Table 1 shows a comparative analysis of the ONS, FoodKG, SPO, and FoodOn ontologies in terms of selected aspects [2].

[3] See https://wiki.openfoodfacts.org/Ingredients_ontology.

**Table 1.** Comparison of the ONS, FoodKG, SPO, and FoodOn ontologies [2]

| Selected aspect | ONS | FoodKG | SPO | FoodOn |
|---|---|---|---|---|
| Class defining a recipe | ✓ | ✓ | ✓ | ✓ |
| Class defining a meal | ✓ | ✓ | ✗ | ✓ |
| Class defining a component | ✓ | ✓ | ✗ | ✗ |
| Class defining a product substitute | ✗ | ✗ | ✗ | ✓ |
| Class defining food | ✓ | ✓ | ✓ | ✓ |
| Classes regarding drinking | ✓ | ✗ | ✓ | ✓ |
| Classes regarding processed food | ✓ | ✓ | ✗ | ✓ |
| Classes describing process of making food | ✓ | ✗ | ✓ | ✓ |
| Classes regarding diet | ✓ | ✗ | ✓ | ✓ |
| Classes regarding user preferences | ✓ | ✗ | ✓ | ✓ |
| Classes regarding product quality | ✓ | ✓ | ✓ | ✓ |
| Classes regarding taste | ✓ | ✓ | ✗ | ✓ |

## 4 Ontological Reasoning in Food Domain

A significant aspect of ontologies lies in their practical applications. Through the process of querying ontologies, one can retrieve necessary information that is already present within the ontology. Furthermore, ontology inference enables the extraction of data that is not explicitly provided in the ontology.

Let us analyze the problem of looking for substitution in a food recipe. Based on the Food Recipe Ingredient Substitution ontology design pattern [15] for the question "What vegan product can be substituted for beef in a roast romaine recipe?" an example query in SPARQL might looks as follows [2]:

```
SELECT  DISTINCT ?recipe ?food_item
    WHERE{ ?recipe_ingr_sub rdf:type food:food_recipe_ingr_subst_spec.
        ?recipe rdf:type food:food_recipe.
        ?set rdf:type food:ingredient_set_specification.
        ?spec rdf:type food:ingredient_specification.
        ?spec2 rdf:type food:ingredient_specification.
        ?food_item rdf:type food:food_item.
        ?set_trans rdf:type food:ingredient_set_trans_spec.

        ?recipe_ingr_sub food:has_part ?recipe.
        ?recipe_ingr_sub food:has_part food:pieczen_rzymska.
        food:pieczen_rzymska food:has_component ?set.
        ?set food:has_member ?spec.
        ?spec food:is_about food:wolowina.
        ?recipe_ingr_sub food:has_part ?set_trans.
```

```
    ?set_trans food:has_member ?spec2.
    ?spec2 food:is_about ?food_item.
    ?food_item food:has_quality food:weganski.
}
```

The result of running the HermiT reasoner [9] is a vegan product that can be substituted for beef: chickpeas. These queries can be even more specific and further refined to not only look at the characteristics of the product itself but also take into account the user's preferences.

The ontology's structure needs to be formalized to facilitate automatic processing, as ontology inference plays a crucial role in deriving data that is not explicitly stated. The inference was conducted using the Protégé application, employing the Pellet reasoner, supporting the OWL-DL language and ontology inference with instances [24].

Let us analyze the following example. The class 'food_item' is linked to quality through the relationship 'has_quality' and 'has_no_quality'. Both the ObjectProperties 'has_quality' and 'has_no_quality' in their description have the 'food_item' class in the domain and the 'quality' class in the value range. A new instance of 'wieprzowina' ('pork') was introduced into the ontology, without assigning it to any class, but linking it to instances of the 'quality' class using the 'has_quality' and 'has_no_quality' relationships. Before running the reasoner, one can see in the `Individuals (by type)` window that the pork does not belong to any class. After running it in the `Individuals by type (inferred)` window, the pork is already assigned as an instance of the 'food_item' class, as shown in Fig. 1.

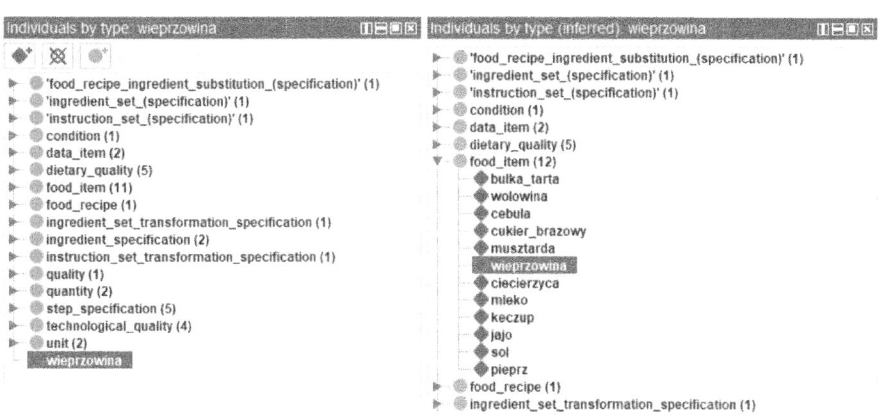


**Fig. 1.** Inference result after adding a new unclassified instance to an ontology.

# 5 Integrating Existing Knowledge with Machine-Learned Information About Recipes

It is commonly known that a healthy diet prevents disease and promotes a long, happy life. As people have different allergies and dietary requirements, which is why very specific diets are becoming more popular, they frequently upload, share, and record food photographs, recipes, cooking films, and food diaries on the Internet and social networks. As a result, a large portion of textual information is now published in open online repositories and available in digital form. Despite having access to such vast amounts of information, constructing diets and catering to individual nutritional needs can still be challenging. However, with the development of technology and artificial intelligence, there is potential for innovative solutions. One such idea is analyzing and understanding the ingredients in recipes and linking them to formal knowledge bases on which logical reasoning can be performed.

A recipe is a valuable source of data for artificial intelligence due to its structure and unambiguity. Cooking instructions usually consist of specific steps, amounts of ingredients, and cooking times, which makes them ideal for analysis. Recipes are a specific source of data that may be used to train language models, make culinary suggestions, examine cooking trends, and generate recipes automatically. The rules and semantics of the various sections of the recipe text can be modeled quite effectively if they are carefully examined and expressed. AI systems can comprehend and interpret a recipe with the use of named entity recognition (NER) and entity linking. Ingredients, cooking times, and other crucial components of a recipe can all be identified and labeled with the use of NER, which is the process of automatically detecting and identifying named entities in text. Due to entity linking, which is a technique that involves assigning the recognized named entities to corresponding entities in a knowledge base or ontology, ingredients can be connected with their descriptions and properties, such as dietary implications, culinary style, nutritional value, and ingredient substitutes.

## 5.1 Named Entity Recognition from Culinary Recipes

Named Entity Recognition (NER) is a valuable tool in food computing that can be used to extract insights from unstructured text data related to food and nutrition. Entity extraction can be used to identify ingredients, cooking methods, and measurements in recipes which makes possible to categorize recipe, substitute ingredients and analyze nutritional value. Similarly, in menu descriptions, NER can be employed to detect food and beverage items including the names of dishes, types of cuisine, and drink options, to help with menu recommendations, personalized menu suggestions, and dietary restrictions. Entity identification can be also applied to social media posts, online forums, and product reviews to extract information about food-related entities. This can provide valuable insights into consumer preferences and sentiment towards food products and inform marketing and product development strategies.

In 2012, S. Mori, T. Sasada, Y. Yamakata, and K. Yoshino [17] published their research on the subject of a novel approach to extract recipe-specific information, such as ingredient names, quantities, and cooking procedures, using machine learning algorithms. Researcher Yuzhe Chen, from University of Pittsburgh in 2017 presented a statistical machine learning approach to generating graph structures from food recipes [5]. The main aim of the study was to generate recipe graphs that capture the underlying structure of recipes, including ingredient relationships, preparation steps, and cooking methods. In 2020, a paper [21] was published on the subject that covers various Named Entity Recognition (NER) methods used in the food field and compares their performance on FoodBase corpus dataset [22], which consists of 1000 recipes annotated with food concepts. The recipes were chosen from the most popular recipe-sharing social network - Allrecipes. During the studies, two distinct methodologies: FoodIe and NCBO were utilized to extract food entities from each recipe.

### 5.2 Linking the Recognized Entities with Knowledge Bases

Entity Linking (EL) has promising achievements in food computing. Researchers have been able to extract significant information and insights from food-related data sources by applying various named-entity disambiguation strategies. Interestingly, entity linking has made significant strides in assessing the nutritional composition of recipes. EL-based algorithms can compute the nutritional value of a meal, including calories, macronutrients, and micronutrients, by integrating information about food products with their nutrient information. This helps individuals and food corporations make more educated decisions about the nutritional value of food products.

One of the most intriguing advances in food data science is the use of entity linking in recipe recommendation systems. Named-entity disambiguation algorithms, in essence, can connect the elements in a recipe to a knowledge base, allowing for more intelligent recipe recommendations. Entity linking can offer alternate ingredients or recipes that better meet an individual's dietary restrictions, tastes, and item availability by understanding the context of a recipe. For instance, if a person is allergic to peanuts, an EL-powered tool can offer alternative nut kinds of butter, for example, almond or cashew butter. One example of such a recommendation system is the FoodKG platform developed by researchers at the University of Bonn [11]. The system employs entity linking to analyze the ingredients in chosen recipes and suggest alternatives that share similar ingredients or flavor profiles. In addition, the FoodKG platform provides nutritional information about each recipe - its calorie and nutrient content from the recipe's ingredients, which are linked to a database of food items and their nutrient information. In 2022, researchers from Poland presented TASTEset - a dataset of food-related text, including recipes and ingredient lists, that can be used for training and evaluating entity recognition and linking models [28]. The TASTEset includes over 700 recipes with 3,788 ingredients and above 13,000 entities of different types. The dataset includes information about ingredient names, quantities, and units, as well as other relevant information such as cooking methods and preparation instructions.

### 5.3 Development of an Integrated Knowledge Graph

By using the above-described techniques, namely Named Entity Recognition and Entity Linking, we have developed a knowledge graph – an integrated knowledge base that consists of data about recipes, the ingredients required to prepare the described dish, as well as the nutrients of the required ingredients. A list of ingredients with nutritional information was gathered in JSON format from the FoodData Central website. Moreover, we have linked the food entities identified in the recipes with the entries in selected existing ontologies; this way enriching our knowledge graph with information already defined in the ontologies. Thanks to this, the entities, identified in the recipes obtain broader context and can be reasoned upon, using the relations defined in the ontologies. For instance, knowing that a string 'apple' in a recipe denotes an entity 'FOODON_00002473'[4] we can use its properties defined in FoodON to infer more properties and understand its taxonomic information (e.g., subclassing certain types of food that can be either forbidden or prescribed in a certain dietary plan).

To obtain data about recipes, a scraper was implemented in Python. The data was downloaded from the website of the Complex Systems Lab at Indraprastha Institute of Information Technology Delhi (IIIT Delhi)[5]. The scraper collected approximately 900,000 recipes from the initial source. Recipes with ingredients and their quantities were saved in JSON files. After preprocessing operations 61,577 different recipes were gathered. The final collection of recipes included 2,930 different ingredients, 2,891 of which had names that were no longer than five words. Only entities with less than 5 words were selected for further work.

The implementation of ingredient recognition in the recipe's text was based on a machine-learning approach. The implemented NER model was created using the Spacy library and the "en_core_web_lg" pre-trained language model[6]. To implement customized NER that could recognize ingredients in a recipe's text, it was retrained to recognize additional custom entity types based on specific requirements. To achieve that, a new label called "ingredient" was added to the scope of entity labels. Following the training, nearly 62,000 recipes were fed into the model to recognize things in step-by-step instructions. To improve the results, things identified as ingredients were tokenized, and only words relevant to the notion of food were additionally chosen based on their WordNet synsets.

Following the entity recognition step, the entity linking process was employed to establish connections between the recognized words and objects from knowledge bases. The entity linking tool used SPARQL queries to find corresponding entries in selected knowledge bases for identified named entities. Using a Python

---

[4] See http://purl.obolibrary.org/obo/FOODON_00002473.

[5] See https://cosylab.iiitd.edu.in/.

[6] See release en_core_web_sm-3.6.0 Spacy model: https://github.com/explosion/spacy-models/releases/tag/en_core_web_sm-3.6.0.

script, the tool queries the FoodON and Wikidata databases to find relevant information for each recognized ingredient. Due to their differing structures, separate queries are designed to ensure optimal searching in both knowledge bases. The queries are intended to look for synonyms and particular labels relevant to the food domain. In total, 428 ingredients were successfully linked to the FoodOn ontology, and 329 ingredients were linked to the Wikidata knowledge base. A total of 597 components were obtained, each of which had at least one link to either FoodOn ontology or the Wikidata knowledge base. Furthermore, within the 597 components, 160 entities had the distinction of having links to both the FoodOn ontology and the Wikidata knowledge base. This indicates a substantial overlap and agreement between the two ontologies for these specific entities, further reinforcing the reliability and consistency of the obtained results.

The entity-linking process successfully connected recognized ingredients to relevant entities in both the FoodOn ontology and the Wikidata knowledge base. The resulting collection of components with links to these ontologies provided enriched information and insights, contributing to a deeper understanding of the ingredients' attributes, properties, and relationships in the broader culinary and nutritional contexts.

### 5.4 A Graph Knowledge Base for Nutrients and Recipes

Upon the completion of the named entity recognition, linking process, and integration of datasets, four final files were obtained. These resources were used in consolidating the processed information and facilitating further analysis. The content of the four files is as follows:

- recipes data collected by the scrapper
- unique ingredient's nutritional values based on FoodCentral data unified with the master dataset
- mapped entities with FoodOn knowledge base's identifiers
- mapped entities with WikiData knowledge base's identifiers

These four final files represented the culmination of the data processing and integration steps, providing structured and consolidated data for further analysis and graph database creation.

The final graph database structure revolves around two main types of nodes: recipes and ingredients (see Figs. 2 and 3). Each recipe node is mandated to have properties such as name and instructions, providing essential information about the recipe itself. Ingredient nodes are equipped with a name property and can potentially include additional properties such as fat, carbohydrate, protein, and energy, as well as Wikidata link, and FoodOn link. These properties capture specific details about the nutrient composition of the ingredients.

By combining data from two sources, namely the master database and the ingredient nutritional values set, a total of 4,847 distinct items related to recipe components were obtained. These items represented a comprehensive collection of ingredients and nutrients used in the cooking recipes. Through the consolidation and merging of data from two distinct sources of knowledge, a total of 1,437

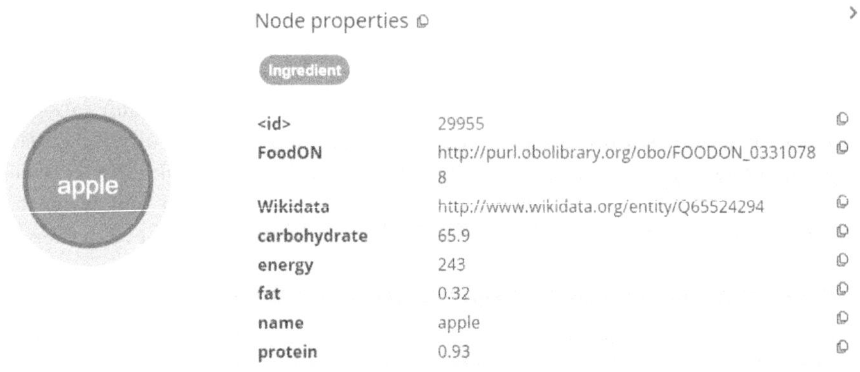


**Fig. 2.** Example ingredient node with properties

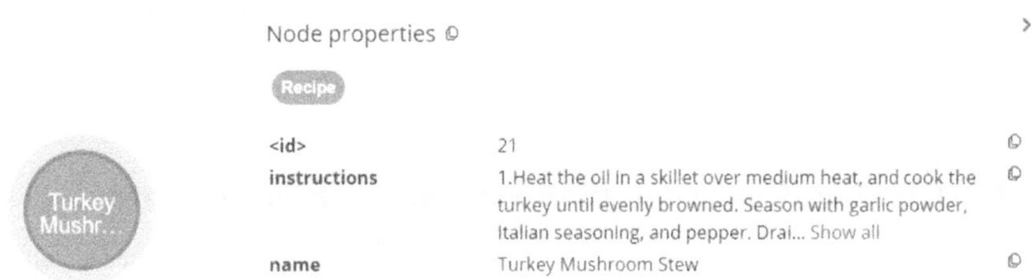


**Fig. 3.** Example recipe node with properties

recipe ingredients were identified that were common to both datasets. After a series of import queries, a total of 65,784 nodes were created, comprising 4,847 ingredient nodes and 60,937 recipe nodes. These nodes formed the backbone of the graph database, representing the distinct items extracted from the dataset. In addition to the creation of nodes, there were also 625,109 relationships between nodes. These relationships captured the associations and connections between ingredients and recipes, forming a network within the graph database. Out of the total number of ingredients analyzed, a subset of 3,357 components was found to have properties associated with nutritional values. Among these components, 1,441 are linked to recipes. Furthermore, the analysis revealed that a total of 2,931 ingredient nodes were linked to recipe nodes.

A successfully created database provides a powerful framework for capturing the nature of the recipe components and their nutritional attributes, facilitating advanced data analysis, querying, and visualization (see Fig. 4). It also provides a structured representation of the relationships between ingredients and recipes, enabling a more comprehensive understanding of culinary compositions.

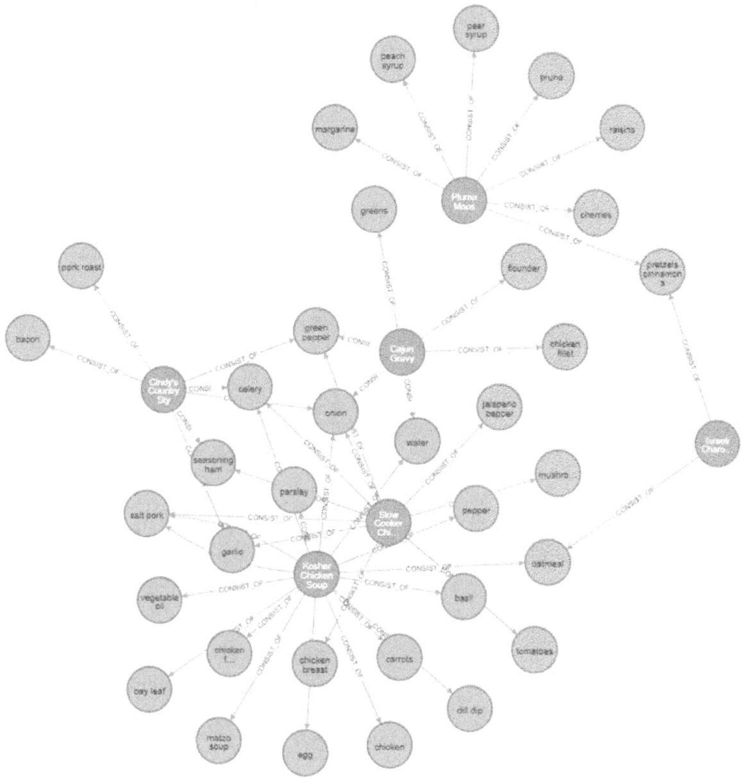


**Fig. 4.** Visualization of dependencies between nodes for selected recipes

For instance, to get the recipe with the highest number of ingredients, the following query can be posed in Cypher:

```
MATCH (r:Recipe)
RETURN r, SIZE((r)--()) AS cnt
ORDER BY cnt DESC
LIMIT 1
```

This dish (illustrated in Fig. 5) boasts an array of 30 distinct ingredients, forming a complex network of 41 relationships. What makes this particular case intriguing is the presence of repeated ingredients, like water or garlic, which give rise to multiple relationships with different "amount" properties from a single ingredient node within the recipe content. This unique situation adds an interesting layer of complexity to the culinary composition, underscoring the significance of these ingredients in the overall profile of the dish.

**Fig. 5.** Recipe with highest number of ingredients

# 6 Conclusions

In this paper, we argued that AI with ontologies can contribute to sustainability in the food sector. We emphasized the role of food ontologies in providing structured data to enhance the capabilities of AI applications. We also highlighted the versatility of ontologies in the food domain and demonstrated how ontological reasoning can extract implicit knowledge in complex scenarios. The combination of AI methods and food ontologies has been recognized as a significant contributor to sustainability, impacting areas such as biodiversity, precision farming, waste reduction, and supply chain efficiency.

This integration aligns with the objectives of three key Sustainable Development Goals: Zero Hunger, Good Health and Well-being, and Responsible Consumption and Production. Concerning Zero Hunger (Goal 2), we discussed how ontology-driven AI can enhance agricultural productivity and food security through precision agriculture. Concerning Good Health and Well-being (Goal 3), the paper discusses the benefits of personalized diets and sustainable food choices, facilitated by AI and ontologies, in promoting better health outcomes and nutritional awareness. Concerning Responsible Consumption and Production (Goal 12), we highlighted how sustainable food systems can be achieved by optimizing food production, minimizing waste, and promoting overall sustainability in the food chain.

To provide a proof-of-concept solution, the ontology based on the ontology design pattern for ingredient substitution was developed. Moreover, we have developed a knowledge graph that integrates data about recipes and nutritional information about different types of food and provides links of the identified ingredients to existing food ontologies. In the future, we plan to use the newly created knowledge graph and the ontology built for substitution support to further develop ontology-based intelligent recommendations for personalized diets and contribute to the evolving concept of the Internet of Food. Through continuous enhancement and integration with existing ontologies, we aim to expand the applications and benefits of AI in the food sector.

## References


1. Abbas, F., Najjar, N., Wilson, D.: Exploring the effect of recipe representation on critique-based conversational recommendation. In: Keane, M.T., Wiratunga, N. (eds.) ICCBR 2022. LNCS, vol. 13405, pp. 96–110. Springer, Cham (2022). https://doi.org/10.1007/978-3-031-14923-8_7
2. Adrian, W.T., Pyrczak, K., Kluza, K., Ligęza, A.: Food ontologies and ontological reasoning for sustainability. In: Nowaczyk, S., et al. (eds.) ECAI 2023. CCIS, vol. 1948, pp. 262–268. Springer, Cham (2024). https://doi.org/10.1007/978-3-031-50485-3_28
3. Aggarwal, A., Tam, C.C., Wu, D., Li, X., Qiao, S.: Artificial intelligence-based chatbots for promoting health behavioral changes: systematic review. J. Med. Internet Res. **25**, e40789 (2023)
4. Babaie, H., Davarpanah, A., Dhakal, N.: Projecting pathways to food-energy-water systems sustainability through ontology. Environ. Eng. Sci. **36**(7), 808–819 (2019)
5. Chen, Y.Z.J.: A statistical machine learning approach to generating graph structures from food recipes (2017)
6. Dooley, D.M., Griffiths, E.J., Gosal, G.S., et al.: Foodon: a harmonized food ontology to increase global food traceability, quality control and data integration. NPJ Sci. Food **2**(1), 23 (2018). https://doi.org/10.1038/s41538-018-0032-6
7. d'Aquin, M., Motta, E., Nikolov, A., Thomas, K.: Realizing networks of proactive smart products. In: ten Teije, A., et al. (eds.) EKAW 2012. LNCS, vol. 7603, pp. 337–352. Springer, Heidelberg (2012). https://doi.org/10.1007/978-3-642-33876-2_30
8. World Commission on Environment and Development: Our Common Future. Oxford Paperbacks, Oxford University Press (1987)
9. Glimm, B., Horrocks, I., Motik, B., Stoilos, G., Wang, Z.: Hermit: an owl 2 reasoner. J. Autom. Reason. **53**(3), 245–269 (2014)
10. Griffiths, E.J., Dooley, D.M., Buttigieg, P.L., Hoehndorf, R., Brinkman, F.S., Hsiao, W.W.: Foodon: a global farm-to-fork food ontology. In: ICBO/BioCreative, pp. 1–2 (2016)
11. Haussmann, S., et al.: FoodKG: a semantics-driven knowledge graph for food recommendation. In: Ghidini, C., et al. (eds.) ISWC 2019. LNCS, vol. 11779, pp. 146–162. Springer, Cham (2019). https://doi.org/10.1007/978-3-030-30796-7_10
12. Holden, N.M., White, E.P., Lange, M.C., Oldfield, T.L.: Review of the sustainability of food systems and transition using the internet of food. NPJ Sci. Food **2**(1), 18 (2018)

13. Jachimczyk, B., Tkaczyk, R., Piotrowski, T., Johansson, S., Kulesza, W.: IoT-based dairy supply chain-an ontological approach. Elektronika ir Elektrotechnika **27**(1), 71–83 (2021)
14. Joshi, S., et al.: Artificial intelligence assisted food science and nutrition perspective for smart nutrition research and healthcare. Syst. Microbiol. Biomanufact. 1–16 (2023)
15. Ławrynowicz, A., Wróblewska, A., Adrian, W.T., Kulczyński, B., Gramza-Michałowska, A.: Food recipe ingredient substitution ontology design pattern. Sensors **22**(3), 1095 (2022)
16. Mazac, R., Tuomisto, H.L.: The post-anthropocene diet: navigating future diets for sustainable food systems. Sustainability **12**(6), 2355 (2020)
17. Mori, S., Sasada, T., Yamakata, Y., Yoshino, K.: A machine learning approach to recipe text processing (2012)
18. Mortazavi, B.J., Gutierrez-Osuna, R.: A review of digital innovations for diet monitoring and precision nutrition. J. Diabetes Sci. Technol. **17**(1), 217–223 (2023)
19. Ngo, Q.H., Le-Khac, N.A., Kechadi, T.: Ontology based approach for precision agriculture. In: Kaenampornpan, M., Malaka, R., Nguyen, D., Schwind, N. (eds.) MIWAI 2018. LNCS, vol. 11248, pp. 175–186. Springer, Cham (2018). https://doi.org/10.1007/978-3-030-03014-8_15
20. Popov, P.: The power of ontologies and knowledge graphs: practical examples from the financial industry (2023). https://www.ontotext.com/blog/the-power-of-ontologies-and-knowledge-graphs-for-the-financial-industry/
21. Popovski, G., Seljak, B.K., Eftimov, T.: A survey of named-entity recognition methods for food information extraction. IEEE Access **8**, 31586–31594 (2020)
22. Popovski, G., Seljak, B.K., Eftimov, T.: Foodbase corpus: a new resource of annotated food entities. Database **2019**, baz121 (2019). https://doi.org/10.1093/database/baz121
23. UN Publications: The Sustainable Development Goals Report 2023. United Nations Fund for Population Activities (2023)
24. Sirin, E., Parsia, B., Grau, B.C., Kalyanpur, A., Katz, Y.: Pellet: a practical OWL-DL reasoner. J. Web Semant. **5**(2), 51–53 (2007)
25. Stojanov, R., et al.: Food waste ontology: a formal description of knowledge from the domain of food waste. In: 2019 IEEE International Conference on Big Data (Big Data), pp. 5190–5194. IEEE (2019)
26. Vitali, F., et al.: ONS: an ontology for a standardized description of interventions and observational studies in nutrition. Genes Nutr. **13**(1), 1–9 (2018)
27. Vrandečić, D., Krötzsch, M.: Wikidata: a free collaborative knowledgebase. Commun. ACM **57**(10), 78–85 (2014). https://doi.org/10.1145/2629489
28. Wróblewska, A., Kaliska, A., Pawłowski, M., Wiśniewski, D., Sosnowski, W., Ławrynowicz, A.: Tasteset – recipe dataset and food entities recognition benchmark (2022)

# The Use of Semantic Networks for the Categorization of Prosumers: Expanded Version

Iwona Chomiak-Orsa[1], Andrzej Grenczuk[1](✉), Kamila Łuczak[1], and Dorota Jelonek[2]

[1] Wroclaw University of Economics and Business, 53-345 Wroclaw, Poland
{iwona.chomiak-orsa,andrzej.grenczuk,kamila.luczak}@ue.wroc.pl
[2] Czestochowa University of Technology, 42-201 Czestochowa, Poland
dorota.jelonek@pcz.pl

**Abstract.** Business continuity is possible through maintaining market position, while growth requires gaining competitive advantage. This can only be achieved through systematic attention to the consumer and the development of the product offering. These factors primarily determine the success of an organization. Against this backdrop, the trend towards personalization of goods delivered to consumers is becoming increasingly evident. The answer to these business problems is the creation of buy-erseller relationships in which the consumer becomes a prosumer: a consumer who provides opinions, suggests solutions, tests and evaluates the advantages and disadvantages of the product. Therefore, the search for methods and tools that allow for the identification of groups of consumers susceptible to cooperation with the organization - to varying degrees - becomes a very important scientific and business problem. This is why the authors of this article defined the aim of the article as the analysis of the possibility of using semantic networks for the categorization of consumers and defining the category of prosumers. The results presented in the article were obtained through the application of triangulation of research methods, such as analytical literature review, computer simulation conducted using Protégé software, and research experiment consisting of simulation of selected problem situations. This paper is an expanded version of an article published as part of the ECAI 2023 conference proceedings.

**Keywords:** prosumers · semantic networks · competitiveness

## 1 Introduction

The concept of sustainability is not only about the environment, but also about people and all the social aspects involved. Prosumers, representing consumers, can contribute to so-called "eco-prosumption". Eco-prosumption refers to ways of producing and acquiring value in a socially and environmentally responsible form [15].


Published by Springer Nature Switzerland AG 2024
E. Mercier-Laurent et al. (Eds.): AI4KMES 2023, IFIP AICT 693, pp. 55–67, 2024.
https://doi.org/10.1007/978-3-031-61069-1_5

The evolution of market conditions in which modern enterprises operate has determined changes in the concepts of creating relationships and directions of cooperation with customers, who are the final consumers of manufactured goods [3,27]. Purchasing relationships are evolving into relationships based on customer experience [17,32]. When creating marketing strategies, companies move away from actions aimed at seeking and acquiring passive customers, whose relationship with the organization is limited only to the purchase transaction [26,29].

Interactive customers are at the center of attention, creating active relationships that enable cooperation and strengthen the exchange of information between the parties to the purchase-sale relationship. Interactive communication between the company and the customer can contribute to the development of the goods offered by the company [4,6,21].

An active customer has the opportunity to share experiences resulting from the use of goods offered by the company, as well as to report their needs related to new product attributes that have not been offered before. Such a customer becomes a prosumer [2,18,35,39].

The information obtained in this way is a key stimulus for the organization to enrich and develop the product offer, often contributing to innovative actions [21,25,37] carried out mainly within the framework of open innovation models [21,24,41]. The search for mechanisms "stimulating" customers to actively participate in trade relations becomes one of the concepts of organization development, which is increasingly important and attention is paid to it in scientific studies [7,9,16].

On the other hand, not every customer is willing to change their attitude from passive to interactive, that is, to become a prosumer. There are people who treat the purchasing relationship as a way to satisfy their needs, and will only stop at this action. Satisfying the need through the purchased product/service will end their relationship with the organization.

The above determinants contribute to the fact that identifying groups of customers who may become potential prosumers becomes a very important problem for organizations. In order to correctly identify potential prosumers, it is necessary to develop tools supporting the processes of classifying and clustering customers. Such tools can be semantic networks [11,13,19,31,36], which allow the classification and clustering of groups of customers by searching for phraseological relationships and relations resulting from possessing specific similarities and equations. Semantic networks show strong versatility in application. It can be pointed out, moreover, that semantic networks can be a source for Artificial Intelligence algorithms that will treat it as input. In addition, these algorithms can update its content [30].

The above scientific observations as well as the authors' business experiences have contributed to considering the possibility of developing patterns for selected consumer groups and the relationships they can create in their interactions with an organization through the use of semantic networks. As a result, the authors of this article have defined the following research problem: Can semantic networks be used to categorize consumers in order to identify their potential to transform into prosumers? Therefore, the aim of this article is to analyze the potential use of a semantic network for the categorization of consumers and the definition of prosumer categories. To achieve the designated goal of the article, the following specific research questions have been defined:

1. How can semantic networks be used to represent prosumer categories?
2. Can the designed network be mapped using concept maps (topics)?
3. What IT tools can be used to design the target semantic network?

The research presented in the article was conducted using the following research methods:

1. Computer simulation in the form of building a semantic network in the Protégé program.
2. An experiment conducted in the form of scenario analysis to preliminarily verify the proposed solution.

As a result of the above triangulation of research methods, the authors verified the research problem and achieved the designated goal of the article.

We also want to emphasize that this paper is an expanded version of the article published as part of the European Conference on Artificial Intelligence (ECAI) 2023 conference proceedings.

## 2 Identification of the Scope of Publications

This section presents a quantitative identification of the range of publications in the area of the application of artificial intelligence tools such as semantic networks to categorise prosumer attitudes. By conducting bibliometric analysis, it can be observed that the concepts of "prosumption" and "prosumer" were first proposed by Alvin Toffler [39] and had their beginnings in literature in the 1980s. In scientific studies, prosumption is defined as a value-creation activity carried out by customers, while this activity produces the products they ultimately consume and becomes their consumption experience [42]. There are also various conceptualizations of prosumers, from Toffler's definition [39] as someone who creates goods, services or experiences for their own use or satisfaction, to adding to the definition that prosumers are those who create value for everyone in their community (not just for themselves) and share it globally [37,38], to the latest definitions that define prosumers as "individuals who consume and create value, either for their own consumption or for consumption by others, and may receive hidden or explicit incentives from organizations involved in the exchange" [28]. In the era of dynamic development of social networks and social media, it is worth expanding the definition: prosumers are knowledgeable, empowered consumers who use digital technology (Web 2.0) to collaborate and participate in product or service design, conception, testing, and usage, and they have a significant influence on their social networks and communities [37].

The concept of prosumption has been discussed by researchers in various fields, such as economics [2], business [20], and incorporating prosumer participation in business processes [43]. As additional areas of research, marketing strategies and actions [10] as well as the broad sociological and social trend [14,34,35] can be distinguished. Since the early 2000s, scholars have highlighted prosumers as "co-creators," and this phenomenon has been called value co-creation [33]. Value co-creation is possible through the sharing and exchange of internal resources of prosumers, through the interaction and communication of prosumers, and through the use of prosumers' actions [22]. The aim of many scientific studies was to identify motivators for prosumers' involvement in co-creation processes [16] in service experiences [7] , and in the development of e-entrepreneurship [23].

D. Jelonek [21] identified the following roles for prosumers: consultant experts, product and brand promoters, external human resources of the enterprise, and innovators. The list of potential roles for prosumers has been expanded, emphasizing the use of Web 2.0 for collaboration and participation in product or service design, conception, testing, and usage [37].

Watson and Shove [40] used the term "do-it-yourself" to describe practices in which consumers simultaneously act as constructors, designers, controllers, and evaluators of what they produce and then consume for their own use. Marketing experts have long used prosumers as promoters of products, services, or brands, particularly their engagement in virtual brand communities [5]. Recommendations have also been developed for effectively engaging prosumers as consultants in the development of marketing strategies [29], particularly in digital marketing strategy and integrated approaches to online marketing activities [26]. A new trend in this area is designing customer experiences, and prosumers are also valuable contributors to these efforts [17,32]. Prosumers are also creative creators of brand content [8]. For the most part, transmedia brands use storytelling to collaborate with prosumers to actively consume and produce brand content and, in doing so, positively influence the brand [12].

Research on prosumers is particularly valuable when focusing on their potential as innovators [4,41], innovation models [24], and benefits for businesses [6]. The development of ICT and Web 2.0, as well as the migration of traditional business to the online space and new e-business models, mean that scientific research on prosumption increasingly focuses on virtual communities and social media [1]. The topic of managing relationships with prosumers is still relevant, but with the use of new tools such as Google Analytics [25] or big data [3].

The multidimensionality and multiaspect nature of research on prosumption show that it is not only an important phenomenon in the contemporary digital world, but also a scientific category with a solid position in the fields of economics, business, and sociology. Businesses also recognize the potential of prosumption and prosumers and, depending on their needs, want to establish cooperation relationships with prosumer-innovators, prosumer-testers, prosumer-experts, or prosumer-promoters.

Moreover, indicating quantitative trends in published scientific works in databases such as Scopus and Web of Science (WoS), it can be concluded that the concept still enjoys great popularity and is increasingly associated with such areas as organizational management, customer relationship management, or even innovation. The content analysis of the databases was based on establishing the leading keyword as "prosumer*". The use of the symbol "*" allows for the matching of the suffix of the term “prosumer”. The query was then defined in the databases by specifying that the leading keyword should appear in the title, abstract, and/or keywords. In Scopus, 4,628 records were obtained, while in WoS, 3,277 results were obtained. The set of results was then narrowed down by applying limitations to the query:

- Language = “English”,
- Document type = “Article” and “Conference paper”,
- Years = 2010–2022.

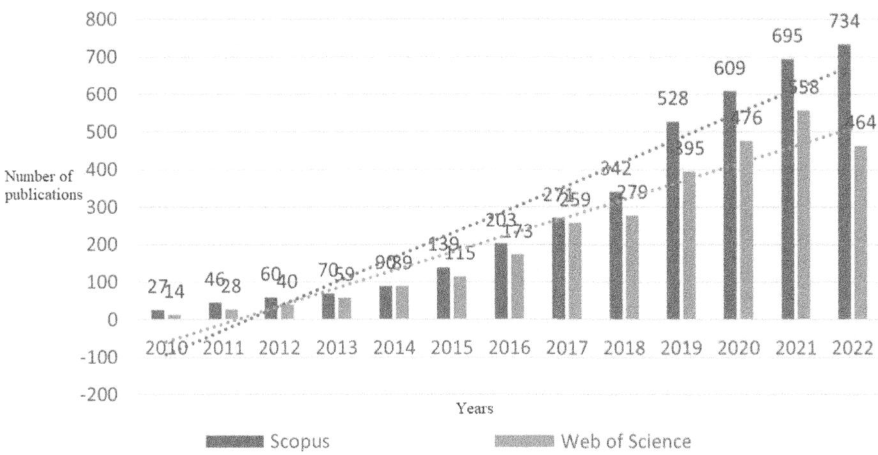


**Fig. 1.** Number of publications from 2010 to 2022.

On Fig. 1, it can be observed that the number of publications increases from year to year. It is worth noting that this increase is significantly greater in the Scopus database compared to the WoS database.

## 3 Method and Research Procedure

The research method used was a research experiment, consisting of developing the assumptions of a semantic network and basic concepts with their relationships. The construction of the semantic network was based on the analysis of scientific papers (documentary method). Then, a computer simulation was used to create an ontology as a method of knowledge representation. The simulation was conducted using the Protégé ontology editor.

To develop the semantic network, the following steps were taken:

1. Analysis of scientific publications on prosumers,
2. Extraction and analysis of the scope of concepts,

3. Development of:
   (a) Taxonomic relations,
   (b) Semantic relation words,
   (c) Semantic relations of concepts,
4. Introduction of concepts into the Protégé program,
5. Testing and verification of the semantic network by performing defined scenarios.

## 4 Research Results

As a result of the previously presented research procedure, an ontology was created with the purpose of categorizing prosumers. The categorization of prosumers depends on different criteria, which can be divided into characteristics related to the product and personal characteristics of the prosumers. Figure 2 presents the developed semantic network, which was shown using a concept map stored in the ontology.

The relation that connects the presented concepts is a taxonomic relation. After developing the semantic network in the form of a concept map, it is necessary to present the meaning of all concepts (Table 1).

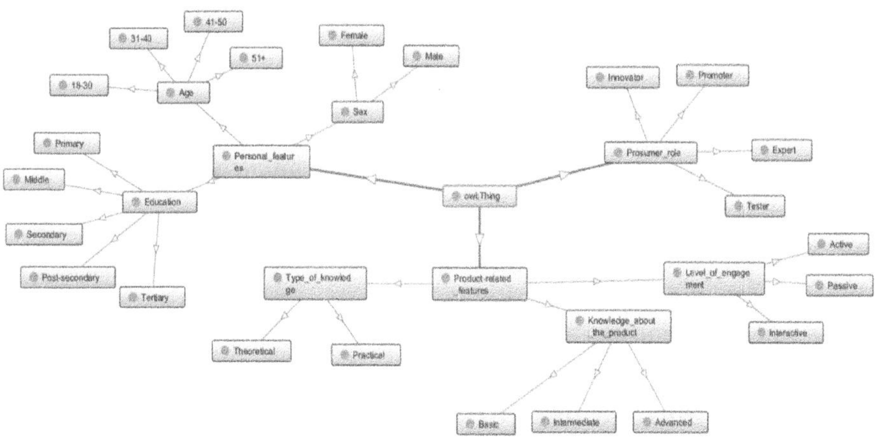


**Fig. 2.** Presentation of semantic network mapping using concept map.

Table 2 presents the taxonomic relations identified within the developed semantic network. After defining the taxonomic relations, it is necessary to define the semantic relations. In the case of the considered problem, one semantic relation was defined: "is called as".

In the next step, selected concepts were connected by the developed semantic relation. To achieve the aim of this article, three scenarios were developed and

**Table 1.** Simplified definitions of concepts

| Concept name | Meaning |
|---|---|
| Prosumer role | Type of prosumer developed based on their behaviour |
| Innovator | A customer who suggests new ideas for improving the product |
| Expert | A customer who has advanced knowledge about the product |
| Promoter | A customer who promotes the brand |
| Tester | A customer who enjoys testing products and services |
| Personal features | Personal characteristics of prosumers |
| Age | The number of years the prosumer has been alive |
| Education | The level of education attained by the prosumer |
| Sex | The gender of the prosumer |
| Product-related features | Prosumer characteristics related to product use |
| Knowledge about the product | The information the customer has about the product |
| Level of engagement | The level of engagement of the customer while using the product |
| Type of knowledge | The type of knowledge that the prosumer has related to the product |
| 18–30 | Prosumers who are 18–30 years old |
| 31–40 | Prosumers who are 31–40 years old |
| 41–50 | Prosumers who are 41–50 years old |
| 51+ | Prosumers who are 51 years old or older |
| Primary | Prosumers who have completed primary school |
| Middle | Prosumers who have completed vocational school |
| Secondary | Prosumers who have completed high school or technical college |
| Post-secondary | Prosumers who have completed post-secondary school |
| Tertiary | Prosumers who have completed higher education |
| Female | Prosumers who identify as female |
| Male | Prosumers who identify as male |
| Basic | Prosumers with basic knowledge about the product |
| Intermediate | Prosumers with intermediate knowledge about the product |
| Expert | Prosumers with expert knowledge about the product |
| Theoretical | Prosumers who know the product from a theoretical standpoint |
| Practical | Prosumers who know the product from a practical standpoint |
| Active | A prosumer who is active after purchase and comments on the product/service |
| Interactive | A prosumer who engages in the development of the product by sharing ideas |

implemented. However, presented is only one scenario, which reflects the idea. Table 3 presents a fragment of the semantic relation in the developed network.

The developed scenarios aim to verify whether it is possible to obtain answers to the given questions in the selected area. The Protégé editor and OntoGraf plugin were used to implement the scenarios. The developed scenarios will be presented in the further part of the article.

**Scenario No. 1.** An organization wants to identify prosumers among its clients. It has collected some personal characteristics of prosumers and those related to the product (Fig. 3).

**Table 2.** Taxonomic relations

| Taxonomy | Component concepts |
|---|---|
| Prosumer role | Innovator, Expert, Tester, Promoter |
| Personal feature | Age, Education, Sex |
| Product-related features | Knowledge about the product, level of engagement, Type of knowledge |
| Age | 18–30, 31–40, 41–50, 51+ |
| Education | Primary, Middle, Secondary, Post-secondary, Tertiary |
| Sex | Male, Female |
| Knowledge about the product | Basic, Intermediate, Advanced |
| Level of engagement | Active, Interactive, Passive |
| Type of knowledge | Theoretical, Practical |

**Table 3.** Semantic relations

| Concept | Relation | Target concept |
|---|---|---|
| 18-30 | is called as | Tester |
| 31-40 | is called as | Innovator |
| Primary | is called as | Expert |
| Primary | is called as | Innovator |
| Primary | is called as | Promoter |
| Middle | is called as | Tester |
| Secondary | is called as | Expert |
| Secondary | is called as | Innovator |
| Female | is called as | Tester |
| Male | is called as | Expert |
| Intermediate | is called as | Innovator |
| Advanced | is called as | Expert |
| Interactive | is called as | Tester |
| Theoretical | is called as | Expert |
| Theoretical | is called as | Promoter |
| Practical | is called as | Expert |
| Practical | is called as | Innovator |

**PROCEDURE:** From the semantic network, "owl: Thing" should be selected, followed by: "Personal_features" -> "Sex" -> "Female", "Personal_features" -> "Education" -> "Tertiary," "Personal_features" -> "Age" -> "31–40," "Product-related_features" -> "Knowledge_about_the_product" ->

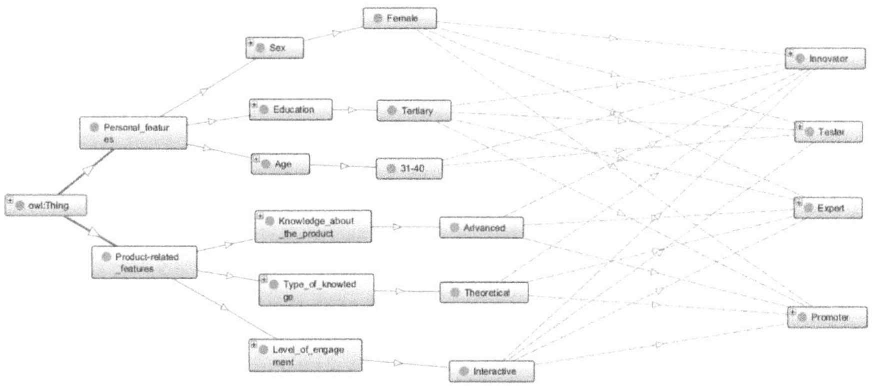


**Fig. 3.** Results obtained from scenario 1.

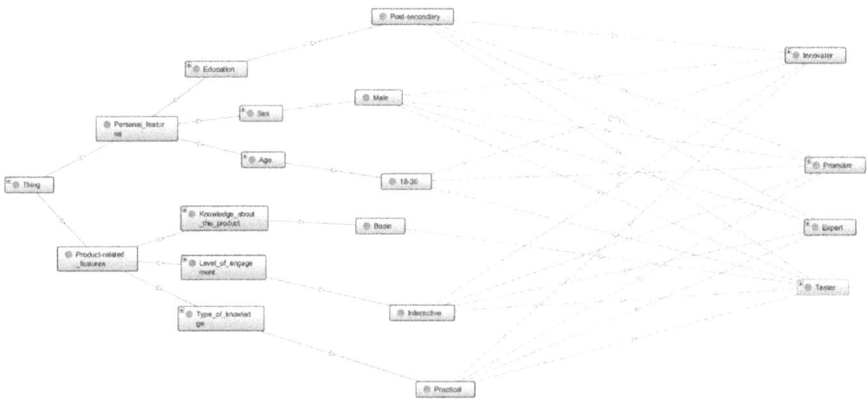


**Fig. 4.** Results obtained from scenario 2.

"Advanced," "Product-related_features" -> "Type_of_knowledge" -> "Theoretical," and "Product-related_features" -> "Level_of_engagement" -> "Interactive."

**RESULT:** As a result of scenario 1 implementation, the organization can determine that based on the indicated characteristics, the prosumers are likely to be innovators.

**Scenario No. 2.** The company wants to identify prosumers among its customers. It has gathered certain personal characteristics of the prosumers as well as those related to the product (Fig. 4).

**PROCEDURE:** From the semantic network, "owl: Thing" should be selected, and then in parallel: "Personal_features" -> "Sex" -> "Male", "Personal_features" -> "Education" -> "Post-secondary", "Personal_features" -> "Age" -> "18–30", "Product-related_features" -> "Knowledge_about_the_product" -

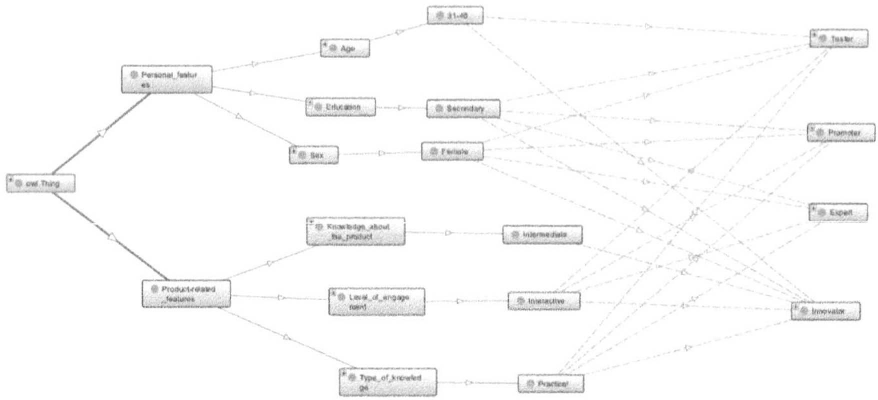


**Fig. 5.** Results obtained from scenario 3.

> "Basic", "Product-related_features" -> "Type_of_knowledge" -> "Practical", "Product-related_features" -> "Level_of_engagement" -> "Interactive".

**RESULT:** As a result of implementing scenario 2, the company can determine that based on the indicated features, consumers are likely to be testers.

**Scenario No. 3:** The company wants to identify prosumers among its customers. It has collected certain personal characteristics of prosumers as well as those related to the product (Fig. 5).

**PROCEDURE:** From the semantic network, select "owl: Thing", and then in parallel: "Personal_features" -> "Sex" -> "Female", "Personal_features" ->"Education" -> "Secondary", "Personal_features" -> "Age" -> "31-40", "Product-related_features" -> "Knowledge_about_the_product" -> "Intermediate", "Product-related_features" -> "Type_of_knowledge" -> "Practical", "Product-related_features" -> "Level_of_engagement" -> "Interactive".

**RESULT:** As a result of implementing scenario 3, the company can conclude that based on the indicated characteristics, consumers are likely to be innovators.

## 5 Conclusions

The goal defined in this article by the authors was to analyze the possibilities of using a semantic network for categorizing consumers and defining prosumer categories. Furthermore, the authors defined detailed research questions to support the goal. As a result of the conducted and presented research, the authors obtained the following answers:

1. Semantic networks can be a very useful tool for categorization and visualization of customer categorization into appropriate prosumer segments.
2. The designed networks can be mapped using a concept map, which is a very useful complementary tool for visualizing researched problems.

3. One of the very useful tools for designing target semantic networks is the Protégé program, which was used by the authors of this article during the research and preparation of research results.

Obtaining answers to all research questions posed by the authors is equivalent to achieving the goal, which was to analyze the possibilities of using semantic networks in the categorization of prosumers.

By extending the article previously published in ECAI 2023 conference proceedings, we were able to present a more complete picture of the theoretical foundations, the developed semantic network, as well as sample scenarios for using the developed concept of using the semantic network to categorize prosumers.

## References


1. Buzzetto-More, N.: Social media and prosumerism. Issues Informing Sci. Inf. Technol. **10**, 067–080 (2013). https://doi.org/10.28945/1796
2. Alderete, M.V.: The age of prosumerism: some micro-economic analysis. J. Theor. Appl. Electron. Commer. Res. **12**(3), 1–12 (2017). https://doi.org/10.4067/S0718-18762017000300002
3. Anshari, M., Almunawar, M.N., Lim, S.A., Al-Mudimigh, A.: Customer relationship management and big data enabled: personalization & customization of services. Appl. Comput. Inform. **15**(2), 94–101 (2019). https://doi.org/10.1016/j.aci.2018.05.004
4. Asión-Suñer, L., López-Forniés, I.: Prosumer and product design through digital tools. In: Cavas-Martínez, F., Sanz-Adan, F., Morer Camo, P., Lostado Lorza, R., Santamaría Peña, J. (eds.) Advances in Design Engineering, pp. 23–30. Springer, Cham (2020). https://doi.org/10.1007/978-3-030-41200-5_3
5. Brodie, R.J., Ilic, A., Juric, B., Hollebeek, L.: Consumer engagement in a virtual brand community: an exploratory analysis. J. Bus. Res. **66**(1), 105–114 (2013). https://doi.org/10.1016/j.jbusres.2011.07.029
6. Bustinza, O.F., Gomes, E., Vendrell-Herrero, F., Baines, T.: Product-service innovation and performance: the role of collaborative partnerships and R&D intensity: product-service innovation and performance. R&D Manag. **49**(1), 33–45 (2019). https://doi.org/10.1111/radm.12269
7. Chandler, J., Chen, S.: Prosumer motivations in service experiences. J. Serv. Theory Pract. **25**(2), 220–239 (2015). https://doi.org/10.1108/JSTP-09-2013-0195
8. Comor, E.: Contextualizing and critiquing the fantastic prosumer: power, alienation and hegemony. Crit. Sociol. **37**(3), 309–327 (2011). https://doi.org/10.1177/0896920510378767
9. Cova, B., Cova, V.: On the road to prosumption: marketing discourse and the development of consumer competencies. Consum. Markets Cult. **15**(2), 149–168 (2012). https://doi.org/10.1080/10253866.2012.654956
10. Cova, B., Dalli, D.: Working consumers: the next step in marketing theory? Mark. Theory **9**(3), 315–339 (2009). https://doi.org/10.1177/1470593109338144
11. Drieger, P.: Semantic network analysis as a method for visual text analytics. Procedia Soc. Behav. Sci. **79**, 4–17 (2013). https://doi.org/10.1016/j.sbspro.2013.05.053

12. Du Plessis, C.: Prosumer engagement through story-making in transmedia branding. Int. J. Cult. Stud. **22**(1), 175–192 (2019). https://doi.org/10.1177/1367877917750445
13. Dudycz, H.: Mapa pojęć jako wizualna reprezentacja wiedzy ekonomicznej =: topic map as a visual representation of economic knowledge. No. nr 229 in Monografie i Opracowania - Uniwersytet Ekonomiczny we Wrocławiu, Wydawnictwo Uniwersytetu Ekonomicznego, Wrocław (2013)
14. Dusi, D.: Investigating the exploitative and empowering potential of the prosumption phenomenon. Sociol. Compass **11**(6), e12488 (2017). https://doi.org/10.1111/soc4.12488
15. Eizenberg, E., Jabareen, Y.: Social sustainability: a new conceptual framework. Sustainability **9**(1), 68 (2017). https://doi.org/10.3390/su9010068
16. Fernandes, T., Remelhe, P.: How to engage customers in co-creation: customers' motivations for collaborative innovation. J. Strateg. Mark. **24**(3–4), 311–326 (2016). https://doi.org/10.1080/0965254X.2015.1095220
17. Gentile, C., Spiller, N., Noci, G.: How to sustain the customer experience. Eur. Manag. J. **25**(5), 395–410 (2007). https://doi.org/10.1016/j.emj.2007.08.005
18. Gržanić, M., Capuder, T., Zhang, N., Huang, W.: Prosumers as active market participants: a systematic review of evolution of opportunities, models and challenges. Renew. Sustain. Energy Rev. **154**, 111859 (2022). https://doi.org/10.1016/j.rser.2021.111859
19. Hills, T.T., Kenett, Y.N.: Is the mind a network? Maps, vehicles, and skyhooks in cognitive network science. Top. Cogn. Sci. **14**(1), 189–208 (2022). https://doi.org/10.1111/tops.12570
20. Humphreys, A., Grayson, K.: The intersecting roles of consumer and producer: a critical perspective on co-production, co-creation and prosumption: intersecting roles of consumer and producer. Sociol. Compass **2**(3), 963–980 (2008). https://doi.org/10.1111/j.1751-9020.2008.00112.x
21. Jelonek, D.: The innovative potential of prosumption and the results of enterprises. In: Proceedings of the 7th Conference on Performance Measurement and Management Control, p. 18 (2013)
22. Jelonek, D.: Prosumption and co-creating value. In: Modern Management in the 21st Century. Theoretical and Practical Issues, pp. 127–131. GARMOND, Nitra (2013)
23. Jelonek, D.: The role of open innovations in the development of e-entrepreneurship. Procedia Comput. Sci. **65**, 1013–1022 (2015). https://doi.org/10.1016/j.procs.2015.09.058
24. Jelonek, D., Moczała, A. (eds.): Metody i Techniki Projektowania Innowacji. NPI Nauka i Praktyka Innowacji, Państwowe Wydawnictwo Ekonomiczne, Warszawa (2020)
25. Jelonek, D., Turek, T.: Opportunities for the use of google analytics for management of relations with prosumers. In: Book of Proceedings ICoM 2018. 8th International Conference on Management "Leadership, Innovativeness and Entrepreneurship in a Sustainable Economy", pp. 318–323. Wydawnictwo Wydziału Zarządzania Politechniki Częstochowskiej, Częstochowa (2018)
26. Kingsnorth, S.: Digital Marketing Strategy: An Integrated Approach to Online Marketing, 3rd edn. Kogan Page Inc, New York (2022)
27. Kumar, V., Reinartz, W.: Customer Relationship Management. Springer Texts in Business and Economics. Springer, Heidelberg (2018). https://doi.org/10.1007/978-3-662-55381-7

28. Lang, B., Dolan, R., Kemper, J., Northey, G.: Prosumers in times of crisis: definition, archetypes and implications. J. Serv. Manag. **32**(2), 176–189 (2021). https://doi.org/10.1108/JOSM-05-2020-0155
29. Mothersbaugh, D.L., Hawkins, D.I., Kleiser, S.B., Mothersbaugh, L.L., Watson, C.F.: Consumer Behavior: Building Marketing Strategy, 14 edn, International Student Edition. McGraw-Hill Education, New York (2020)
30. Navigli, R., Ponzetto, S.P.: BabelNet: the automatic construction, evaluation and application of a wide-coverage multilingual semantic network. Artif. Intell. **193**, 217–250 (2012). https://doi.org/10.1016/j.artint.2012.07.001
31. Odlanicka-Poczobutt, M.: Significance of semantic web – pitfalls and benefits of use in the common judiciary. Comparative Legilinguistics **40**(1), 21–41 (2019). https://doi.org/10.14746/cl.2019.40.2
32. Palmer, A.: Customer experience management: a critical review of an emerging idea. J. Serv. Mark. **24**(3), 196–208 (2010). https://doi.org/10.1108/08876041011040604
33. Prahalad, C., Ramaswamy, V.: Co-creation experiences: the next practice in value creation. J. Interact. Mark. **18**(3), 5–14 (2004). https://doi.org/10.1002/dir.20015
34. Ritzer, G.: The "new" world of prosumption: evolution, "return of the same," or revolution? Sociol. Forum **30**(1), 1–17 (2015). https://doi.org/10.1111/socf.12142
35. Ritzer, G., Dean, P., Jurgenson, N.: The coming of age of the prosumer. Am. Behav. Sci. **56**(4), 379–398 (2012). https://doi.org/10.1177/0002764211429368
36. Scott, P.B.: Knowledge workers: social, task and semantic network analysis. Corporate Commun. Int. J. **10**(3), 257–277 (2005). https://doi.org/10.1108/13563280510614519
37. Seran (Potra), S., Izvercian, M.: Prosumer engagement in innovation strategies: the prosumer creativity and focus model. Manag. Decis. **52**(10), 1968–1980 (2014). https://doi.org/10.1108/MD-06-2013-0347
38. Tapscott, D., Williams, A.: Wikinomics: How Mass Collaboration Changes Everything. Penguin Publishing Group (2008)
39. Toffler, A.: The Third Wave, 1st edn. Morrow, New York (1980)
40. Watson, M., Shove, E.: Product, competence, project and practice: DIY and the dynamics of craft consumption. J. Consum. Cult. **8**(1), 69–89 (2008). https://doi.org/10.1177/1469540507085726
41. West, J., Bogers, M.: Leveraging external sources of innovation: a review of research on open innovation: leveraging external sources of innovation. J. Prod. Innov. Manag. **31**(4), 814–831 (2014). https://doi.org/10.1111/jpim.12125
42. Xie, C., Bagozzi, R.P., Troye, S.V.: Trying to prosume: toward a theory of consumers as co-creators of value. J. Acad. Mark. Sci. **36**(1), 109–122 (2008). https://doi.org/10.1007/s11747-007-0060-2
43. Ziemba, E., Eisenbardt, M.: Prosumers' participation in business processes. Online J. Appl. Knowl. Manag. **3**(1), 114–127 (2015)

# Methods for Mitigating Gender Bias in Binary Classification Models – A Comparative Analysis

Andrzej Małowiecki(✉) and Iwona Chomiak-Orsa

Wrocław University of Economics and Business, Wrocław, Poland
andrzej.malowiecki@ue.wroc.pl

**Abstract.** Inequality is one of the problems of the modern world. Discrimination of various kinds can affect many areas of life. The growing importance of data in the modern world makes it all the more important to ensure that the methods used to analyze it do not return results in which unfairness is present. Unfortunately, there may be situations where there is unfairness in the predictions of machine learning models. Over the years, researchers in this field of artificial intelligence have developed methods for mitigating bias in models. The purpose of this article is to identify gender bias in selected dataset and compare which of the selected solutions achieves the best result while used for mitigating impact of this type of unfairness on model's predictions. The following research methods were used: literature review, experiment and comparative analysis. The evaluation of methods will be based on the value of measures: disparity in recall and disparity in selection rate for the column containing information about the person's gender. The values of these measures, achieved by binary classification models in which different methods for mitigating bias were implemented, will be compared in order to identify which of the methods is best suited for mitigating gender bias in binary classification models.

**Keywords:** Fairlearn · resampling · gender bias · binary classification

## 1 Introduction

Today's world is witnessing a dynamic increase in the importance of artificial intelligence. The different categories of this scientific field are integrated into human life in various ways. One of the most popular categories of artificial intelligence is machine learning, which beginnings date back to the middle of the previous century. Nowadays decisions made by machine learning models have a significant impact on human life. Therefore, it is crucial that the predictions of the created models are reliable and devoid of various types of social biases. Situations in which the negative decision of the model was mainly influenced by characteristics such as age, gender, race or origin are unfair and against the established sustainability goals.

Throughout recent history a handful of ideas were explored with an aim of ensuring that machine learning models are unbiased. This has led to the creation of methods


Published by Springer Nature Switzerland AG 2024
E. Mercier-Laurent et al. (Eds.): AI4KMES 2023, IFIP AICT 693, pp. 68–79, 2024.
https://doi.org/10.1007/978-3-031-61069-1_6

that allow users to reduce bias in both the dataset itself and the model. An example of a solution to reduce unfairness in a dataset is resampling, which makes it possible to synthetically generate or reduce the number of observations in order to guarantee greater balance in the data.

In recent years, there have been increasing signs that transforming only the dataset is not sufficient, as the predictions of machine learning models still tend to be unfair. Among many solutions created in order to mitigate this problem there is Fairlearn, an open-source, community-driven project with an associated Python library. Originally, it was created with the purpose of helping to mitigate unfairness in machine learning models (Dudik et al. 2020). This library provides access to various types of algorithms and parity constraints that can be used on different types of machine learning models to ensure that regardless of the given dataset, created predictions should be fair and unbiased.

The purpose of this article is to identify gender bias in selected dataset and compare which of the selected solutions achieves the best result while used for mitigating impact of this type of unfairness on model's predictions. The following research methods were used: literature review, experiment and comparative analysis. The evaluation of methods will be based on the value of measures: disparity in recall and disparity in selection rate for the column containing information about the person's gender. The values of these measures, achieved by binary classification models in which different methods for mitigating bias were implemented, will be compared in order to identify which of the methods is best suited for mitigating gender bias in binary classification models.

The experiment will be conducted according to the following procedure: initially, a binary classification model will be created and evaluated on the original dataset, then the same steps will be followed for models using resampled data and ThresholdOptimizer models. At the end the evaluation metrics of all models will be compared to find the best performing one.

## 2 Gender Bias in Machine Learning Models

Nowadays, the need for sustainable development is being increasingly promoted, especially by the youngest generations (Rzemieniak and Wawer, 2021). In this regard the problem of reducing inequalities becomes one of the biggest challenges of today's world. Among 17 sustainable development goals, 2 of them were established with the purpose of overcoming this problem:

- goal 5 – gender equality,
- goal 10 – reduced inequalities (SDG FUND, 2015).

Nowadays the use of machine learning in decision-making processes is becoming more widespread, covering a variety of fields (Butryn et al. 2021). With the growing role of this technology in everyday life, it is important to ensure that the model adheres to these sustainable development goals. This means that no sensitive characteristics should affect predictions made by them. Unfortunately, there are examples where models tend to make unfair or biased predictions (Barocas, Hardt, Narayanan, 2017, Mittelstadt, Wachter, Russell, 2023, Yang, Wang, Ton, 2023, Tolan et al., 2019). There are many factors that can affect model's fairness, including ethnicity, gender, age or race (Mehrabi et al., 2021, Pessach, Shmueli, 2022).

This article focuses on gender bias in machine learning models. This type of unfairness was identified in numerous algorithms. One of the examples is an algorithm that was used in order to deliver ads, designed with the purpose of promoting job opportunities in the Science, Technology, Engineering and Math fields. Even though the ads were supposed to be gender-neutral, the majority of viewers were men. The simple explanation of this behaviour would be that the algorithm just imitated supposed user behaviour, which means that, due to the fact that women were supposedly less likely to click on an ad, it was displayed to fewer of them. This assumption turned out to be incorrect because women were more likely to click on an ad after it was displayed to them (Lambrecht, Tucker, 2019). This means that there were other reasons which can be summarized as a difference in "price" between both demographics. For a given example, women were considered a "prized demographic" due to the fact that they are more likely to engage with advertising than men, even though the stereotypical assumption can be made that these types of ads would not interest them (Lambrecht, Tucker, 2019).

There are two factors that allow users to check whether models learning model are making unfair predictions:

- Disparity in predictions – predictions comparison for each group within a selected sensitive feature, measured using selection rate. In binary classification selection rate is used to measure what fraction of data points is assigned the value of 1 for each of the classes. The greater the disparity in the selection rate, the more unfair are the predictions made by the model.
- Disparity in prediction performance – predictive performance metrics comparison for each group within a selected sensitive feature. In binary classification metrics such as accuracy, precision or recall can be used to measure the disparity between both classes. The greater the disparity in the performance metrics, the more unfair are the predictions made by the model. (Microsoft, 2023).

When any of the disparity values is significant, then the assumption can be made that the given model is lacking fairness. The reason for this may be:

- Data imbalance – in binary classification it is a situation in which one of the classes has significantly more instances than the other one. This is often the case in the datasets used for fraud detection because the vast majority of observations are not examples of fraudulent activities. There are certain techniques that can be used to mitigate the impact of data imbalance, the most popular being data resampling.
- Indirect correlation between features – a situation in which two or more variables are indirectly correlated through the other variable or the combination of variables.
- Other societal biases – sensitive features, such as age, gender, ethnicity or race (Pagano et al., 2023).

Correct identification of the reason is very important when implementing mitigation methods. For the purpose of this article selected dataset will be tested for possible data imbalance and evaluated using both mentioned performance factors. In case of possible data imbalance being detected selected dataset will be resampled using available algorithms. If significant disparities in predictions and predictions performance are achieved, it will be necessary to use tools that allow the impact of societal biases on the predictions made to be negated. Fairlearn is an example of a tool that can be used to achieve this.

## 3 Resampling

Data resampling is a data level method used to change the number of observations in unbalanced classes. Resampling techniques are applied at the pre-processing stage. Their use causes the structure of the dataset to be altered in order to effectively deal with the data imbalance problem. To some extent, this type of action contributes to improving the predictive ability of the model, learned from the resampled dataset (Lee, 2014).

Within resampling, there are three different approaches that can be used to change the number of observations. These are:

- undersampling – a type of resampling, in which the number of observations belonging to the more numerous classes is reduced to the level of the least numerous class while retaining relevant information from the perspective of the model learning process,
- oversampling – a type of resampling, in which the number of observations belonging to the less numerous classes is increased to the level of the most numerous class while retaining relevant information from the perspective of the model learning process,
- hybrid sampling – a type of resampling that combines undersampling and oversampling methods in order to reduce the negative consequences of using only one of them (Alam et al., 2021).

None of the types mentioned above is ideal. The biggest problem of undersampling is that the application of its methods means that some observations containing important information may be removed from the dataset, thus negatively affecting its quality. The variety of filtering rules within the various undersampling methods is intended to reduce the occurrence of such negative rejection of important observations, but then another problem arises, which is the selection of an appropriate method for the data (Małowiecki, 2023.a, 2023.b).

In oversampling, new observations are generated on top of existing in order to achieve a more balanced distribution of them between classes. The negative effect of this is that model overfitting can occur. In machine learning, overlearning is when a model 'fits' too well to the training data. This causes its ability to make predictions based on previously unseen data from the test set to be impaired, so that it *de facto* loses the essence of its function, which is to make predictions based on unknown data. The risk of overfitting increases when the training set is too small in terms of the number of observations. This is the case when oversampling methods are used, because once they are used, the number of observations for a smaller class may appear large, but they are mostly 'artificial' observations generated from a small set of existing ones. This causes the model learning process to actually take place on the original sample augmented by derivatives of the observations belonging to it. The effect of this is that overfitting can occur (Małowiecki, 2023.a, 2023.b).

Examples of data resampling methods include:

- Random Over- / Under-Sampling – data resampling methods, which use randomness to reduce the number of observations of a more numerous class or to generate new observations for a less numerous class. Both methods are characterised by the fact that they are simple to use, but this makes them less effective than others.

- Edited Nearest Neighbors (ENN) – an undersampling method based on the K-Nearest Neighbours (KNN) algorithm, which assigns observations to classes based on the class membership of their k nearest neighbours. Within the ENN method, each observation belonging to the more numerous classes is tested using KNN. Observations that are misclassified by the KNN are then removed from the dataset.
- Tomek Links – an undersampling method based on the identification of so-called Tomek Links, i.e. pairs of instances that are simultaneously their nearest neighbours and belong to two different classes. If successfully identified, an observation that is simultaneously one of the Tomek Links and belongs to the more numerous class is removed from the dataset. This way, undersampling takes place by removing boundary instances.
- Adaptive Synthetic – an oversampling method that uses a weighted distribution of the smaller class to generate synthetic data, i.e. artificial observations used to improve the performance of a machine learning model. The method uses the KNN algorithm for each observation belonging to the smaller class to define its nearest neighbourhood. This is followed by the calculation of the normalised domination factor of the more numerous class for each neighbourhood. This is used to determine the number of instances of the less numerous class to be generated for each neighbourhood in order to achieve an identical abundance of all classes. New observations for the less numerous class are generated based on a linear combination of two randomly selected observations that belong to that class and are within the same neighbourhood. A common procedure is to add white noise to the generated instances in order to avoid too much linear dependence between observations within a class that is oversampled.
- Synthetic Minority Oversampling Technique (SMOTE) – oversampling method, in which synthetic data for a minority class are generated by interpolating the k nearest neighbours for each observation belonging to that class. The operation scheme of the SMOTE method is very susceptible to that of Adaptive Synthetic, with the important difference that the local distribution of the minority class does not affect the number of instances generated for each neighbourhood. This results in a simpler implementation of SMOTE. The first step of the method is to randomly select one of the observations included in the minority class for which to find the k nearest neighbours. Then, one of these neighbours, which at the same time also belongs to the smaller class, should be selected. The next step is to define a synthetic point on the line that connects the two selected observations. Each such point is a generated instance of a class that is oversampled. Consequently, this process has to be repeated until the class counts are balanced (Alam et al., 2021, James et al., 2023).

The hybrid resampling approach combines oversampling and undersampling methods to reduce the negative impact of the disadvantages of both approaches. A common combination of methods within hybrid resampling is the simultaneous use of SMOTE and ENN methods, as well as SMOTE and Tomek Links (Alam et al., 2021).

## 4 Fairlearn Overview

Fairlearn was originally started in 2018 as a Python package created for the purpose of a connected research paper by Miro Dudik with the aim of providing data scientists with a toolkit to mitigate unfairness in their machine learning models (Dudik et al., 2020).

The basis of fairness consists of two types of algorithms that allow unfairness mitigation in machine learning models:

- postprocessing algorithms – algorithms that transform predictions created by a trained model,
- reduction algorithms – algorithms that iteratively re-weight data points and retrain the model in order for the final version of it to have the best performance and at the same time comply with the selected constraint (Dudik et al. 2020).

Fairlearn offers its users the possibility to use both types of algorithms. Algorithms available within this package include:

- Threshold Optimizer – a postprocessing algorithm which establishes different decision thresholds for each group within a selected sensitive feature so that the model complies with the selected constraint.
- Exponentiated Gradient – a reduction algorithm that iteratively updates a set of weights associated with different actions or decisions in a way that minimizes the cumulative loss over time.
- Grid Search – a reduction algorithm used to find the most optimal values of hyperparameters in the model by re-creating models with different sets of hyperparameters obtained from a user-defined grid (Dudik et al. 2020).

Both types have advantages and disadvantages that make their use vary depending on the given use case. In general, reduction algorithms are more flexible and compliant due to the fact that they allow the use of a wider range of metrics and do not require access to sensitive features during deployment (which often can be forbidden by the law) (Dudik et al., 2020). On the other hand, postprocessing algorithms are easier and faster to use due to the fact that there is no need to make any changes to the model, just to its predictions. Its performance should also be better as there is no need to re-create models with different hyperparameters.

Besides algorithms, Fairlearn consists of other features that are designed with the purpose of helping people detect and mitigate unfairness in machine learning models. A good example of this is a group of special metrics that can be used to more accurately identify unfairness in predictions. One of them is selection rate, which is used to measure the proportion of positive predictions for each group within a selected sensitive feature (Microsoft, 2023, Pandey, 2022).

In Fairlearn, parity constraints are constraints that a model has to satisfy in order for it to be considered fair. There are different types of constraints that are designed in a way so that the user is able to choose whichever is best suitable for the given machine learning task and specific fairness criteria[1].

[1] Available parity constraints are mostly algorithm-agnostic, which means that they should be able to work with both types of Fairlearn algorithms. One of the exceptions is error rate parity, which is a constraint example that works only with reduction algorithms.

Among many available Fairlearn parity constraints, ones that will be used for the purpose of this article are:

- Demographic parity – constraint designed to assure that an equal number of positive predictions is being made for each group within a selected sensitive feature,
- True positive rate parity – constraint designed to assure that a comparable proportion of true positive predictions is being made for each group within a selected sensitive feature,
- False positive rate parity – constraint designed to assure that a comparable proportion of false positive predictions is being made for each group within a selected sensitive feature,
- Equalized odds – constraint designed to assure that a comparable proportion of true positive and false positive predictions is being made for each group within a selected sensitive feature (Dudik et al., 2020).

Some of the selected constraints are designed for the purpose of reducing specific unfairness factors, e.g., the use of demographic parity should reduce mainly the disparity in the model's predictions, while equalized odds should concentrate on reducing the disparity in its prediction performance.

# 5 Comparative Analysis of Methods for Mitigating Gender Bias in Binary Classification Models

Machine learning models are used for the purpose of supporting the decision-making process in many areas, such as financial services, marketing or health care. Companies in every industry have the opportunity to benefit from the use of this technology in decision-making by using its models in the hiring process. As machine learning algorithms are increasingly being used at every stage of this process, it is all the more important to ensure that the decisions they make are not unfair (Schumann et al., 2020).

## 5.1 Experiment Overview

For the following experiment, "Utrecht Fairness Recruitment dataset" dataset was selected. This dataset was created by Sieuwert van Otterloo, AI researcher at Vrije Universiteit and Utrecht University of Applied Sciences. The owner of it is Utrecht ICT Institute, which has made it available on Kaggle with a license: CC BY-SA 4.0 (Kaggle, 2023).

Selected dataset contains data on recruitment decisions of 4 companies. It consists of over 500 candidates who are described using attributes such as gender, age, nationality, sports background, university grade and previous working experience. A number of sensitive features (such as gender, age or nationality) makes this dataset an appropriate choice for the experiment.

The experiment will be conducted according to the following procedure:

1. Creation of a baseline binary classification model, using the decision tree algorithm.
2. Calculation of evaluation metrics for the baseline model.

3. Calculation of the disparity in evaluation metrics for gender groups in the baseline model.
4. Application of selected resampling methods to the original dataset.
5. Creation of binary classification models based on resampled dataset.
6. Calculation of the disparity in evaluation metrics for gender groups in models based on resampled dataset.
7. Addition of a balancing index to the original training dataset.
8. Creation of ThresholdOptimizer models based on baseline model.
9. Calculation of evaluation metrics for ThresholdOptimizer models.
10. Calculation of the disparity in evaluation metrics for gender groups in the ThresholdOptimizer models.
11. Comparison of disparity in evaluation metrics between baseline model, models based on resampled data and ThresholdOptimizer models.

## 5.2 Baseline Model

The first stage of the experiment was to create a binary classification model, using the decision tree algorithm. Before that, selected dataset was prepared for the given task, which means that all non-numerical attributes were converted using LabelEncoder and all rows with gender values different than "male" or "female" were removed[2]. It is important to mention that the selected dataset is imbalanced – there are 337 more observations where gender is male. This feature of the dataset will be used in the second stage of the experiment, the data resampling part.

After preparation, the dataset was split into training and test sets at a ratio of 2:1. The training set was used during the process of learning the decision tree model. The test set was used to evaluate models using selected evaluation metrics: selection rate, accuracy, recall and precision. After evaluation, disparities in evaluation metrics for gender groups in the baseline model were calculated. Table 1 presents results of the baseline model evaluation.

**Table 1.** Baseline model evaluation results.

| | selection rate | accuracy | recall | precision |
|---|---|---|---|---|
| Female | 0.237374 | 0.801347 | 0.577181 | 0.609929 |
| Male | 0.343348 | 0.818312 | 0.732510 | 0.741667 |
| Disparity | 0.105974 | 0.016965 | 0.155329 | 0.131738 |

According to obtained evaluation results, there is a disparity between the values of selection rate and recall, which means that the model is slightly biased.

[2] There was only one different value for gender – "other". It was removed due to the fact that there were fewer observations of it: 83 to 2127 for "male" and 1790 for "female".

### 5.3 Models Based on Resampled Data

After successful deployment and evaluation of the baseline model and identification of gender bias in its predictions, the next step was to apply selected resampling methods to the original dataset. Of the available methods Synthetic Minority Oversampling Technique (SMOTE) and Edited Nearest Neighbor were implemented as they are examples of different approaches to data resampling, the first one being oversampling and the second one being undersampling (Małowiecki, 2023.a, 2023.b).

The resampled dataset was used to train new instances of decision trees model. After model training and evaluation, disparities in evaluation metrics for gender groups in both models based on the resampled dataset were calculated. Table 2 presents results of models evaluation.

**Table 2.** Comparison of disparities in selection rate and recall between models based on the resampled dataset.

| | disparity in selection rate | disparity in recall |
|---|---|---|
| SMOTE-based model | 0.072916 | -0.001405 |
| ENN-based model | 0.135927 | 0.075045 |

According to obtained evaluation results, SMOTE-based model achieved better results in both metrics.

### 5.4 ThresholdOptimizer Models

After successful deployment and evaluation of the model based on resampled dataset, the next step was to implement a balancing index into the original dataset. This index is used to ensure that in the input there is an equal number of samples that produce the result of 0 and 1. The new, balanced dataset was split again into train and test sets at the same ratio as before.

The newly created train set was used to train ThresholdOptimizer models, which were based on the originally trained model. Of the available parity constraints demographic parity and equalized odds were implemented in created models, as they effectively handle unfairness mitigation in binary classification models (Małowiecki, 2023.a, 2023.b).

After model training and evaluation, disparities in evaluation metrics for gender groups in both ThresholdOptimizer models were calculated. Table 3 presents results of models evaluation.

According to obtained evaluation results, demographic parity constraint achieves better results when mitigating disparity in selection rate, while equalized odds constraint achieves slightly better results when mitigating disparity in recall.

### 5.5 Comparative Analysis

After successful evaluation of ThresholdOptimizer models results for all the models have been collected for the purpose of comparing them. Table 4 presents the comparison of disparities in evaluation metrics between all the created models.

**Table 3.** Comparison of disparities in selection rate and recall between ThresholdOptimizer models.

| | disparity in selection rate | disparity in recall |
|---|---|---|
| Demographic parity | 0.006064 | 0.050224 |
| Equalized odds | 0.083999 | 0.049147 |

**Table 4.** Comparison of disparities in selection rate and recall between all the models.

| | disparity in selection rate | disparity in recall |
|---|---|---|
| Baseline model | 0.105974 | 0.155329 |
| SMOTE-based model | 0.072916 | −0.001405 |
| ENN-based model | 0.135927 | 0.075045 |
| Demographic parity | 0.006064 | 0.050224 |
| Equalized odds | 0.083999 | 0.049147 |

### 5.6 Summary

Among the selected models, ThresholdOptimizer model using demographic parity constraint achieved the lowest value of disparity in selection rate and the third lowest value of disparity in recall. The lowest value of disparity in recall was achieved by the model based on the dataset resampled using SMOTE. Model that was based on the dataset resampled using ENN achieved worse value of disparity in selection rate than the baseline model. The reason for that might be the fact that selected dataset does not contain a lot of records (less than 4000). In this example the use of undersampling techniques may lead to deterioration of model's performance (Dal Pozzolo, Caelen, Bontempi, 2015).

Selected evaluation criteria indicated using demographic parity constraint and SMOTE resampling method as the most suitable methods for a given use case. Because both these techniques are used during different stages of the entire process they can be combined together to ensure the lowest possible disparities in both evaluation metrics.

## 6 Conclusions

In this article the results of comparative analysis of methods that can be used for mitigating gender bias in binary classification models were presented. Created decision tree models were compared using disparity in selection rate and disparity in recall measures.

The comparative analysis indicated ThresholdOptimizer model with demographic parity constraint implemented as most suitable for the given use case. The use of SMOTE resampling method and ThresholdOptimizer model with equalized odds constraint implemented can also be advised as values of both evaluation metrics achieved by them were better than in the baseline model.

In future publications the scope of compared methods could be expanded to include comparison of different Fairlearn algorithms for different machine learning models (not only binary classification but also regression). Additionally, it could be worth trying to detect and mitigate model unfairness in different areas, such as corporate credit risk analysis or markets selection.

## References


Alam, T.M., et al.: A comparative performance analysis of data resampling methods on imbalance medical data. IEEE Access **9**, 109960–109975 (2021)

Barocas, S., Hardt, M., Narayanan, A.: Fairness in machine learning. Nips tutorial, 1 (2017)

Bird, S., et al.: Fairlearn: a toolkit for assessing and improving fairness in AI. Microsoft, Technical report. MSR-TR-2020-32 (2020)

Butryn, B., Chomiak-Orsa, I., Hauke, K., Pondel, M., Siennicka, A.: Application of Machine Learning in medical data analysis illustrated with an example of association rules. Procedia Comput. Sci. **192**, 3134–3143 (2021)

Dal Pozzolo, A., Caelen, O., Bontempi, G.: When is undersampling effective in unbalanced classification tasks? In: Appice, A., Rodrigues, P.P., Santos Costa, V., Soares, C., Gama, J., Jorge, A. (eds.) ECML PKDD 2015, Part I. LNCS (LNAI), vol. 9284, pp. 200–215. Springer, Cham (2015). https://doi.org/10.1007/978-3-319-23528-8_13

James, G., Witten, D., Hastie, T., Tibshirani, R., Taylor, J.: Resampling methods. In: An Introduction to Statistical Learning: With Applications in Python, pp. 201–228. Springer, Cham (2023). https://doi.org/10.1007/978-3-031-38747-0_5

Kaggle (2023). https://www.kaggle.com/datasets/ictinstitute/utrecht-fairness-recruitment-dataset. Accessed 15 July 2023

Lambrecht, A., Tucker, C.: Algorithmic bias? An empirical study of apparent gender-based discrimination in the display of STEM career ads. Manage. Sci. **65**(7), 2966–2981 (2019)

Lee, P.H.: Resampling methods improve the predictive power of modeling in class-imbalanced datasets. Int. J. Environ. Res. Public Health **11**(9), 9776–9789 (2014)

Małowiecki, A.: Metody resamplingu danych w rozwiązaniu problemu nierównowagi danych przy wykrywaniu oszustw związanych z kartami kredytowymi. … (2023)

Małowiecki, A.: Fairlearn parity constraints for mitigating gender bias in binary classification models – comparative analysis (2023)

Mehrabi, N., Morstatter, F., Saxena, N., Lerman, K., Galstyan, A.: A survey on bias and fairness in machine learning. ACM Comput. Surv. (CSUR) **54**(6), 1–35 (2021)

Microsoft.. https://learn.microsoft.com/en-us/training/modules/detect-mitigate-unfairness-models-with-azure-machine-learning/2-consider-model-fairness (2023). Accessed 15 July 2023

Mittelstadt, B., Wachter, S., Russell, C.: The Unfairness of Fair Machine Learning: Levelling down and strict egalitarianism by default. arXiv preprint arXiv:2302.02404 (2023)

Pagano, T.P., et al.: Bias and unfairness in machine learning models: a systematic review on datasets, tools, fairness metrics, and identification and mitigation methods. Big Data Cogn. Comput. **7**(1), 15 (2023)

Pandey, H.: Comparison of the usage of Fairness Toolkits amongst practitioners: AIF360 and Fairlearn (2022)

Pessach, D., Shmueli, E.: A review on fairness in machine learning. ACM Comput. Surv. (CSUR) **55**(3), 1–44 (2022)

Rzemieniak, M., Wawer, M.: Employer branding in the context of the company's sustainable development strategy from the perspective of gender diversity of generation Z. Sustainability **13**(2), 828 (2021)

Schumann, C., Foster, J., Mattei, N., Dickerson, J.: We need fairness and explainability in algorithmic hiring. In: International Conference on Autonomous Agents and Multi-Agent Systems (AAMAS), May 2020

SDG FUND: Sustainable development goals (2015). https://www.un.org/sustainabledevelopment/inequality

Tolan, S., Miron, M., Gómez, E., Castillo, C.: Why machine learning may lead to unfairness: evidence from risk assessment for juvenile justice in Catalonia. In: Proceedings of the Seventeenth International Conference on Artificial Intelligence and Law, pp. 83–92, June 2019

Yang, M., Wang, J., Ton, J.F.: Rectifying unfairness in recommendation feedback loop. In: Proceedings of the 46th International ACM SIGIR Conference on Research and Development in Information Retrieval, pp. 28–37, July 2023

# ChatGPT as a Learning Tool in Business Education. Research on Students' Motivation

Aleksander Binsztok, Beata Butryn, Katarzyna Hołowińska(✉), Mieczysław L. Owoc, and Małgorzata Sobińska

Department of Business Intelligence in Management, Wroclaw University of Economics and Business, Komandorska, Wroclaw, Poland
katarzyna.holowinska@ue.wroc.pl

**Abstract.** The education process is radically changing with changing technology, which fits perfectly into sustainable development. However, how the teachers and students use it depends only on them. The effectiveness of ChatGPT as a learning tool in business education and its impact on student motivation can vary depending on implementation, context, or individual student characteristics. Using ChatGPT as a learning tool in business education can be an innovative approach to engage students and enhance their learning experience. In our research, we would like to create a diagnosis regarding the use of ChatGPT by WUE students (motives, scope of questions/tasks, frequency of use, concerns, satisfaction). The impact of AI (ChatGPT) on the implementation of knowledge verification processes of students at economic universities and the resulting demands for changes in the learning outcomes verification system - diagnosis of an economic university (UEW). Without a doubt, further research and empirical studies are needed to explore these aspects and provide more comprehensive insights.

**Keywords:** ChatGPT · Education · AI · Business Education

## 1 Introduction

The concept of sustainability development has gained considerable attention in various fields including education. As societies strive to create a sustainable future it is crucial to integrate sustainable practices into educational systems. In recent years the application of Artificial Intelligence (AI) in education has emerged as a promising tool to promote sustainability development. The increasing access to tools based on artificial intelligence causes general interest in their use. At the same time, with their development, there are some questions and doubts about their use, starting from technical issues to ethical aspects. That is why the main aim of the research is to present the results of a survey on the motivation of students of economic universities to use ChatGPT and a discussion on the impact of AI (Chat GPT) on learning processes, and education processes, but also verification of education processes and the resulting demands for changes in the context of university teaching.


Published by Springer Nature Switzerland AG 2024
E. Mercier-Laurent et al. (Eds.): AI4KMES 2023, IFIP AICT 693, pp. 80–91, 2024.
https://doi.org/10.1007/978-3-031-61069-1_7

Sustainability education encompasses teaching and learning practices that promote environmental consciousness social responsibility and economic viability. It equips learners with the knowledge skills and values necessary to address sustainability challenges and contribute to a more sustainable future. It involves interdisciplinary approaches encouraging critical thinking and fostering a holistic understanding of the interconnectedness between ecological social and economic systems. ChatGPT an artificial intelligence model has the potential to revolutionize the field of education including sustainability education. It can provide personalized learning experiences instant feedback and access to vast amounts of information. By leveraging ChatGPT educators can enhance student engagement promote critical thinking and facilitate a deeper understanding of sustainability concepts [1].

From 2015 UNESCO as a leader agency provide Global Action Program on Education for Sustainable Development which highlight five main priority areas [2]:

1. Creating favorable climate to allow education for sustainable development to manage to find the potential in permanent changing educational systems. The main goal contains integration between educational for sustainable development idea with educational and sustainability policy-making.
2. Focusing on holistic learning and teaching transformation environments. The main goal was changing main values and structures of institutions connected with education.
3. Developing proper competences among trainers and teachers, to implement the idea of sustainable development in education in practice.
4. Mobilizing and empowering young generation by engaging them in development and implementation of strategies in the area of sustainable development.
5. Promoting the idea of sustainable development at local levels. Creating networks with engagement of different contributions which allows discussions and improvements the quality of area of educational services.

It is very optimistic that this topic is being dealt with such globally significant institutions as UNESCO, which indicates the importance of the issue and allows us to believe that real actions are being taken that indicate a goal that is not indifferent and that should be pursued [3].

## 2 Research Background

When reviewing the literature, it is worth mentioning a completely new phenomenon, namely that the authors of the review publications themselves question the credibility of the cited sources, i.e. they express the hypothesis that perhaps some of the works are the result of the work of artificial intelligence and not the work of man. It can be assumed that such doubts will be more and more frequent and the need to improve tools verifying the authorship of various types of scientific papers is therefore urgent. It seems that allowing dishonest prepared works to "pass" may have serious consequences when it comes to scientific research and ethics in general.

- Searching for information: ChatGPT can be used as a tool to quickly find information about specific concepts, definitions, economic theories, etc. It can be especially useful when writing scientific papers, solving problems, or preparing for exams.

- Understanding difficult concepts: Some economic concepts can be complex and difficult to understand. Students can use ChatGPT to explain these difficult topics in a more accessible way than traditional textbooks or reference materials.
- Help with problem-solving: ChatGPT can support students in solving economics tasks and problems. It can provide tips, suggestions, or examples to help students find the right solutions.
- Creative thinking and generating ideas: ChatGPT can inspire students to think creatively and generate new ideas in the field of economics. By asking questions, discussing and exploring different possibilities, ChatGPT can support students in developing analytical and creative skills.
- Providing students with an interactive and personalized learning environment where active learning methods can be improved. For example, Rudolf et al. [4] propose the use of flipped learning in which students are required to familiarize themselves with the materials before class. This instructional approach can free up class time for group discussion.
- ChatGPT, as a virtual tutor, can help students learn independently online by answering their questions, providing real-time feedback, and improving group dynamics by suggesting a discussion structure [5].

In the discussion of using ChatGPT it also appears that in context of automation writing tools used to reply to customer e-mails, complete documents, prepare reports, etc. are useful, save time and money and serve to optimize certain processes in the organization. Unfortunately, in the context of implementing the same tools in education, this may mean a limitation of developing skills like creativity, ability to thinking, to creating clear and consist contents. That is why it is so important to deploy such tools at a specific stage of development to avoid harmful effects and negative impact [6]. On the other hand thanks to the use of AI, we have the opportunity to model education in a way that is tailored to individual needs, focused on individual interests and predispositions. Moreover, there is the possibility of training teachers, but also of training the model so that it adapts the content, individual methods and tasks based on previously defined principles [7]. The types of AI applications are unlimited, but how this technology will be used and what consequences its use will have depends entirely on us. Some sources demonize the use of AI, emphasizing the independence of this technology, unlimited number of applications, and advantage over human biological capabilities. Undoubtedly, some of the worst-case scenarios may happen, but AI is still a tool in the hands of humans.

## 3 Research Methodology and Analysis

An internet survey tool was used for the research. Surveys are a widely used scientific method for collecting data and information. They are particularly valuable for gathering data on a population's opinions, behaviors, attitudes, and characteristics. The team decided to use an Internet survey mainly because of a broad range of advantages:

Cost efficiency compared to the traditional method of collecting data using printed materials or additional expenses. Moreover, online surveys allow to reach a bigger amount of recipients, and data collection, is also much faster to process and collect data. The survey's main purpose was to diagnose the motives, ways, and scope of using

ChatGPT by students of an economic university. The survey took place at Wroclaw University of Business and Economy between the end of May 2023 and until end of June 2023. The survey was divided into 18 questions, with many options: closed and open questions, with single and multiple choice questions.

93 students took part in the survey, 55% man and 45% woman The vast majority of the participants in the study were students in the second year of master's studies (63%) and most of them attended part-time study (61%). As many as 95% of those responding to the question were of Polish nationality. According to the survey, most of the respondents study computer science in business. More than 91% of surveyed students declared that they are using ChatGPT to prepare for classes at the university. Such a large amount of answers presents how important is ChatGPT as an educational tool. Only 8% who declared that they are not using ChatGPT to prepare for classes also declared that they are not using this tool because most of them are not interested in this solution and don't know anything about ChatGPT or don't trust this technology. At the same time for the question, "What would make you use this tool for educational purposes" 50% of them informed that more credibility of generated data, and 37% declared that allowing chatGPT as an official tool supported didactic processes (Fig. 1).

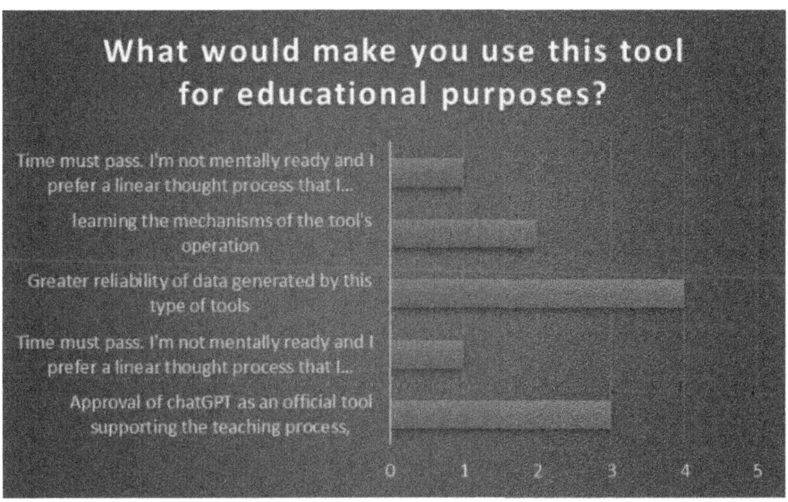


**Fig. 1.** Use chatGPT for educational spurposes. Source: own elaboration.

In the further part of the study, most of the students who declared the use of ChatGPT were using the free version (85%), and only 15% of responders paid option of ChatGPT. The results can be concluded that the paid version is not yet so attractive in the context of education to pay for it. The study concerns people who often do not work, in this situation this type of expense may seem unnecessary to them. Among the respondents, the most popular languages are Polish and English. In the context of frequency, 52% of students answered that they are using ChatGPT for educational activities a few times per month, 25% a few times per week, 17% once a week, and only 5% are using ChatGPT every day. Without a doubt tools like ChatGPT are used for educational reasons even in the early stage of development, which shows how important it is to improve skills in using such a universal instrument and to give the possibility to work with it during the projects, assignments, etc. (Figs. 2 and 3).

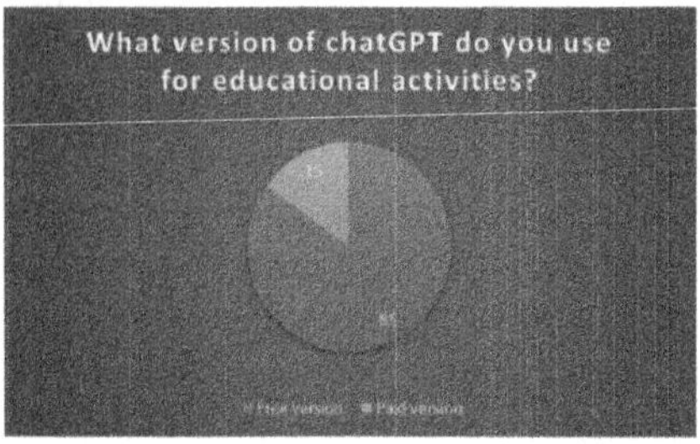


**Fig. 2.** ChatGPT version. Source: own elaboration

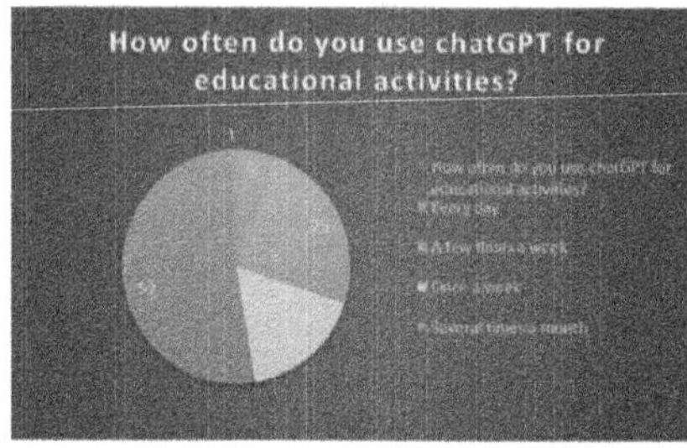


**Fig. 3.** Frequency of using ChatGPT. Source: own elaboration.

In the question "For what purpose do you use ChatGPT" most of the answers were to extend the knowledge, and the second most popular answer was to solve the tasks, also for creating texts, reports, tables, and projects. According to the answers, students choose to support their university obligations by ChatGPT and probably it is something that cannot be avoided or forbidden, but what is extremely important, it would be worth defining the path of use (Fig. 4).

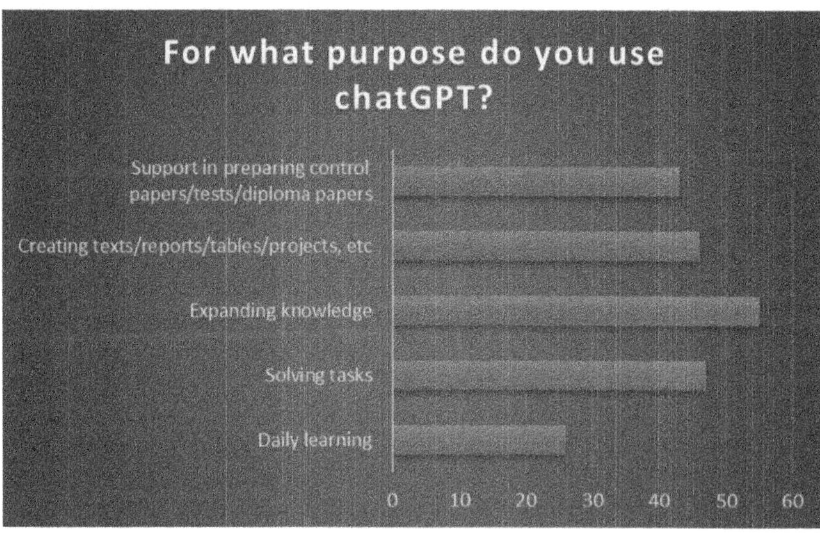


**Fig. 4.** Purpose of using ChatGPT. Source: own elaboration.

According to the survey, the biggest disadvantages of ChatGPT for educational purposes are difficulty/impossible to verify information sources, lack of trust in the information, limitations in understanding contexts, or technology addiction. It is interesting how despite their young age, users are aware of the disadvantages that modern technology may have, which means that the majority of respondents do not use the tool thoughtlessly. This also indicates that when designing and creating this type of tool, expectations are high and users are not satisfied with feedback without sources or taken out of context. Interestingly, the hygiene of using new technologies is also important for young people (Fig. 5).

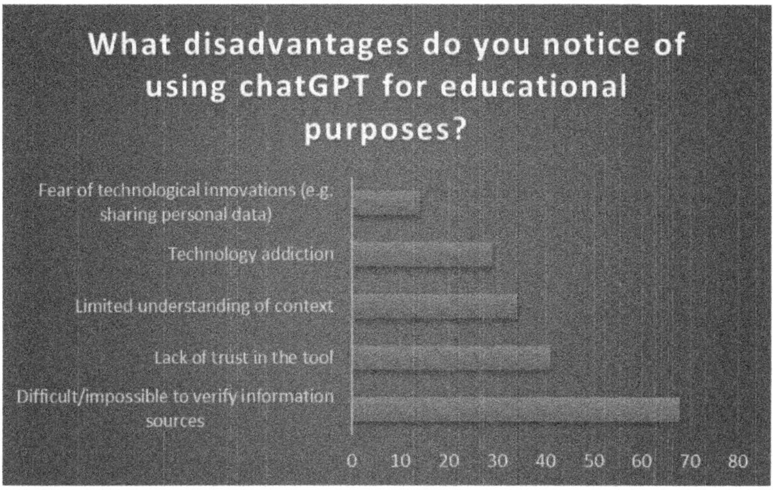


**Fig. 5.** Disadvantages of using ChatGPT. Source: own elaboration.

Respondents in the survey indicated the quick response time, accelerated way of acquiring knowledge, help in solving most problems or using the latest and developing technologies as the main advantage of using chatGPT. Additionally, respondents also indicated a virtual tutor for students and an interactive and personalized learning environment. Undoubtedly, the use of chatGPT in education is quite wide and we are pleased with the fact that users are not limited to just copying information, but that the tool is used creatively (Fig. 6).

For the respondents, the most common fields of acquiring knowledge by using chatGPT are IT, finance, economics, management, and e-business. It is not surprising that the IT field dominates this area, although it is pleasing that the tool is also used in other domains. Perhaps it is worth paying attention when creating lesson programs to increase the possibilities of using chatGPT also in other areas of science (Fig. 7).

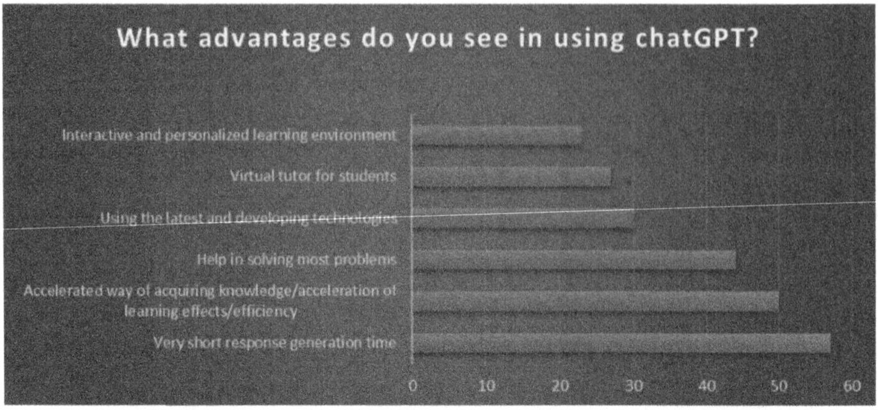


**Fig. 6.** Advantages of using ChatGPT. Source: own elaboration.

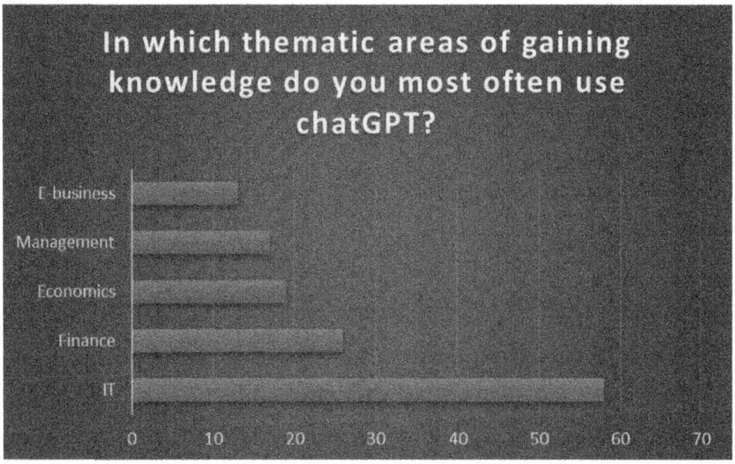


**Fig. 7.** Areas of using ChatGPT. Source: own elaboration.

As part of the fight against AI, some universities have banned the use of tools such as chatGPT, taking into account the answers regarding the assessment of the usefulness of chatGPT in educational activities, it seems that the use of AI in education is inevitable, as many as 43% of respondents found this tool helpful, 26% that it is very helpful, 0% that it does not bring any benefits. Undoubtedly, defining a developmental and clear policy for the use of AI in education is a necessity that universities must cope with as quickly as possible (Fig. 8).

As the main reason for using chatGPT, respondents chose saving time in preparing various types of work, also minimizing effort in connection with the implementation of tasks that are of little interest, but also looking for inspiration, easily obtaining information and the curiosity. This type of answers indicate what chatGPT is most often used for and what activities it supports (Fig. 9).

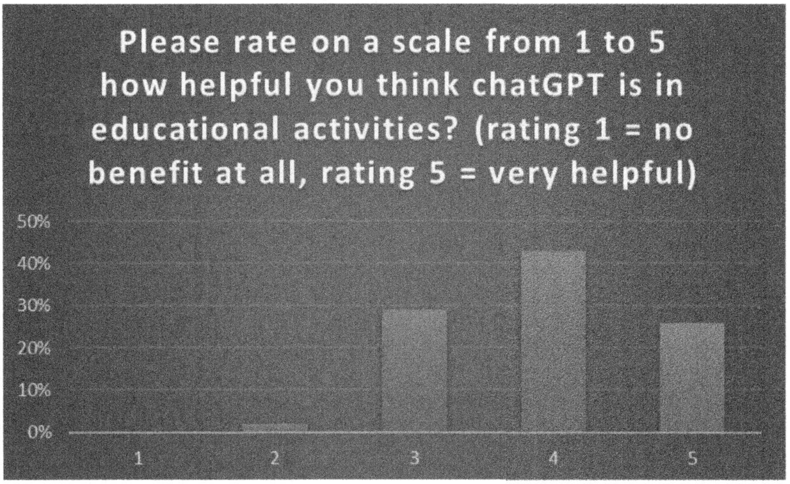


**Fig. 8.** How helpful chat GPT is. Source: own elaboration.

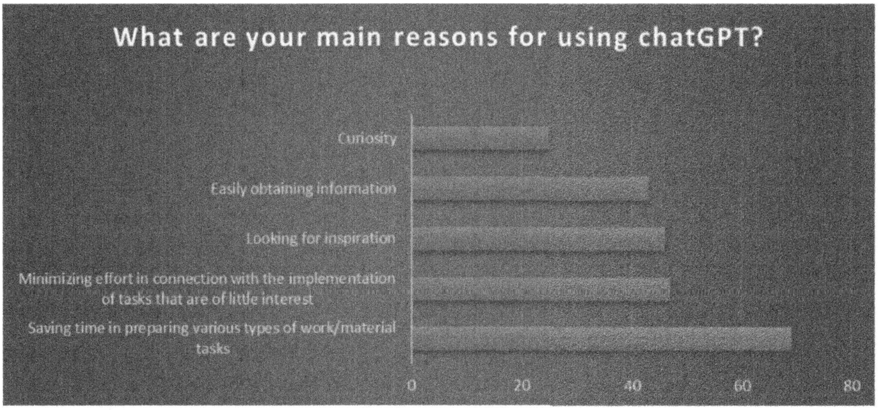


**Fig. 9.** Reasons of using ChatGPT. Source: own elaboration.

The last question of the survey concerned verifying the answers received via chatGPT, the vast majority of respondents, as many as 95%, answered that they verified the information received in this way, and only 5% answered that they did not verify it. This percentage of responses perfectly shows how distant chatGPT is treated as a learning tool. This significantly indicates how much there is still to be done in the context of this tool and perhaps the right direction would be to indicate the full sources of information from which the answers are prepared (Fig. 10).

This type of survey seems to be an interesting form of communication between students and the university, which can inspire interesting conclusions and directions in which educational methods should follow in the context of developing technologies and the needs of the generations that will use these technologies.

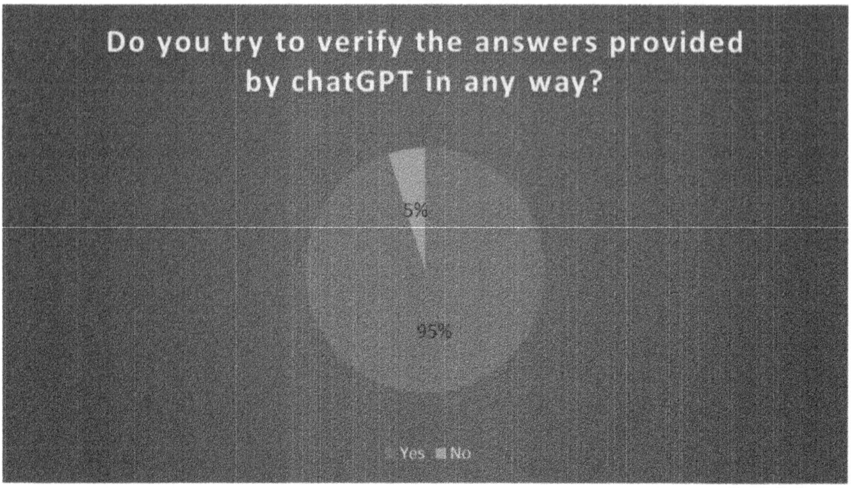


**Fig. 10.** Level of verifying ChatGPT information. Source: own elaboration.

## 4 Future Research Directions and Conclusions

ChatGPT used as a virtual tutor for students raises some concerns related to the generation of incorrect or false information, posing a threat to academic integrity. Undoubtedly, this requires immediate action on the part of the academic community, consisting of the development of new guidelines and rules on academic integrity and the prevention of plagiarism. Both lecturers and students should be trained in the effective use of ChatGP. Academic teachers should be equipped with appropriate plagiarism detection tools/capabilities, and students should be made aware of the limitations of ChatGPT and their potential impact on academic integrity.

However, it should be remembered that the effective use of ChatGPT in education depends on the skillful approach of students and the conscious use of these tools. Students need to understand that ChatGPT does not always provide valid, verified information and that the results generated by the model may contain significant errors and/or oversimplifications. Objective research, critical thinking, and fact-checking should still remain key to effective economic education [8].

There are many benefits of using ChatGPT in sustainability education, but the main of them are:

1. Personalized Learning: ChatGPT can adapt to individual learners' needs and preferences offering tailored educational content and activities. This personalized approach enhances student motivation self-directed learning and overall engagement.
2. Interactive and Immersive Learning: ChatGPT can simulate real-world scenarios enabling learners to explore and experiment with sustainable practices in a safe and controlled environment. This interactive and immersive learning experience fosters active participation and deeper comprehension.
3. Access to Real-Time Information: ChatGPT can provide learners with instant access to up-to-date information on sustainability topics. This enables students to stay

informed about current environmental issues scientific advancements and innovative solutions promoting a more comprehensive understanding of sustainability challenges.

While ChatGPT offers numerous benefits it is important to recognize and address the challenges and limitations associated with its use in sustainability education:

1. Reliability and Accuracy: ChatGPT generates responses based on patterns it has learned from vast amounts of data. However it may sometimes provide inaccurate or biased information. Educators must ensure the accuracy and reliability of the content generated by ChatGPT and guide students in critically evaluating the information provided.
2. Lack of Human Connection: ChatGPT lacks the human touch and empathy that is essential in education, particularly for sensitive topics like sustainability. Developing a genuine connection with students and fostering values and attitudes towards sustainability may be challenging solely through an AI-based tool.
3. Accessibility and Equity: The availability and accessibility of ChatGPT may vary across different educational contexts regions and socioeconomic backgrounds. Ensuring equitable access to ChatGPT and related technologies becomes crucial to avoid exacerbating existing educational disparities [9].

The integration of artificial intelligence (AI) technologies in higher education has gained significant attention in recent years. One such technology ChatGPT has emerged as a promising tool for enhancing learning experiences and promoting sustainable development in educational contexts. With its ability to generate human-like responses and engage in meaningful conversations, ChatGPT presents numerous opportunities for educators and students alike [10]. Recently, it has often been predicted that AI may bring tragic consequences for humanity, there are comments that humans will lose control over machines, everything indicates that sustainable development may be a great opportunity to strike a balance and technology will contribute to finding appropriate solutions that will protect the planet from complete degradation. However, to start this process from scratch, it must be implemented in educational processes and methods [11].

The study showed that students of an economic university willingly use ChatGPT while studying. Undoubtedly, a very important, if not the most important, motivating factor is the temporary fascination with this tool, not only by students but also by lecturers and the general public, which for several months has been testing various ideas with ChatGPT with curiosity equal to disbelief. In addition, the study indicated such reasons for the use of chat by students, such as:

- searching for information,
- understanding difficult concepts,
- assistance in solving problems,
- generating ideas and thus supporting creativity in the preparation of projects, papers, and other types of conceptual work,
- everyday learning, expanding knowledge, support in the preparation of control papers, tests, and diploma theses,
- curiosity, looking for inspiration.

Undoubtedly, students perceive ChatGPT as an interactive and personalized learning environment, helpful in solving most problems. As its advantage, they mention the accelerated way of acquiring knowledge/accelerating the effects/efficiency of learning. It is also worth emphasizing that students are also aware of certain limitations, or even threats, resulting from the use of ChatGPT in the process of acquiring knowledge [12]. The most frequently mentioned are lack of trust in the tool, lack of knowledge about the tool, limitation in understanding the context, and difficult/impossible verification of information sources. In the minority, they also point to ethical doubts or addiction to technology or, on the contrary, fear of technological innovations.

However, saving time in preparing various types of work/tasks of the material, minimizing effort in connection with the implementation of tasks that are of little interest, lack of independent ideas for solving selected problems, and easy acquisition of information, are the main motives of students after reaching for this tool. This may be a somewhat disturbing signal/prophecy as to the way of acquiring knowledge, solving problems, and thus the future of education [13]. Therefore, it would be worth using AI in the context of enhancing creativity, critical thinking, communication and collaboration [14] which are the basic components that a graduate should be equipped with in order to use them not only in professional work but also in everyday life.

## References


1. OpenAI: ChatGPT: Engaging and Creative Conversations (2021). https://openai.com/research/ChatGPT
2. Hauff, M., Kuhnke, C., Sustainable Development Policy: A European Perspective, p. 135 (2017)
3. https://unesdoc.unesco.org/ark:/48223/pf0000246270
4. Rudolph, J., Tan, S., Tan, S.: ChatGPT: bullshit spewer or the end of traditional assessments in higher education? J. Appl. Learn. Teach. **6**, 1–22 (2023)
5. Kasneci, E., et al.: ChatGPT for good? On opportunities and challenges of large language models for education. Learn. Individ. Differ. **103**, 102274 (2023)
6. Reich, R.: Generative AI: perspectives from Stanford HAI How do you think generative AI will affect your field and society going forward? In: Education, a Disaster in the Making, p. 20 (2023)
7. Norvig, P.: Generative AI: perspectives from Stanford HAI How do you think generative AI will affect your field and society going forward? In: Solving Inequalities in the Education System, p. 21 (2023)
8. Cooper, G.: Examining science education in ChatGPT: an exploratory study of generative artificial intelligence. J. Sci. Educ. Technol. **32**, 444–452 (2023). https://doi.org/10.1007/s10956-023-10039-y
9. Chatfield, A.T., Reddick, C.G.: Artificial intelligence in education: promises, ethics, and concerns. Int. J. Publ. Admin. Digit. Age **8**(1), 1–16 (2021)
10. Brown, A., Green, T.D.: The Essentials of Instructional Design: Connecting Fundamental Principles with Process and Practice. Routledge, New York (2016)
11. Mercier-Laurent, E.: Artificial intelligence and sustainability. The use of AI in sustainability initiatives (2020)
12. Malinka, K., Perešíni, M., Firc, A., Hujňák, O., Januš, H.: On the Educational Impact of ChatGPT: Is Artificial Intelligence Ready to Obtain a University Degree? (2023). https://doi.org/10.48550/arXiv.2303.11146

13. Lo, C.K.: What is the impact of ChatGPT on education? A rapid review of the literature. Educ. Sci. **13**, 410 (2023). https://doi.org/10.3390/educsci13040410
14. https://scstemacademy.org/4-cs-of-21st-century-skills/
15. Adams, W.M.: The future of sustainability: re-thinking environment and development in the twenty-first century. Report of the IUCN Renowned Thinkers Meeting, Cambridge, UK, 29–31 January 2006 (2006)

# Integrating Artificial Intelligence into Electric Vehicle Energy Systems: A Survey

Weiqi Hua[1], Daniel Mullen[2], Abdul Wahid[3(✉)], Khadija Sitabkhan[3], and Karl Mason[3]

[1] Department of Electronic, Electrical and Systems Engineering, University of Birmingham, Birmingham B15 2TT, UK
w.hua@bham.ac.uk

[2] School of Engineering, University of Edinburgh, Edinburgh EH9 3DW, UK
d.t.mullen@sms.ed.ac.uk

[3] School of Computer Science, University of Galway, Galway H91 FYH2, Ireland
{abdul.wahid,k.sitabkhan1,karl.mason}@universityofgalway.ie

**Abstract.** Electric vehicles play an important role in the global transition to "Net Zero" and the decarbonisation of point source emissions from road transport, as their market share continues to grow each year. However, integrating these electric vehicles into existing electricity grids, refuelling stations and supply chains presents significant challenges. But most challenges can be effectively addressed through the implementation of artificial intelligence solutions. This paper starts with an introduction to artificial intelligence and an investigation of the challenges associated with the widespread adoption of electric vehicles in society. Then, the paper analyses in detail how artificial intelligence can facilitate the smooth integration of electric vehicles. In addition, the paper provides a detailed investigation of the life-cycle emissions of electric vehicles and examines the limitations of existing research in this area and suggests potential avenues for future research.

**Keywords:** Electric Vehicles · Sustainability · Artificial Intelligence · Decarbonization · Renewable Energy

## 1 Introduction

Road transport is an integral part of modern society. Traditionally, these vehicles have been powered by internal combustion engines (ICEs) burning liquid hydrocarbon fossil fuels such as petroleum. As a result, they directly emit carbon dioxide, the most prevalent greenhouse gas (GHG) in earth atmosphere. This is problematic as nations around the world have committed to cutting GHG emissions in an effort to avoid the worst effects of climate change [65]. ICEs

This paper is an extension of work originally presented ar the Workshop on Artificial Intelligence for Sustainability, ECAI 2023.


Published by Springer Nature Switzerland AG 2024
E. Mercier-Laurent et al. (Eds.): AI4KMES 2023, IFIP AICT 693, pp. 92–115, 2024.
https://doi.org/10.1007/978-3-031-61069-1_8

also directly emit particulate matters which negatively impact human health [8]. These vehicles also produce a significant amount of noise pollution [57].

Electric vehicles (EVs) are considered a promising solution to address the challenges associated with traditional fossil-fuel vehicles. They offer benefits such as reduced noise, low maintenance, zero direct carbon dioxide emissions, and lower particulate matter emissions [75]. However, moving towards large production, acceptance, and integration of EVs into existing energy systems is challenging. One major challenge lies in the production of EV batteries, which rely on rare earth minerals, such as lithium, which are expensive to mine and production often has poor humanitarian record [93]. Further, the establishment of a comprehensive charging infrastructure for EVs poses financial challenges for governments and adds a substantial burden to the electrical grid [11]. The success of EVs in achieving meaningful decarbonization is also hampered by the carbon intensity of power production, as many countries still heavily rely on fossil fuels for power grid. Integrating renewable generation, carbon capture and storage and battery and thermal storage systems into the power grid can provide a solution.

As the world progresses to a more decarbonized and digitalized future, artificial intelligence (AI) is expected to play an important role in integrating EVs into energy system infrastructure. Effectively integrating EVs into the grid requires optimization, planning, forecasting, modeling, etc. To address these challenges, many AI systems have been developed [1,59,73,92]. However, these studies have limitations, requiring new research to address these issues. Rigas et al. conducted a detailed analysis of AI in EV integration [59]. The review covers a wide range of AI applications in EV integration. However, it lacks coverage of current advancements in recent years. In a more recent survey, Zadeh et al. focused specifically on deep learning applications for EVs within microgrids [92]. This review of the applications of deep learning to EVs within microgrids is comprehensive when discussing deep learning only. However, the scope of this study is limited to deep learning only, neglecting the broader spectrum of AI algorithms. Song et al. published a detailed report in 2020, analyzing global EV adoption trends [73]. Despite its detailed analysis of monetary and non-monetary incentives, national targets, and regulatory systems across countries, the paper lacks any discussion on the integration of AI in the context of EVs. In 2021, Abdullah et al. conducted a review specifically on studies evaluating reinforcement learning (RL) for EV charging management [1]. Although this study is detailed, it focuses only on RL for EV charging management systems.

As per our knowledge, there is no review article relating to AI for EV energy-transportation integration that are as comprehensive as this paper. This article makes the following contributions:

1. Providing a comprehensive survey of the applications of AI in the integration of energy-transportation.
2. Discussing the limitations present in the existing literature and identifying potential areas for future research.

3. Identifying and outlining key areas where AI techniques can significantly influence the integration of energy systems in electric vehicles

The paper is structured as follows. Section 2 provides an overview of electric vehicles and their relevance to the energy sector. Section 3 covers the life cycle assessment and life cycle emission of EVs. Section 4 covers AI in general. Section 5 presents a complete analysis of AI applications to EV manufacturers, EV owners, power network operators, charging infrastructure owners, and vehicle-to-grid planners. Section 6 discusses the limitations and future works. Finally, Sect. 7 draws conclusions from this study.

## 2 Electric Vehicles

### 2.1 Overview

EV market share grows annually in several countries [63]. EVs use a battery to store power from the grid or a decentralized source and drive an electric motor as required. The EV drive system is simple, while the battery technology is complex. EV battery packs must match ICEs in range, charging efficiency, operating the lifespan, and the cost. Building the charging infrastructure and decarbonizing the battery supply chain are technological challenges, while public opinion and high prices jeopardize EV adoption. Here are some popular EV configurations:

- **HEV (Hybrid Electric Vehicle):** HEVs, which are the most prevalent type of EV, reduce carbon emissions by combining an ICE with an electric motor [72]. The ability to charge the on-board battery outside to the ICE defines two main HEV subgroups. First, the traditional HEV uses ICE drive train energy to charge the on-board battery, which cannot be charged externally. Thus, increasing thermal efficiency reduces carbon intensity, limited by the Carnot efficiency of the cycle. Another type of HEV is a plug-in hybrid electric vehicle (PHEV) or extended range electric vehicle (E-REV). The main difference between PHEV/E-REV and typical HEVs is that the on-board battery can be charged externally to the ICE and potentially accounts for most of the life-cycle kilometers, with the ICE as a backup for longer trips. Thus, travel carbon intensity depends on power source carbon intensity and battery-to-ICE ratio.
- **BEV (Battery Electric Vehicle):** A BEV relies solely on an externally charged on-board battery for propulsion [62]. BEVs have no ICE backup, unlike PHEVs. This indicates that BEV carbon intensity depends on charging point power and vehicle manufacturing emissions. BEV carbon intensity could be zero if a Net Zero emissions electricity grid and BEV manufacturing emissions were removed or offset. Because BEVs use stored electricity, range per charge and charging time have generally limited their acceptance. Resolving these technical issues will make BEVs more viable as transportation.
- **FCEV (Fuel Cell Electric Vehicle):** FCEVs use electric motors like conventional EVs. In contrast to HEVs and BEVs, the motor is driven by a hydrogen fuel cell, generating electricity without external charge [25]. No emissions

occur when hydrogen is used. They emit no direct emissions. However, hydrogen production method determines travel carbon intensity. Hydrogen must be produced using zero-emission methods like electrolyses with dedicated renewables or methane reforming with carbon capture and storage for zero-emission travel.

### 2.2 Transport and Climate Change

A recent report by the Intergovernmental Panel on Climate Change (IPCC) [34] states that "human activities, principally through emissions of greenhouse gases, have unequivocally caused global warming, with global surface temperature reaching 1.1 °C above 1850–1900 in 2011–2020". A report, published by the UK climate change committee, mentioned that the surface transport emission increased by 3%, but remained 8% below pre-pandemic (2019) levels [15]. Decarbonizing road transport, reliant on carbon-intensive internal combustion engines, poses challenges. While centralized hydrocarbon use can adopt carbon capture and storage, no cost-effective solution exists for decentralized ICEs. Hydrogen and electricity are potential alternatives, with electrification favored for passenger vehicles due to hydrogen's challenges.

BEVs are embraced globally for climate change mitigation and local air quality improvement. BEVs emit no carbon during use, impacting air quality in urban areas. However, their net greenhouse gas reduction depends on factors like power production's carbon intensity and manufacturing emissions, requiring detailed life cycle assessments.

### 2.3 Batteries

For domestic vehicle transportation to meet the energy demands, new battery technologies are essential. While Alessandro Volta's work in 1799 is credited with the invention of electrochemical batteries [26], Gaston Plante's 1859 rechargeable battery introduced reversibility to the electrochemical reaction by using lead acid components [33]. There are many different types of rechargeable batteries available today, such as nickel-metal hydride and nickel-cadmium, but lithium-ion (Li-ion) batteries are the most popular because of their lightweight design, high energy density, and favorable cycle life. Li-ion batteries, which consist of a graphite anode, a lithium metal oxide cathode, and a lithium salt electrolyte, have specific energy densities that range from 90 to 250 Wh/kg. Recent technological advances has led to an average range of 314 km for electric vehicles, with fast charging-enabled BEVs being able to charge from zero to full capacity in less than an hour.

### 2.4 Grid

The electricity required to power EVs is obtained from either distributed renewable sources or the electricity grid. Traditionally, the electrical grid consisted of centralised electricity generation and transmission [42]. Power was produced using a combination of large scale power plants with low flexibility to provide forecasted minimum power requirements or "base load" and more flexible plants to meet variation in demand or "load following". These load following plants typically operated with an excess generation capacity or "operating reserve" to allow increased power generation in times of higher demand while rotational inertia helps smooth out small fluctuations in the grid frequency. When a consumer is connected to a grid, the carbon intensity of electricity supplied is an average of the carbon intensity of all generators currently supplying power to the grid. The development of Smart Grids (SG) offers one potential avenue for addressing challenges associated with the grid. Hence, the domestic battery capacity can function as operational reserve feeding to or drawing from the grid as required. The paradigm of selling electricity from BEVs back to the grid is referred to as the Vehicle-to-Grid (V2G), which would enable EV owners to sell electricity back to the grid during peak hours, reduce peak demands, and earn additional income.

## 2.5 Challenges

The challenges faced by global conversion to BEVs can be broadly characterised into two subsections: consumer adoption and infrastructure development.

**Consumer Adoption:** Consumer acceptance is required in order for BEV's to serve as a viable replacement for ICEs. Barriers to widespread acceptance typically include the range anxiety and cost. Inherent in this barrier is the fact that the BEV recharging time is drastically longer than the time taken to refuel an ICE. However, advanced rapid chargers can fully charge in 30–60 min, which makes mid-trip recharging to be more viable option, while growing battery capacity and increased efficiency continually improve the maximum range [27]. Comparing the cost of BEVs verses ICEs can be complex due to the distribution of expenses over the lifetime of the vehicle. BEVs have higher initial costs and higher rates of depreciation [43]. This can cause consumers to consider them to be more expensive. ICEs typically have higher running costs. In order to more accurately compare BEVs to ICEs, a total cost of ownership (TCO) analysis is required. A TCO analysis calculates the total discounted cost of owning a vehicle over the lifetime of that vehicle to evaluate a net present value for comparisons. As with the potential for climate change mitigation, comparisons require case by case analysis and vary considerably depending on a number of factors e.g., annual millage, fuel/power prices, vehicle lifetime, governmental incentives, initial costs. However, the literature is clear that given the correct economic conditions, BEVs can be more cost effective than ICEs [86] [54] [13] [81].

**Infrastructure Level Challenges:** Aside from the consumer adoption, multiple challenges lay in the development of infrastructure to support a global shift to BEVs. Manufacturing supply chains, primarily those associated with battery production, need to scale up to unprecedented levels to meet the growing demand for BEVs with domestic production in the European union already struggling to meet demand [28]. The building out of sufficient domestic and public charging points also poses a challenge. While adequate charging facilities are required to drive adoption, low use rates due to currently low BEV market penetration and the potential for rapid obsolescence, make investment in charging stations unattractive for the private sector. As a result, development of charging infrastructure often requires governmental backing, necessitating progressive action and strong public support. Due to the growing electrification of our society in an effort to mitigate climate change, a large increase in power production capacity is expected to be required. BEVs are anticipated to contribute to a large portion of this increase. However, the electrification of home heating, industry and hydrogen production via electrolyses are all expected to drive demand.

It is clear that there are many challenges associated with integrating EVs into society, and specifically the grid. AI has received a great deal of interest in both academia and industry recent years. It is expected that AI will play a significant role in addressing the challenges outlined above.

## 3 Life-Cycle of Electric Vehicles

### 3.1 Life-Cycle Assessment

Life-cycle assessment (LCA) is a systematic and comprehensive technique to evaluate the environmental impacts of a product, process, or service over the course of its whole life cycle [56]. When it comes to EVs, LCA takes into account the environmental effects related to the vehicle's manufacturing, usage, and end of life phases. The key phases of LCA for EVs are as follows:

- **Raw Materials:** This phase involves the extraction of raw materials and their processing into a usable form, particularly for EV components, with a primary focus on battery production. The production of BEVs involves a diverse range of raw materials, with significant distinctions from ICEVs arising mainly from the battery, power electronics, and electric motor in a BEV. These rare earth minerals include lithium, cobalt, nickel, etc. However, the extraction of these minerals for use in electric vehicles poses various environmental challenges, such as the potential release of toxic materials into water and soil contamination. Recent LCAs indicate that raw material extraction and processing for Li-ion batteries contribute approximately 20% of the total GHG emissions from battery production [22,30,56].

- **Production:** This stage focuses on addressing environmental concerns associated with the energy-intensive manufacturing of BEVs after raw materials have been processed into a usable form. BEVs differ from ICEVs primarily in their energy storage, propulsion, and braking components. Instead of the traditional fuel tank, engine, gearbox, and exhaust found in ICEVs, BEVs require a battery, an electric motor, and power electronics. Notably, other components like the vehicle body and auxiliary systems may not necessarily differ. Many existing BEVs are adapted from ICEV vehicle bodies to streamline development and capitalize on existing production lines [18]. From a life cycle perspective, GHG and air pollutant emissions during BEV production are generally higher compared to ICEV production, primarily due to the energy-intensive nature of battery manufacturing [56]. According to the Polestar and Rivian Pathway report, battery manufacturing alone accounts for 4 to 6 $tCO_2e$ for small to large BEVs, and 1 $tCO_2e$ for HEVs [29].

Furthermore, the demand for raw materials such as lithium and cobalt, which are required in the production of EV batteries, is skyrocketing, leading in a plethora of social and environmental effects, including human rights violations. According to the research, the Democratic Republic of the Congo (DRC) accounts for two-thirds of total cobalt production. A report by the United Nations Children's Fund (UNICEF), around 20% of cobalt supplied from the DRC comes from artisanal mining where human rights violations have been observed, and up to 40,000 children work in highly unsafe conditions in the mines for meager wages. In Chile, lithium mining consumes about 66% of the water in the Salar de Atamaca region, one of the world's driest desert locations, to pump brines from drilled wells [14]. This has pushed local quinoa producers and llama herders to relocate and abandon their ancestral homelands.

These impacts can be minimized by adopting a circular economy approach by increasing the use of renewable electricity, promoting recycling, encouraging consumer choices favoring smaller vehicle categories through shared mobility services, reducing waste generation, and selecting battery types with lower environmental impact per unit of energy provided.

- **Usage:** During the use phase, BEVs provide many environmental benefits by eliminating all toxic emissions from the engines. When compared to ICE vehicles, the use of BEVs improves air quality by reducing local air pollution. However, emissions occur in the form of electricity generation, accompanied by noise and some particulate matter (PM) pollution resulting from factors like tire wear. According to a recent study [20], a BEV emits less GHG than a comparable diesel vehicle, which emits roughly 244 g/km for the diesel car and 95 g/km for the BEV. Further, in a fully renewable future, BEV lifecycle GHG emissions might reach 10 g/km and ICE vehicles could emit 153 g/km. This reduction can be attributed to the energy efficiency benefits of BEVs and their reliance on electricity sources with lower carbon intensity. While BEVs are generally quieter than ICEVs at lower speeds, distinctions in noise pollution diminish at higher speeds. It is important to note that the per-kilometer emissions during the utilization phase for BEVs are significantly influenced by consumption patterns, usage behaviors, and the electricity generation mix.

To minimize GHG and air pollutant emissions associated with BEV usage, a few measures can be implemented, such as increasing the share of low-carbon electricity in the overall grid mix. Additionally, promoting flexible charging practices becomes essential to capitalize on periods of low-carbon electricity availability and mitigate the risk of creating or exacerbating peaks in demand.

- **End-of-life:** The global market for electric vehicles is experiencing exponential growth, with sales surpassing 10 million units in 2022. Electric vehicle sales have increased by over threefold in the past three years, from approximately 4% in 2020 to 14% in 2022 [2]. While this phase has the least impact on total life cycle emissions when considered in isolation, promoting sustainable practices during this stage can provide many benefits across the whole life cycle [56]. These advantages include a diminished demand for virgin materials, thereby reducing the environmental impacts associated with mining and production. Sustainable practices also contribute to a decreased or deferred need for disposal, leading to a reduction in the environmental impacts related to landfilling. Additionally, embracing a more circular economy is achievable through the reuse, remanufacture, and recycling of batteries or their components, fostering a sustainable approach to material recovery.

In order to maximize the effectiveness and sustainability of end-of-life processes, further research is required. Major efforts entail advancing the cause of standardization to facilitate widespread recycling and reuse procedures, devising mechanisms to extract rare earth elements from magnets, and performing real-world assessments of battery second-use applications.

### 3.2 Life Cycle Emissions

The life cycle emissions of a product are calculated by aggregating emissions in three major stages: *production*, *usage phase*, and *end-of-life*. Production emissions are the emissions from vehicle and battery production resulting from new cars sold in a given year. Emissions from all vehicles in operation that year are captured using phase emissions, which include emissions from fuel/electricity production, tailpipe, and maintenance. Finally, end-of-life emissions occur when a vehicle's life cycle is complete and include recycling credits. The life cycle emissions of medium-sized battery electric, hybrid electric, and ICE vehicles in each step of their life cycles are shown in Table 1. Here, emission during the end-of-life stage represents emission "credits" related with recycling vehicles. These values are based on a 16-year use period and a distance of 240,000 km.

As we move toward an economy with no carbon emissions, BEVs can help cut $CO_2$ emissions around the world. Although BEVs don't have tailpipe emissions, it's important to note that many stages of their life cycle still produce a lot of emissions, especially when it comes to manufacturing and energy production. Therefore, making battery production less harmful to the environment while promoting the use of clean energy sources can help lower the emissions of BEVs even more, leading to better sustainability in the transportation sector.

This section explored at how BEVs can help to reduce GHG emissions and local air pollution. However, there are situations where BEVs may have a negative impact, such as during the raw material extraction stage. It is clear that

**Table 1.** Life Cycle Emissions: Electric vs. ICE Vehicles.

| Vehicle Types | BEV | HEV | ICE |
|---|---|---|---|
| Battery Management | 5 | 1 | – |
| Vehicle Manufacturing | 9 | 9 | 10 |
| Fuel/Electricity Production | 26 | 12 | 13 |
| Tailpipe Emission | – | 24 | 32 |
| Maintenance | 1 | 2 | 2 |
| End-of-life | −2 | −1 | −1 |
| **Total Emission** ($tCO_2e$) | **39** | **47** | **56** |

as more electric vehicles are deployed, the transportation and energy sectors will become increasingly intertwined. The importance of low-carbon energy is a theme that affects all stages of the life cycle. There will be a need to manage and optimize the higher energy consumption associated with the operation of electric vehicles. Low-carbon electricity will also help to reduce the environmental impact of battery and vehicle manufacturing, as well as raw material mining.

# 4 Artificial Intelligence

## 4.1 Overview

Artificial Intelligence (AI) dates back to the 1950's. Broadly speaking, AI refers to enabling machines to behave in an intelligent manner, either by imitating human behaviour or otherwise [61]. There is a wide range of algorithms that fall under the category of AI algorithms. One of the most prominent sub-fields of AI is the machine learning (ML). ML consists of a wide range of techniques, e.g., computer vision, natural language processing (NLP), neural networks, reinforcement learning (RL), etc. In addition to ML, other AI sub-fields include: multi-agent systems, fuzzy logic, evolutionary algorithms, and robotics. The purpose of this section is to give a broad and high level overview of AI techniques. AI topics such as NLP will be omitted from this review as it is unrelated to integrating EVs into energy systems.

## 4.2 Machine Learning

ML is a sub-field of AI. ML algorithms learn automatically through experience [49]. Prior to ML, traditional AI approaches consisted of hand-crafted rules, e.g., expert systems. In ML, the algorithm is presented with a data set or environment. The machine then learns what to do by interacting with the dataset or environment. ML algorithms can be broadly categorized as the supervised learning, unsupervised learning, semi-supervised learning, and RL.

In the supervised learning, the data is labelled and the ML algorithms need to learn the optimum model that produces the correct outputs, close to the labels, for given inputs. In the unsupervised learning problems, the data does not have labels. For these problems, the goal is to identify patterns in the dataset using algorithms such as clustering techniques [64]. Semi-supervised learning relates to datasets with a mixture of labelled and unlabelled data. RL algorithms learn an optimal policy that determines what actions to take for a given environment state [79].

### 4.3 Reinforcement Learning

RL consists of an agent interacting with an environment and learning what actions it should take to maximize its reward, e.g., learning to navigate a maze. At the time step $t$, the agent will observe the state $s_t$ of the environment and take an action $a_t$ based on its policy $\pi$. The environment will transition to its next state $s_{t+1}$ and the agent will receive a reward $R$ based on a reward function. RL problems are often modelled as a Markov decision process. This is a discrete time decision making framework.

One of the most prominent RL algorithms is Q-Learning [84]. The Q-Learning algorithm represents the policy $\pi$ using a Q-table. The values in the Q table determine what actions should be taken for a given state. The deep Q-network algorithm extends the Q-learning algorithm to problems with continuous state spaces by representing the agents policy using a neural network (NN) [50]. The deep deterministic policy gradient algorithm is an example of an RL algorithm that can operate in environments with continuous actions [39].

### 4.4 Neural Networks and Deep Learning

NNs are ML models that are inspired by the brain [71]. NNs operate by reading in a signal through the input layer of processing units, often refereed to as 'neurons'. This signal is passed through to subsequent hidden layers of processing units in the network by weighted connections. Finally, the signal is outputted through the output layer of the NN. NNs with more than one hidden layer of processing units are referred to as deep NNs.

The processing units consist of an activation function. Commonly used activation functions include the Sigmoid and ReLu functions, outlined in Equations (1) and (2), respectively. The output of the processing unit, $f(x)$, is calculated based on the sum of the weighted signals passed to the processing unit, $x$.

$$f(x) = \frac{1}{1 + e^{-x}} \tag{1}$$

$$f(x) = max(0, x) \tag{2}$$

NNs are commonly trained using methods based on the backpropagation by gradient decent algorithm. This involves calculating the error between the observed and expected outputs, and passing this error back through the network to update the weights.

### 4.5 Multi-agent Systems

Multi-agent systems (MAS) are systems that comprise of multiple autonomous goal orientated agents, capable of observing and interacting with the environment and other agents [88]. Figure 1 illustrates multiple agents interacting with their environment. There are many factors that can dictate the dynamics of the MAS:

- *Cooperative vs competitive environments:* Decision making tasks can be cooperative, competitive or a combination of both. Each results in different emergent system behaviour.
- *Homogeneous vs heterogeneous agents:* There are many problems in which agents are identical to another, e.g., drone coordination [10]. Heterogeneous agents refer to agents that vary from one another in some way.
- *Information availability:* Not all agents have complete environmental information available to them.
- *Resource competition:* The resources available within the environment also affect the system's dynamics. In zero sum games, one agent gains in resources directly corresponds to another agent loss in resources.

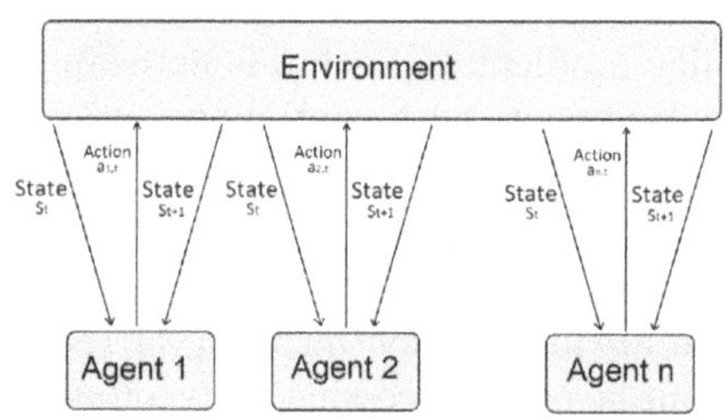


**Fig. 1.** Agent environment interaction for multi-agent system.

## 5 Applications of Artificial Intelligence to Electric Vehicles

Artificial Intelligence has seen increasing industrial and academic applications in the field of EVs. This section reviews the state-of-the-art research for such applications from the perspective of EV producers, end users, power system operators, infrastructure owners, policy makers and V2G planners. The stakeholders, specific functions, and studies for applying the AI into the field of EVs are summarised in Table 2, with details provided in the following subsections.

**Table 2.** Stakeholders, functions, and studies for applying the AI into the field of EVs.

| Stakeholders | Functions | Studies |
|---|---|---|
| EV producers | Range efficiency | [46,78,91] |
| | Battery efficiency | [7,40,53] |
| End users | Adoption | [6,60] |
| | Behaviours | [9,89] |
| | Scheduling | [38,99] |
| Power system operators | Intrusive load monitoring | [3,12] |
| | Non-intrusive load monitoring | [51,58,95,98] |
| | Management | [19,35,37,66] |
| Infrastructure owners | Planning | [36,48,55,77] |
| | Scheduling | [21,80,96] |
| Policy makers | Digitalisation | [16] |
| Vehicle-to-grid planners | Prediction | [69,70] |
| | Scheduling | [67,85] |

### 5.1 Electric Vehicle Producers

AI can support EV producers in many ways, including; range prediction, improvement of range efficiency, optimisation of battery usage, improvement of charging efficiency, reducing production cost, enhancing EV performance, and adjusting the manufacturing process accordingly.

Several studies have implemented AI for range prediction and improvement of range efficiency. Yavasoglu *et al* developed an AI based range estimation approach through which the driver profiles and road types were estimated using a decision tree and periodogram of jerk trace, respectively [91]. Sun *et al* developed a gradient boosting decision tree algorithm to improve the prediction accuracy of the driving range from the conventional multiple linear regression methods [78]. Meng *et al* implemented the online sequential extreme learning machine for online efficiency-optimisation control of extended range EVs in achieving a trade-off of the carbon emissions, driving performance, battery life, and driving range [46].

AI has demonstrated great capacity to optimise battery usage and improve charging efficiency. Lin *et al* proposed a nested learning framework to learn the limits on the state of charge range and optimal actions on the gear ratio and mode options for the hybrid EVs, in order to reduce the fuel and battery replacement cost [40]. Tejaswini and Sivraj implemented the coulomb counting approach, support vector machine, and optimal feed-forward artificial neural network to estimate the state of charge of lithium-ion batteries under various storage temperatures, initial conditions, and stress tests [53]. Bhatt *et al* exploited the second-life of batteries after retired from the EVs as storage applications in other domains, in which the remaining capacity and operational characteristics of the retired batteries were estimated through using deep neural networks [7].

## 5.2 End Users

In terms of end users, there are many examples in the literature where AI has been implemented to analyse EV adoption and charging behaviours for a variety of EV users and to help individual users schedule their charging activities. For predicting the adoption of EVs, de Rubens investigated the motivations of adoption and potential waves of EV buyers through using the k-means method, and found that the price and V2G were the key factors for the EV adoption, in particular for financially and environmentally-sensitive consumers [60]. Bas *et al* identified key factors of the EV adoption and classified potential EV purchasers through comparing various ML techniques, including the SVM, deep neural networks, gradient boosting models, distributed random forests, and extremely randomised forests [6].

For estimating the user behaviours of EVs, Xiong *et al* proposed an EV user modelling technique based on real-world datasets of EV charging behaviours, through combining the clustering algorithm with multilayer perceptron [89]. Chung *et al* assembled the support vector regression, random forest regression and diffusion-based kernel density estimator to predict charging behaviours of EV users, under various entropy-to-sparsity ratios of datasets, and applied the prediction into the EV charging scheduling to reduce the peak load, load variation, and operating costs [9].

For assisting users to schedule their EV charging activities, Li *et al* proposed a deep RL method that responds to time-of-use prices for the cost reduction, in which the charging problem was modelled as a Markov decision process and solved by the deep deterministic policy gradient algorithm [38]. Zhou *et al* proposed a long short-term memory recurrent neural network based ML algorithm to schedule the charging and discharging of EVs in a commercial building to improve the computational efficiency from conventional optimisation based methods [99].

## 5.3 Power System Operators

From a power systems operations perspective, load monitoring has attracted increasing attention from distribution network operators in terms of the supply-demand balance, energy conservation, and grid resilience. This is particularly important with the increasing penetration of EVs, roof-top solar panels, and air-source heat pumps. Load monitoring can be categorised as intrusive load monitoring (ILM) and non-intrusive load monitoring (NILM). ILM relies on the metering devices at the edge of power networks. Hoffmann *et al* developed deep learning methods to detect EVs from hourly smart meter data [24]. Their model detected the presence of EV charging with an accuracy of 90%. Dang *et al* extracted key features from the EV charging profiles and exploited these features to formulate a decision tree, so as to detect the EV profiles from high-resolution metering data of households [12]. Ahmed *et al* investigated the impacts of EV profiles on the household level smart meter data through using a ML based clustering algorithm, in which the EV loads were separated from non-EV loads by the change in the cluster membership [3]. There are many benefits of ILM, however it is dependent on the large scale rolling-out of smart meters and sensors with high granularity, which results in significant costs for power system operators, energy suppliers, and consumers.

Another approach, NILM is capable of identifying the power consumption of individual appliances through analysing aggregated meter readings at the substation level with the assistance of the AI. Jaramillo *et al* developed a NILM for the DSO through using the principal component analysis and random forest to detect EV charging at the distribution networks [51]. Rehman *et al* proposed an event based NILM approach based on support vector machines in combination with the genetic algorithm and GridSearchCV [58]. Zhao *et al* exploited the duration of the power consumption event and the interval between adjacent events to characterise charging patterns of EVs and developed an event detection method based on the skipping power difference, upon which a NILM algorithm was proposed based on the bounding-box fitting and load signatures [98]. A NILM algorithm driven by deep generative models was proposed by Wang *et al* for the extraction of EV charging profiles, which improved the computational efficiency and accuracy compared to hidden Markov models [83]. Zhang *et al* proposed a sequence-to-point learning algorithm to overcome the issue of sliding windows in the NILM problems and developed convolutional neural networks to learn signatures of appliances including EVs [95].

In addition to the aforementioned studies, AI can assist power system operators to manage the grid operation with the integration of EVs. Lei and Mohammadi proposed a secured energy management architecture based on a hybrid ML approach to manage the operations of microgrids with the integration of plug-in hybrid EVs, in order to minimise the operational cost of microgrids and prevent potential cyber-attacks [35]. Li *et al* formulated a distributed locational marginal pricing for the distribution network operator to alleviate congestions caused by the EV loads through solving the social welfare optimisation problem [37]. Ding *et al* developed an optimal EV charging strategy in a distribution network to maximise the profits of distribution system operators while maintaining physical system constraints through using the Markov decision model and policy gradient based RL to capture uncertainties of charging behaviours [19]. Shao *et al* exploited the charging management and vehicle-to-grid control as distributed storage of power networks through using the partial decomposition method based on the Lagrangian relaxation framework [66].

### 5.4 Owners of EV Charging Infrastructure

AI methods can assist with the planning and scheduling of EV charging infrastructure, in order to reduce the investment cost, improve the utilisation efficiency of infrastructure, and enhance the coordination of EV charging behaviour.

In order to enhance infrastructure planning of EV charging, Straka *et al* exploited the geographic information system data which describes the urban context and activities near charging infrastructures to investigate the popularity of charging infrastructures through using the $l_1$ penalty, random forests and gradient boosted regression trees [77]. Pevec *et al* exploited data on transactions, geographical locations, and distances to predict the utilisation of charging stations and find the optimal location to build new charging stations, for the purposes of maximising the utilisation of overall charging networks and increasing the number of chargers in scarcely populated areas [55]. Micari *et al* designed a planning scheme for EV charging infrastructure to determine the number and location of the charging points in a road network through using the graph based algorithm [48]. Li *et al* developed a multi-relation graph convolutional network based encoder-decoder deep architecture for planning the size and number of the EV charging infrastructures [36].

Many studies have considered implementing AI to schedule the charging behaviours of public infrastructures. Zhang *et al* formulated the scheduling problem for public EV charging infrastructures as a Markov decision process solved by the deep RL, in order to minimise the total charging time and reduce the origin-destination distance [96]. Ejaz *et al* proposed an internet of vehicles based framework, incorporating deployment into the scheduling of the EV charging infrastructures, to minimise the travel distance and charging costs while maintain system constraints and resources of charging stations [21]. Vanitha *et al* developed ML algorithms to schedule the coordination of EV charging infrastructure by identifying fast charging ports with the minimum waiting time [80].

Many of these previous studies consider AI algorithms to enhance some aspect of EV charging infrastructure. There have been multiple studies that have investigated applications of autonomous AI robots for EV integration [31] [52] [87]. These studies demonstrate the applicability of robotics for EV integration, in addition to AI algorithms.

## 5.5 Policy Makers

AI is capable of digitalising and visualising massive data describing multiple dimensions of EVs. This provides information to policy makers and aids them when making regulatory decisions. Asensio *et al* developed a classification algorithm and cloud-based data visualization tool to support policy making and planning of EV charging infrastructure [5]. This facilitates the conversion of large datasets into human understandable visualisations used by policy makers and general public. Debnath *et al* investigated EV adoption from the political, economic, social, technological, legal, and environmental dimensions through analysing the social media data from Facebook by the social network analysis and ML-based topic modelling [16]. This approach enables policy makers and planners to design contextualised energy policy to increase EV adoption.

### 5.6 Vehicle-to-Grid Planners

Vehicle-to-Grid (V2G) enables EV owners to sell extra power from EV batteries back to utility grids when the EV is unused. V2G can help with demand response and reduce peak energy demand. Incorporating AI into V2G has been well documented in the literature for both predicting EV behaviour and scheduling V2G.

For predicting the V2G behaviours, Shipman *et al* implemented automated ML to predict the location and time for V2G through using historical data from vehicle tracking services [70]. To estimate V2G behaviours for future EV owners, Shipman *et al* implemented the time series forecasting neural networks to predict the state of charge and available capacity of EV batteries based on the historical trip data [69]. Shipman *et al* also developed a machine learning algorithm to investigate the factors affecting users' EV usages and predict the available capacity from a pool of EVs at a certain time [68].

When scheduling V2G, Shibl *et al* proposed an EV management system for both charging and V2G [67]. This study compared decision trees, random forest, support vector machines, k-nearest neighbours, long short-term memory, and deep neural networks. Sortomme and El-Sharkawi developed a V2G algorithm to schedule the provisions of energy and ancillary services from EVs in providing the load shaving for power system operators and low-cost charging for EV owners [74]. Wei *et al* proposed an optimisation-based planning framework to capture the stochastic features of the EVs and schedule the V2G in an integrated energy system, in which the optimisation problem was solved by intelligent algorithms [85].

## 6 Discussion

### 6.1 Limitations

There are a number of limitations with many of the studies that have applied the AI to the EV integration.

**Practicality.** One of the primary limitations is that the vast majority of the studies in the literature apply AI to an aspect of EV integration in simulation only. Battery charging management [67] and EV charge point location scheduling [21] are examples of this. These studies provide proof of concept for applying the AI to various tasks related to the EV integration. Further work is required to demonstrate their effectiveness in reality.

There are examples in the literature of studies that utilise the real world EV data. For example, Wang et al. applied the policy iteration to optimise the charging scheduling of a fleet of electric busses using the real-world data from Shenzhen in China and reported a cost reduction of 23.7% [82]. There are limited case studies in the literature where AI has been deployed for the EV integration. In a 2022 study by Mahdy et al., the authors collaborated with Winchester City Council to apply multi-criteria decision analysis for the optimisation of EV charge point placement in Winchester, UK [44].

**Vehicle-to-Grid.** Another limitation of the current literature is that technologies such as V2G has not yet been realised. There are examples of V2G pilot programmes. However this technology has yet to be widely adopted. One such pilot programme was announced by EDF Energy in the UK in collaboration with Nissan and Nuvve [45]. This indicates a willingness of industry to embrace V2G.

**Willingness of Control.** A vital consideration when utilising the AI to manage aspects of the EV integration is the willingness of consumers to relinquish control of the EV charging to an AI system. Some consumers may feel hesitant due to lack of understanding of AI technologies. A 2019 survey into the attitudes of Americans towards AI found that 22% of Americans strongly oppose the development of the AI [94]. This may hinder the uptake of this technology for EV integration.

**Explainability.** There is a wider concern in the field of the AI that is directly relevant to the AI for theEV integration, namely explainability. There is often resistance to the black box approach to developing AI systems. This is where the system makes some decisions based on some input, and the reasoning as to why the system makes that decision is opaque or non-comprehensible to a human. This can be problematic in safety critical systems or more broadly in circumstances where an explanation for the decision is required. Explainable AI is a sub-field of the AI that aims to make AI models explainable to humans [90]. It is likely that a more explainable AI would increase the adoption for the EV integration. Explainable AI has recently made its way into the literature relating to power systems. A 2022 study by Zhang et al. proposed an explainable AI approach for power system emergency control [97]. In time, explainable AI will also be adopted by EV researchers.

**Trustworthy.** Related to the concept of explainable AI is trustworthy AI [32]. Trustworthy AI consists of developing AI systems that are robust and reliable. If an AI system is to be developed that is responsible for EV charging/discharging, the consumer would require that the system is reliable and will manage the battery of the EV in a manner that aligns with the preferences of the user. There is a distinct lack of studies in the literature that have investigated this topic.

## 6.2 Future Directions

There are a number of trends that future research in the AI for the EV integration will follow:

- The effectiveness of AI algorithms is constantly increasing. Breakthroughs and achievements are occurring regularly, e.g., RL successfully controlling the magnetic field in nuclear fusion [17]. As these advanced AI algorithms are developed, they will be applied to overcome various challenges of EV integration. This trend will continue into the future.

- As homes are fitted with advanced metering infrastructure, an ever larger amount of data will be collected relating to the usage of EVs and other appliances [23]. Gathering, storing, processing and gaining insight from this data will require developments in AI algorithms, and also how they are deployed and integrated into the home.
- As outlined in Sect. 6.1, there is a gap in the research into explainable and trustworthy AI and their application to the EV integration. Recent studies have begun to investigate their impact on power systems [97]. It is expected that future studies will also analyse these methods in the context of the EV integration.
- The capacity of EV batteries is increasing over time. For example, the 2012 Nissan Leaf had a capacity of 24 kWh. This has increased to 40 kWh in the 2019 Nissan Leaf [76]. Larger batteries will result in greater power demand for the EV charging. This will also increase the benefits of demand response from the V2G. A 2021 study by Alfaverh estimated that a RL controlled charging system with V2G could reduce peak demand by 23% and 15% in the morning and evening, respectively, in a residential area with 100 homes and 50 EVs [4]. Studies such as this one that have quantified the benefits of V2G in terms of peak shaving may observe greater peak demand reductions in the future when larger EV battery capacities are more prevalent.
- The paradigm of Peer-to-Peer (P2P) energy trading facilitated by technologies such as blockchain, has received a significant amount of interests in recent years [41]. The Brooklyn Microgrid is a well known example of such a P2P network [47]. The amount of research published applying the AI to the EV battery management with P2P networks will increase over time, along with the number of P2P implementations.

## 7 Conclusion

This article presents a comprehensive overview of the challenges connected with EV grid integration, EV life cycle emissions, and the intersection of these problems with Artificial Intelligence (AI). Further, it provides a comprehensive analysis of the application of artificial intelligence in the integration of electric vehicle (EV) grids. It also addresses the existing limitations of research and suggests potential directions for future investigations. The following are the main findings of this review:

1. AI has great potential for improving numerous aspects of EV integration, such as battery management.
2. Understanding EV life cycle emissions provides insights into areas where reductions can be made, contributing to a more sustainable EV landscape.
3. The implementation of AI solutions in the real world is critical for validating their efficacy beyond simulation contexts and demonstrating their practical effectiveness.

4. Emerging technologies such as peer-to-peer energy trading, blockchain, and vehicle-to-grid (V2G) connectivity give great opportunities for employing AI approaches to accelerate EV integration.

## References


1. Abdullah, H.M., Gastli, A., Ben-Brahim, L.: Reinforcement learning based EV charging management systems-a review. IEEE Access **9**, 41506–41531 (2021)
2. AGENCY, I.E.: Global ev outlook 2023 (2023). https://iea.blob.core.windows.net/assets/dacf14d2-eabc-498a-8263-9f97fd5dc327/GEVO2023.pdf
3. Ahmed, S., Khan, Z.A., Gul, N., Kim, J., Kim, S.M.: Machine learning-based clustering of load profiling to study the impact of electric vehicles on smart meter applications. In: 2021 Twelfth International Conference on Ubiquitous and Future Networks (ICUFN), pp. 444–447. IEEE (2021)
4. Alfaverh, F., Denai, M., Sun, Y.: Electrical vehicle grid integration for demand response in distribution networks using reinforcement learning. IET Electr. Syst. Transport. (2021)
5. Asensio, O.I., Mi, X., Dharur, S.: Using machine learning techniques to aid environmental policy analysis: a teaching case regarding big data and electric vehicle charging infrastructure. Case Stud. Environ. **4**(1), 961302 (2020)
6. Bas, J., Cirillo, C., Cherchi, E.: Classification of potential electric vehicle purchasers: a machine learning approach. Technol. Forecast Soc. Change **168**, 120759 (2021)
7. Bhatt, A., Ongsakul, W., Madhu, N.: Machine learning approach to predict the second-life capacity of discarded ev batteries for microgrid applications. In: Vasant, P., Zelinka, I., Weber, G.W. (eds.) ICO 2020. LNCS, vol. 1324, pp. 633–646. Springer, Heidelberg (2020). https://doi.org/10.1007/978-3-030-68154-8_55
8. Choma, E.F., Evans, J.S., Hammitt, J.K., Gómez-Ibáñez, J.A., Spengler, J.D.: Assessing the health impacts of electric vehicles through air pollution in the united states. Environ. Int. **144**, 106015 (2020)
9. Chung, Y.W., Khaki, B., Li, T., Chu, C., Gadh, R.: Ensemble machine learning-based algorithm for electric vehicle user behavior prediction. Appl. Energy **254**, 113732 (2019)
10. Cimino, M.G., Lazzeri, A., Vaglini, G.: Combining stigmergic and flocking behaviors to coordinate swarms of drones performing target search. In: 2015 6th International Conference on Information, Intelligence, Systems and Applications (IISA), pp. 1–6. IEEE (2015)
11. Coignard, J., MacDougall, P., Stadtmueller, F., Vrettos, E.: Will electric vehicles drive distribution grid upgrades?: the case of california. IEEE Electrificat. Maga. **7**(2), 46–56 (2019)
12. Dang, Q., Huo, Y., Sun, C.: Privacy preservation needed for smart meter system: a methodology to recognize electric vehicle (ev) models. In: 2018 IEEE Innovative Smart Grid Technologies - Asia (ISGT Asia), pp. 1016–1020 (2018). https://doi.org/10.1109/ISGT-Asia.2018.8467822
13. Danielis, R., Giansoldati, M., Rotaris, L.: A probabilistic total cost of ownership model to evaluate the current and future prospects of electric cars uptake in Italy. Energy Policy **119**, 268–281 (2018)
14. Darroch, G.: Un news: Global perspective human stories. United Nations. https://news.un.org/en/story/2020/06/1067272

15. Deben, L., Bell, K., Davies, M., Forster, P., FRS, C., CMG, N.: Progress in reducing UK emissions 2023 report to parliament (2023). https://www.theccc.org.uk/wp-content/uploads/2023/06/Progress-in-reducing-UK-emissions-2023-Report-to-Parliament-1.pdf
16. Debnath, R., Bardhan, R., Reiner, D.M., Miller, J.: Political, economic, social, technological, legal and environmental dimensions of electric vehicle adoption in the united states: A social-media interaction analysis. Renew. Sust. Energy Rev. **152**, 111707 (2021)
17. Degrave, J., et al.: Magnetic control of tokamak plasmas through deep reinforcement learning. Nature **602**(7897), 414–419 (2022)
18. Delogu, M., Zanchi, L., Dattilo, C., Pierini, M.: Innovative composites and hybrid materials for electric vehicles lightweight design in a sustainability perspective. Mater. Today Commun. **13**, 192–209 (2017)
19. Ding, T., Zeng, Z., Bai, J., Qin, B., Yang, Y., Shahidehpour, M.: Optimal electric vehicle charging strategy with Markov decision process and reinforcement learning technique. IEEE Trans. Ind. Appl. **56**(5), 5811–5823 (2020). https://doi.org/10.1109/TIA.2020.2990096
20. Doust, M., Otkur, M.: Carbon footprint comparison analysis of passenger car segment electric and ice-propelled vehicles in Kuwait. Alex. Eng. J. **79**, 438–448 (2023)
21. Ejaz, W., et al.: IOV-based deployment and scheduling of charging infrastructure in intelligent transportation systems. IEEE Sens. J. **21**(14), 15504–15514 (2021). https://doi.org/10.1109/JSEN.2020.3006706
22. Ellingsen, L., Hung, C.: Research for tran committee-resources, energy, and lifecycle greenhouse gas emission aspects of electric vehicles. Policy Department for Structural and Cohesion Policies, European Parliament, Brussels (2018)
23. Gold, R., Waters, C., York, D.: Leveraging advanced metering infrastructure to save energy. American Council for an Energy-Efficient Economy (ACEEE), Washington DC (2020)
24. Hoffmann, V., Fesche, B.I., Ingebrigtsen, K., Christie, I.N., Engelstad, M.P.: Automated detection of electric vehicles in hourly smart meter data (2019)
25. Hong, B.K., Kim, S.H.: Recent advances in fuel cell electric vehicle technologies of Hyundai. ECS Trans. **86**(13), 3 (2018)
26. Hu, E., Yang, X.Q.: Rejuvenating zinc batteries. Nat. Mater. **17**(6), 480–481 (2018)
27. IEA: Electric car models available globally and average range (2021). https://www.iea.org/data-and-statistics/charts/electric-car-models-available-globally-and-average-range-2015-2020-2
28. IEA: Global ev outlook 2021 (2021). https://www.iea.org/reports/global-ev-outlook-2021
29. Kearney: Polestar and rivian pathway report (2023). https://www.kearney.com/industry/automotive/article/-/insights/polestar-and-rivian-pathway-report-
30. Kim, H.C., Wallington, T.J., Arsenault, R., Bae, C., Ahn, S., Lee, J.: Cradle-to-gate emissions from a commercial electric vehicle li-ion battery: a comparative analysis. Environ. Sci. Technol. **50**(14), 7715–7722 (2016)
31. Kong, P.Y.: Extending energy storage lifetime of autonomous robot-like mobile charger for electric vehicles. IEEE Access **8**, 106811–106821 (2020)
32. Kumar, A., Braud, T., Tarkoma, S., Hui, P.: Trustworthy AI in the age of pervasive computing and big data. In: 2020 IEEE International Conference on Pervasive Computing and Communications Workshops (PerCom Workshops), pp. 1–6. IEEE (2020)

33. Kurzweil, P.: Gaston planté and his invention of the lead-acid battery-the genesis of the first practical rechargeable battery. J. Power Sources **195**(14), 4424–4434 (2010)
34. Lee, H., Romero, J.e.: Ipcc, 2023: Summary for policymakers (2023)
35. Lei, M., Mohammadi, M.: Hybrid machine learning based energy policy and management in the renewable-based microgrids considering hybrid electric vehicle charging demand. Int. J. Electr. Power **128**, 106702 (2021)
36. Li, C., Dong, Z., Chen, G., Zhou, B., Zhang, J., Yu, X.: Data-driven planning of electric vehicle charging infrastructure: a case study of Sydney, Australia. IEEE Trans. Smart Grid **12**(4), 3289–3304 (2021). https://doi.org/10.1109/TSG.2021.3054763
37. Li, R., Wu, Q., Oren, S.S.: Distribution locational marginal pricing for optimal electric vehicle charging management. IEEE Trans. Power Syst. **29**(1), 203–211 (2014). https://doi.org/10.1109/TPWRS.2013.2278952
38. Li, S., Hu, W., Cao, D., Dragičević, T., Huang, Q., Chen, Z., Blaabjerg, F.: Electric vehicle charging management based on deep reinforcement learning. J. Mod. Power Syst. Clean Energy **10**, 719–730 (2021)
39. Lillicrap, T.P., et al.: Continuous control with deep reinforcement learning. In: ICLR (Poster) (2016)
40. Lin, X., Bogdan, P., Chang, N., Pedram, M.: Machine learning-based energy management in a hybrid electric vehicle to minimize total operating cost. In: 2015 IEEE/ACM International Conference on Computer-Aided Design (ICCAD), pp. 627–634 (2015). https://doi.org/10.1109/ICCAD.2015.7372628
41. Liu, H., Zhang, Y., Zheng, S., Li, Y.: Electric vehicle power trading mechanism based on blockchain and smart contract in v2g network. IEEE Access **7**, 160546–160558 (2019)
42. Liu, J., Wang, J., Cardinal, J.: Evolution and reform of UK electricity market. Renew. Sustain. Energy Rev. **161**, 112317 (2022)
43. Liu, Z., et al.: Comparing total cost of ownership of battery electric vehicles and internal combustion engine vehicles. Energy Policy **158**, 112564 (2021)
44. Mahdy, M., Bahaj, A.S., Turner, P., Wise, N., Alghamdi, A.S., Hamwi, H.: Multi criteria decision analysis to optimise siting of electric vehicle charging points-case study Winchester district, UK. Energies **15**(7), 2497 (2022)
45. Manthey, N.: EDF launches V2G service for Nissan fleet customers in the UK (2021). https://www.electrive.com/2021/08/02/edf-launches-v2g-service-for-nissan-fleet-customers/. Accessed 07 April 2023
46. Meng, B., Wang, Y., Yang, Y.: Efficiency-optimization control of extended range electric vehicle using online sequential extreme learning machine. In: 2013 IEEE Vehicle Power and Propulsion Conference (VPPC), pp. 1–6 (2013)
47. Mengelkamp, E., Gärttner, J., Rock, K., Kessler, S., Orsini, L., Weinhardt, C.: Designing microgrid energy markets: a case study: the brooklyn microgrid. Appl. Energy **210**, 870–880 (2018)
48. Micari, S., Polimeni, A., Napoli, G., Andaloro, L., Antonucci, V.: Electric vehicle charging infrastructure planning in a road network. Renew. Sustain. Energy Rev. **80**, 98–108 (2017)
49. Mitchell, T.: Machine Learning. McGraw Hill, New York (1997)
50. Mnih, V., et al.: Human-level control through deep reinforcement learning. Nature **518**(7540), 529–533 (2015)

51. Moreno Jaramillo, A.F., Laverty, D.M., del Rincón, J.M., Hastings, J., Morrow, D.J.: Supervised non-intrusive load monitoring algorithm for electric vehicle identification. In: 2020 IEEE International Instrumentation and Measurement Technology Conference (I2MTC), pp. 1–6 (2020). https://doi.org/10.1109/I2MTC43012.2020.9128529
52. Ouya, A., De Aragon, B.M., Bouette, C., Habault, G., Montavont, N., Papadopoulos, G.Z.: An efficient electric vehicle charging architecture based on lora communication. In: 2017 IEEE International Conference on Smart Grid Communications (SmartGridComm), pp. 381–386. IEEE (2017)
53. Tejaswini, P., Sivraj, P.: Artificial intelligence based state of charge estimation of li-ion battery for EV applications. In: 2020 5th International Conference on Communication and Electronics Systems (ICCES), pp. 1356–1361 (2020)
54. Palmer, K., Tate, J.E., Wadud, Z., Nellthorp, J.: Total cost of ownership and market share for hybrid and electric vehicles in the UK, US and Japan. Appl. Energy **209**, 108–119 (2018)
55. Pevec, D., Babic, J., Kayser, M.A., Carvalho, A., Ghiassi-Farrokhfal, Y., Podobnik, V.: A data-driven statistical approach for extending electric vehicle charging infrastructure. Int. J. Energy Res. **42**(9), 3102–3120 (2018)
56. Pridemore, A., et al.: Electric vehicles from life cycle and circular economy perspectives. European Environment Agency, Copenhagen, Denmark (2018)
57. Qin, Y., et al.: Noise and vibration suppression in hybrid electric vehicles: state of the art and challenges. Renew. Sustain. Energy Rev. **124**, 109782 (2020)
58. Rehman, A.U., Lie, T.T., Vallès, B., Tito, S.R.: Non-invasive load-shed authentication model for demand response applications assisted by event-based non-intrusive load monitoring. Energy AI **3**, 100055 (2021)
59. Rigas, E.S., Ramchurn, S.D., Bassiliades, N.: Managing electric vehicles in the smart grid using artificial intelligence: a survey. IEEE Trans. Intell. Transp. Syst. **16**(4), 1619–1635 (2014)
60. de Rubens, G.Z.: Who will buy electric vehicles after early adopters? using machine learning to identify the electric vehicle mainstream market. Energy **172**, 243–254 (2019)
61. Russell, S., Norvig, P.: Artificial intelligence: a modern approach (2002)
62. Safari, M.: Battery electric vehicles: looking behind to move forward. Energy Policy **115**, 54–65 (2018)
63. Sanguesa, J.A., Torres-Sanz, V., Garrido, P., Martinez, F.J., Marquez-Barja, J.M.: A review on electric vehicles: technologies and challenges. Smart Cities **4**(1), 372–404 (2021)
64. Saxena, A., et al.: A review of clustering techniques and developments. Neurocomputing **267**, 664–681 (2017)
65. Scott, V., Geden, O.: The challenge of carbon dioxide removal for EU policy-making. Nat. Energy **3**(5), 350–352 (2018)
66. Shao, C., Wang, X., Shahidehpour, M., Wang, X., Wang, B.: Partial decomposition for distributed electric vehicle charging control considering electric power grid congestion. IEEE Trans. Smart Grid **8**(1), 75–83 (2017). https://doi.org/10.1109/TSG.2016.2595494
67. Shibl, M., Ismail, L., Massoud, A.: Electric vehicles charging management using machine learning considering fast charging and vehicle-to-grid operation. Energies **14**(19), 6199 (2021)
68. Shipman, R., Naylor, S., Pinchin, J., Gough, R., Gillott, M.: Learning capacity: predicting user decisions for vehicle-to-grid services. Energy Inform. **2**(1), 1–22 (2019)

69. Shipman, R., Roberts, R., Waldron, J., Naylor, S., Pinchin, J., Rodrigues, L., Gillott, M.: We got the power: predicting available capacity for vehicle-to-grid services using a deep recurrent neural network. Energy **221**, 119813 (2021)
70. Shipman, R., Waldron, J., Naylor, S., Pinchin, J., Rodrigues, L., Gillott, M.: Where will you park? predicting vehicle locations for vehicle-to-grid. Energies **13**(8), 1933 (2020)
71. Shrestha, A., Mahmood, A.: Review of deep learning algorithms and architectures. IEEE Access **7**, 53040–53065 (2019)
72. Singh, K.V., Bansal, H.O., Singh, D.: A comprehensive review on hybrid electric vehicles: architectures and components. Journal of Modern Transportation **27**(2), 77–107 (2019)
73. Song, R., Potoglou, D.: Are existing battery electric vehicles adoption studies able to inform policy? a review for policymakers. Sustainability **12**(16), 6494 (2020)
74. Sortomme, E., El-Sharkawi, M.A.: Optimal scheduling of vehicle-to-grid energy and ancillary services. IEEE Trans. Smart Grid **3**(1), 351–359 (2012). https://doi.org/10.1109/TSG.2011.2164099
75. Sovacool, B.K.: A transition to plug-in hybrid electric vehicles (phevs): why public health professionals must care (2010)
76. Specifications, E.: Nissan leaf sl specifications (2022). https://www.evspecifications.com/en/model/96744. Accessed 08 Apr 2023
77. Straka, M., et al.: Predicting popularity of electric vehicle charging infrastructure in urban context. IEEE Access **8**, 11315–11327 (2020)
78. Sun, S., Zhang, J., Bi, J., Wang, Y.: A machine learning method for predicting driving range of battery electric vehicles. J. Adv. Transp. **2019** (2019)
79. Sutton, R.S., Barto, A.G.: Reinforcement Learning: An Introduction. MIT press, Cambridge (2018)
80. Vanitha, V., Resmi, R., Reddy, K.N.S.V.: Machine learning-based charge scheduling of electric vehicles with minimum waiting time. Comput. Intell. **37**(3), 1047–1055 (2021)
81. Velzen, A., Annema, J.A., de Kaab, G., Wee, B.: Proposing a more comprehensive future total cost of ownership estimation framework for electric vehicles. Energy Policy **129**, 1034–1046 (2019)
82. Wang, G., Xie, X., Zhang, F., Liu, Y., Zhang, D.: bcharge: data-driven real-time charging scheduling for large-scale electric bus fleets. In: 2018 IEEE Real-Time Systems Symposium (RTSS), pp. 45–55. IEEE (2018)
83. Wang, S., Du, L., Ye, J., Zhao, D.: A deep generative model for non-intrusive identification of EV charging profiles. IEEE Trans. Smart Grid **11**(6), 4916–4927 (2020). https://doi.org/10.1109/TSG.2020.2998080
84. Watkins, C.J., Dayan, P.: Q-learning. Mach. Learn. **8**(3–4), 279–292 (1992)
85. Wei, H., Zhang, Y., Wang, Y., Hua, W., Jing, R., Zhou, Y.: Planning integrated energy systems coupling v2g as a flexible storage. Energy **239**, 122215 (2022)
86. Weldon, P., Morrissey, O'Mahony, M.P.: Long-term cost of ownership comparative analysis between electric vehicles and internal combustion engine vehicles. Sustain. Cities Soc. **39**, 578–591 (2018)
87. Weng, Y., Liao, Y., Ilic, M., Srinivasan, D.: Electric vehicle robot-based testbed for future grid's evaluation. In: 2017 IEEE Conference on Energy Internet and Energy System Integration (EI2), pp. 1–6. IEEE (2017)
88. Wooldridge, M.: An Introduction to Multiagent Systems. John Wiley & Sons, Hoboken (2009)

89. Xiong, Y., Wang, B., Chu, C.C., Gadh, R.: Electric vehicle driver clustering using statistical model and machine learning. In: 2018 IEEE Power Energy Society General Meeting (PESGM), pp. 1–5 (2018). https://doi.org/10.1109/PESGM.2018.8586132
90. Xu, F., Uszkoreit, H., Du, Y., Fan, W., Zhao, D., Zhu, J.: Explainable AI: a brief survey on history, research areas, approaches and challenges. In: Tang, J., Kan, M.Y., Zhao, D., Li, S., Zan, H. (eds.) NLPCC 2019. LNCS, vol. 11839, pp. 563–574. Springer, Heidelberg (2019). https://doi.org/10.1007/978-3-030-32236-6_51
91. Yavasoglu, H., Tetik, Y., Gokce, K.: Implementation of machine learning based real time range estimation method without destination knowledge for bevs. Energy **172**, 1179–1186 (2019)
92. Zadeh, P.T., Joudaki, M., Ansari, A.: A survey on deep learning applications for electric vehicles in micro grids. In: 2021 5th International Conference on Internet of Things and Applications (IoT), pp. 1–6. IEEE (2021)
93. Zeng, X., Li, M., Abd El-Hady, D., Alshitari, W., Al-Bogami, A.S., Lu, J., Amine, K.: Commercialization of lithium battery technologies for electric vehicles. Adv. Energy Mater. **9**(27), 1900161 (2019)
94. Zhang, B., Dafoe, A.: Artificial intelligence: American attitudes and trends. SSRN 3312874 (2019)
95. Zhang, C., Zhong, M., Wang, Z., Goddard, N., Sutton, C.: Sequence-to-point learning with neural networks for non-intrusive load monitoring. In: Proceedings of the AAAI Conference on Artificial Intelligence, vol. 32 (2018)
96. Zhang, C., Liu, Y., Wu, F., Tang, B., Fan, W.: Effective charging planning based on deep reinforcement learning for electric vehicles. IEEE Trans. Intell. Transp. Syst. **22**(1), 542–554 (2021). https://doi.org/10.1109/TITS.2020.3002271
97. Zhang, K., Zhang, J., Xu, P.D., Gao, T., Gao, D.W.: Explainable AI in deep reinforcement learning models for power system emergency control. IEEE Trans. Comput. Soc. Syst. (2021)
98. Zhao, H., Yan, X., Ma, L.: Training-free non-intrusive load extracting of residential electric vehicle charging loads. IEEE Access **7**, 117044–117053 (2019). https://doi.org/10.1109/ACCESS.2019.2936589
99. Zhou, H., et al.: Lstm-based energy management for electric vehicle charging in commercial-building prosumers. J. Mod. Power Syst. Clean Energy **9**(5), 1205–1216 (2021). https://doi.org/10.35833/MPCE.2020.000501

# Towards Sustainable Power Systems: Exploring the Opportunities of Multi-task Learning for Battery Degradation Forecasting

Emilie Grégoire(✉) and Sam Verboven

Data Analytics Laboratory, Vrije Universiteit Brussel, Ixelles, Belgium
{emilie.gregoire,sam.verboven}@vub.be

**Abstract.** The task of developing a reliable and long-lasting battery system remains a major obstacle to the expansion of the electric vehicle fleet and the improvement of storage systems in renewable energy plants. To overcome this challenge, improving battery ageing models to accurately forecast the battery degradation trajectory is a complex but critical step. In this work, we introduce a novel sequence-to-sequence multi-task learning (MTL) method. Empirical results on battery ageing datasets show that our model enhances the data efficiency and precision of capacity and power degradation forecasts for lithium-ion battery cells. Furthermore, our model generates new insights into the trade-offs and key decisions for incorporating battery ageing models into the MTL paradigm.

**Keywords:** Lithium-ion Battery · Time Series Forecasting · Multi-Task Learning

## 1 Introduction

The electrification of the transportation industry is a crucial factor in driving towards a carbon-neutral future [14,25]. Thanks to their high efficiency and long life [39], the development of lithium-ion batteries has played a prominent role in the electrification of the automotive sector [36]. Although lithium-ion batteries currently power the majority of electric vehicles on the road [25], significant improvements in battery performance and reliability are needed for the increased significance of battery-driven electric vehicles in the vehicle market [2,22]. Furthermore, a longer battery lifespan would not only be crucial for electric vehicle adoption but also for the improvement of the infrastructure for smart grids and renewable energy [26,42]. Accurate prediction of lithium-ion battery degradation, a key aspect in the monitoring and enhancement of battery performance, is essential. This degradation is characterized by indicators such as loss of capacity and an increase in internal resistance [23,26,28]. Although much attention has been given to this problem, accurately modeling the aging of


Published by Springer Nature Switzerland AG 2024
E. Mercier-Laurent et al. (Eds.): AI4KMES 2023, IFIP AICT 693, pp. 116–133, 2024.
https://doi.org/10.1007/978-3-031-61069-1_9

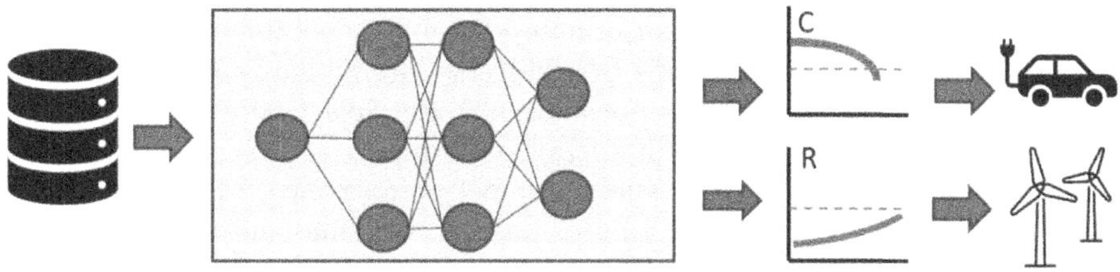


**Fig. 1.** Data-driven methods have become increasingly important in forecasting battery degradation, which is of crucial importance to ensure further use of electric vehicles and sustainable power systems.

lithium-ion batteries remains challenging due to many cell-specific electrochemical processes, degradation mechanisms [38,46], and a large variation in operating conditions. Ideally, physics-based (PB) models, designed to simulate electrochemical and degradation processes through mathematical representations, could be employed [24]. However, PB models face significant challenges in accurately predicting long-term degradation [2]. To overcome these limitations, there has been a shift towards data-driven, machine learning-based approaches [42,44]. Various machine learning techniques, such as Gaussian process machine learning [53], Support Vector Machines (SVM) [37] and deep neural networks [21] have been utilized to forecast critical battery health indicators such as the end-of-life (EOL), remaining useful lifetime (RUL), state of health (SOH), and state of charge (SOC) [6]. Notably, in the field of battery health estimation, Recurrent Neural Networks (RNN) are gaining prominence, demonstrating state-of-the-art results [5,51].

RNNs distinguish themselves from other machine learning techniques by their ability to accurately capture the temporal dynamics inherent in battery degradation trajectories. Encoder-decoder architectures in particular facilitate accurate point-to-sequence and sequence-to-sequence (Seq2Seq) prediction, allowing for the forecasting of entire future degradation sequences rather than isolated time points [16]. This capability is crucial for monitoring battery states that continuously evolve over time, thus enabling more realistic scenario assessments [5]. Despite these advancements, RNNs are hindered by high computational demands and limited generalizability. Additionally, most current predictive systems are primarily focused on capacity degradation, neglecting power fade which is also critical in applications such as hybrid and electric vehicles, as well as energy grids [4,47]. Addressing these limitations, multi-task learning (MTL) [45] has been proposed to concurrently predict both capacity and power degradation [28]. MTL, as a paradigm, has demonstrated its efficacy in enhancing generalizability and robustness across various fields including natural language processing [13], computer vision [27], reinforcement learning [50] and time series forecasting [35]. Recent studies [3,28] have successfully applied MTL in battery degradation forecasting, demonstrating MTL's capability to improve generalisability and reduce computing costs. Nonetheless, the joint optimization of multiple tasks is complex and can also degrade performance [20,49]. A notable cause of performance degradation in MTL stems from adverse interactions among tasks that can detrimentally affect model performance [32,40]. Specifically, conflicting gradients between tasks may result in inferior performance [41,52]. To mitigate the impact of these adverse interactions on model performance, careful consideration should be given to the selection of tasks to combine and the appropriate weighting of their contributions during training [18,19,27]. In this study, we delve into the essential trade-offs and critical decisions concerning the mitigation of the possible negative impact of task interactions, which have not yet been addressed in optimizing the promising application of MTL to the problem of battery degradation forecasting (Fig. 1).

The paper is structured as follows. In Sect. 2, we introduce the problem setting of applying multi-task learning to sequence-to-sequence problems. Next, the battery degradation data used for conducting the experiments is presented in Sect. 3, supplemented by a discussion of the statistical properties of the capacity and power degradation curves. In Sect. 4, the design and optimisation choices concerning the application of the encoder-decoder multi-task model are introduced. Finally, the corresponding results are presented in Sect. 5.

## 2 Problem Setting

### 2.1 Multi-task Learning

In multi-task learning, multiple tasks are optimized jointly. In its deep learning instantiation, this generally involves sharing a subset of parameters among the tasks in an encoder, while task-specific decoders are composed of layers that are specifically parametrized for each task, as illustrated in Fig. 2. In the standard practice of MTL, all layers are trained jointly, i.e., single-stage training. Alternatively, multi-stage training involves separate stages of training during which the parameters of one or more components (e.g., A, B, or C in Fig. 2) are temporarily frozen during training [28,34].

In MTL, the model parameters are updated using the signal of the composite loss $\mathcal{L}_{Tot}$, which for this paper corresponds to the weighted sum of the task-specific capacity and resistance losses, denoted by $\mathcal{L}_C$ and $\mathcal{L}_R$ respectively,

$$\mathcal{L}_{Tot} = w_C \mathcal{L}_C + w_R \mathcal{L}_R. \tag{1}$$

The coefficients $w_C$ and $w_R$ are the corresponding task-specific weights. The resulting multi-task learning paradigm is flexibly applicable to (combinations of) regression and classification tasks.

### 2.2 Multi-task Sequence-to-Sequence Models

In the context of sequence-to-sequence learning (Seq2Seq), encoder-decoder architectures have demonstrated excellent performance [11,17]. In such an encoder-decoder Seq2Seq model [43], the encoder transforms a (multi-dimensional) sequence $\mathbf{X}(t)$, into a temporary vector representation $\mathbf{V}_T(t)$ of

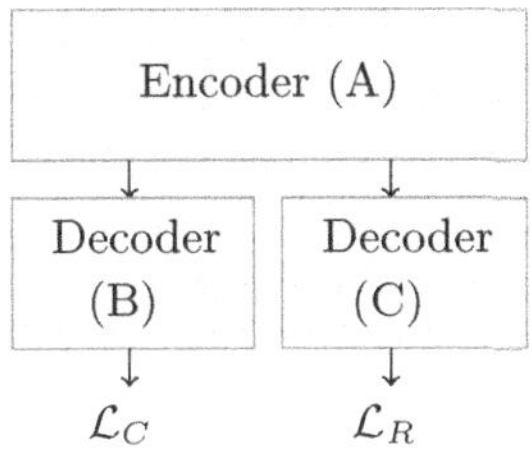


**Fig. 2.** Multi-task learning encoder-decoder architecture. The shared encoder (A) is employed across all tasks, while the decoders (B and C) are utilized for task-specific predictions. Each decoder generates a task-specific loss, $L_C$ and $L_R$, related to the predictions on the capacity and resistance tasks respectively.

a fixed dimension that corresponds to the final hidden state at the last hidden layer. Additionally, a decoder enables the transformation from the temporary vector to the future sequence $\mathbf{y}(t)$.

In multi-task learning, encoder-decoder Seq2Seq models can be used to predict multiple future sequences $\mathbf{y}_i(t)$ simultaneously [28,33]. To this end, multiple task-specific decoders are added on top of the encoder, each transforming the temporary vector representation $\mathbf{V}_T(t)$ to a task-specific sequence. In Fig. 2 an example of such an architecture is visualized for the simultaneous prediction of capacity $y(t)_C$ and resistance $y(t)_R$ sequences. In the remainder of this work we will refer to such a model as an encoder-decoder multi-task model.

### 2.3 Task Weighting

The accurate calibration of task-specific weights, as delineated in equation (1), is pivotal in the optimization of a multi-task learning model. A notable drawback of optimizing static task weights is the consequential rise in the number of hyperparameter configurations over which to optimize. Furthermore, it is widely acknowledged in MTL literature that tasks exhibit dynamic interactions during training: learning a task can be helpful for learning another task at early stages in training, but become harmful later on [19,31,49]. In response to these insights, recent studies have proposed algorithms that dynamically adjust task weights $w_i$ in equation (1),

$$w_i \rightarrow w_i(t), \tag{2}$$

where $t$ can be an epoch or an individual training step, based on a quantifiable metric that evaluates the mutual impact of task signals on each other. There is a diverse range of dynamic weighting algorithms documented in the literature. A substantial subset of these algorithms concentrates on the direct adaptation of task weights, wherein adjustments are made based on criteria such as geometric loss [10], inverse validation loss [1], and uncertainty [12]. Other algorithms directly adjust the task-specific gradient directions and/or magnitudes [9]. Approaches include masking gradients with a sign that is opposite to the

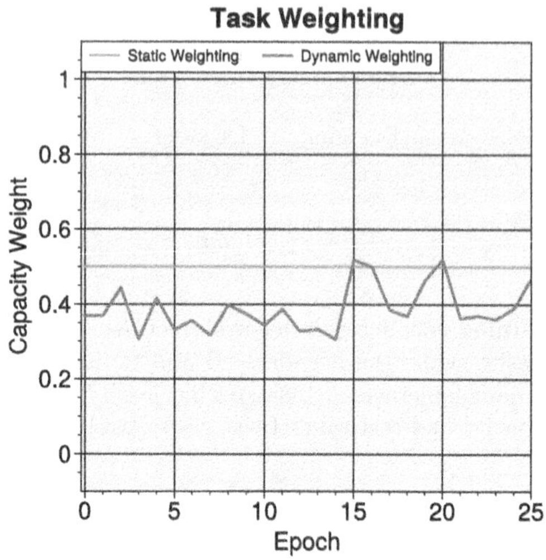


**Fig. 3.** Comparison of static and dynamic weighting. The use of uniform task weights yields a constant capacity and resistance weight equal to 0.5 (green line). In contrast, dynamic weighting algorithms adapt the task-weights during the epochs (blue line). (Color figure online)

most frequent gradient sign of that update, projecting gradients with a negative cosine similarity with respect to other gradients onto the normal plane of another task [52] or an optimized direction vector [41]. A complete overview is provided by [19,48]. The conceptual difference between static and dynamic weighting is illustrated in Fig. 3.

### 2.4 Research Gap

Building upon this foundation, our study delves into the design choices of MTL networks tailored for battery degradation forecasting and aims to quantify the effects of key design choices. Specifically, our research compares the efficacy of single-stage training against multi-stage training. Additionally, we examine the impacts of different static task weighting strategies as outlined in equation (1), as well as the implications of employing advanced dynamic task weighting algorithms in the context of battery degradation forecasting.

## 3 Battery Degradation Data

The experiments are performed on an open-source dataset corresponding to data from battery aging experiments conducted by RWTH Aachen University[1]. The data consists of capacity $C$ and resistance $R$ sequences, reflecting the energy and

[1] The dataset from RWTH Aachen is publicly available here: https://doi.org/10.18154/RWTH-2021-04545.

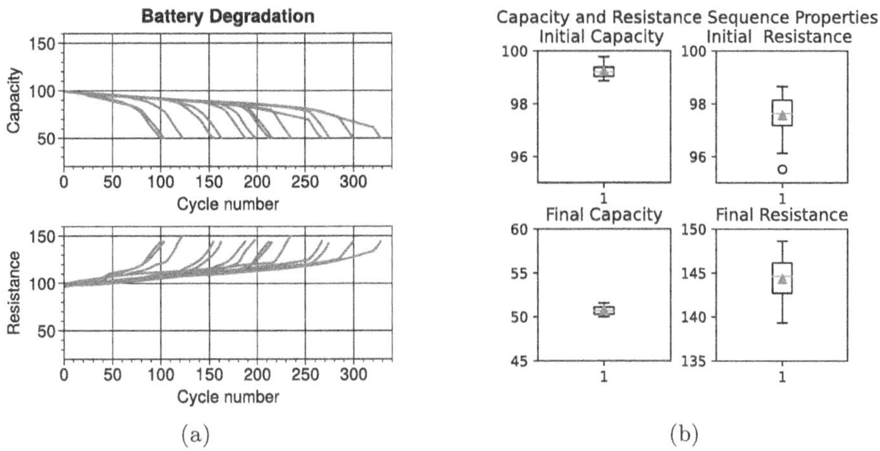


**Fig. 4.** To conduct the experiments, we employed the dataset obtained from RWTH Aachen University [28]. A small subset of the data is visualized on the left (a), showing capacity and resistance sequences. The boxplots on the right (b) are computed based on the entire dataset and reflect the variance and scales of both tasks at the beginning and end of the curves.

power fade of 48 Lithium-ion batteries. As shown in Fig. 4(a), battery degradation results in an increase in the resistance and a decrease in capacity. Despite undergoing the same aging scenarios, the Lithium-ion battery cells exhibit distinct variations in the trajectories of capacity and resistance. The similarity between the statistical properties of the capacity and power sequences, which correspond to distinct forecasting tasks combined within the multi-task model, can serve as an indicator of task similarity. Furthermore, it may offer insights into potential challenges that could arise during their joint training. Figure 4(b) shows the variance in the initial and final values of the capacity and resistance throughout the entire dataset. A comparative analysis of the capacity and resistance plots reveals a more pronounced variability in the resistance measurements. Additionally, based on Figs. 4 (a) and (b), a substantial difference in scale is observable towards the end of the sequences. These scale differences between the tasks could lead to imbalances in the task gradients. Such imbalance can prohibit optimal model training when tasks are given the same task weight in equation (1) [9]. The actual implications of these variance and scale differences will be further explored empirically in the subsequent sections.

### 3.1 Data Preprocessing

The preprocessing of capacity and resistance sequences, as illustrated in Fig. 4 (a), follows the methodology described in [28]. Concretely, the number of input sequences, corresponding to earlier cycles of the degradation curves, was augmented by applying an increasing window of size 20 with stride equal to one.

The output sequences were created by applying a decreasing window, containing the remaining pieces of the sequences obtained after applying the window with fixed length. We note that one should also optimize the size of the input window concerning computation time and generalization performance. Additionally, when inputting these sequences into a Recurrent Neural Network (RNN), it is necessary to ensure uniformity in sequence lengths. This can be achieved by padding the preprocessed sequences with zeros. However, it is crucial to confirm that both the model and the evaluation metrics can ignore these artificially introduced values.

# 4 Empirical Setup

In this section we elaborate about the empirical setup, used to conduct the experiments. First, we introduce the base encoder-decoder Seq2Seq multi-task learning architecture used for performing experiments on battery ageing data in Subsect. 4.1. Then, in Subsect. 4.2, we specify the design choice space that will be used for benchmarking in the empirical study.

## 4.1 The Encoder-Decoder Multi-task Model

To simultaneously predict future capacity and resistance sequences (Fig. 4), we use an encoder-decoder Seq2Seq multi-task learning architecture as proposed by [28]. The model consists of a shared encoder that transforms a two-dimensional sequence $\mathbf{X}(t)$, resulting from the concatenation of historical capacity $X_C(t)$ and resistance $X_R(t)$ sequences, into a temporary vector representation $\mathbf{V}_T$ of a fixed dimension. Additionally, two task-specific decoders are added to the model to enable the transformation from the temporary vector to future capacity $y_C(t)$ an resistance sequences $y_R(t)$.

Both encoder and decoders (Fig. 2) contain layers $k$, which consist of LSTM units that each produce a hidden state $h_k^t$ and cell state $c_k^t$ which are produced by each layer and timestep $t$ according to:

$$c^t = f^t \odot c^{t-1} + i^t \odot g^t \tag{3a}$$
$$h^t = o^t \odot \tanh(c^t) \tag{3b}$$

with

$$i^t = \sigma(W^i x^t + U^i h^{t-1} + b^i) \tag{3c}$$
$$f^t = \sigma(W^f x^t + W^f h^{t-1} + b^f) \tag{3d}$$
$$o^t = \sigma(W^o x^t + W^o h^{t-1} + b^o) \tag{3e}$$
$$g^t = \tanh(W^g x^t + W^g h^{t-1} + b^g), \tag{3f}$$

where superscripts $i$, $f$, $o$, and $g$ indicate that the parameter matrices $W$ or $b$ are specific to the input, forget, output, and cell gates respectively. The $t$ superscripts correspond to the time steps. Dropout is applied to the layers of both the encoder and decoders. The dimension of the hidden states, the number of LSTM units, the number of LSTM- layers, and the dropout rate are hyperparameters to be optimized both for the shared encoder and task-specific decoders. The optimal hyperparameter configurations are presented in the Appendix.

## 4.2 Exploration Space

In this section we introduce some key design choices of the encoder-decoder MTL model, introduced in Subsect. 4.1. The results are reported in Sect. 5.

**Multi-stage Training.** We compare the standard single-stage training regime to the multi-stage training regime. In [28], the encoder-decoder model, illustrated in Fig. 2, is trained in three steps. The task-specific decoders (B and C) are temporarily frozen (i.e., their corresponding parameters are not updated) one by one during the first two stages, followed by a final step where all modules are updated. We compare this approach to the standard single-stage approach where the parameters of each component (A-B-C) are continuously updated throughout training.

**Static Weighting.** We analyze the impact of different task weights of the capacity and resistance forecasting tasks while satisfying

$$w_C + w_R = 1. \tag{4}$$

This ensures that the task weights do not affect the total learning rate. Furthermore, we perform a grid search over the following weight combinations ($w_C = 0.2, 0.4, 0.6, 0.8$), as visualized in Fig. 5, and report the generalization performance on the test set.

**Dynamic Weighting.** We compare the performance of static uniform weighting, which is a standard baseline with static and uniformly assigned task weights, with four state-of-the-art weighting algorithms for which we summarize the approach shortly:

- PCGrad [52]: An algorithm that projects conflicting gradient directions of a task to the normal plane of any other task it negatively interferes with.
- CAGrad [31]: Conflict-Averse Gradient descent that aims to simultaneously minimize the average loss and leverages the worst local improvement of individual tasks.
- OL-AUX [30]: An algorithm that uses auxiliary task gradient directions, computed on previous batches to update auxiliary task weights as to optimize a task of interest. The gradient directions are computed on past batches and updated with gradient descent every few steps.

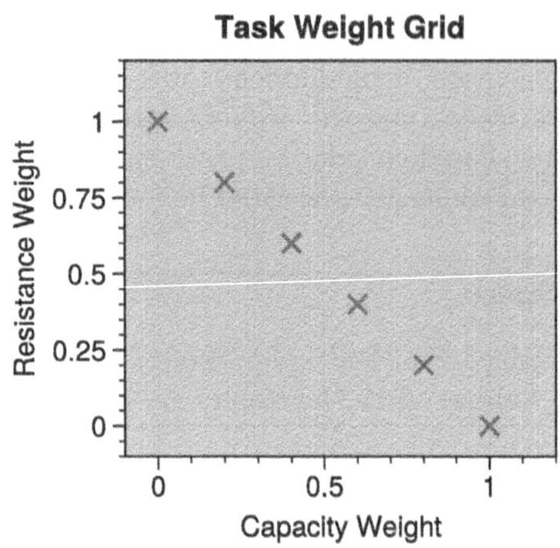


**Fig. 5.** The generalization performance of training with several weight combinations is analyzed through a grid search.

- Random Weighting (RW) [29]: A simple weighting method that is trained with randomly assigned weights while yielding remarkable performance results.

The selection of the baseline algorithms was performed based on the width of adoption and current state-of-the-art performance in MTL literature.

### 4.3 Loss Function and Evaluation Metrics

Consistent with previous research [28], the multi-task model in our experiments is trained using the Mean Squared Error (MSE) as the loss function. The MSE is mathematically defined as:

$$MSE = \frac{1}{n}\sum_{i=1}^{n}\left(Y_i - Y_i^{GT}\right)^2, \tag{5}$$

where $n$ represents the number of samples, $Y_i$ is the predicted value, and $Y_i^{GT}$ is the corresponding ground truth value. Additionally, we also evaluate the generalization performance using the Mean Absolute Percentage Error (MAPE). The MAPE is defined as follows:

$$MAPE = \frac{100}{n}\sum_{i=1}^{n}\left|\frac{Y_i^{GT} - Y_i}{Y_i^{GT}}\right|. \tag{6}$$

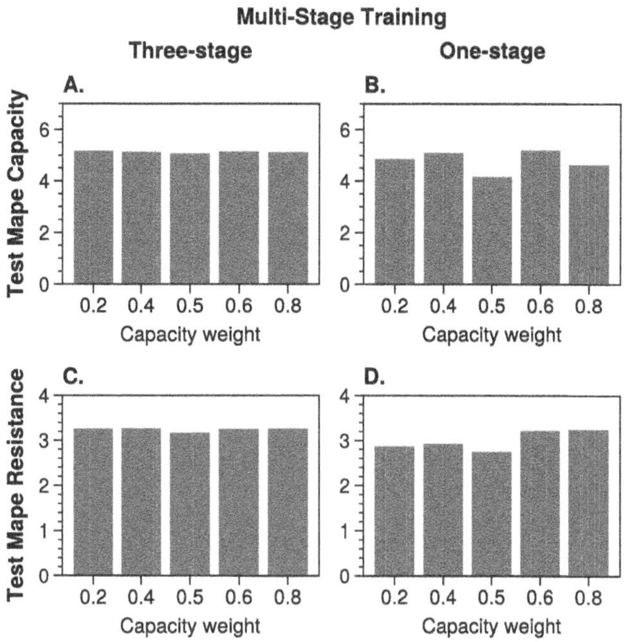


**Fig. 6.** The Mean Average Percentage Error for the forecasting of both capacity (first row A-B) and resistance (second row C-D) sequences are compared for models trained in three stages (first column A-C) and one stage (second column B-D). The MAPE is shown for different task weight combinations. The x-axes represent the capacity weight $w_C$ and the corresponding resistance weight $w_R$ is equal to 1-w$_C$.

## 5 Results

In this section, we present the results of the experiments discussed in Sect. 4.

### 5.1 Comparing Single-Stage with Three-Stage Training

Figure 6 reports the Mean Average Percentage Errors (MAPE) for the capacity and resistance tasks on the test set obtained after three-stage training (left panels) and single-stage training (right panels). Comparing the left (A and C) to the right (B and D) plots shows that single-stage training consistently achieves equal or lower MAPE scores than three-stage training. Furthermore, altering the task-specific weights has a minor impact on the MAPE for three-stage training while a significant impact can be observed for single-stage training. These results indicate that the added complexity of multi-stage training has no immediate significant performance benefits for the setup under study.

### 5.2 Analyzing Static Task Weighting

Figure 6 presents the different Mean Average Percentage Errors corresponding to different task weight configurations as bars. Both plot $B$ and plot $D$, corre-

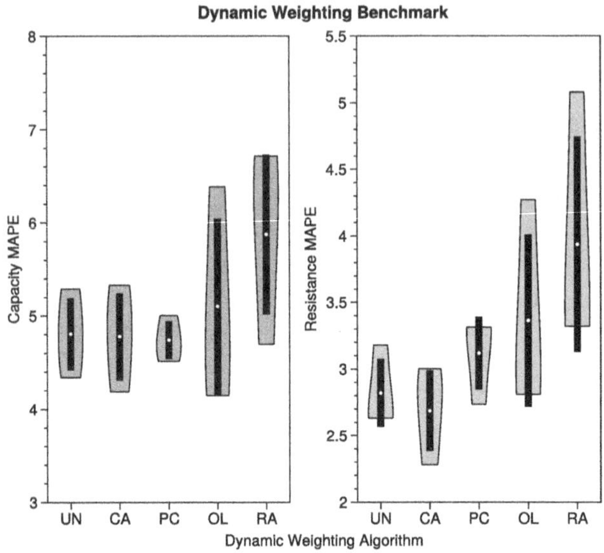


**Fig. 7.** The test Mean Average Percentage Errors for both capacity and resistance tasks are compared for different dynamic weighting algorithms (CAGrad (CA), PCGrad (PC), Olaux (OL) and Random weighting (RA)) using Uniform weighting (UN) as a baseline. The violin plots represent the mean and variance of the optimized weighting algorithms corresponding to five different initializations.

sponding to the performance of the capacity and resistance tasks respectively, show that altering task weights influences the MAPE and convergence rate in single-stage training. However, the uniform configuration $w_C = w_R = 0.5$ seems favorable for both forecasting tasks. The learning curves for different task weight combinations ($w_C$ and $w_R$) are presented on Fig. 8 in the Appendix.

### 5.3 Comparing Dynamic Task Weighting Algorithms

The different dynamic task weighting algorithms presented in Sect. 4.2 are optimised and the resulting generalization performances are compared in Fig. 7, where the mean and variance of the MAPE for five different initializations are visualised. The final hyperparameters for each algorithm are reported in the Appendix.

The empirical results indicate that, on average, CAGrad surpasses static (uniform) weighting in both forecasting tasks, demonstrating the effectiveness of dynamic task weighting. Other dynamic algorithms, such as PCGrad and Olaux, achieve performance levels comparable to static weighting, while some (like the random approach) fare worse. An analysis of the violin plot shapes further reveals that dynamic weighting algorithms introduce additional stochasticity compared to static weighting. It is thus important to consider the trade-offs between performance, variance and computational budget when choosing the right approach.

## 6 Conclusion

This work presents an investigation into the crucial modelling decisions for multi-task learning for battery degradation forecasting.

From a practitioner's perspective, several observations can be made. The findings indicate that, although it may not deliver the optimal outcome, the simple single-stage, static weighting approach remains a viable and competitive option for multi-task learning for battery degradation forecasting, especially when computational limitations apply. Conversely, in the absence of computational restrictions, practitioners should carefully test several algorithms, as the optimal choice may be dataset-dependent. Another important trade-off is the cost of increased stochasticity of dynamic weighting against moderate performance gains. Finally, based on our observations, there is no apparent evidence supporting the superiority of three-stage training over single-stage training. Therefore, one might assert that the latter is relatively more straightforward. These insights can help practitioners make more informed decisions when designing a practically feasible and performant solution.

From a researcher's perspective, important reflections on recent research can be posited, and several avenues for future research discerned. While multi-task learning has recently been introduced in the research field of data-driven Battery degradation forecasting, many opportunities for optimization still exist. Although we address many of the crucial choices concerning the design of multi-task learning models for battery degradation forecasting, further research and in-depth ablations across multiple datasets are required to dissect where performance increases originate. Firstly, the encoder-decoder architecture can be used with different RNN such as Gated Recurrent Unit (GRU) networks or attention-based models. These showed promising results in the single task setup [8,15] and could similarly be successful in the MTL setup. Furthermore, the emergence of hybrid-based models, which amalgamate the strengths of both physics-based and machine learning-based models, has been noted as a promising development [2,7]. These physics-inspired models could be interesting to integrate within the multi-task learning paradigm. In relation to dynamic task weighting, there is a need for expanded benchmarking involving a broader array of algorithms. Additionally, conducting in-depth investigations to clarify the reasons behind performance disparities is crucial for a deeper understanding of these models' efficacy.

## Data and Code Availability

The used data is publicly available here: https://doi.org/10.18154/RWTH-2021-04545. More details about the Lithium-ion battery ageing experiments that generated the dataset can be found in [28]. The models and dynamic weighting algorithms were implemented with Pytorch and the resulting code will be made available on https://github.com/vub-dl/.

## Competing Interests

The authors declare they do not have any competing interests.

## Appendix

In this Appendix, we provide additional details of the experiments.

**Data.** For the preprocessing of the data, we follow the same approach as the one presented in [28] and described in Sect. 3. The output capacity and resistance sequences have lengths 86. Seventy percent of the dataset was allocated for the purpose of training, while 15 percent was designated for both validation and testing, respectively.

**Hyperparameters.** We systematically optimized the hyperparameters, including the number of LSTM layers, learning rate, and batch size. Furthermore, a comparative analysis was undertaken, assessing the efficacy of Stochastic Gradient Descent in contrast to ADAM, as well as evaluating the performance distinction between bidirectional and standard LSTM layers. The results revealed ADAM as the optimal optimizer across all weighting methodologies, with a consistent preference for bidirectional LSTM layers over their standard counterparts. The optimal hidden dimension for both the shared encoder and decoder LSTM layers was determined to be 64, while the dimension of the hidden vector was set at 128. The dropout rate in the LSTM layers of the encoder and decoder was fine-tuned under the uniform weighting configuration and subsequently fixed at 0.3 for experiments employing dynamic weighting algorithms (Table 1).

**Table 1.** Optimal hyperparameters for each weighting method.

| Algorithm | Batch Size | Learning Rate | Shared Layers | Task-Specific Layers |
|---|---|---|---|---|
| Uniform | 256 | 0.001 | 4 | 4 |
| OLAUX | 256 | 0.001 | 3 | 3 |
| PCGrad | 512 | 0.001 | 3 | 3 |
| CAGrad | 512 | 0.001 | 4 | 4 |
| Random | 512 | 0.001 | 4 | 4 |

**Additional Figure.** On the next page, we include an additional Fig. 8, depicting the learning curves corresponding to experiments with different task-specific weights (Sect. 5.2).

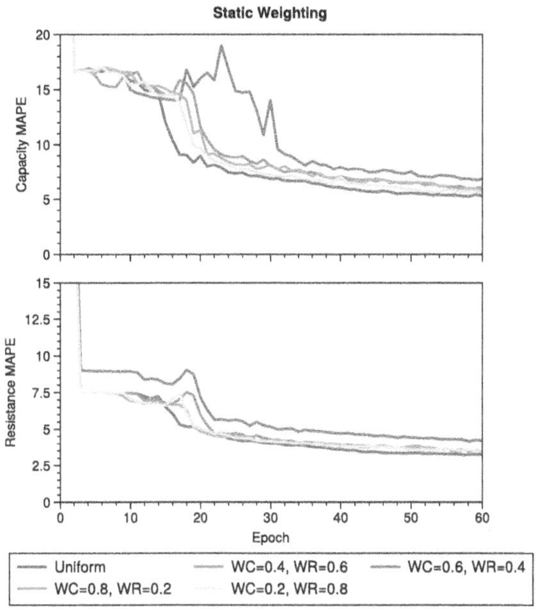


**Fig. 8.** The learning curves corresponding to different task weight configurations are compared for the capacity (top plot) and resistance tasks (bottom plot).

## References


1. Abbas, W., Tap, M.: Adaptively weighted multi-task learning using inverse validation loss. In: ICASSP 2019 - 2019 IEEE International Conference on Acoustics, Speech and Signal Processing (ICASSP), pp. 1408–1412 (2019)
2. Aykol, M., et al.: Perspective-combining physics and machine learning to predict battery lifetime. J. Electrochem. Soc. **168**(3), 030525 (2021). https://doi.org/10.1149/1945-7111/abec55
3. Bao, X., Liu, Y., Liu, B., Liu, H., Wang, Y.: Multi-state online estimation of lithium-ion batteries based on multi-task learning. Energies **16**(7) (2023). https://doi.org/10.3390/en16073002
4. Belt, J.R., Ho, C.D., Motloch, C.G., Miller, T.J., Duong, T.Q.: A capacity and power fade study of li-ion cells during life cycle testing. J. Power Sources **123**(2), 241–246 (2003)
5. Bian, C., He, H., Yang, S., Huang, T.: State-of-charge sequence estimation of lithium-ion battery based on bidirectional long short-term memory encoder-decoder architecture. J. Power Sources **449**, 227558 (2020). https://doi.org/10.1016/j.jpowsour.2019.227558
6. Chandran, V., Patil, C., Karthick, A., Ganeshaperumal, D., Rahim, R., Ghosh, A.: State of charge estimation of lithium-ion battery for electric vehicles using machine learning algorithms. World Electr. Veh. J. **12**, 38 (2021). https://doi.org/10.3390/WEVJ12010038

7. Chen, D., et al.: An empirical-data hybrid driven approach for remaining useful life prediction of lithium-ion batteries considering capacity diving. Energy **245**, 123222 (2022). https://doi.org/10.1016/j.energy.2022.123222
8. Chen, J., Feng, X., Jiang, L., Zhu, Q.: State of charge estimation of lithium-ion battery using denoising autoencoder and gated recurrent unit recurrent neural network. Energy **227**, 120451 (2021)
9. Chen, Z., Badrinarayanan, V., Lee, C.Y., Rabinovich, A.: GradNorm: gradient normalization for adaptive loss balancing in deep multitask networks. In: ICML, pp. 793–802 (2018)
10. Chennupati, S., Sistu, G., Yogamani, S.K., Rawashdeh, S.A.: Multinet++: multi-stream feature aggregation and geometric loss strategy for multi-task learning. In: 2019 IEEE/CVF Conference on Computer Vision and Pattern Recognition Workshops (CVPRW), pp. 1200–1210 (2019)
11. Cho, K., van Merrienboer, B., Gülçehre, Ç., Bougares, F., Schwenk, H., Bengio, Y.: Learning phrase representations using RNN encoder-decoder for statistical machine translation. CoRR **abs/1406.1078** (2014). http://arxiv.org/abs/1406.1078
12. Cipolla, R., Gal, Y., Kendall, A.: Multi-task learning using uncertainty to weigh losses for scene geometry and semantics. In: 2018 IEEE/CVF Conference on Computer Vision and Pattern Recognition, pp. 7482–7491 (2018)
13. Collobert, R., Weston, J.: A unified architecture for natural language processing: deep neural networks with multitask learning. In: Proceedings of the 25th International Conference on Machine Learning, pp. 160–167 (2008)
14. Costa, C., Barbosa, J., Gonçalves, R., Castro, H., Campo, F.D., Lanceros-Méndez, S.: Recycling and environmental issues of lithium-ion batteries: advances, challenges and opportunities. Energy Storage Mater. **37**, 433–465 (2021). https://doi.org/10.1016/j.ensm.2021.02.032, https://www.sciencedirect.com/science/article/pii/S2405829721000829
15. Cui, S., Joe, I.: A dynamic spatial-temporal attention-based GRU model with healthy features for state-of-health estimation of lithium-ion batteries. IEEE Access **9**, 27374–27388 (2021)
16. Cui, S., Yong, X., Kim, S., Hong, S., Joe, I.: An LSTM-based encoder-decoder model for state-of-charge estimation of lithium-ion batteries. In: Silhavy, R. (ed.) CSOC 2020. AISC, vol. 1224, pp. 178–188. Springer, Cham (2020). https://doi.org/10.1007/978-3-030-51965-0_15
17. Das, S., Tariq, A., Santos, T., Kantareddy, S.S., Banerjee, I.: Recurrent Neural Networks (RNNs): Architectures, Training Tricks, and Introduction to Influential Research, pp. 117–138. Springer US, New York, NY (2023). https://doi.org/10.1007/978-1-0716-3195-9_4
18. Fifty, C., Amid, E., Zhao, Z., Yu, T., Anil, R., Finn, C.: Efficiently identifying task groupings for multi-task learning. Adv. Neural. Inf. Process. Syst. **34**, 27503–27516 (2021)
19. Gong, T., et al.: A comparison of loss weighting strategies for multi task learning in deep neural networks. IEEE Access **7**, 141627–141632 (2019). https://doi.org/10.1109/ACCESS.2019.2943604
20. Grégoire, E., Chaudhary, H., Verboven, S.: Sample-level weighting for multi-task learning with auxiliary tasks. arXiv preprint arXiv:2306.04519 (2023)
21. Hong, J., Lee, D., Jeong, E.R., Yi, Y.: Towards the swift prediction of the remaining useful life of lithium-ion batteries with end-to-end deep learning. Appl. Energy **278**, 115646 (2020)

22. Hosen, M.S., Jaguemont, J., Van Mierlo, J., Berecibar, M.: Battery lifetime prediction and performance assessment of different modeling approaches. iScience **24**(2), 102060 (2021). https://doi.org/10.1016/j.isci.2021.102060
23. Hossain Lipu, M., Hannan, M., Karim, T.F., Hussain, A., Saad, M.H.M., Ayob, A., Miah, M.S., Indra Mahlia, T.: Intelligent algorithms and control strategies for battery management system in electric vehicles: progress, challenges and future outlook. J. Cleaner Prod. **292**, 126044 (2021). https://doi.org/10.1016/j.jclepro.2021.126044, https://www.sciencedirect.com/science/article/pii/S095965262100264X
24. Jin, S., Sui, X., Huang, X., Wang, S., Teodorescu, R., Stroe, D.I.: Overview of machine learning methods for lithium-ion battery remaining useful lifetime prediction. Electronics **10**(24) (2021). https://doi.org/10.3390/electronics10243126, https://www.mdpi.com/2079-9292/10/24/3126
25. Jones, P.K., Stimming, U., Lee, A.A.: Impedance-based forecasting of lithium-ion battery performance amid uneven usage. Nature News (2022). https://www.nature.com/articles/s41467-022-32422-w#citeas
26. Karger, A., Wildfeuer, L., Aygül, D., Maheshwari, A., Singer, J.P., Jossen, A.: Modeling capacity fade of lithium-ion batteries during dynamic cycling considering path dependence. J. Energy Storage **52**, 104718 (2022). https://doi.org/10.1016/j.est.2022.104718
27. Kendall, A., Gal, Y., Cipolla, R.: Multi-task learning using uncertainty to weigh losses for scene geometry and semantics. In: Proceedings of the IEEE Conference on Computer Vision and Pattern Recognition, pp. 7482–7491 (2018)
28. Li, W., Zhang, H., van Vlijmen, B., Dechent, P., Sauer, D.U.: Forecasting battery capacity and power degradation with multi-task learning. Energy Storage Mater. **53**, 453–466 (2022)
29. Lin, B., Ye, F., Zhang, Y., Tsang, I.W.: Reasonable effectiveness of random weighting: a litmus test for multi-task learning. arXiv preprint arXiv:2111.10603 (2021)
30. Lin, X., Baweja, H., Kantor, G., Held, D.: Adaptive auxiliary task weighting for reinforcement learning. In: Wallach, H., Larochelle, H., Beygelzimer, A., d'Alché-Buc, F., Fox, E., Garnett, R. (eds.) Advances in Neural Information Processing Systems, vol. 32. Curran Associates, Inc. (2019)
31. Liu, B., Liu, X., Jin, X., Stone, P., Liu, Q.: Conflict-averse gradient descent for multi-task learning. In: Ranzato, M., Beygelzimer, A., Dauphin, Y., Liang, P., Vaughan, J.W. (eds.) Advances in Neural Information Processing Systems, vol. 34, pp. 18878–18890. Curran Associates, Inc. (2021)
32. Liu, S., Liang, Y., Gitter, A.: Loss-balanced task weighting to reduce negative transfer in multi-task learning. In: Proceedings of the AAAI Conference on Artificial Intelligence **33**(01), 9977–9978 (2019). https://doi.org/10.1609/aaai.v33i01.33019977, https://ojs.aaai.org/index.php/AAAI/article/view/5125
33. Luong, M.T., Le, Q.V., Sutskever, I., Vinyals, O., Kaiser, L.: Multi-task sequence to sequence learning. arXiv preprint arXiv:1511.06114 (2015)
34. Mehmood, T., Gerevini, A.E., Lavelli, A., Serina, I.: Combining multi-task learning with transfer learning for biomedical named entity recognition. Procedia Comput. Sci. **176**, 848–857 (2020). https://doi.org/10.1016/j.procs.2020.09.080, knowledge-Based and Intelligent Information & Engineering Systems: Proceedings of the 24th International Conference KES2020
35. Nikentari, N., Wei, H.L.: Multi-task learning for time series forecasting using NARMAX-LSTM. In: 2022 27th International Conference on Automation and Computing (ICAC), pp. 1–6 (2022). https://doi.org/10.1109/ICAC55051.2022.9911071

36. Nykvist, B., Nilsson, M.: Rapidly falling costs of battery packs for electric vehicles. Nat. Clim. Chang. **5**, 329–332 (2015)
37. Patil, M.A., .: A novel multistage support vector machine based approach for li ion battery remaining useful life estimation. Appl. Energy **159**, 285–297 (2015). https://doi.org/10.1016/j.apenergy.2015.08.119, https://www.sciencedirect.com/science/article/pii/S0306261915010557
38. Rieger, L.H., et al.: Uncertainty-aware and explainable machine learning for early prediction of battery degradation (2022). https://doi.org/10.26434/chemrxiv-2022-h1g21
39. Scrosati, B., Garche, J.: Lithium batteries: status, prospects and future. J. Power Sources **195**(9), 2419–2430 (2010). https://doi.org/10.1016/j.jpowsour.2009.11.048, https://www.sciencedirect.com/science/article/pii/S0378775309020564
40. Sener, O., Koltun, V.: Multi-task learning as multi-objective optimization. In: Advances in Neural Information Processing Systems, vol. 31 (2018)
41. Senushkin, D., Patakin, N., Kuznetsov, A., Konushin, A.: Independent component alignment for multi-task learning. In: Proceedings of the IEEE/CVF Conference on Computer Vision and Pattern Recognition (CVPR), pp. 20083–20093 (2023)
42. Sharma, P., Bora, B.J.: A review of modern machine learning techniques in the prediction of remaining useful life of lithium-ion batteries. Batteries **9**(1), 13 (2022). https://doi.org/10.3390/batteries9010013
43. Sutskever, I., Vinyals, O., Le, Q.V.: Sequence to sequence learning with neural networks. In: Advances in Neural Information Processing Systems, vol. 27 (2014)
44. Tang, T., Yuan, H.: An indirect remaining useful life prognosis for li-ion batteries based on health indicator and novel artificial neural network. J. Energy Storage **52**, 104701 (2022)
45. Thung, K.H., Wee, C.Y.: A brief review on multi-task learning. Multimedia Tools Appl. **77**, 29705–29725 (2018)
46. Tian, J., Xiong, R., Shen, W., Lu, J.: Data-driven battery degradation prediction: forecasting voltage-capacity curves using one-cycle data. EcoMat **4**(5) (2022). https://doi.org/10.1002/eom2.12213
47. Tomaszewska, A., et al.: Lithium-ion battery fast charging: a review. eTransportation **1**, 100011 (2019). https://doi.org/10.1016/j.etran.2019.100011, https://www.sciencedirect.com/science/article/pii/S2590116819300116
48. Vandenhende, S., Georgoulis, S., Van Gansbeke, W., Proesmans, M., Dai, D., Van Gool, L.: Multi-task learning for dense prediction tasks: a survey. IEEE Trans. Pattern Anal. Mach. Intell. **44**(7), 3614–3633 (2022). https://doi.org/10.1109/TPAMI.2021.3054719
49. Verboven, S., Chaudhary, M.H., Berrevoets, J., Ginis, V., Verbeke, W.: Hydalearn: Highly dynamic task weighting for multitask learning with auxiliary tasks. Appl. Intell. **53**(5), 5808–5822 (2023)
50. Vithayathil Varghese, N., Mahmoud, Q.H.: A survey of multi-task deep reinforcement learning. Electronics **9**(9), 1363 (2020)
51. Yang, F., Yang, F., Li, W., Li, C., Miao, Q.: State-of-charge estimation of lithium-ion batteries based on gated recurrent neural network. Energy (2019). https://doi.org/10.1016/J.ENERGY.2019.03.059

52. Yu, T., Kumar, S., Gupta, A., Levine, S., Hausman, K., Finn, C.: Gradient surgery for multi-task learning. In: Larochelle, H., Ranzato, M., Hadsell, R., Balcan, M., Lin, H. (eds.) Advances in Neural Information Processing Systems, vol. 33, pp. 5824–5836. Curran Associates, Inc. (2020)
53. Zhang, Y., Tang, Q., Zhang, Y., Wang, J., Stimming, U., Lee, A.A.: Identifying degradation patterns of lithium ion batteries from impedance spectroscopy using machine learning. Nat. Commun. **11**(1), 1–6 (2020)

# Classification Tree Based AI System for Short Term Prediction for Heat and Power Plants

Małgorzata Markowska[1], Andrzej Sokołowski[2(✉)], Grzegorz Migut[3], and Danuta Strahl[4]

[1] Wrocław University of Economics and Business, Wrocław, Poland
malgorzata.markowska@ue.wroc.pl
[2] Collegium Humanum – Warsaw Management University, Warsaw, Poland
sokolows@uek.krakow.pl
[3] StatSoft Poland, Kraków, Poland
g.migut@statsoft.pl
[4] WSB University, Dąbrowa Górnicza, Poland
danuta.strahl@ue.wroc.pl

**Abstract.** Companies supplying electrical energy rely mainly on long term agreements with electricity producers, but on the other hand the actual demand should be precisely predicted for 48 h ahead, to take into account the actual weather conditions. The same type of analysis is important also for heat and power plants, but this time the temperature of returning water is the most interested. Some time series models can be used for forecasting. However in daily practice – more popular are average profiles showing the distribution over 24 h. We propose to build an AI system to choose the future profile. First – from the historical data – daily profiles are obtained, by cutting the time series into 24-h periods. Then, these empirical profiles are clustered with hierarchic and non-hierarchic clustering procedures to form homogeneous groups (types of profiles). Finally the classification methods are applied using weather data and observed demand from previous days (up to one week backwards). The measure for the forecasting evaluation has been proposed. Out of the two tested classification methods, CART classification tree performed better.

**Keywords:** Electricity Demand · Heat and Power Plant · Forecasting Models · Clustering

## 1 Introduction

During United Nations summit in 2015, with 160 heads of state, the document "Transforming Our World: The 2030 Agenda for Sustainable Development" [26] has been approved. Sustainable Development Goals assumes actions to change the world in which the needs of current generation will be fulfilled in a balanced way. According to Goal 7 we should ensure access to affordable, reliable, sustainable and modern energy for all, and Goal 12 tells us to ensure sustainable consumption and production patterns. With


Published by Springer Nature Switzerland AG 2024
E. Mercier-Laurent et al. (Eds.): AI4KMES 2023, IFIP AICT 693, pp. 134–149, 2024.
https://doi.org/10.1007/978-3-031-61069-1_10

10% of world population without access to modern electric energy we have to work on effective energy production and consumption in every country, and on every level. One possible way is to forecast the demand for electricity or characteristics important for heat and power plants within existing system of production and distribution. Artificial Intelligence systems can help to forecast them, and optimize production.

## 2 Literature Remarks

Books and papers on heat and power plants (CHP) are usually concentrated on technical aspect of production, and its operational and economic efficiency [6, 12, 20, 28]. Some studies are devoted specially to a given geographic area: Denmark [19], Beijing [17], Riga [3]. Among methods used, artificial neural networks [8] and linear programming [2] are popular. The closest to water temperature forecasting are [3, 17, 20].

Historical data is typically used in building forecasting systems. In electric energy industry prices are forecasted on hourly basis [7] and in long-term horizon [8, 18, 32] show that in last 10 years more than 170 papers were published on that subject. Probabilistic energy forecasting [11] and short-term load forecasts are important for production system and energy markets [1]. Among methods used for forecasting we can name some examples: data-driven modelling [8, 32], artificial neural networks: ANN [13, 16, 21], Deep Feed-Forward [30], deep neural networks [7], hybrid models with SSN and wavelet transform [1, 5, 22], seasonal and non-seasonal autoregressive moving average models (SARIMA/ARIMA) [15, 24], quantile regression [9], Ordinary Least Squares Regression [27], machine learning Random Forests [23], models merging Singular Spectral Analysis, Cuckoo Search and Support Vector Machine [31].

## 3 Method

The aim of the paper is to propose the methodological structure of AI system for forecasting hourly temperature of return water in the heat and power plant, and demand for electrical energy - using classical classification trees. The research is based on an empirical time series. The most popular approach in short term hourly forecasting is based on time series analysis. We propose to forecast not the individual hours but daily profiles. Different daily profiles are used in forecasting practice. Analysis presented here is based on concrete real data, but the shape of profiles are more or less similar in a homogeneous regions.

Daily profiles have been first clustered by Ward [29] agglomerative method with squared Euclidean distance used to measure distances between groups on the consecutive stages of agglomerative process, and final partition have been obtained by k-means method [25]. Cluster analysis makes possible to group objects, variables and time units. In our study daily profiles are objects defined in 24-dimensional space. Hierarchical Ward method, and the dendrogram obtained, help to identified the number of group of profiles (typical profiles). Profiles are grouped by non-hierarchical, k-means clustering procedure.

Different methods have been proposed in the literature to stop the agglomeration process and obtain the final partition. We decided to use the procedure based on the relative increase of the agglomerative distance. i.e. the distance which is used to identify which groups should be merged on the given step. The increase of this distance is somehow smooth until objects or small groups belonging to the same large group are merged. The distance visibly increased when we join together groups lying far from each other in the multidimentional space. It means that it would be fair to stop the agglomeration process before distant groups are put together. There is an additional criterion for the number of groups. If there are too many groups than the practical simplicity of forecasting profiles - not the time series - is lost.

Two types of classification trees are used: CART (Classification and Regression Trees, also known as C&RT) [4] and CHAID (Chi-squared Automatic Interaction Detector) [14].

In order to measure the quality of prediction we propose measure M defined by (1).

$$M = 1 - \frac{\sum_{i=1}^{k}\sum_{j=1}^{k} n_{ij}d_{ij}}{\sum_{j=1}^{k} n_{.j}\sum_{i=1}^{k} p_j d_{ij}} \tag{1}$$

The above measure is based on two matrices: **N** – classification matrix obtained by a given classification method. **D** – matrix of weights (distances between day means per hour in the profiles or distances between profiles). The idea of M is to compare the results of a given method with random assignment defined by the observed probability distribution for profiles, or assuming that all profiles have equal probability to occur in a given day. Probability distributions are estimated on the basis of learning set.

All calculations have been performed on STATISTICA software.

## 4 Temperature of Return Water from Heat and Power Plant

Heat and Power plant, according to its name, produce heat and electricity. In this section we concentrate on heat provided for the city. The temperature of water leaving the plant for the city (supply water) can be controlled and in fact it is set by the plant. What is the most interesting for the plant are the hourly forecasts of the return water. This of course can make possible to calculate the amount of heat provided to the city.

In this section we use data from one of the big cities (population greater than 500000) in Poland. The time span is 14 and a half months, which is 440 days, or 10560 h. January 1 was the starting day. The average profile of the temperature of return water is presented at Fig. 1, with standard errors as whiskers. The last 15 days (profiles) are treated as test data.

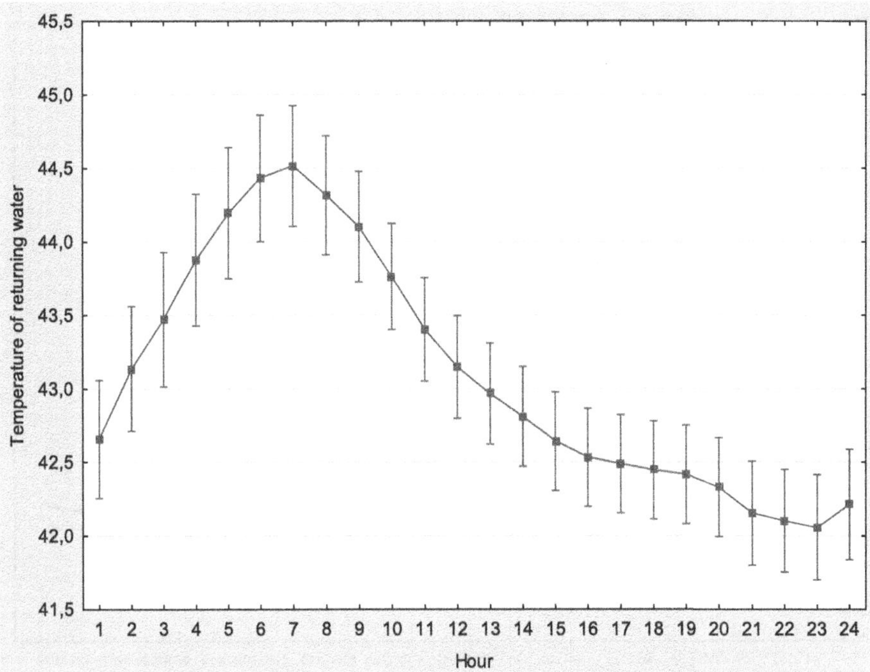


**Fig. 1.** The average profile of the temperature of return water

To find clusters of individual day profiles we used Ward's method to identify number of clusters and k-means method to obtain the final partition. The number of clusters has been found as 9, and the average profiles of these clusters are presented on Fig. 2, and the mean temperatures of the whole day are in Table 1.

**Table 1.** Daily average return water temperature for profiles

| | Profile | | | | | | | | |
|---|---|---|---|---|---|---|---|---|---|
| | 1 | 2 | 3 | 4 | 5 | 6 | 7 | 8 | 9 |
| n | 21 | 34 | 43 | 41 | 36 | 49 | 92 | 37 | 72 |
| Av. Temp. | 54.2 | 49.4 | 46.4 | 44.1 | 42.3 | 42.1 | 40.8 | 40.5 | 39.3 |
| Probability | 0.049 | 0.08 | 0.101 | 0.096 | 0.085 | 0.115 | 0.216 | 0.087 | 0.169 |

Source: own calculations

The following variables have been consider as potential predictors: day of the month (as number), month, day of the week, working day/holiday, average daily temperature, hour temperature, wind speed, sky (sunny/variable cloud cover/cloudy). While preparing predictions for one day or two days ahead we do not know what will be the temperature of supply water, so this very important variable cannot be included in our model.

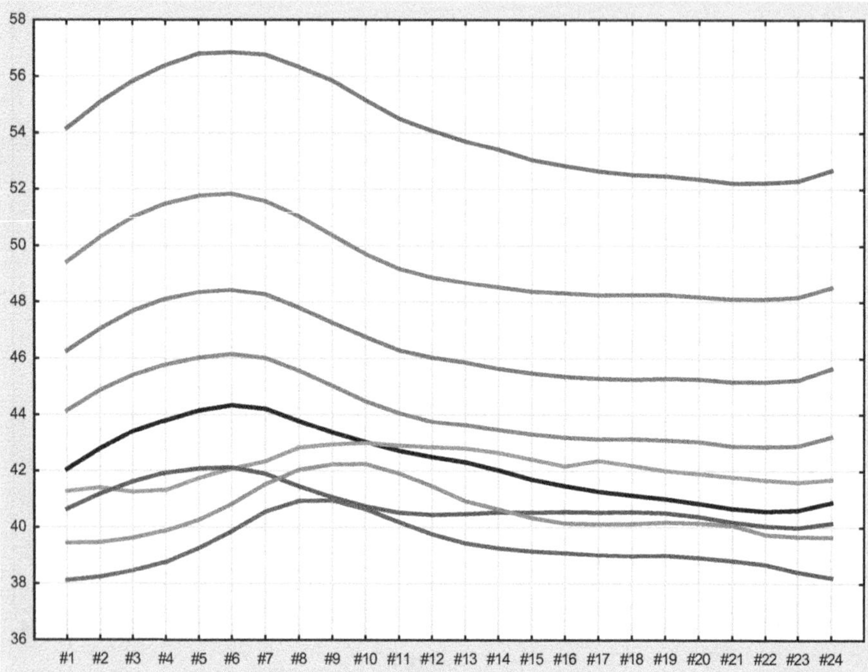


**Fig. 2.** Profiles of return water temperature

To validate the importance of some individual variables and secure their coding as the possible predictors, we estimated standardized regression models with backward stepwise elimination procedure using significance level of 0.05 as the criterion for inclusion. Variable with the highest p-value, but greater than significance level, has been eliminated at each step (just one at a time) until all remaining variables were statistically significant. Models were estimated separately for each hour, based on learning set, and adjusted for temperature of supply water.

Coefficients in Table 2 are comparable and one can evaluate the importance of variables. It is rather surprising that cloudiness is practically unimportant, considered as dummy variables with clear sky as a reference variant. So the only dummy variable used in classification trees is working day (coded as 1), opposite to holiday of any kind. Three quantitative variables serve as diagnostic variables: mean daily (24 h) temperature, average temperature between 10–22, average wind speed between 8–18.

**Table 2.** Standardized regression results

| Hour | Working day | Mean daily temp. | Hourly temp. | Wind speed | Partially cloudy | Cloudy | $R^2$ |
|---|---|---|---|---|---|---|---|
| 01 | | −0.15 | | | | | 0.900 |
| 02 | | −0.20 | | | 0.03 | | 0.904 |
| 03 | | −0.37 | 0.17 | | | | 0.878 |
| 04 | | −0.24 | | | | | 0.932 |
| 05 | | −0.21 | | | | | 0.942 |
| 06 | | −0.18 | | | | | 0.946 |
| 07 | | −0.09 | | | | | 0.952 |
| 08 | −0.05 | | | −0.03 | | | 0.887 |
| 09 | −0.06 | 0.08 | | | | | 0.922 |
| 10 | −0.05 | | 0.13 | −0.05 | | 0.04 | 0.907 |
| 11 | | −0.68 | 0.26 | −0.04 | | | 0.956 |
| 12 | | −0.37 | 0.36 | −0.05 | | | 0.878 |
| 13 | | −0.55 | 0.49 | | | | 0.866 |
| 14 | 0.04 | −0.58 | 0.47 | −0.05 | | | 0.874 |
| 15 | 0.04 | −0.84 | 0.36 | −0.03 | | | 0.962 |
| 16 | 0.05 | −0.56 | 0.40 | −0.07 | | | 0.892 |
| 17 | 0.04 | −0.69 | 0.26 | −0.04 | | | 0.963 |
| 18 | 0.05 | −0.42 | 0.30 | −0.04 | | | 0.891 |
| 19 | 0.05 | −0.43 | 0.35 | | | | 0.901 |
| 20 | 0.04 | −0.46 | 0.40 | | | | 0.902 |
| 21 | | −0.54 | 0.51 | | | | 0.849 |
| 22 | | −0.42 | 0.39 | | | | 0.901 |
| 23 | | −0.07 | | | | | 0.896 |
| 24 | | −0.38 | 0.28 | −0.04 | | | 0.893 |

Source: own calculations

The evaluation of the tree performance on learning set (See Table 3) shows that CART performed better than CHAID, so detailed structure of CART tree is the only one presented. None of the method used month and day numbers, mainly because the same information is provided by temperature and working day variables. The general CART layout is on Fig. 3, and split variables and values in Table 4. If the split variable assumes value smaller or equal to split constant, you go to the left branch, if bigger – to the right one. If the dummy variables assumes split category than the movement on the tree is to the left branch.

**Table 3.** Accuracy of return water profile prediction – M measure (learning set)

| Probabilities | Weighted by distances between means | | Weighted by distances between profiles | |
|---|---|---|---|---|
| | CART | CHAID | CART | CHAID |
| equal | 0.894 | 0.741 | 0.980 | 0.978 |
| distribution | 0.877 | 0.700 | 0.869 | 0.695 |

Source: own calculations

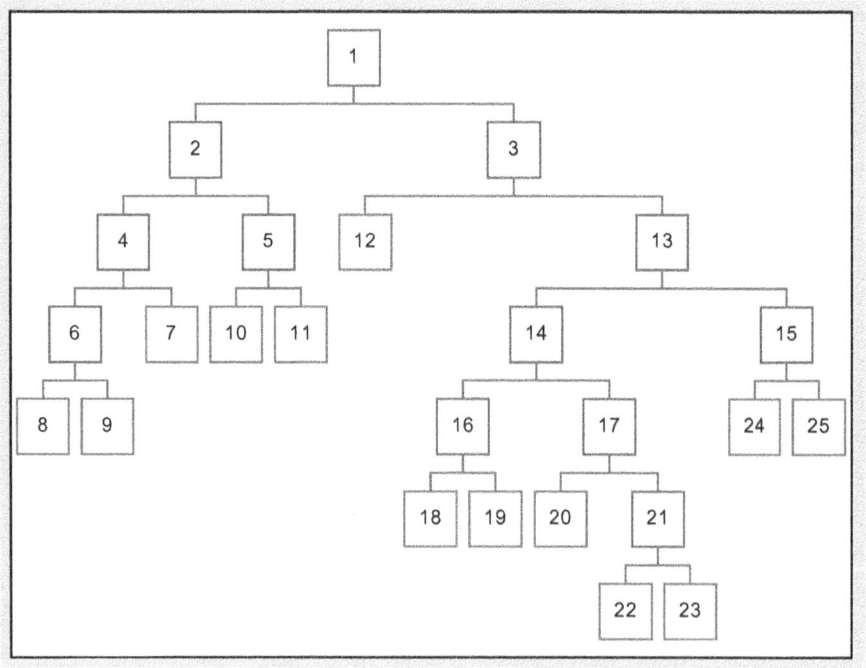


**Fig. 3.** CART layout for returning water

Test set consisted of 15 profiles. 11 (73.3%) of them had been identified precisely. M measures in Table 5 are much better because they take into account the "size" of false identification – how far is a predicted profile from the true one.

**Table 4.** CART tree structure for return water

| Node | Left branch | Right branch | Node size | Selected profile | Split variable | Split constant |
|---|---|---|---|---|---|---|
| 1 | 2 | 3 | 425 | 7 | Aver. daily temp. | 3.5 |
| 2 | 4 | 5 | 157 | 3 | Aver. daily temp. | −0.2 |
| 4 | 6 | 7 | 97 | 3 | Aver. daily temp. | −3.9 |
| 6 | 8 | 9 | 46 | 2 | Aver. daily temp. | −9.5 |
| 8 | | | 17 | 1 | | |
| 9 | | | 29 | 2 | | |
| 7 | | | 51 | 3 | | |
| 5 | 10 | 11 | 60 | 4 | Temp. 10–22 | 3.1 |
| 10 | | | 40 | 4 | | |
| 11 | | | 20 | 5 | | |
| 3 | 12 | 13 | 268 | 7 | Aver. daily temp. | 9.6 |
| 12 | | | 93 | 7 | | |
| 13 | 14 | 15 | 175 | 9 | Aver. daily temp. | 18.6 |
| 14 | 16 | 17 | 103 | 9 | Aver. daily temp. | 13.3 |
| 16 | 15 | 19 | 46 | 9 | Working day | working |
| 18 | | | 29 | 7 | | |
| 19 | | | 17 | 9 | | |
| 17 | 20 | 21 | 57 | 9 | Aver. daily temp. | 15.0 |
| 20 | | | 12 | 9 | | |
| 21 | 22 | 23 | 45 | 9 | Temp. 10–22 | 18.8 |
| 22 | | | 18 | 8 | | |
| 23 | | | 27 | 9 | | |
| 15 | 22 | 25 | 72 | 6 | Wind 8_18 | 3.7 |
| 24 | | | 61 | 6 | | |
| 25 | | | 11 | 8 | | |

Source: own calculations

**Table 5.** Accuracy of return water profile prediction by CART – M measure (Test set)

| Probability | Weighted by distances between means | Weighted by distances between profiles |
|---|---|---|
| Equal | 0.894 | 0.980 |
| distribution | 0.877 | 0.869 |

Source: own calculations

## 5 Demand for Electricity at a Given Area

Our empirical time series of electricity demand covers the period from October, until May two years later (15312 h) for small region in Poland. This time series has been transformed into multivariable data set (each variable representing one hour). Each object (table row) represents one day. 21 days have been randomly selected as a test data – not the consecutive days, but spread all over time series. So the learning set consists of 617 days.

Daily profiles have been clustered by Ward agglomerative method with squared Euclidean distance used to measure distances between groups on the consecutive stages of agglomerative process. According to the first important jump of linkage distance, 14 clusters were identified. The final partition was obtained by k-means method. The average demand profile is presented on Fig. 4, and its decomposition into 14 clusters on Fig. 5. Averages for whole profiles, calculated from 24 h are in Table 6.

**Table 6.** Clusters of electricity demand

| | Profile | | | | | | |
|---|---|---|---|---|---|---|---|
| | 1 | 2 | 3 | 4 | 5 | 6 | 7 |
| n | 26 | 58 | 66 | 22 | 76 | 69 | 19 |
| Av. Profile | 760.2 | 722.8 | 693.3 | 666.5 | 664.9 | 634.3 | 611.3 |
| Probability | 0.041 | 0.093 | 0.107 | 0.036 | 0.123 | 0.112 | 0.031 |
| | Profile | | | | | | |
| | 8 | 9 | 10 | 11 | 12 | 13 | 14 |
| n | 46 | 88 | 27 | 26 | 33 | 22 | 39 |
| Av. Profile | 608.6 | 592.2 | 576.4 | 566.2 | 554.4 | 538.5 | 520.2 |
| Probability | 0.075 | 0.143 | 0.044 | 0.042 | 0.054 | 0.036 | 0.063 |

Source: own calculations

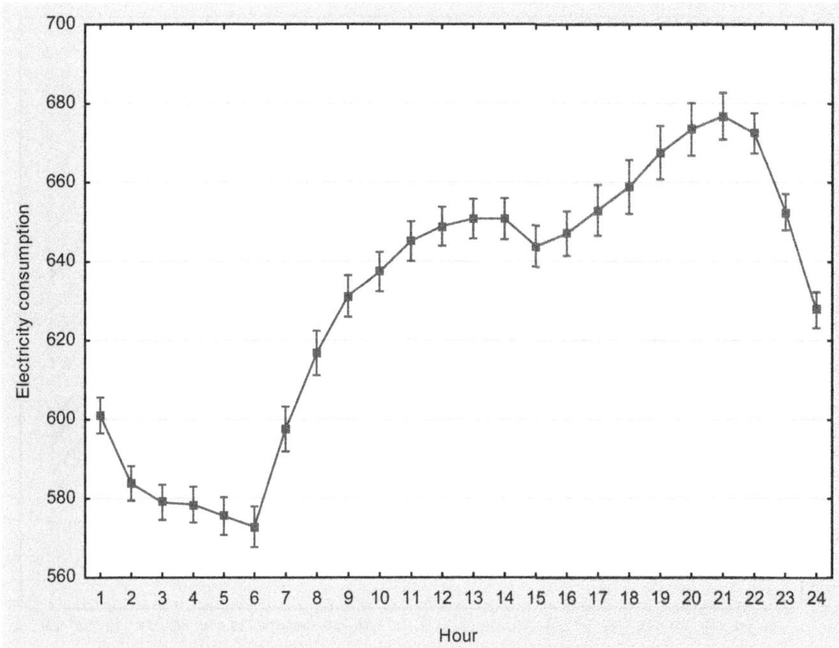


**Fig. 4.** Average profile of demand for electricity

For the forecasting (identifying future profiles), the following explaining variables have been used:

- qualitative variable: week day
- dummy variables: day before holiday different from Sunday, day of the holiday, day after the holiday
- quantitative variables: average day temperature, average night temperature, seven lagged demand variables from the days of previous seven days

Accuracy of profile prediction by CART and CHAID are summarized in Tables 7 and 8.

Generally CART was again superior to CHAID. Its layout is presented on Fig. 6, and tree structure in Table 8 (Table 9).

Demand for electricity from the previous day was the most important diagnostic variable (importance = 1). The next four variables where also autoregressive – days (−4), (−6), (−7), (−5) – with importance from [0.855–0.963] range. The internal inertia of electricity demand process is somehow natural. On the other hand, in some cases, the forecasts for two days ahead are the most wanted, so Day(-1) variable cannot be used. The next variables in order of importance are: average day temperature (0.830), average night temperature (0.764), Day (-3) (0.757), Day (-2) (0.677), week day (0.662), holiday (0.272), day after holiday (0.171), day before holiday (0.132).

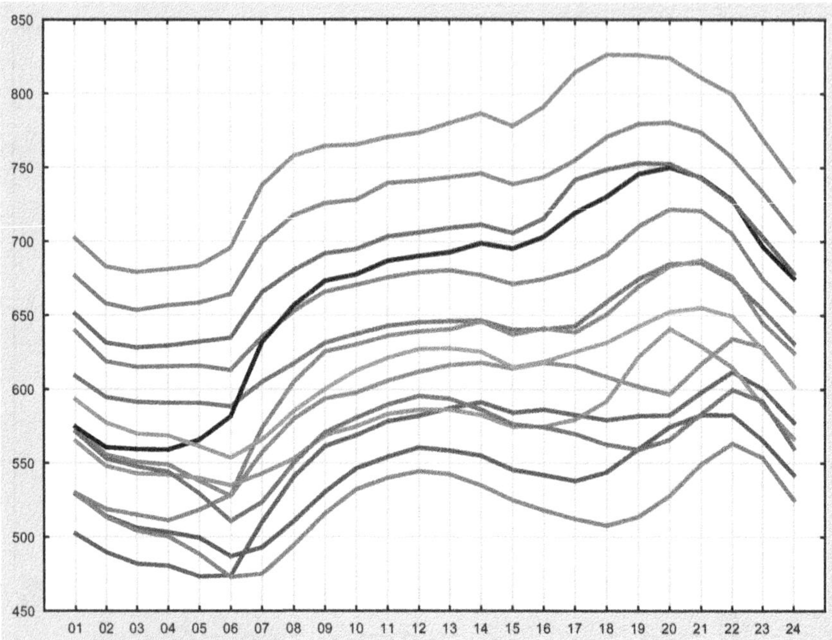


**Fig. 5.** Averages of Clustered profiles of electricity demand

**Table 7.** Accuracy of electricity demand prediction – M measure (learning set)

| Probabilities | Weighted by distances between means | | Weighted by distances between profiles | |
|---|---|---|---|---|
| | CART | CHAID | CART | CHAID |
| equal | 0.715 | 0.545 | 0.991 | 0.993 |
| distribution | 0.718 | 0.587 | 0.835 | 0.730 |

Source: own calculations

**Table 8.** Accuracy of electricity demand prediction by CART – M measure (test set)

| Probability | Weighted by distances between means | Weighted by distances between profiles |
|---|---|---|
| equal | 0.711 | 0.819 |
| distribution | 0.670 | 0.831 |

Source: own calculations

**Table 9.** CART tree structure for electricity demand

| Node | Left branch | Right branch | Size of node | Selected profile | Split variable | Split constant |
|---|---|---|---|---|---|---|
| 1 | 2 | 3 | 610 | 9 | Day(-1) | 623.5 |
| 2 | 4 | 5 | 295 | 9 | Week day | Mon/Sat/Sun |
| 4 | 6 | 7 | 148 | 14 | Week day | Sat/Sun |
| 6 | 8 | 9 | 80 | 14 | Day(-1) | 580.1 |
| 8 | | | 38 | 14 | | |
| 9 | | | 42 | 11 | | |
| 7 | 10 | 11 | 68 | 12 | Day(-7) | 549.9 |
| 10 | | | 34 | 12 | | |
| 11 | | | 34 | 4 | | |
| 5 | 12 | 13 | 147 | 9 | Aver. night temp. | 8.5 |
| 12 | | | 42 | 6 | | |
| 13 | 14 | 15 | 105 | 9 | Holiday | No |
| 14 | 16 | 17 | 100 | 9 | Day (-1) | 557.6 |
| 16 | | | 8 | 13 | | |
| 17 | 18 | 19 | 92 | 9 | Day (-4) | 609.1 |
| 18 | 20 | 21 | 87 | 9 | Day (-5) | 510.2 |
| 20 | | | 9 | 9 | | |
| 21 | 22 | 23 | 78 | 9 | Day (-1) | 619.7 |
| 22 | | | 77 | 9 | | |
| 23 | | | 1 | 11 | | |
| 19 | | | 5 | 8 | | |
| 15 | | | 5 | 14 | | |
| 3 | 24 | 25 | 315 | 5 | Day (-1) | 714.8 |
| 24 | 26 | 27 | 245 | 5 | Day (-7) | 662.9 |
| 26 | 28 | 29 | 123 | 6 | Week day | Sun |
| 28 | | | 36 | 8 | | |
| 29 | 30 | 31 | 87 | 5 | Day (-1) | 633.9 |
| 30 | | | 24 | 6 | | |
| 31 | 32 | 33 | 63 | 5 | Day (-6) | 677.8 |
| 32 | | | 60 | 5 | | |
| 33 | | | 3 | 3 | | |

*(continued)*

**Table 9.** (*continued*)

| Node | Left branch | Right branch | Size of node | Selected profile | Split variable | Split constant |
|---|---|---|---|---|---|---|
| 27 | 34 | 35 | 122 | 3 | Aver. day temp. | 6.5 |
| 34 | 36 | 37 | 69 | 3 | Day (-4) | 679.8 |
| 36 | | | 28 | 3 | | |
| 37 | | | 41 | 2 | | |
| 35 | | | 53 | 5 | | |
| 25 | 38 | 39 | 70 | 2 | Day (-1) | 739.9 |
| 38 | | | 42 | 2 | | |
| 39 | | | 28 | 1 | | |

Source: own calculations

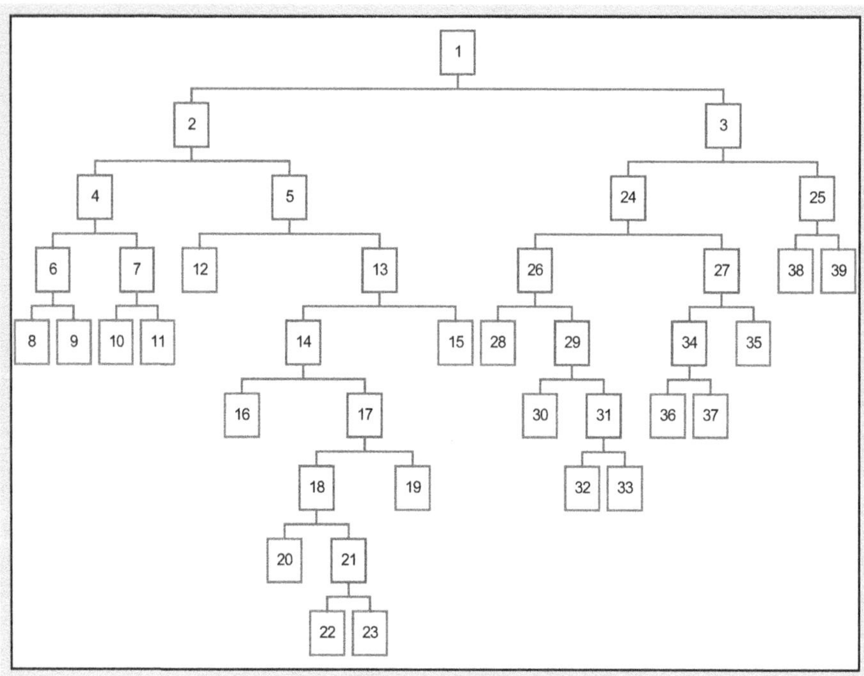


**Fig. 6.** CART layout for electricity demand

## 6 Conclusions

The staff responsible for ordering the hourly amount of electricity or the temperature of return water are sometimes not experts in statistical forecasting, having just weather forecast for the next two days and past demand from last seven days. So AI system would be very helpful for them, suggesting which profile they can use for ordering demand. Such a profile defines the size and hourly distribution of demand or other interesting characteristic. In the paper we proposed the procedure which can be applied as a core for AI forecasting system. Time series analysis and forecasting models are the most popular approach, but the procedure proposed here can be interesting and simpler. Generally, the forecasting task is heavily data driven. In our problem the results, the best method and forecasting accuracy depend on the structure of the analysed area (urban, rural, industrial, etc.). The first part of the proposed method is the analysis of historical data of a given region to identify the typical profiles. This can be done by applying cluster analysis methods, especially the most popular ones – Ward method and k-means. Then the forecasting of future profiles is performed by tree based classification methods. It was found that CART classification trees performed better than CHAID in both considered examples. To achieve goals of sustainable development named in Agenda 2030 we need the support of research based AI systems in the decision process. The analysis presented here can be used in the construction of AI system forecasting profiles as an alternative to typical time series forecasting. The future study should look for some other predictors, assuming that they are available for next two days on hourly or daily basis.

**Acknowledgements.** The project is funded under the program of the Minister of Science and Higher Education titled "Regional Initiative of Excellence" in 2019–2023, project number 018/RID/2018/19, the amount of funding PLN 10 788 423.16.

## References

1. Amjady, N., Keynia, F.: Short-term load forecasting of power systems by combination of wavelet transform and neuro-evolutionary algorithm. Energy **34**(1), 46–57 (2009)
2. Aringhieri, R., Malucelli, F.: Optimal operations management and network planning of a district heating system with combined heat and power plant. Ann. Oper. Res. **120**, 173–199 (2003)
3. Bolonina, A., Bolonins, G., Blumberga, D.: Analysis of the impact of decreasing district heating supply temperature on combined heat and power plant operation. Environ. Clim. Technol. **14**(1), 41–46 (2014)
4. Breiman L., Friedman J.H., Olshen R.A., Stone C.J.: Classification and Regression Trees, Wadsworth & Brooks/Cole Advanced Books & Software (1984)
5. Chang, Z., Zhang, Y., Chen, W.: Electricity price prediction based on hybrid model of adam optimized LSTM neural network and wavelet transform. Energy **187**, 115804 (2019)
6. Dai, Y., et al.: Dispatch model of combined heat and power plant considering heat transfer process. IEEE Trans. Sustain. Energy **8**(3), 1225–1236 (2017)
7. Dombi, G., Dulai, T.: Hourly electricity price forecast for short-and long-term, using deep neural networks. Acta Universita Sapientiae Informatica **14**(2), 208–222 (2022). https://doi.org/10.2478/ausi-2022-0013

8. Fast, M., Palme, T.: Application of artificial neural networks to the condition monitoring and diagnozis of a combined heat and power plant. Energy **35**(2), 1114–1120 (2010)
9. Gabrielli, P., Wüthrich, M., Blume, S., Giovanni, S.: Data-driven modeling for long-term electricity price forecasting. Energy **244** (2022). https://doi.org/10.1016/j.energy.2022.123107
10. Hagfors, L.I., Bunn, D., Kristoffersen, E., Staver, T.T., Westgaard, S.: Modeling the UK electricity price distributions using quantile regression. Energy **102**, 231–243 (2016)
11. Hong, T., Pinson, P., Fan, S., Zareipour, H., Troccoli A., Hyndman R.: Probabilistic energy forecasting: Global Energy Forecasting Competition 2014 and beyond. Int. J. Forecast. **32** (2016). https://doi.org/10.1016/j.ijforecast.2016.02.001
12. Horlock J.H.: Combined heat and power, United States (1987)
13. Jasiński, T.: Use of new variables based on air temperature for forecasting day-ahead spot electricity prices using deep neural networks: a new approach. Energy **213**, 118784 (2020)
14. Kass, G.V.: An exploratory technique for investigating large quantities of categorical data. Appl. Stat. **29**, 119–127 (1980)
15. Kristiansen, T.: Forecasting Nord Pool day-ahead prices with an autoregressive model. Energy Policy **49**, 328–332 (2012)
16. Lago, J., De Ridder, F., Vrancx, P., Bart De Schutter, B.: Forecasting day-ahead electricity prices in Europe: the importance of considering market integration. Appl. Energy **211**, 890–903 (2018)
17. Lin, F., Yi, J., Weixing, Y., Xuzhong, Q.: Influence of supply and return water temperatures on the energy consumption of a district cooling system. Appl. Therm. Eng. **21**(4), 511–521 (2001)
18. Lu, H., Ma, X., Ma, M., Zhu, S.: Energy price prediction using data-driven models: a decade review. Comput. Sci. Rev. **39**, 100356 (2021)
19. Lund, R., Mathiesen, B.V.: Large combined heat and power plants in sustainable energy systems. Appl. Energy **142**, 389–395 (2015)
20. Nesheim, S.J., Ertesvag, I.S.: Efficiencies and indicators to promote combined heat and power. Energy Convers. Manage. **48**, 1004–1015 (2007)
21. Nitin, S., Soumya, R.M., Rishabh, D.S.: Short term electricity price forecast based on environmentally adapted generalized neuron. Energy **125**, 127–139 (2017)
22. Qiao, W., Yang, Z.: Forecast the electricity price of U.S. using a wavelet transform-based hybrid model. Energy **193**, 116704 (2020)
23. Romero, A., Dorronsoro, J.R., Diaz, J.: Day-ahead price forecasting for the Spanish electricity market. Int. J. Interact. Multimedia Artif. Intell. **5**(4), 42–50 (2019)
24. Shafie-khah, M., Parsa, M.M., Sheikh-El-Eslami, M.K.: Price forecasting of day-ahead electricity markets using a hybrid forecast method. Energy Convers. Manage. **52**(5), 2165–2169 (2011)
25. Steinhaus, H.: Sur la division des corps materiels en parties. Bulletin De L'Academie Polonaise Des Sciences, CL.III, **IV**, 12, 801–804 (1956)
26. Transforming our world: the 2030 Agenda for Sustainable Development, United Nations (2015). https://sdgs.un.org/2030agenda
27. Uniejewski, B., Weron, R., Ziel, F.: Variance stabilizing transformations for electricity spot price forecasting. IEEE Trans. Power Syst. **33**(2), 2219–2229 (2017)
28. Wang, J., You, S., Zong, Y., Traeholt, C., Dong, Z.Y., Zhou, Y.: Flexibility of combined heat and power plant: a review of technologies and operation strategies. Appl. Energy **252**, 113445 (2019)
29. Ward, J.H.: Hierarchical grouping to optimize an objective function. J. Am. Stat. Assoc. **58**, 236–244 (1963)
30. Windler, T., Busse, J., Rieck, J.: One month-ahead electricity price forecasting in the contex of production planning. J. Clean. Prod. **238**, 117910 (2019)

31. Zhang, X., Wang, J., Gao, Y.: A hybrid short-term electricity price forecasting framework: Cuckoo search-based feature selection with singular spectrum analysis and SVM. Energy Econ. **81**, 899–913 (2019)
32. Ziel, F., Steinert, R.: Probabilistic mid- and long-term electricity price forecasting. Renew. Sustain. Energy Rev. **94**, 251–266 (2019)

# The Influence of Neural Networks on Hydropower Plant Management in Agriculture: Addressing Challenges and Exploring Untapped Opportunities

C. Coelho[1(✉)], M. Fernanda P. Costa[1], and L. L. Ferrás[1,2]

[1] Centre of Mathematics (CMAT), University of Minho, Braga, Portugal
cmartins@cmat.uminho.pt, mfc@math.uminho.pt

[2] Department of Mechanical Engineering (Section of Mathematics) - FEUP, University of Porto, Porto, Portugal
lferras@fe.up.pt

**Abstract.** Hydropower plants are crucial for stable renewable energy and serve as vital water sources for sustainable agriculture. However, it is essential to assess the current water management practices associated with hydropower plant management software. A key concern is the potential conflict between electricity generation and agricultural water needs. Prioritising water for electricity generation can reduce irrigation availability in agriculture during crucial periods like droughts, impacting crop yields and regional food security. Coordination between electricity and agricultural water allocation is necessary to ensure optimal and environmentally sound practices. Neural networks have become valuable tools for hydropower plant management, but their black-box nature raises concerns about transparency in decision making. Additionally, current approaches often do not take advantage of their potential to create a system that effectively balances water allocation.

This work is a call for attention and highlights the potential risks of deploying neural network-based hydropower plant management software without proper scrutiny and control. To address these concerns, we propose the adoption of the Agriculture Conscious Hydropower Plant Management framework, aiming to maximise electricity production while prioritising stable irrigation for agriculture. We also advocate reevaluating government-imposed minimum water guidelines for irrigation to ensure flexibility and effective water allocation. Additionally, we suggest a set of regulatory measures to promote model transparency and robustness, certifying software that makes conscious and intelligent water allocation decisions, ultimately safeguarding agriculture from undue strain during droughts.

**Keywords:** Ethical AI · Transparent AI · Deep Learning · Sustainability · Agriculture · Hydropower


Published by Springer Nature Switzerland AG 2024
E. Mercier-Laurent et al. (Eds.): AI4KMES 2023, IFIP AICT 693, pp. 150–160, 2024.
https://doi.org/10.1007/978-3-031-61069-1_11

# 1 Introduction

Hydropower plants play a vital role in our renewable energy infrastructure by harnessing the kinetic energy of flowing water to generate electricity. The efficiency of these power plants is often enhanced through the construction of reservoirs and dams, which serve as essential components for controlling and optimising the energy derived from water sources. Dams serve as effective barriers that impound substantial volumes of water within reservoirs, creating a regulated water supply.

In addition to electricity generation, some reservoirs also serve as vital water sources that support irrigation systems to promote sustainable agriculture. The provision of water for irrigation is of paramount significance, given its pivotal role in ensuring global food security and supporting agriculture, which forms the backbone of numerous economies. Irrigation systems are instrumental in increasing natural rainfall and meeting the water requirements of crops, particularly in regions characterised by erratic or insufficient precipitation. Effective irrigation practices not only enhance crop yields, but also facilitate the cultivation of a wider variety of crops and allow year-round agricultural production. Consequently, these measures contribute to stabilising food production, increasing food availability, and reducing the susceptibility of communities to food shortages and price fluctuations [10].

Governments play a crucial role in regulating the availability of irrigation water by setting minimum water guidelines for reservoirs associated with hydropower plants. These guidelines are formulated to address a range of critical objectives, including the preservation of agricultural productivity, which is fundamental for ensuring food security and economic stability. Moreover, these regulations are designed to safeguard the natural ecosystems and aquatic life within the reservoir and downstream areas. Failure to meet these minimum guidelines leads to fines applied to the respective management company [8].

Traditionally, hydropower plant management has relied heavily on software solutions that incorporate traditional optimisation algorithms. These software tools are designed to ensure the efficient utilisation of available water resources for electricity generation, thus making real-time decisions about water release, reservoir levels, and electricity generation. These tools analyse various factors such as water inflow forecasts, electricity demand, and environmental constraints to determine the most advantageous operational strategies [5,8].

With the success of Neural Networks (NNs) as powerful predictors, several works in the literature have shown NNs can be powerful tools for hydropower plant management [1,7]. However, concerns arise due to their inherent black-box nature, lacking transparency in decision making. This raises doubts about the adherence to minimum water guidelines for maintaining agricultural and ecosystem preservation water levels, posing threats to food security and natural life. To address potential fines and regulatory issues, one strategy is to deduct minimum water guidelines required for agriculture and ecosystem preservation from the inflows before giving them as input to the NN, prioritising energy production, and overlooking optimising agricultural water usage.

In both traditional optimisation-based and NN-based software, the predominant training objective frequently centres around the maximisation of revenue, possibly overlooking the broader considerations of sustainability and social aspects in water resource management. This is achieved through the definition of objective functions that primarily reward electricity generation or revenue without adequately promoting prudent and strategic water storage for irrigation purposes. Given the critical role of hydropower plants in ensuring stable renewable energy and their importance as vital water sources for sustainable agriculture, it is essential to assess the current water management practices associated with these systems. A key concern is the potential conflict between electricity generation and agricultural water needs. Prioritising water for electricity generation can reduce the availability of irrigation water during crucial periods such as droughts, impacting crop yields and regional food security. Coordination between energy and agricultural water allocation is necessary to ensure optimal and environmentally sound practices.

In this work, our main goal is to draw attention to the potential harms associated with deploying NN hydropower plant management software in production without proper scrutiny and control. We also aim to highlight the missed opportunity to integrate electricity generation with agriculture sustainability and food security. To address these concerns, we propose the adoption of the Agriculture Conscious Hydropower Plant Management framework (ACHPM) as a novel approach for developing these software. The importance of our research lies in recognising that the uncontrolled and unregulated deployment of NN-based hydropower management software may have adverse consequences on both economic and environmental fronts. Furthermore, current practices fail to take advantage of the full capabilities of NNs. By highlighting the importance of this issue, we hope to inspire a shift towards more responsible and sustainable practices in the field of hydropower management with NN models.

The structure of this paper is outlined as follows. In Sect. 2, we provide a brief exploration of approaches to hydropower plant management, using traditional optimisation techniques, and more contemporary approaches, using NNs. Section 3 delves into the proposed ACHPM framework and underscores the importance of regulating and scrutinising black-box models before their deployment. Finally, in Sect. 4 we conclude this paper by summarising the key takeaways and insights and discuss some future work.

## 2 Hydropower Plant Management

Hydropower plants are crucial for renewable energy generation and some play an equally important role as a water source for agriculture. Thus, the efficient management of hydropower plants is crucial to optimise their performance, ensure a stable electricity supply to consumers, preserve the surrounding ecosystem, and promote agricultural sustainability. Over time, companies responsible for hydropower plants have relied on software solutions for management. Initially, these software solutions were based on traditional constrained optimisation techniques aimed at maximising total revenue while satisfying specific constraints [6]. Note that many software still use this type of approach [11].

However, with the rise of NNs and their remarkable performance across various tasks, the landscape of software for hydropower plant management is undergoing a shift towards NN-based solutions, as evidenced by various examples in the literature [2,3]. In this section, we provide a brief overview and a general mathematical formulation of the management problem when solved using constrained optimisation techniques and NNs. We also emphasise the distinctions between these two approaches and delineate the challenges associated with each strategy.

### 2.1 Constrained Optimisation Approach

The problem of managing a hydropower plant is generally formulated as the constrained optimisation problem (1) in which the goal is to maximise an objective function $l(\boldsymbol{\theta})$, typically defined by the amount of electricity generated, *i.e.* the company's profit, while satisfying some constraints [5,6]. In this work, we focus on the constraints related to meeting the electricity demand and minimum water guidelines for irrigation and ecosystem preservation. In general, the formulation of the optimisation problem is defined by:

$$\begin{aligned} \underset{\boldsymbol{\theta}\in\mathbb{R}^{n_\theta}}{\text{maximize}} \quad & l(\boldsymbol{\theta}), \\ \text{subject to} \quad & P(\boldsymbol{\theta}) \geq P_{demand}, \\ & Q_{river}(\boldsymbol{\theta}) \geq Q_{river}^{\min}, \\ & Q_{irrigation}(\boldsymbol{\theta}) \geq Q_{irrigation}^{\min}, \end{aligned} \tag{1}$$

where $\boldsymbol{\theta} \in \mathbb{R}^{n_\theta}$ are the parameters to optimise, $l$ is the objective function, $P$ is the electricity generated, $P_{demand}$ the electricity required to meet consumer needs, $Q_{river}$ the amount of water for the preservation of ecosystems, $Q_{river}^{\min}$ the minimum water guideline for ecosystem preservation, $Q_{irrigation}$ the amount of water allocated for irrigation and $Q_{irrigation}^{\min}$ the minimum water guideline for irrigation.

In general, a common behaviour observed when solving (1) is that traditional optimisation algorithms' solution only allocate the minimum water guidelines for irrigation and ecosystem preservation since the objective is to maximise electricity generation. Since there is no direct incentive or reward for allocating more water to these other purposes, in the mathematical formulation (1), the optimal solution prioritise electricity production. Allocating strictly the minimum water guidelines for irrigation and ecosystem preservation allows for more water to be available for electricity generation, which, in turn, increases the value of the objective function.

This outcome underscores a potential limitation of such optimisation approaches, as they may not inherently account for suitable broader social and environmental considerations associated with water resource management.

### 2.2 Neural Networks Approach

Analysing a NN training process from the perspective of traditional optimisation, one can draw parallels to an algorithm for solving the unconstrained problem (2). This view is based on the fact that during NN training, the primary objective is to minimise an objective function $l(\boldsymbol{\theta})$, that measures the error between the predicted and ground-truth values.

The optimisation problem is given by:

$$\underset{\boldsymbol{\theta} \in \mathbb{R}^{n_\theta}}{\text{minimize}} \qquad l(\boldsymbol{\theta}), \tag{2}$$

where $l$ is the objective function used in NN training, commonly referred to as the loss function. $\boldsymbol{\theta} \in \mathbb{R}_{n_\theta}$ are the NN parameters to be optimised.

In general, in this type of approach, there are not constraints on the parameters of the problem (2). Furthermore, if necessary, incorporating constraints can be nontrivial and may not align with the standard practice of NN training.

The NN approach has been extensively used for hydropower plant management in which the goal is mainly to predict electricity generation given a set of input data [2,3]. However, few works can also be found in the literature that solve the problem incorporating constraints on parameters $\boldsymbol{\theta}$ (1) [9].

To the best of our knowledge, there has been a significant gap between optimising irrigation water allocation and electricity generation. The existing approaches, which focuses primarily on electricity generation and profit maximisation, are limited in their capacity to make conscious, balanced decisions regarding water management for irrigation. This limitation poses risks to society as it does not account for the critical role that water plays in supporting agriculture and food security.

Expanding the NN framework to include the optimisation of irrigation water in the loss function is a crucial step towards addressing these limitations. This approach would enable more informed and responsible decision making in water resource management, allowing for a comprehensive assessment of trade-offs between electricity generation and the needs of agriculture, thus promoting a more sustainable and equitable allocation of this valuable resource.

## 3 The Proposal

In this section, we introduce the ACHPM framework as an innovative approach aimed at conscious and balanced hydropower plant management. The ACHPM framework seeks to address the limitations of existing software by integrating ethical considerations, promoting sustainability, and providing a more comprehensive model for managing water.

Additionally, we emphasise the importance of regulating and scrutinising these software solutions before they enter the production stage. Such regulatory measures are essential to ensure that the software is not only effective but also ethical and transparent. By taking these steps, we can better tackle the challenges posed by climate change, which directly impact agriculture and food security. This approach reflects a commitment to responsible and sustainable management of our valuable water resources and their crucial role in addressing the pressing challenges of our time.

### 3.1 The Agriculture Conscious Hydropower Plant Management Framework

As discussed previously, existing hydropower management approaches predominantly prioritise maximising electricity production, offering no explicit incentives to allocate more water for irrigation, indirectly penalising such allocations. Given the current era marked by climate change, which alters the seasonality of ecosystems and introduces instability in rainfall patterns essential for crop growth, it has become increasingly clear that this management approach is inadequate and overly simplistic.

The existing state of management software in many hydropower plant management companies typically adheres to government-imposed minimum water guidelines. This rigid approach underscores the missed opportunity to intelligently allocate water for irrigation based on predictive models that account for the likelihood of dry or wet periods. The proposed ACHPM framework seeks to address this deficiency by advocating for an approach that not only maximises electricity production but also prioritises the provision of a stable source of irrigation for agriculture. By anticipating higher or lower irrigation needs and adjusting water allocation accordingly, this framework aims to establish a resilient water supply for agriculture, especially during drought periods that can lead to crop loss, food scarcity, rising food prices, and, ultimately, food poverty.

The ACHPM framework, Fig. 1, comprises an ensemble of NNs organised into three components with different goals:

(1) **Water inflow predictor:** A NN to forecast reservoir water inflow using historical data and climate patterns, enabling anticipation of water availability during dry and wet seasons. The information given by this NN forms the foundation for informed decision making in hydropower management;
(2) **Water manager for electricity generation:** A NN tasked with optimising the allocation of water for electricity generation. It takes into account the predictions of water inflows provided by the water inflow predictor NN, along with other input data such as electricity demand, turbine efficiency, operational constraints, among others;
(3) **Water manager for irrigation:** A NN dedicated to optimising the allocation of water for crop irrigation. It relies on the forecasts of water inflows made by the water inflow predictor NN, in addition to input data such as soil moisture levels, atmospheric conditions, and the water needs of the targeted crops. The objective here is to allocate water resources efficiently to support agricultural sustainability.

The training approach for the ensemble of neural networks in the ACHPM framework involves a two-stage process:

- *First Stage - water inflow predictor training:* In this initial stage, the focus is on optimising the water inflow predictor NN. This NN is trained using the loss function (2), that measures the error between the predicted and the ground-truth values, enabling the NN to learn a model that accurately captures the patterns of water inflows over time;
- *Second Stage - water manager for electricity generation and irrigation training:* The second stage is characterised by the joint training of the water manager for electricity generation and the water manager for irrigation NNs. Both of these NNs share a loss function $\text{Loss}_{\text{total}}$. Both NNs receive as input, the output of the water inflow predictor NN and specific input data for each NN. The two NNs must balance water resource allocation to minimise the shared loss function. It important to note that, in this stage, the reward is not solely based on electricity generation. Instead, it is extended to include the goal of securing sufficient irrigation water to meet demand over time. The shared loss function guides the training process by having the contributions of each NN ensuring maximisation of electricity generation, $\text{Loss}_2(\boldsymbol{\theta}_2)$, and clever water allocation for irrigation, $\text{Loss}_3(\boldsymbol{\theta}_3)$. $\boldsymbol{\theta}_2, \boldsymbol{\theta}_3$ are the parameters of the water manager for electricity generation and for irrigation NNs, respectively.

This two-stage training approach equips the ACHPM framework with the capacity to make informed and balanced decisions in hydropower management, considering both economic and agricultural objectives while predicting and adapting to changing environment conditions.

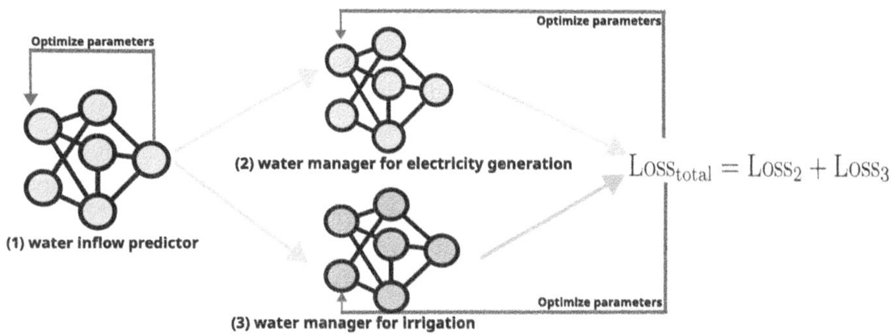


**Fig. 1.** The ACHPM framework training process.

It should be noted that, upon initial examination, it might appear that implementing such a framework would result in reduced water availability for electricity generation. However, the existing practice of maintaining minimum water guidelines allocations, even during wet periods, is often unnecessary and could be used more efficiently to benefit both agriculture and the profitability of hydropower companies.

One of the concerns associated with using NNs in hydropower management is the perception that the traditional training process resembles an unconstrained optimisation problem. Furthermore, the black-box nature of NNs can make it challenging to ensure that critical constraints, such as minimum water guidelines for ecosystem preservation, are consistently maintained. This is a significant issue as violating these constraints may pose a risk to natural life and lead to fines imposed by governments on management companies.

To address this challenge, we propose an approach in which the constraints are explicitly incorporated into the ACHPM framework. This can be achieved using established methods found in the literature that enable to solve a constrained optimisation problem during NN training. By explicitly integrating these constraints into the training process, we can ensure that the NNs are not only optimised for their primary objectives but also guarantee that the constraints are consistently satisfied [4].

### 3.2 Software Regulation

In addition to presenting the ACHPM framework, we strongly advocate for the implementation of regulations governing hydropower plant management software. The development of this framework has been influenced by the shortcomings of existing approaches in achieving a balance between electricity generation and the allocation of water for irrigation. Our advocacy centres on the need to reconsider the current reliance on minimum water guidelines for irrigation imposed by governments, as they often introduce inflexibility and may be exploited by companies, leading to suboptimal water allocation for agriculture.

We propose the adoption of regulations that mandate management software to prioritise conscious and adaptive water allocation for irrigation. This approach requires management software to respond to the actual needs of agriculture by successfully adjusting the allocation of water as conditions demand. In doing so, these software solutions can actively promote agricultural sustainability and contribute to a stable food supply, ensuring the well-being of populations. This shift in focus reflects a commitment to a more responsive and equitable approach to hydropower management in the face of changing environmental conditions and evolving societal needs.

To ensure the successful implementation of hydropower management software that prioritises conscious water allocation for irrigation and electricity generation, transparency and accountability are vital. We advocate regulating entities to promote:

- **Transparency:** It is imperative that the architectures and training procedures of the NNs used in these software solutions are transparent and well documented. This transparency allows for the validation of imposed requirements;
- **Evaluation:** The creation of robust evaluation metrics is essential for assessing the performance of the software in real-world scenarios. These metrics should measure the software's ability to predict drought periods and efficiently allocate water, penalising instances where the software pressures the irrigation system when it could have allocated more water for irrigation during unconstrained electricity generation periods;

- **Regular auditing and compliance checks:** Due to the high variability of atmospheric conditions due to climate change, to ensure that the management software continues to adhere to the requirements, regular auditing and compliance checks should be conducted. This prevents outdated software and helps holding management companies accountable for their software's performance.

These measures collectively contribute to the responsible and sustainable management of water resources, achieving the dual goals of efficient electricity production and robust support for agriculture, especially during critical periods such as droughts. This approach reflects a commitment to addressing the challenges of climate change while ensuring the availability of essential resources like a stable food supply.

## 4 Conclusion and Future Work

This work is a call for attention to the impact of current and future NN-based approaches for hydropower plant management software in agriculture. We highlighted the common goal of management companies to maximise the electricity generation while limiting the allocation of water to irrigation to the minimum guidelines issued by the government as to avoid fines.

The impact of climate change on water availability and agricultural sustainability requires a more sophisticated and adaptive approach to hydropower management. Such an approach should be based on broader social needs, including agriculture and food security. It is crucial to move beyond the naive optimisation of electricity production and embrace a more holistic and environmentally conscious strategy that recognises the intricate interplay between hydropower and agriculture in the face of climate variability.

To fix this issue, we proposed the ACHPM framework, designed to promote responsible software capable to balance water resource allocation. Thus, the proposed framework is an ensemble of three NNs working together. The first NN acts as a water inflow predictor, modelling the behaviour of the inflows over time giving the ability of predicting dry and wet periods. The second and third NNs are trained jointly using a shared loss function in which one dedicated to managing water for electricity generation and the other for irrigation. The shared loss function must be chosen so that the models balance the allocation of water resources. Given the inherent black-box nature of NNs and their limitations in guaranteeing constraint satisfaction, such as the minimum water guideline for ecosystem preservation, we suggest using an approach that explicitly introduces constraints during NN training.

Furthermore, this work underscores the need for regulations governing hydropower management software, including evaluation and certification processes by regulatory entities prior to production. It emphasises the importance of transparency in model architectures and training procedures to ensure that software objectives align with societal needs rather than just profit maximisation. Creating evaluation metrics to assess the software's ability to balance water allocation and conducting regular auditing and compliance checks are also crucial steps in promoting responsible management.

As future work, we encourage the practical application of the ACHPM framework to real data and performance analysis to refine and enhance the framework's effectiveness. In addition, the development of shared loss functions that further promote balanced water usage and the establishment of comprehensive evaluation metrics remain open challenges to ensure the robustness of such systems in addressing the complex interplay of electricity generation and agriculture sustainability.

**Acknowledgments.** The authors acknowledge the funding by Fundação para a Ciência e Tecnologia (Portuguese Foundation for Science and Technology) through CMAT projects UIDB/00013/2020 and UIDP/00013/2020 and the funding by FCT and Google Cloud partnership through projects CPCA-IAC/AV/589164/2023 and CPCA-IAC/AF/589140/2023.

C. Coelho would like to thank FCT the funding through the scholarship with reference 2021.05201.BD. L.L. Ferrás would also like to thank the funding by FCT through the project 2022.06672.PTDC

## References

1. Abdulkadir, T., Sule, B., Salami, A.: Application of artificial neural network model to the management of hydropower reservoirs along river Niger, Nigeria. Ann. Fac. Eng. Hunedoara **10**(3), 419 (2012)
2. Barzola-Monteses, J., Gómez-Romero, J., Espinoza-Andaluz, M., Fajardo, W.: Hydropower production prediction using artificial neural networks: an Ecuadorian application case. Neural Comput. Appl. **34**(16), 13253–13266 (2022). https://doi.org/10.1007/s00521-021-06746-5
3. Bordin, C., Skjelbred, H.I., Kong, J., Yang, Z.: Machine learning for hydropower scheduling: state of the art and future research directions. Procedia Comput. Sci. **176**, 1659–1668 (2020). https://doi.org/10.1016/j.procs.2020.09.190
4. Coelho, C., Costa, M.F.P., Ferrás, L.L.: Prior knowledge meets neural ODEs: a two-stage training method for improved explainability. In: Proceedings of the International Conference on Learning Representations (2023)
5. Feng, Z.K., Niu, W.J., Zhou, J.Z., Cheng, C.T.: Multiobjective operation optimization of a cascaded hydropower system. J. Water Resour. Plan. Manag. **143**(10), 05017010 (2017). https://doi.org/10.1061/(ASCE)WR.1943-5452.0000824
6. Grygier, J., Stedinger, J.: Algorithms for optimizing hydropower system operation. Water Resour. Res. - Water Resour. **21**, 1–10 (1985). https://doi.org/10.1029/WR021i001p00001
7. Lin, Y., et al.: Revenue prediction for integrated renewable energy and energy storage system using machine learning techniques. J. Energy Storage **50** (2022). https://doi.org/10.1016/j.est.2022.104123
8. Schaffer, L.E., Adeva-Bustos, A., Bakken, T.H., Helseth, A., Korpas, M.: Modelling of environmental constraints for hydropower optimization problems – a review. In: 2020 17th International Conference on the European Energy Market (EEM),

pp. 1–7. IEEE, Stockholm, Sweden (2020). https://doi.org/10.1109/EEM49802.2020.9221918
9. Shaw, A.R., Smith Sawyer, H., LeBoeuf, E.J., McDonald, M.P., Hadjerioua, B.: Hydropower optimization using artificial neural network surrogate models of a high-fidelity hydrodynamics and water quality model. Water Resour. Res. **53**(11), 9444–9461 (2017). https://doi.org/10.1002/2017WR021039
10. Tilmant, A., Goor, Q., Pinte, D.: Agricultural-to-hydropower water transfers: sharing water and benefits in hydropower-irrigation systems. Hydrol. Earth Syst. Sci. **13**(7), 1091–1101 (2009). https://doi.org/10.5194/hess-13-1091-2009
11. Zhang, J., Cheng, C., Yu, S., Su, H.: Chance-constrained co-optimization for day-ahead generation and reserve scheduling of cascade hydropower–variable renewable energy hybrid systems. Appl. Energy **324**, 119732 (2022). https://doi.org/10.1016/j.apenergy.2022.119732

# Usability of Honeybee Algorithms in Practice. Towards Nature-Inspired Sustainable Development

Mieczysław L. Owoc(✉)

Department of Business Intelligence in Management, Wroclaw University of Economics and Business, Komandorska, Wroclaw, Poland
Mieczyslaw.Owoc@ue.wroc.pl

**Abstract.** Honeybee algorithms (HBAs), inspired by the collective intelligence of bee colonies, have garnered increasing attention for their potential to solve complex problems (especially focused on optimization aspects). This abstract delves into the practical usability of these algorithms, exploring their strengths and limitations in real-world applications, particularly within the context of sustainable development. Advantages of the approaches in problem solutions relate to efficiency (HBAs demonstrate impressive performance in finding optimal solutions, particularly for large-scale and dynamic problems), adaptability (their decentralized nature allows them to handle changes in the environment effectively, and sustainability (often require fewer resources compared to traditional optimization methods, contributing to a more sustainable approach). Some examples of implementation in sustainable development embrace resource optimization: which can optimize energy usage in buildings, transportation networks, and industrial processes, waste management: which can aid in designing efficient waste collection and recycling systems, and renewable energy integration: optimizing the placement and operation of renewable energy sources like solar panels and wind turbines.

The article, aimed at popularizing bee algorithms, presents issues related to their usefulness in the context of sustainable development. Previous research related to the essence and research directions of bee algorithms, the origins and basic assumptions of these algorithms qualified as collective intelligence, and actually relating to concepts of swarm algorithms known from nature. The main part concerns the application areas and types of tasks that can be supported by such approaches. We can observe the continuous development of the original concepts of the discussed algorithms, directions of further research will be included in the summary of the article.

**Keywords:** Honeybee algorithms · artificial bee colony algorithm · collective intelligence · swarm algorithms · sustainable development · complex problems · nature-inspired solutions


Published by Springer Nature Switzerland AG 2024
E. Mercier-Laurent et al. (Eds.): AI4KMES 2023, IFIP AICT 693, pp. 161–176, 2024.
https://doi.org/10.1007/978-3-031-61069-1_12

## 1 Introduction

The study of honeybee algorithms and their application in practice represents an intriguing convergence of biology-inspired computational techniques and sustainable development goals. This interdisciplinary research approach draws its genesis from the observation of honeybees' foraging behavior, translating these natural processes into algorithms that can solve complex human problems. This introduction aims to elucidate the origin, development, and significance of honeybee algorithms within the context of nature-inspired sustainable development. The inception of honeybee algorithms is deeply rooted in the field of biomimicry, where biological processes and systems observed in nature are emulated in solving human engineering and design challenges. Specifically, honeybee algorithms are inspired by the foraging behavior of honeybees, which exhibit an extraordinary ability to find the most efficient routes to flower patches and communicate this information to their hive-mates. This behavior, characterized by decentralized decision-making and remarkable efficiency, sparked interest among researchers to develop algorithms that mimic these traits for optimization problems. Early research into honeybee behavior provided insights into their decision-making processes, notably the "waggle dance," a form of communication that bees use to inform others in the hive of the location, distance, and quality of food sources. This discovery laid the groundwork for developing algorithms that could apply similar principles to optimize network routing, resource allocation, and other complex computational problems.

The importance of honeybee algorithms extends beyond their novelty; they represent a crucial tool in the pursuit of sustainable development. By harnessing the efficiency, adaptability, and decentralized decision-making processes observed in honeybees, these algorithms offer innovative solutions to problems in various domains, including agriculture, energy management, urban planning, and environmental conservation. Their application is particularly relevant in the context of sustainability, where the optimization of resources and minimization of waste are paramount.

In agriculture, for instance, honeybee algorithms have been used to optimize crop pollination strategies and irrigation systems, leading to better resource management and reduced environmental impact. In energy management, they contribute to the development of smart grids, optimizing energy distribution and reducing consumption. Urban planning also benefits from honeybee algorithms through the optimization of traffic flow and public transportation networks, reducing congestion and pollution.

The adoption of honeybee algorithms in practice is a testament to the growing recognition of nature-inspired solutions to human challenges. This approach not only emphasizes the efficiency and resilience of natural systems but also advocates for a symbiotic relationship between technological advancement and environmental stewardship. As research in this field progresses, the integration of honeybee algorithms into more aspects of human endeavor holds the potential to significantly contribute to sustainable development goals.

The exploration of honeybee algorithms is a vibrant example of how interdisciplinary research, bridging biology, computer science, and environmental science, can lead to innovative solutions that are both effective and sustainable. It underscores the importance of looking to nature for inspiration, leveraging the evolutionary-tested strategies of non-human actors like honeybees to address some of the most pressing challenges facing humanity today. As this research continues to evolve, it promises to offer new pathways towards achieving a balance between technological progress and the preservation of our planet's ecological balance.

## 2 Research Background and Methodology

Honeybee society seems to be very attractive subject of scientific research. In my opinion, the following areas can be defined as crucial topics of research honey colonies: interdisciplinary investigation of the survival of this society across millions of years, honeybee colonies and democracy, and key (in this research) implementation of honeybee algorithms.

The adoption of honeybee algorithms in various practical applications has marked a significant milestone in the quest for solutions inspired by nature, particularly in the pursuit of sustainable development. This literature review synthesizes insights from a selection of studies that have explored the usability of honeybee algorithms in practice, emphasizing their role in driving nature-inspired sustainable development. These studies collectively demonstrate the versatility, efficiency, and effectiveness of honeybee algorithms across different domains, from optimization tasks to solving complex computational problems.

Honeybee algorithms are inspired by the foraging behaviour of honeybees, particularly their methods of communication, such as the waggle dance, to inform the hive of promising flower patches. This behaviour has been abstracted into computational algorithms aimed at solving optimization problems. Duc Truong Pham and colleagues [2–4] were pioneers in modelling these behaviours into what is known as the Bees Algorithm, illustrating its potential in solving complex optimization problems by simulating the natural foraging patterns of bees.

The usability of honeybee algorithms extends across various fields, demonstrating their capacity to tackle multi-dimensional and complex optimization problems efficiently. For instance, Habib Shah et al. [1] applied a hybrid global crossover bees algorithm to solve Boolean function classification tasks, showcasing the algorithm's effectiveness in handling computational tasks with high precision. Similarly, Wenping Zou et al. [7] utilized the Artificial Bee Colony algorithm for solving multi-objective optimization problems, further emphasizing the algorithm's adaptability and efficiency in navigating complex problem spaces.

In the realm of data science and cloud computing, honeybee algorithms have shown significant promise in enhancing data clustering and task scheduling processes. Ajit Kumar et al. [5] provided a comprehensive review of Artificial Bee Colony algorithms and their applications to data clustering, highlighting the algorithm's ability to improve the accuracy and efficiency of clustering methods. Likewise, Medhat A. Tawfeek et al. [9] demonstrated the utility of these algorithms in cloud task scheduling, improving resource allocation and operational efficiency in cloud environments.

Beyond optimization and computational tasks, honeybee algorithms have also been instrumental in advancing swarm intelligence and multirobot coordination. Floriano De Rango and Mauro Tropea [8] explored multirobot coordination through bio-inspired strategies, including those inspired by honeybees, underlining the potential of these algorithms in facilitating efficient and autonomous multirobot systems. This area of research highlights the algorithms' relevance in robotics and autonomous systems, promoting collaboration and intelligence distribution among multiple agents.

The integration of honeybee algorithms into practical applications not only solves immediate technical challenges but also aligns with broader sustainability goals. By optimizing resource use, enhancing efficiency, and reducing waste, these algorithms contribute to sustainable practices across various sectors, including agriculture, energy management, and urban planning. The research surveyed, particularly by Kuldeep Kaswan [12] and others, underscores the potential of honeybee algorithms in driving innovations that harmonize technological advancement with environmental stewardship.

The literature on honeybee algorithms reveals a robust framework for solving complex problems through nature-inspired solutions. These algorithms' applications, ranging from optimization, data clustering, and task scheduling to swarm intelligence and multi-robot coordination, demonstrate their versatility and effectiveness. As research in this domain continues to evolve, honeybee algorithms stand out as a promising avenue for promoting sustainable development, embodying the principles of efficiency, adaptability, and minimal environmental impact that are crucial for the future of both technology and environmental conservation.

The research methodology employed across the studies on the usability of honeybee algorithms in practice, focusing on nature-inspired sustainable development, incorporates a variety of approaches, each tailored to the specific aspects of algorithm development, optimization, and application in solving real-world problems. This section outlines the methodologies used in the referenced sources, highlighting key approaches, experimental designs, and evaluation metrics that collectively contribute to the advancement of honeybee algorithm research.

So, the first approach is focused on algorithm development and enhancement which denotes analysis of hybrid global crossover HBAs and modelling and finding optimal or near-optimal solutions within a reasonable computational time (see: H. Shah et al. and Duc Truong Pan et al.)

The second direction refers to considering the implementation of the bee algorithms in solving specific problems like: data clustering and task scheduling connected with more globally interpreted multi-objective optimization. These research involve HBAs where defining problem, resource utilization and efficiency become crucial in methodology according to the proposals of Ajit Kumar et al. and Wenping Zou et al.)

The next orientation in research methodology relates to evaluation and comparative analysis. Studies of performance evaluation with setting up comparative experiments and assessing performance with applying swarm intelligence proposed by Dervis Karaboga and Bahriye Basturk with a separate investigation involving bio-inspired strategies performed by Floriano de Rango and Mauro Tropea.

The last significant approach in research methodology can be defined as cross-domain applications. Supporting technically advanced networks and promoting sustainable development based on HBAs are good examples of this approach offered by Yinggao Ye et al. and Kuldeep Kaswan.

Across the studies, the research methodologies share common elements of problem identification, algorithm adaptation or development, rigorous testing, and performance evaluation. These methodologies underscore the interdisciplinary nature of honeybee algorithm research, encompassing computer science, engineering, and environmental science.

## 3 Fundamentals of Honeybee Algorithms

Nature-inspired algorithms are a fascinating branch of computer science that draws inspiration from natural phenomena to solve complex problems. These algorithms mimic the behaviours and processes found in animals, plants, and ecosystems, offering unique approaches to optimization and problem-solving.

Among these nature-inspired solutions, the honeybee algorithm stands out as a prime example of swarm intelligence. This class of algorithms leverages the collective behaviour of groups, like ant colonies or bird flocks, to achieve complex tasks efficiently. The general taxonomy of nature-inspired algorithms is depicted in Fig. 1.

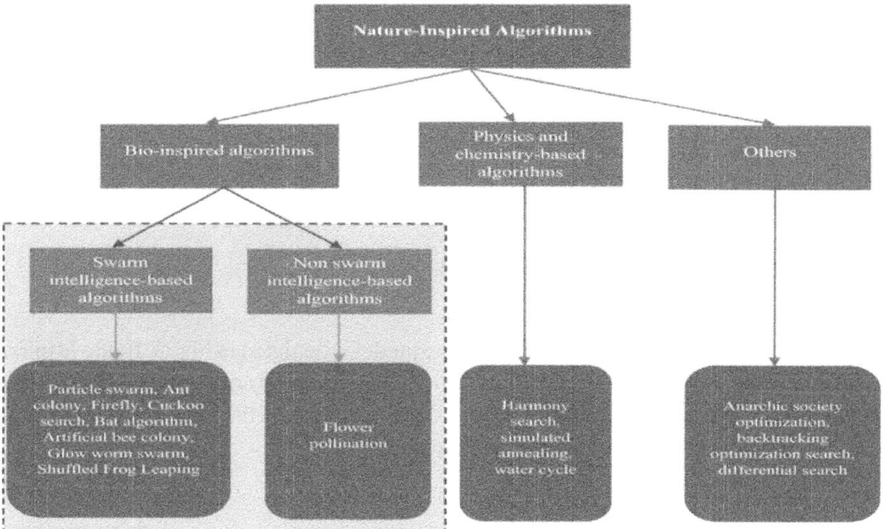


**Fig. 1.** Diversification of nature-inspired algorithms. Source: [14]

The main properties of swarm intelligence can be expressed as follows (compare [13]):

- decentralized and self-organized - what denotes no single leader or central control dictates the swarm's behaviour. Individuals react locally to their environment and each other, leading to emergent global behaviour,
- simple individuals, complex collective - with the ability that individual members of the swarm follow simple rules of behaviour. But through their interactions, the swarm as a whole can exhibit complex and intelligent behaviour,
- emergent intelligence - the collective intelligence of the swarm is greater than the sum of its parts. Complex solutions and adaptations arise from the interactions, not pre-programmed into each individual,

– adaptation and learning - swarms can adapt to changing environments and learn from experience. Individuals may adjust their behaviour based on past successes and failures, leading the swarm to collectively adapt over time.
– robustness and fault tolerance - if one individual fails, the swarm can usually continue functioning. This resilience makes them ideal for complex and dynamic environments.

These properties make swarm intelligence a powerful tool for solving complex problems in various fields, what is presented in Fig. 2.

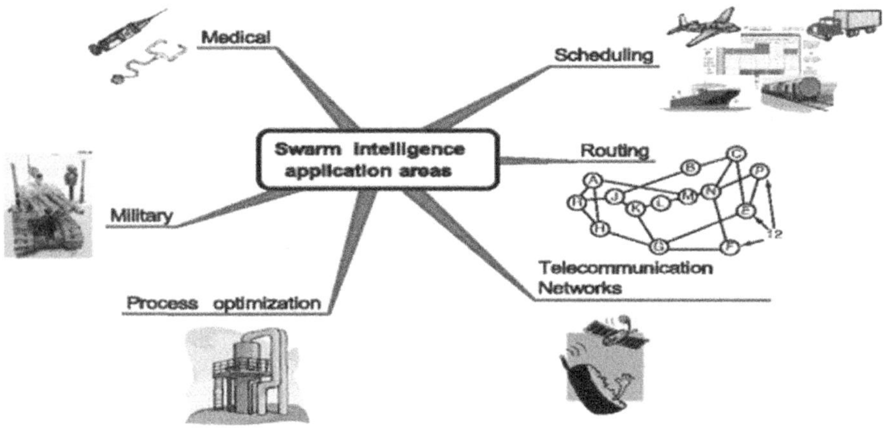


**Fig. 2.** Applications of swarm intelligence in various fields. Source [15]

The general idea of the swarm intelligence model is depicted in Fig. 3. Being inspired by nature, especially based on observation of functioning swarms (crucial importance plays earlier mentioned swarm properties), developers create the model which is tested and finally designed for the determined purposes.

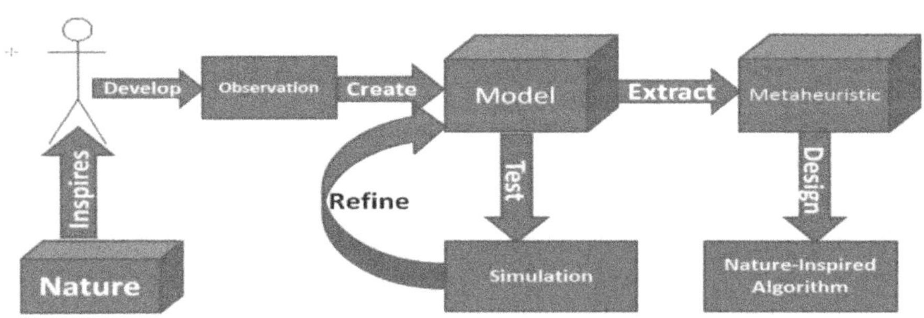


**Fig. 3.** Model of swarm intelligence. Source [13]

Let's consider an example of searching for forage are able to identify potential sources of nectar. The scouts looking for good sites prepare several alternatives and proclaim them to the colony. Communication in the colony is made using waggle dance informing about the power and distance to the site. After a short debate (having several alternatives) a group of workers following the most convincing scout fly to the chosen site. Concluding, the honeybee swarm becomes a cognitive entity (Fig. 4).

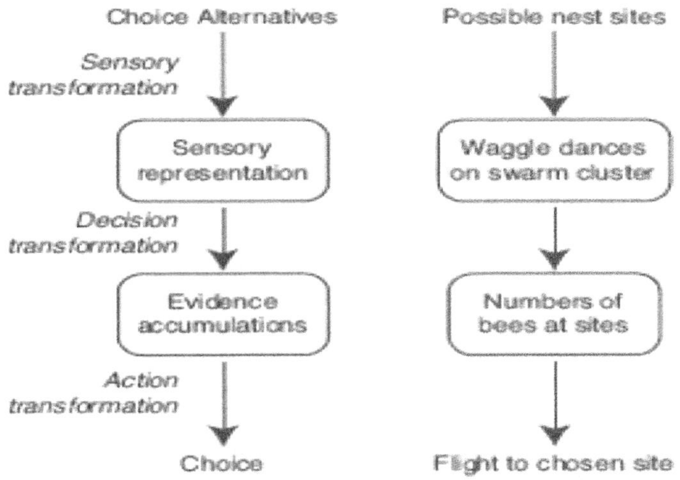


**Fig. 4.** Honeybee swarm as cognitive entity. Source: [16]

The very sensitive and essential step in the swarm intelligence entity is the decision making process. Contextual landscape of this step is demonstrated in Fig. 5.

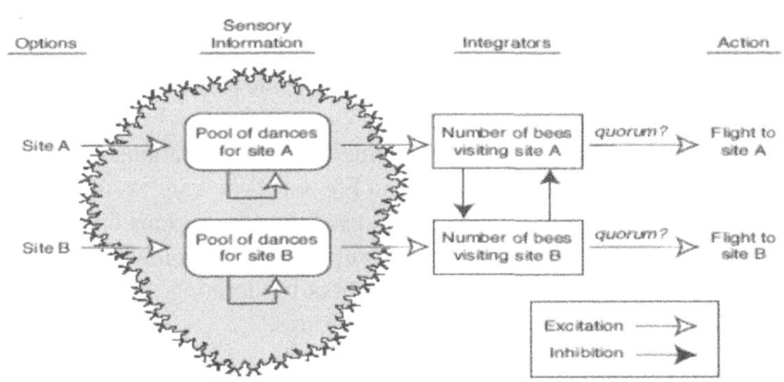


**Fig. 5.** Conceptual framework for decision making in honeybee swarm. Source [13]

The final decision of the honeybee swarm (marked as an Action) is preceded by an analysis of potential options (Site A and Site B, respectively), which, after a kind of debate and mutual "convincing", come down to choosing one of the sites. Symbolically, the final decisions are the result of mixed "Excitation" and "Inhibition" operations. Communication accompanying the debate takes place in the area marked "Sensory information" and takes the form of "dances" with the transfer of information regarding the parameters of the sources of nectar.

Described above concept of swarm intelligence was inspiration for invention of Artificial Intelligence Colony (ABC) algorithm proposed by Dervis Karaboga in 2005 (see [18]). The ABC algorithm is a swarm based meta-heuristic algorithm based on foraging behaviour of honeybee colonies. Three groups of honeybee workers play the dominant role in ABC algorithm: scouts, onlookers and employed bees. Below is a breakdown of how the three bee groups contribute.

***Employed Bees*** - represent solutions already found in the "colony's memory." Each employed bee is associated with a single food source (solution). They exploit their existing knowledge by locally modifying their food source (solution) using a random step in the solution space. The quality (fitness) of the modified solution is evaluated. If the new solution is better, it replaces the old one.

***Onlooker Bees*** - represent the "unemployed" bees waiting for promising leads. They observe the "dance" of employed bees, where the dance intensity reflects the quality of the food source (solution). Based on the dance and a probabilistic selection process, onlookers choose food sources (solutions) to explore further. They exploit the information from employed bees but introduce some exploration by modifying chosen solutions using smaller random steps. Similar to employed bees, the modified solutions are evaluated, and better ones replace the original ones.

***Scout Bees*** - play the crucial role of exploration and preventing the algorithm from getting stuck in local optima. When an employed bee fails to improve its food source (solution) for a certain number of iterations, it becomes a scout. Scout bees abandon their old food source and randomly search for a new one in the entire solution space.

This introduces diversification and helps the colony explore new areas of the search space, potentially leading to better solutions. The combined efforts of these three bee groups create a robust and efficient optimization process. Employed bees exploit existing knowledge, onlookers leverage the information shared by others, and scouts explore uncharted territory. This balance between exploitation and exploration allows the algorithm to converge towards optimal solutions while avoiding getting stuck in local traps.

The ideogram of the ABC algorithm, including basic operations that "imitate" the behavior of these three groups, is presented in Fig. 6.

Artificial Bee Colony (ABC) algorithm is used to solve various optimization problems in different areas. Figure 7 shows the operators, control parameters and usage areas of the ABC algorithm. The ABC algorithm works by iterating through the following phases with participations of earlier mentioned groups:

- **Initialization:** An initial population of food sources is generated.
- **Employed bee phase:** Each employed bee visits the food source that it was assigned to and evaluates its quality.
- **Onlooker bee phase:** Each onlooker bee chooses a food source to visit based on the information it receives from employed bees.
- **Scout bee phase:** If a food source is abandoned by its employed bee, a scout bee is generated to replace it.
- **Memorization phase:** The best food source found so far is memorized.
- **Termination:** The algorithm terminates when a stopping criterion is met.

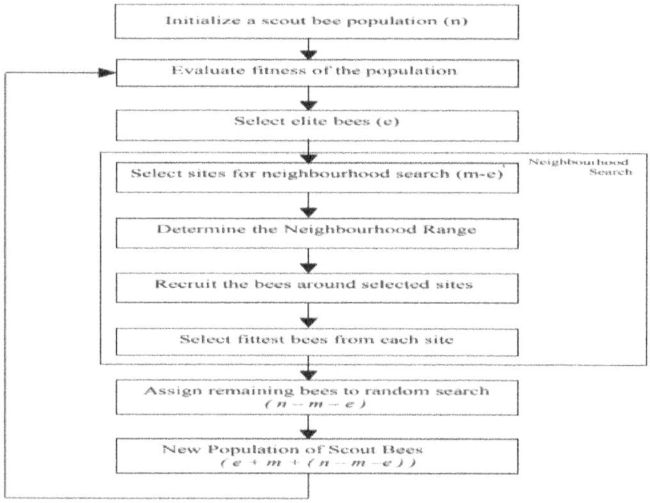


**Fig. 6.** Steps of Artificial Bee Colony Algorithm. Source [3]

The main assumptions of the ABC algorithm are: the problem being optimized can be represented as a continuous search space, the quality of a solution can be evaluated by a fitness function, and there is no limit to the number of food sources that can be explored. The ABC algorithm has been shown to be effective in solving a wide range of optimization problems, including: classification, segmentation, training NN and other problems with the similar assumptions.

The main strengths of the ABC algorithm are its simplicity, ease of implementation, and robustness. However, it can be slow to converge and may not be suitable for problems with a large number of dimensions.

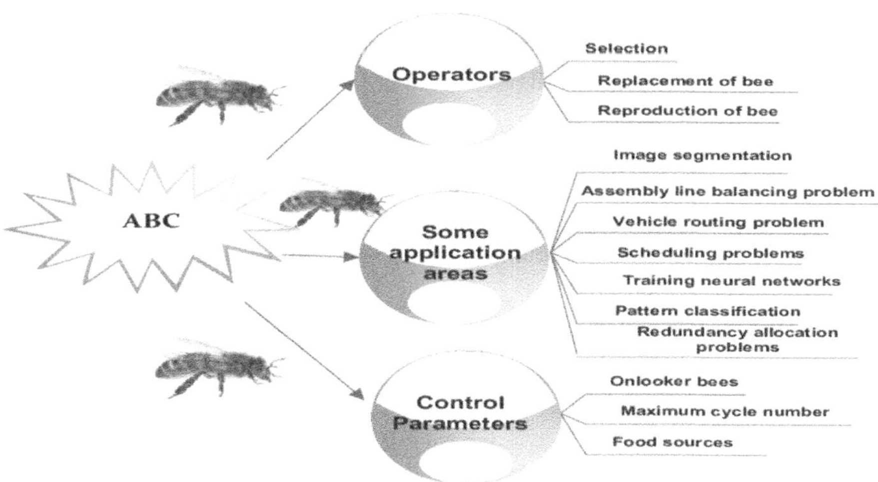


**Fig. 7.** An essence of Artificial Bee Colony Algorithm. Source [17]

## 4 Chosen Artificial Bee Colony Algorithms in Practice

There are several approaches presenting the usability of ABC algorithms in different areas and supporting variety tasks. This section contains an overview of the most valuable examples of the discussed algorithms confirming the effectiveness of this concept and ability to implement essential key characteristics of swarm intelligence: decentralization, self-organization, adaptability, scalability and robustness (compare [19]).

The first category of applications are demonstrated by G.M. Kakandikar in [20]. It is rather random itemizing of ABC algorithm applications stressing different directions of its implementation. It covers the following categories of tasks:

- **Benchmarking Optimization:** This could involve using ABC to find the best possible configuration for a benchmark function, or to compare the performance of different algorithms on a benchmark problem.
- **Bioinformatics application:** This could involve using ABC to solve problems in biology, such as protein folding or gene expression.
- **Scheduling Applications:** This could involve using ABC to schedule tasks or resources in a way that optimizes some objective, such as minimizing makespan or flow time.
- **Clustering and Mining Applications:** This could involve using ABC to group data into clusters or to find patterns in data.
- **Image processing Applications:** This could involve using ABC to improve the quality of images or to extract features from images.
- **Economic Dispatch Problems:** This could involve using ABC to find the optimal way to generate electricity, taking into account factors such as cost, efficiency, and reliability.
- **Engineering Designs and Applications:** This could involve using ABC to design structures or machines that are optimal for a particular purpose.

The list does not explicitly show the usability of ABC algorithms, but it does suggest that they are a versatile tool that can be used in a wide range of applications.

More detailed picture of ABC algorithms focused on implementation in electrical engineering can be depicted as follows (see [21]):

- **Power systems:** ABC algorithms have been successfully applied to solve various power system optimization problems, including:

  - **Distribution system loss minimization:** As mentioned in the figure, ABC can be used to find the optimal placement of sectionalizing switches to minimize power losses in distribution systems.
  - **Capacitor placement:** ABC can be used to find the optimal placement of capacitors in distribution systems to improve voltage profile and reduce power loss.
  - **Economic dispatch:** ABC can be used to find the optimal generation schedule for power plants that minimizes the total cost of generation while meeting system security and reliability constraints.

- **Power electronics:** ABC algorithms can be used to design and optimize power electronic circuits, such as:
  - **Parameter optimization of multi-pass milling process:** ABC can be used to find the optimal settings for the cutting speed, feed rate, and depth of cut in a multi-pass milling process to minimize machining time or cost while ensuring product quality.
  - **Parameter optimization of ultrasonic machining process:** ABC can be used to find the optimal settings for the amplitude, frequency, and power of the ultrasonic vibrations in an ultrasonic machining process to achieve the desired machining accuracy and surface finish.
- **Control systems:** ABC algorithms can be used to design and optimize control systems for various applications, such as:
  - **Modelling and optimization of process parameters of wire electrical discharge machining:** ABC can be used to find the optimal settings for the pulse current, pulse duration, and pulse interval in wire electrical discharge machining to achieve the desired machining accuracy and surface finish.
  - **Optimization of mechanical draft counter flow wet-cooling tower:** ABC can be used to find the optimal design parameters for a mechanical draft counter flow wet-cooling tower to maximize its cooling efficiency.

These are just a few examples of how ABC algorithms can be used in electrical engineering. In general, ABC algorithms are well-suited for solving optimization problems that are nonlinear, non-convex, and continuous. Overall, ABC algorithms are a versatile tool that can be used to solve a wide range of optimization problems in electrical engineering. However, it is important to note that they are not a one-size-fits-all solution, and other optimization algorithms may be more suitable for certain problems.

More general survey on implementation ABC algorithm was prepared by K. Kaswan and expressed in [12]. The research devoted to the implementation of the ABC algorithm encompasses its application across various domains as illustrated in the provided image. The ABC algorithm is central to the survey, branching out to various application fields like:

- Optimization Algorithm Development
- Constrained Problem Optimization
- Structural Optimization
- Cluster Analysis
- Parameter Estimation in Software Reliability Models
- Software Testing
- Advisory Systems
- Wireless Sensor Network
- Bioinformatics
- MR Brain Image Classification
- Face Poses Estimation

- General Assignment Problem
- Numerical Assignment Problem
- Multilevel Thresholding

Each application area is connected to the ABC algorithm, indicating that the ABC algorithm is utilized as a foundational tool to address optimization and search problems in these diverse fields. The applications leverage the algorithm's ability to mimic the foraging behaviour of honey bees to find efficient solutions.

Ajit Kumar's research [5] explores the use of Artificial Bee Colony algorithms for data clustering tasks. Below is a breakdown of their usability based on the findings.

Advantages of ABC for Data Clustering are:

- ***Addresses limitations of conventional methods:*** ABC avoids drawbacks like dependence on initial cluster selection and slow convergence, common in K-means and other conventional algorithms.
- ***Swarm intelligence*:** Mimicking bee foraging behaviour, ABC offers efficient exploration and exploitation of data, leading to potentially better quality clusters.
- ***Flexibility:*** The algorithm can be adapted to various clustering scenarios by modifying its parameters and incorporating domain knowledge.
- ***Parallelization:*** Its decentralized nature allows for parallelization, improving computation speed for large datasets.

Specific findings from Kumar's research relate to:

- ***Improved performance:*** studies show that ABC variants often outperform traditional algorithms in terms of cluster quality and convergence speed.
- ***Versatility:*** ABC has been successfully applied to diverse datasets and clustering tasks across various domains like image segmentation, gene expression analysis, and customer segmentation.
- ***Hybrid approaches*:** combining ABC with other techniques can further enhance its effectiveness, as seen in studies combining it with K-means or fuzzy clustering.

However, usability considerations also exist and embrace: parameter tuning (setting optimal parameters for ABC requires careful consideration and may vary depending on the data and problem), computational complexity (compared to simpler algorithms), ABC can be computationally more expensive, especially for large datasets, and limited theoretical understanding (while effective in practice, the theoretical underpinnings of ABC's success are still evolving).

Overall, based on Kumar's research and broader studies, ABC emerges as a promising and usable option for data clustering, offering advantages in terms of efficiency, flexibility, and adaptability. However, its usability is influenced by factors like parameter tuning, computational cost, and the specific clustering task.

It is also worth to stress many improvements of ABC algorithms – a list of new variants of solutions for Data Clustering problem is presented in Table 1.

Main trends of the proposal more advanced version of algorithms can be formulated in the following manner:

- ***Hybrid approaches (as above):*** integrating ABC with other techniques like fuzzy logic, crossover operators, and local search are popular for enhanced performance.

- ***Parameter adjustments:*** modifying existing parameters or introducing new ones (e.g., cognitive learning factor) are common to improve exploration/exploitation balance or adapt to specific problems.
- ***Bee phases:*** optimizing specific bee phases (employed, onlooker, scout) is explored, including eliminating certain phases (scout) or enhancing their roles (exploitation in onlooker, exploration in scout).
- ***Problem-specific adaptations:*** discrete versions for specific problems (e.g., flow shop scheduling) and interactive approaches tailored to user inputs are proposed.

**Table 1.** Variants of Solutions for Data Clustering

| Author | ABC Algorithm Modification |
|---|---|
| D. Karaboga | Implementing in fuzzy clustering for various tests performed in medical data |
| I. Fister | Formulating a new crossover operator and mutation techniques to enhance ABC performance |
| J.C. Bansal | Elaborating Memetic ABC: adding extra search phase and using neighbourhood aspects |
| S. Kumar | Introducing new parameters during local search phase |
| M. Koijima | Eliminating scout bee phase and improving employed and onlooker bees |
| I. Brajevic | Enhancing the exploitation in onlooker bees and exploration in scout bees |
| Q.K. Pan | Proposing discrete version of ABC to solve flow shop scheduling problems |
| P.W. Tsai | Proposing interactive ABC with applying of the law of universal gravitation in onlooker bees |
| J.C. Bansal | introducing a new control parameter: cognitive learning factor |
| D. Yazdani | Modifying the neighbour search process of employed and onlooker bees by use roulette wheel selection and a random number of dimensions in choosing targets |
| J.C. Bansal | Defining three modifications for optimization:<br>• Self-adaptive step size in employed bee phase,<br>• Updates in two components with modified step size in onlooker bee phase,<br>• Limit parameter based on fitness of solutions in scout bee phase |

Source: own elaboration based on [5]

The Artificial Bee Colony algorithm has potential to support actions identified with Sustainable Development due to its unique characteristics and adaptability. The following three quests can be formulated for conjunction ABC and sustainable development (compare: [12, 22–24]):

**1. Optimizing Resource Allocation and Planning**

- ***Sustainable energy management***: ABC can optimize energy distribution, renewable energy integration, and resource allocation in micro-grids, reducing environmental impact and promoting clean energy adoption.
- ***Waste management***: It can optimize waste collection routes, recycling processes, and resource recovery, minimizing waste generation and promoting circular economy principles.

- ***Sustainable agriculture*****:** ABC can optimize crop planting patterns, irrigation systems, and fertilizer usage, maximizing resource efficiency and crop yield while minimizing environmental damage.

2. **Analyzing and Modeling Complex Systems**

- **Climate change mitigation:** ABC can analyze and model climate change scenarios, helping identify optimal strategies for carbon emission reduction and adaptation measures.
- **Biodiversity conservation:** It can analyze complex ecological systems, optimize habitat management strategies, and support conservation efforts for endangered species.
- **Urban sustainability:** ABC can model urban systems, optimize traffic flow, build energy consumption, and waste management, leading to more sustainable and livable cities.

3. **Facilitating Decision-Making and Stakeholder Engagement**

- ***Multicriteria decision analysis*****:** ABC can handle problems with multiple conflicting objectives, helping decision-makers choose sustainable solutions that balance environmental, economic, and social considerations.
- ***Interactive ABC versions:*** These allow incorporating user preferences and feedback into the optimization process, promoting transparency and participation in sustainable development initiatives.

Main challenges relate to:

- ***Data availability and quality*****:** Sustainable development problems often involve complex and limited data, requiring careful data collection and pre-processing.
- ***Problem formulation:*** Accurately translating sustainability goals into quantifiable objectives suitable for ABC optimization is crucial.
- ***Computational complexity*****:** For large-scale problems, ABC's computational demands can be significant, requiring efficient implementations or parallelization techniques.

Overall, ABC has promising potential to support sustainable development actions by optimizing resource allocation, analyzing complex systems, and facilitating decision-making. However, addressing data challenges, problem formulation, and computational complexity is essential for its effective application. Specific examples of ABC applications in sustainable development are emerging, and further research is needed to evaluate their effectiveness and broader adoption. Combining ABC with other techniques like machine learning or agent-based modelling can enhance its capabilities for tackling complex sustainability challenges.

## 5 Conclusions and Future Research Directions

Honeybee algorithms offer a promising approach to sustainable development by providing efficient and adaptable solutions to complex problems. However, addressing their limitations and ensuring user-friendliness are crucial for wider adoption and maximizing their impact. This paper encourages further research and development to bridge the gap between theory and practice, enabling honeybee algorithms to contribute significantly to a more sustainable future. The following arguments support the continuation of research on the use of ABC algorithms in various areas.

- Following nature swarm intelligence and particularly Bee algorithms were the inspiration for inventors of new solutions in various areas.
- From the very beginning ABC algorithms provided very attractive alternatives for different complex tasks as the results of many advantages: simplicity, flexibility and robustness, ability to explore local solutions, easiness of implementation, and populations of solutions.
- Discovered limitations of Bee algorithms like: lack of use of secondary information, the requirement of new fitness tests on new algorithm parameters, and a high number of objective function parameters resulted in a big number of research leading to many extensions and variants of ABC solutions.
- Comparison to other swarm algorithms confirmed the usability of ABC algorithms in many areas and for different goals.

## References

1. Shah, H., Tairan, N., Mashwani, W.K., Al-Sewari, A.A., Jan, M.A., Badshah, G.: Hybrid global crossover bees algorithm for solving Boolean function classification task. In: Huang, D.-S., Hussain, A., Han, K., Gromiha, M.M. (eds.) ICIC 2017. LNCS (LNAI), vol. 10363, pp. 467–478. Springer, Cham (2017). https://doi.org/10.1007/978-3-319-63315-2_41
2. Pham, D.T., Castellani, M., Le-Thi, H.A.: The bees algorithm: modelling nature to solve complex optimisation problems. In: Proceedings of the 11th International Conference on Manufacturing Research (ICMR2013), 19th–20th September 2013, pp. 481–488. Cranfield University, UK (2013)
3. Pham, D.T., Chamran, A.G.S., Koç, E., Otri, S.: The Bee Algorithm A Novel Approach to Function OptimisationBees Algorithm. Cardiff University Technical Note: MEC 0501 (2005)
4. Yuce, B., Packianather, M.S., Mastrocinque, E., Pham, D.T., Lambiase, A.: Honey bees inspired optimization method: the bees algorithm. Insects **4**, 646–662 (2013). https://doi.org/10.3390/insects4040646
5. Kumar, A., Kumar, D., Jarial, S.K.: A review on artificial bee colony algorithms and their applications to data clustering. Cybernet. Inf. Technol. **17**(3), 3–28 (2017). https://doi.org/10.1515/cait-2017-0027
6. Witkowski, T.: Particle swarm optimization and discrete artificial bee colony algorithms for solving production scheduling problems. Tech. Sci. **22**(1), 61–74 (2019). ISSN:1505-4675
7. Zou, W., Zhu, Y., Chen, H., Zhang, B.: Solving multiobjective optimization problems using artificial bee colony algorithm. Hindawi Publ. Corp. Discrete Dyn. Nat. Soc. **2011**, 569784 (2011). https://doi.org/10.1155/2011/569784
8. De Rango, F., Tropea, M.: Multirobot coordination through bio-inspired strategies. In: Nature-Inspired Computation and Swarm Intelligence (2020). https://doi.org/10.1016/C2019-0-00628-0
9. Tawfeek, M.A., El-Sisi, A., Keshk, A.E., Torkey, F.A.: Artificial bee colony algorithm for cloud task scheduling. Int. J. Comput. Inf. (2015). https://doi.org/10.21608/ijci.2015.33956
10. Yue, Y., Li, J., Fan, H., Qin, Q.: Optimization-based artificial bee colony algorithm for data collection in large-scale mobile wireless sensor networks. Hindawi Publ. Corp. J. Sens. **2016**, 7057490 (2016). https://doi.org/10.1155/2016/7057490

11. Karaboga, D., Basturk, B.: A powerful and efficient algorithm for numerical function optimization: artificial bee colony (ABC) algorithm. J. Glob. Optim. **39**, 459–471 (2007). https://doi.org/10.1007/s10898-007-9149-x
12. Kaswan, K.: Applications of artificial bee colony optimization technique survey. In: Conference: Proceedings of the 9th INDIACom; INDIACom-2015; IEEE Conference ID: 35071; 2015 2nd International Conference on Computing for Sustainable Global Development (2015)
13. Ahmed, H.R., Glasgow, J.I.: Swarm intelligence: concepts, models and application. In: Conference: Queen's University, School of Computing Technical Reports At: Kingston, Canada Volume: Technical Report 2012-585 (2012). https://doi.org/10.13140/2.1.1320.2568
14. Yadav, A., Vishwakarma, D.K.: A comparative study on bio-inspired algorithms for sentiment analysis. Clust. Comput. (2020). https://doi.org/10.1007/s10586-020-03062-w
15. Gunavathi, C., Premalatha, K.: A comparative analysis of swarm intelligence. Techniques for feature selection in cancer classification. Sci. World J. **713**, 12 (2014). https://www.hindawi.com/journals/tswj/2014/693831/
16. Seeley, T.D.: Honeybee Democracy. Princeton University Press (2010)
17. Chinnasamy, R., Kandasamy, G.: Investigation on bio-inspired population based metaheuristic algorithms for optimization problems in ad hoc networks. In: World Academy of Science, Engineering and Technology International Journal of Mathematical, Computational, Natural and Physical Engineering, vol. 9, no. 3 (2015)
18. Karaboga, D.: An idea based on honey bee swarm for numerical optimization. Technical Report-TR06, Erciyes University, Engineering Faculty, Computer Engineering Department (2005)
19. Swarm Intelligence: The Power of the Collective: Swarm Intelligence in AI. https://fastercapital.com/content/Swarm-Intelligence--The-Power-of-the-Collective--Swarm-Intelligence-in-AI.html#Key-Characteristics-of-Swarm-Intelligence
20. Kakandikar, G.K.: Artificial Bee Colony Algorithm. A seminar by Nayak V.R. https://www.academia.edu/35041742/_Artificial_Bee_Colony_Algorithm
21. Kakandikar, G.S.: Artificial Bee Colony Algorithm and Applications in Mechanical Engineering. A Seminar by Veve Abishek. https://www.slideshare.net/AbhishekNeve/application-of-abc-algorithm
22. Altin, C.: Artificial bee colony algorithm based very fast renewable energy system optimization tool design. In: 2023 27th International Conference Electronics, Palanga, pp. 1–6 (2023). https://doi.org/10.1109/IEEECONF58372.2023.10177657
23. Abu-Mouti, F.S., El-Hawary, M.E.: Optimal distributed generation allocation and sizing in distribution systems via artificial bee colony algorithm. IEEE Trans. Power Deliv. 26(4), 2090–2101 (2011). https://doi.org/10.1109/TPWRD.2011.2158246
24. Farooq, M.U., Salman, Q., Arshad, M., Khan, I., Akhtar, R., Kim, S.: An artificial bee colony algorithm based on a multi-objective framework for supplier integration. Appl. Sci. **9**, 588 (2019). https://doi.org/10.3390/app9030588

# Automatic Coral Morphotypes Detection with YOLO: A Deep Learning Approach for Efficient and Accurate Coral Reef Monitoring

Younes Ouassine[1(✉)], Jihad Zahir[1], Noël Conruyt[2], Mohsen Kayal[3,4,5], Philippe A. Martin[2], Eric Chenin[6], Lionel Bigot[2], and Regine Vignes Lebbe[7]

[1] Computer Science Department, LISI, Cadi Ayyad University, Marrakesh, Morocco
younes.ouaasine99@gmail.com, j.zahir@uca.ac.ma
[2] EA2525 LIM, I.T. Department, University of La Réunion, 97400 Saint-Denis, France
{noel.conruyt,philippe.martin,Lionel.Bigot}@univ-reunion.fr
[3] ENTROPIE, IRD, IFREMER, CNRS, Paris, France
mohsen.kayal@ird.fr
[4] University of La Reunion, University of New Caledonia, Noumea, New Caledonia
[5] Marine Science Institute, University of California, Santa Barbara, CA 93106, USA
[6] Institut de Recherche pour le Développement (IRD), Paris, France
eric.chenin@ird.fr
[7] Institut de Systématique, Evolution, Biodiversité (ISYEB), SU, MNHN, CNRS, EPHE, UA - CP 48, 57 Rue Cuvier, 75005 Paris, France
regine.vignes_lebbe@sorbonne-universite.fr

**Abstract.** Coral reefs harbor a large portion of marine biodiversity but are declining rapidly. Conservation efforts rely on monitoring coral abundance and composition as predominant indicators of ecosystem health and management success. However, manual monitoring of coral abundance proves arduous where artificial intelligence-based automatization can help improve efficiency and accuracy. This paper presents a methodology using YOLOv5-based deep learning for automatic detection of corals and classification by morphotype, representing an important step toward streamlining machine-assisted coral reef monitoring. The research addresses the escalating need for precise and timely ecosystem assessments amidst increasing ecological shifts of coral reefs. Using state-of-the-art object detection techniques, the study strives to streamline the detection and classification of diverse coral morphotypes, which is essential for understanding reef dynamics and assessing conservation efforts. To train and evaluate our system, we use a dataset consisting of 280 original underwater coral reef images. We increased the number of annotated images to 388 by manipulating images using data augmentation techniques, which can improve model performance by providing more diverse examples for training. Our system leverages the YOLOv5 algorithm's real-time object detection capabilities, enabling efficient and accurate coral detection. We used YOLOv5 to extract discriminating features from the annotated dataset, enabling the system to generalize, including previously unseen underwater images. The successful implementation of the automatic coral morphotypes detection system


Published by Springer Nature Switzerland AG 2024
E. Mercier-Laurent et al. (Eds.): AI4KMES 2023, IFIP AICT 693, pp. 177–188, 2024.
https://doi.org/10.1007/978-3-031-61069-1_13

with YOLOv5 on our original image dataset highlights the potential of advanced computer vision techniques for coral reef research and conservation.

**Keywords:** Machine Learning · Deep Learning · Underwater ecosystems · Corals · Object Detection · YOLOv5

## 1 Introduction

Coral reefs, intricate ecosystems teeming with life, thrive in warm, shallow waters and stand as vital contributors to marine biodiversity [1]. Comprising an assortment of coral species, they serve as the cornerstone of marine ecosystems, fostering an unparalleled diversity of fishes, invertebrates, and other marine organisms. These vibrant ecosystems are of immense ecological importance, providing critical habitats and nurseries for numerous marine species, supporting fisheries, and contributing significantly to global biodiversity. Moreover, coral reefs offer invaluable ecosystem services, including shoreline protection, nutrient recycling, and carbon sequestration. However, these ecosystems face unprecedented threats due to human-induced factors such as climate change, overfishing, pollution, and habitat destruction [2]. As a result, monitoring coral reefs is imperative to evaluate their health, track changes, and implement timely conservation measures [3, 4]. Continuous monitoring helps scientists, conservationists, and policymakers assess the impact of stressors, identify areas for intervention, and formulate strategies to preserve these invaluable ecosystems for future generations [5–7].

Manual coral monitoring confronts a myriad of challenges inherent to underwater observation. The logistical complexities of diving operations present hurdles in accessing remote or challenging reef locations, coupled with safety concerns and the need for specialized equipment [8]. Moreover, human subjectivity in data collection and interpretation introduces potential biases, impacting the consistency and reliability of observations. These traditional methods, inherently time-intensive and costly, demand extensive resources for meticulous measurements and documentation, limiting both the spatial coverage and frequency of monitoring efforts.

Deep learning, a subset of artificial intelligence, revolutionizes machine learning by enabling systems to glean intricate patterns from extensive datasets. This technology, primarily reliant on neural networks inspired by the human brain, plays a pivotal role in computer vision tasks, notably object detection [9]. Object detection involves the identification and precise localization of multiple objects within images or video frames. One prominent technique in this realm is the YOLO (You Only Look Once) algorithm, celebrated for its real-time processing capabilities, swiftly categorizing and pinpointing objects in a single pass. YOLO's unique strength lies in its holistic view of images during analysis, ensuring rapid and accurate identification of diverse objects [10].

The primary aim of this paper is to introduce and demonstrate the efficacy of using YOLOv5, an upgraded version of the YOLO (You Only Look Once) algorithm, for the automatic detection and classification of coral morphotypes in underwater imagery. The research endeavors to leverage the advanced capabilities of YOLOv5, known for its enhanced accuracy and speed, to streamline the process of identifying and categorizing various coral morphotypes present in complex underwater environments. By harnessing the power of deep learning and object detection techniques offered by YOLOv5, this study seeks to contribute a robust and efficient approach to coral reef monitoring and conservation efforts.

## 2 Related Works

The paper [11] focuses on the classification of bleached and unbleached corals using visual vocabulary, which is a combination of spatial, texture, and color features. The authors propose a methodology that involves feature extraction techniques and classifiers such as Support Vector Machine (SVM) with a linear kernel. The experimental results show that the bag of features (BoF) with a linear kernel of SVM classifier achieves the highest accuracy of 99.08% for binary classification and 98.11% for multi-class classification. The BoF approach also demonstrates high precision and recall. The paper compares the classification accuracy, specificity, and sensitivity of SVM kernels and deep convolutional neural networks. The results highlight the superiority of the BoF approach over other methods.

The authors in [12] Compares two supervised machine learning methods for detecting and recognizing coral reef fish in underwater videos. The authors present the Deep Learning method and the HOG + SVM method and evaluate their performance. The paper discusses the use of histograms of oriented gradients (HOG) for feature extraction and support vector machines (SVM) for classification in the HOG + SVM method. The Deep Learning method utilizes a deep neural network for both feature extraction and classification. The authors compare the F-measure of both methods on a dataset of underwater videos, for the HOG + SVM approach, the F-measure ranges from 0.28 to 0.49, while for the Deep Learning method, it ranges from 0.62 to 0.65.

The authors of [13] Introduces a new method for detecting and assessing the health of coral reefs using underwater images and videos. The researchers found that previous studies focused mainly on coral image classification and lacked coral health detection. To address this gap, they developed a hardware-based autonomous monitoring system for coral-reef health detection. The proposed method, called MAFFN-YOLOv5, consists of a backbone, neck, and head network architecture. The authors obtained 0.83 in the precision measure for a dataset of 3049 high-quality images.

This paper [14] presents an approach to coral reef monitoring using artificial intelligence. The authors use deep learning and image analysis techniques to detect and measure the presence of halos, which are indicators of key ecological processes in coral reef ecosystems. The approach involves the use of a high-performance GPU running a deep learning framework and integration into ArcGIS software for easy accessibility. The authors provide a detailed analysis of halos in space and time on a global scale, highlighting the unique nature of halos and their potential as indicators of ecosystem health. The approach and model developed in this study are made freely available, enabling other researchers and organizations to use them for coral reef conservation efforts. The article concludes by stressing the importance of understanding the mechanisms underlying the creation of halos and using them as indicators of ecological processes.

The paper [15] delves into the outcomes of the ImageCLEFcoral 2020 challenge, centered on automating coral reef image annotation. Utilizing SSD and Mask R-CNN, pre-trained on Pascal VOC 2007, the study aimed to detect and categorize diverse coral and marine organisms in images. Experimenting with offline and online data augmentations, the authors observed superior results with online augmentations, employing techniques like flipping, color filtering, blur, and random cropping. SSD notably outperformed Mask R-CNN in localization, boasting higher mean average precision (mAP), though both models surprisingly excelled more on the test set than the validation set, a puzzling outcome due to limited access to the test set. Analysis of average precision (AP) for specific classes showed varied performance; SSD excelled in classes like sponge barrel, while Mask R-CNN performed better in soft coral. Despite modest overall results, the authors suggest future enhancements like larger training sets and knowledge distillation techniques to bolster outcomes in automated detection. Metrics showcased SSD achieving a validation mAP of 14.94% and a test mAP of 49.0%, while Mask R-CNN achieved a validation mAP of 10.18% and a test mAP of 24.3%. Notably, the highest AP for Mask R-CNN was in Hard coral boulder at 25.76%, whereas SSD excelled in Sponge barrel at 62.17%.

## 3 Datasets

We used a dataset designed explicitly for morphotype detection, encompassing six distinct classes: "branched", "encrusting", "free-living", "massive", "sub-branched" and "tabular". This data set includes 388 underwater images meticulously selected for this very purpose. Within this collection, 280 images serve as originals, and 108 result from image treatments to increase the breadth and depth of the training data. The images were captured using underwater cameras during targeted research expeditions covering various coral reefs around Reunion Island and the Scattered Islands in the southwestern Indian Ocean. The images encompass a broad spectrum of coral reef health, diverse habitats, depths and lighting conditions, ensuring a comprehensive representation of underwater environments. The data set provides an extensive representation of different coral species, colony sizes and orientations, presenting an authentic and detailed description of the coral reef ecosystem (Fig. 1).

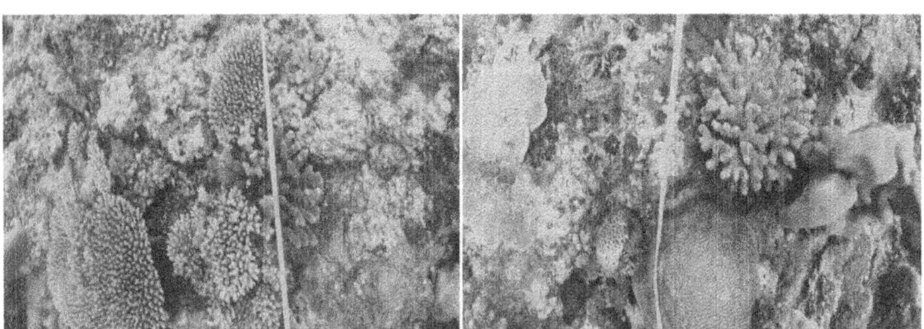

**Fig. 1.** Sample images from the dataset

For training and evaluating our automatic coral morphotypes detection system, we manually annotated the images using the Label Studio tool. The annotation process involved drawing bounding boxes around individual coral colonies and assigning them one of morphotype labels "branched", "encrusting", "free-living", "massive", "sub-branched" or "tabular". This annotation scheme simplifies the task by focusing on identifying coral colonies specifically, with a morphologic rather than taxonomic resolution.

**Fig. 2.** Sample annotated images from the dataset

The Fig. 3 depicts a histogram of the dataset labels. This visualization showcases the frequency of different coral morphology labels present within the dataset. The image on the right is a graphical representation of different bonding box sizes for morphotype annotations.

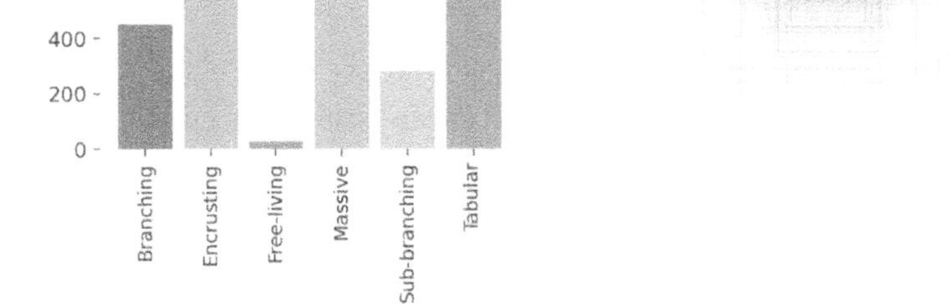


**Fig. 3.** Data set label details

*The entirety of our data is publicly available. Feel free to reach out to Younes Ouassine for further details or access.

## 4 YOLOv5

YOLOv5, like other neural networks designed for image processing, is built upon convolutional layers. The architecture of YOLOv5 can be divided into three distinct parts, as illustrated in Fig. 3. These parts can be considered as sets of layers that form functional units. Each part serves a specific role and is composed of modified versions of existing network components found in the literature. These modified layers were carefully selected and tailored to suit the requirements of YOLOv5's architecture.

- Backbone: The backbone is the initial part of the network responsible for optimizing the feature extraction process. It typically consists of a series of convolutional layers arranged in a hierarchical manner. These layers process the input image, extract low to high-level features, and enhance the gradient descent process, ultimately improving the network's ability to recognize objects efficiently. The efficiency of the backbone contributes significantly to achieving fast inference times, making YOLOv5 suitable for real-time applications.
- Neck: The neck component focuses on generating feature pyramids. Feature pyramids are multi-scale representations of features extracted from different levels of the backbone. These pyramids help in detecting objects of various sizes and scales by providing a hierarchical set of features. YOLOv5 employs PANet (Path Aggregation Network), a feature pyramid approach that allows for better feature representation and information exchange across different scales. This enhances the model's capability to generalize and detect objects robustly across diverse scales and sizes, thereby improving overall accuracy and performance.
- Head: The head is the final stage of the model responsible for generating output predictions. It takes the multi-scale features from the neck and produces bounding boxes, object probabilities, and class predictions. The head utilizes anchor boxes, predefined boxes of different aspect ratios and scales, as reference templates. These anchor boxes aid in accurately localizing objects within the input image and assigning class probabilities to the detected objects. The output vectors produced by the head contain information about the presence of objects, their classes, and precise bounding box coordinates (Fig. 4).

Note:

- The Cross Stage Partial Network (CSPNet) is an architecture designed to enhance information flow and gradient propagation in deep neural networks, specifically in convolutional neural networks (CNNs), for better performance in tasks like object detection and semantic segmentation.
- Spatial Pyramid Pooling (SPP) is a technique primarily used in convolutional neural networks (CNNs) for handling input images of varying sizes and aspect ratios. It enables the network to effectively process images of different dimensions by dividing the feature maps into a fixed number of levels and generating fixed-size representations regardless of the input size.

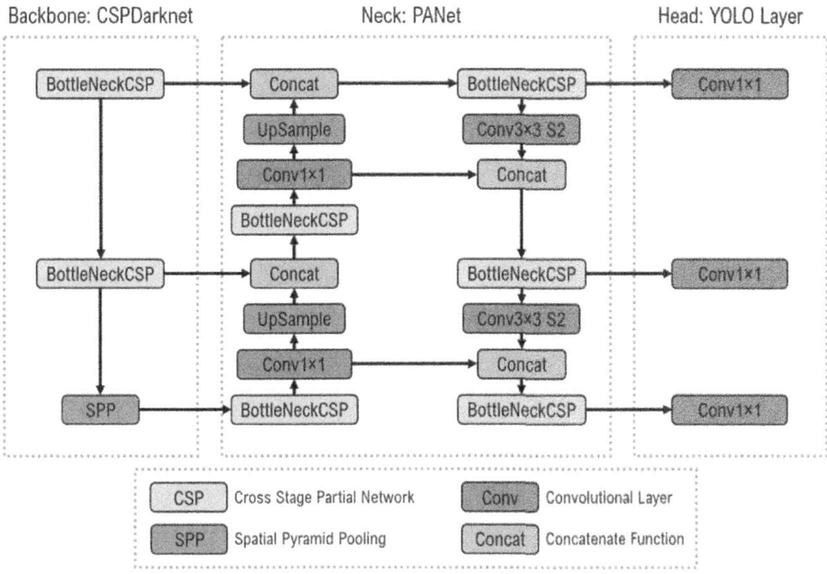


**Fig. 4.** YOLOv5 architecture

- A Conv1 × 1, often referred to as a pointwise convolution, is a type of operation in convolutional neural networks (CNNs) used for dimensionality reduction and feature transformation. Unlike traditional convolutions that involve larger filter sizes, a 1 × 1 convolutional layer employs a filter size of 1 × 1 pixels.
- Up sampling is a technique used in machine learning and deep learning, particularly in convolutional neural networks (CNNs) and image processing, to increase the spatial dimensions or resolution of an image. It's the opposite of down sampling or pooling, where the image's dimensions are reduced.

YOLOv5 is available in four primary versions, namely small (s), medium (m), large (l), and extra-large (x), each tailored to offer incremental improvements in accuracy rates. Alongside this enhancement in accuracy, each variant requires a different duration for training. These variations in model sizes cater to different needs and trade-offs.

Smaller versions tend to train faster but might sacrifice some accuracy compared to larger counterparts. On the other hand, larger versions often offer superior accuracy but might demand more computational resources and time for training due to their increased complexity. The choice among these versions typically depends on the specific requirements of the application, balancing the need for accuracy against the available computational resources and the desired speed of training (Fig. 5).

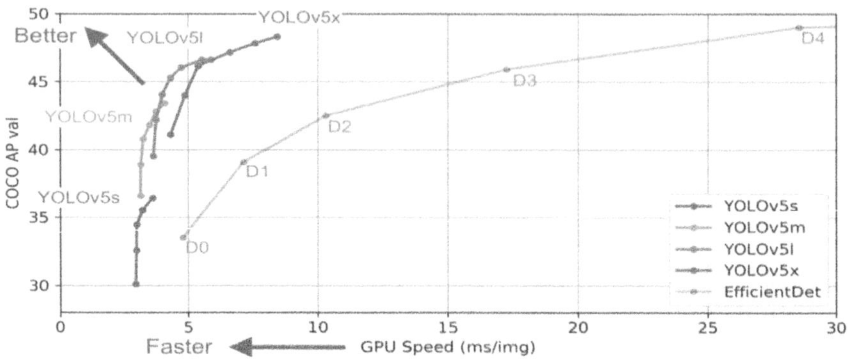


**Fig. 5.** YOLOv5 versions

# 5 Results and Analysis

The Table 1 presents a comparison of various models in the YOLOv5 family specifically designed for coral morphotypes detection tasks. Each model is evaluated based on its size, precision, recall, mean average precision, and inference time. Here is a description of each column:

**Table 1.** Comparison of YOLOv5 models for coral detection

| Model | Size | Precision | Recall | mean Average Precision | Inference time |
|---|---|---|---|---|---|
| Yolov5n | 3.9 MB | 72.7% | 62.1% | 68.3% | 50 ms |
| Yolov5s | 14.4 MB | 77.6% | 70.4% | 70.1% | 85 ms |
| Yolov5m | 42.2 MB | 81.5% | 68.3% | 70.1% | 180 ms |
| Yolov5l | 92.8 MB | 83.9% | 66.8% | 71.5% | 320 ms |

- Model: This column displays the different YOLOv5 models specifically tailored for coral morphotypes detection that are being compared.
- Size: This column indicates the file size of each YOLOv5 model, which represents the amount of storage required for the model.
- Precision: Precision measures the accuracy of the model's predictions for coral morphotypes detection. It calculates the ratio of true positive predictions to all positive predictions made by the model.
- Recall: Recall quantifies the ability of the model to correctly identify coral instances in the dataset. It represents the ratio of true positive predictions to all actual positive instances present.
- Mean Average Precision: mean Average Precision is a widely used metric in object detection tasks, including coral detection. It calculates the average precision across different levels of detection confidence thresholds. Higher values indicate better overall performance in terms of precision and recall.

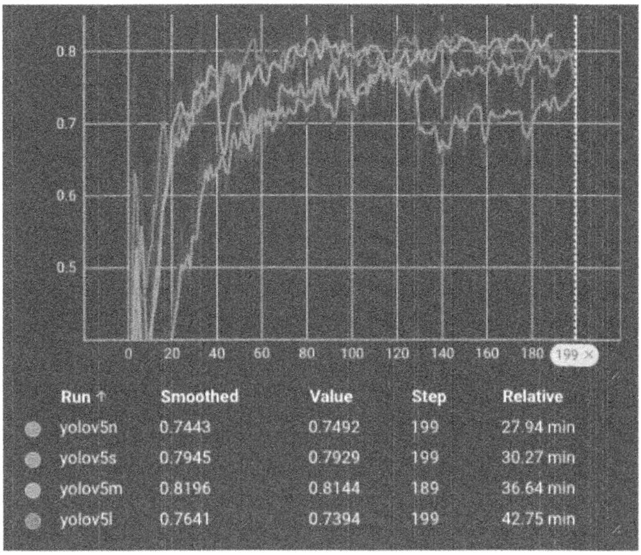


**Fig. 6.** Precision curves

- Inference Time: This column represents the time taken by each YOLOv5 model to process an input image and generate the corresponding coral detection results. It is measured in milliseconds (ms) (Figs. 6 and 7).

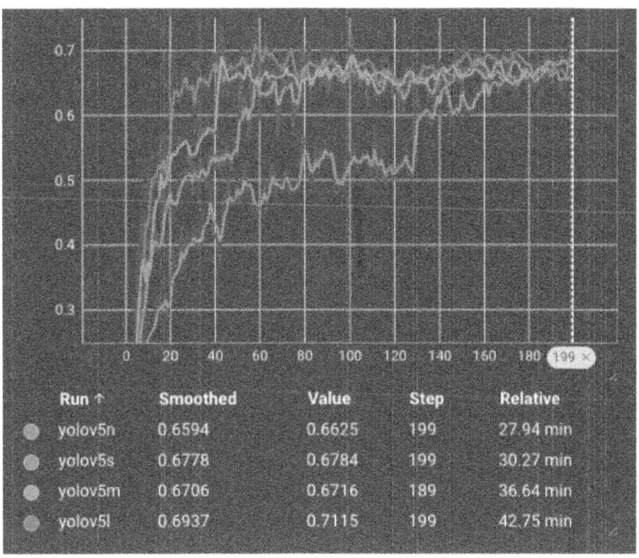


**Fig. 7.** Recall curves

## 6 Discussion

The performance evaluation of various YOLOv5 models reveals intriguing trade-offs between model size, inference speed, and object detection accuracy.

- **Accuracy vs. Model Size:** YOLOv5l outperforms other variants in precision, achieving an 83.9% precision rate, albeit with a larger model size of 92.8 MB. However, this increase in precision is not without compromise, as the recall rate diminishes slightly compared to smaller models.
- **Performance vs. Inference Time:** YOLOv5s demonstrates respectable accuracy, achieving a precision of 77.6% and recall of 70.4%, while maintaining a relatively lower model size of 14.4 MB. This model's inference time of 85 ms indicates its suitability for real-time applications where faster detections are imperative.

The choice of YOLOv5 model must align with the specific requirements of the application. For scenarios demanding high precision at the cost of larger model sizes and increased inference times, YOLOv5l could be the preferred choice. Conversely, for applications prioritizing real-time detection with acceptable accuracy, YOLOv5s stands out as a viable option.

In our study, when examining different YOLOv5 models, we discovered a variety of strengths in comparison to the MAFFN-YOLOv5 [13] approach for detecting coral reef health. These models display a spectrum of precision rates, with the YOLOv5l model standing out at 83.9%, similar to the 83.0% precision attained by MAFFN-YOLOv5. The YOLOv5 models in our analysis exhibit markedly superior accuracy rates compared to the SSD and Mask R-CNN models, showcasing accuracy values spanning from 72.7% to 83.9% across various model sizes. This signifies a significant leap in accuracy compared to the validation and test mAP values achieved by SSD and Mask R-CNN in the ImageCLEFcoral challenge [15].

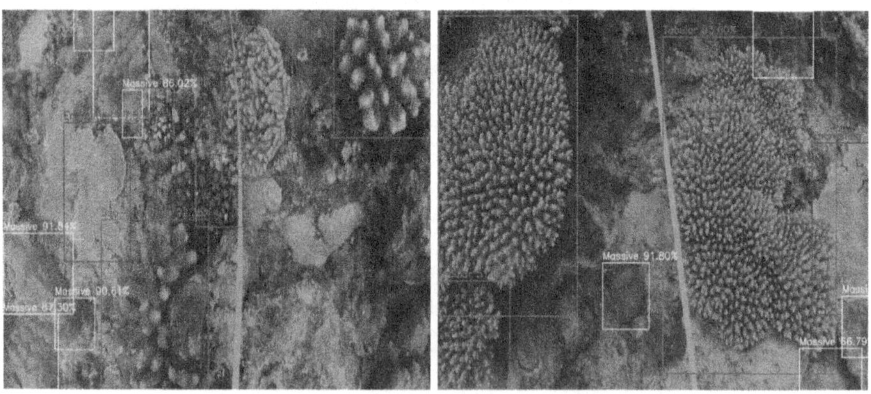


**Fig. 8.** Examples of coral morphotypes detection results

## 7 Conclusion

In this paper, we have presented an automatic coral morphotypes detection system using the You Only Look Once (YOLO) algorithm, a state-of-the-art deep learning approach for efficient and accurate object detection. Our proposed system addresses the need for scalable and accurate coral reef monitoring, a critical task for understanding and conserving these vulnerable ecosystems. Our approach is specifically tailored to handling difficult image data, including corals with various shapes and sizes, as well as images featuring an uneven distribution of corals.

While the use of our dataset comprising 388 manually annotated underwater images with precise bounding boxes has been beneficial for training and evaluating the automatic coral morphotypes detection system, it is important to acknowledge some limitations. Currently, our approach primarily focuses on images with a relatively low concentration of corals (but see Figs. 2 and 8). To improve the system's effectiveness in detecting corals in images with a high concentration of corals, future work involves annotating more images and data specifically targeting such scenarios. This expansion of annotated data will enhance the model's ability to accurately detect and analyze densely populated coral areas. By automating coral morphotype detection with YOLOv5, we provide a means to gather timely and accurate data, enabling a deeper understanding of coral reef dynamics and facilitating prompt actions in response to threats. This enhanced understanding allows developing targeted conservation strategies, allocate resources efficiently, and implement adaptive management practices.

Our research contributes to the broader field of computer vision and deep learning in marine biology and environmental sciences, fostering innovation and collaboration to tackle pressing sustainability challenges. By successfully applying YOLOv5 to coral morphotypes detection, we pave the way for scalable and cost-effective monitoring solutions, thereby supporting long-term coral reef resilience and biodiversity preservation.

## References


1. Fisher, R., et al.: Species richness on coral reefs and the pursuit of convergent global estimates. Curr. Biol. **25**(4) 500–505 (2015)
2. Hughes, T.P., et al.: Coral reefs in the anthropocene. Nature **546**(7656), 82–90 (2017)
3. Adjeroud, M., et al.: Recovery of coral assemblages despite acute and recurrent disturbances on a South Central Pacific reef. Sci. Rep. **8**(1), 9680 (2018)
4. Kayal, M., Mevrel, E., Ballard, J.: Coral demographic performances in New Caledonia, a video transect approach to operationalize imagery-based investigation of population and community dynamics. arXiv preprint bioRxiv: 2023-05 (2023)
5. Chabanet, P., et al.: Coral reef monitoring in the Iles Eparses, Mozambique Channel (2011–2013). Acta Oecol. **72**, 62–71 (2016)
6. Chabanet, P., et al.: Monitoring of coral reefs on contrasting sites (Mayotte and Iles Eparses) in the Mozambique Channel, Indian Ocean: application to management. In: WIOMSA 11th Scientific Symposium (2021)
7. Kayal, M., Adjeroud, M.: The war of corals: patterns, drivers and implications of changing coral competitive performances across reef environments. Roy. Soc. Open Sci. **9**(6), 220003 (2022)

8. Rogers, C.S., et al.: Coral Reef Monitoring Manual for the Caribbean and Western Atlantic. Virgin Islands National Park (1994)
9. LeCun, Y., Bengio, Y., Hinton, G.: Deep learning. Nature **521**(7553), 436–444 (2015)
10. Jiang, P., et al.: A review of yolo algorithm developments. Procedia Comput. Sci. **199**, 1066–1073 (2022)
11. Jamil, S., Rahman, M., Haider, A.: Bag of features (BoF) based deep learning framework for bleached corals detection. Big Data Cognit. Comput. **5**(4), 53 (2021)
12. Villon, S., et al.: Coral reef fish detection and recognition in underwater videos by supervised machine learning: comparison between deep learning and HOG+ SVM methods. In: International Conference on Advanced Concepts for Intelligent Vision Systems. Springer, Cham (2016)
13. Rajan, S.K.S., Damodaran, N.: MAFFN_YOLOv5: multi-scale attention feature fusion network on the YOLOv5 model for the health detection of coral-reefs using a built-in benchmark dataset. Analytics **2**(1), 77–104 (2023)
14. Franceschini, S., et al.: A deep learning model for measuring coral reef halos globally from multispectral satellite imagery. Remote Sens. Environ. **292**, 113584 (2023)
15. Gruber, I., Straka, J.: Automatic coral detection using neural networks. In: CEUR Workshop Proceedings (2020)

# Answering Key Questions About Air Pollution Dynamics in Ho Chi Minh City: A Spatiotemporal Analysis Using the XAI-SHAP Clustering Approach

Polat Goktas[1,2(✉)], Rajnish Rakholia[1,2], and Ricardo S. Carbajo[1,2]

[1] UCD School of Computer Science, University College Dublin, Belfield, Dublin, Ireland
{polat.goktas,rajnish.rakholia,ricardo.simoncarbajo}@ucd.ie
[2] CeADAR: Ireland's Centre for Applied Artificial Intelligence, Clonskeagh, Dublin, Ireland

**Abstract.** This study investigates the impact of various air pollutants in Ho Chi Minh City (HCMC), Vietnam, employing a supervised clustering approach that integrates Shapley Additive exPlanations (SHAP) values with a publicly available outdoor air quality dataset. The research focuses on identifying influential pollutant factors, affected city regions, their impact on surrounding areas, and the effectiveness of supervised clustering using SHAP values in pinpointing intersections between impacted stations. A feature set from Rakholia et al. (2023) is utilized in conjunction with tree-based machine learning models for each target time series. This approach provides insights into the contribution of different variables through the lens of eXplainable artificial intelligence (XAI)-SHAP methodology. The study also explores intersections between affected areas using the Uniform Manifold Approximation and Projection technique. Key findings indicate a pronounced influence of Nitrogen Dioxide ($NO_2$) and Temperature on morning air quality, largely attributed to traffic congestion. Conversely, Carbon Monoxide (CO) and Ozone ($O_3$) significantly affect the afternoon air quality, influenced by solar radiation and industrial activities. Spatial and temporal analysis of air pollution variables suggests that mapping interference between monitoring stations can enhance categorization accuracy in certain city's parts. This research provides valuable insights that can significantly benefit urban planning, time-sensitive policy development, and targeted intervention strategies. These findings are intended to support policymakers and stakeholders in addressing air pollution in HCMC more effectively.

**Keywords:** Air quality · Shapley Additive exPlanations (SHAP) · Spatiotemporal Analysis · Vietnam · XAI


Published by Springer Nature Switzerland AG 2024
E. Mercier-Laurent et al. (Eds.): AI4KMES 2023, IFIP AICT 693, pp. 189–203, 2024.
https://doi.org/10.1007/978-3-031-61069-1_14

## 1 Introduction

Air quality significantly influences human health and environmental ecosystems. In recent times, air pollution has emerged as a critical concern globally, posing serious health hazards such as an increase in heart disease, asthma, and lung cancer, and contributing to broader environmental issues like global warming, acid rain, and the depletion of the ozone layer [1–4]. These challenges are exacerbated by factors such as rapid urbanization, unregulated traffic, and industrial emissions [5]. According to the World Health Organization (WHO), an alarming majority of the global population, approximately 9 out of 10 people, reside in areas where air pollution levels surpass WHO's recommended limits [6]. A study has underscored the grave implications of outdoor air pollution, with a particular focus on Particulate Matter ($PM_{2.5}$), attributing it to millions of premature deaths across the globe each year [7].

Ho Chi Minh City (HCMC), Vietnam's largest city, faces major challenges with air pollution. Each year, the city registers more than 60,000 deaths attributable to diseases linked to this issue [8]. HCMC, known for its high population density, has experienced a rapid increase in $PM_{2.5}$ levels, which poses a significant health risk to its inhabitants. This matter is compounded by the city's economic growth and urbanization trends, with projections suggesting a 30% increase in $PM_{2.5}$ levels by 2030 [9].

The city's air quality is further compromised by pollutants like Nitrogen Dioxide ($NO_2$), Ozone ($O_3$), Sulfur Dioxide ($SO_2$), and Carbon Monoxide (CO), which frequently exceed WHO's safe limits, presenting serious risks to both human health and the environment [10, 11]. High concentrations of $NO_2$ and $SO_2$ adversely affect the human respiratory system, especially in children and the elderly [11]. Short $NO_2$ exposures can lead to asthma and hospital visits, while long-term exposure can cause respiratory infections. $NO_2$ creates acid rain [12], and $SO_2$ generates tiny particles [13], both harmful to human health and the environment. Higher $O_3$ concentrations impact children, the elderly, outdoor enthusiasts, and asthmatics, and are associated with various health issues such as inflammation, chronic lung damage, and breathing difficulties [14]. In addition, elevated CO levels reduce oxygen supply and affect critical organs like the brain and heart [15]. Thus, it is essential to comprehend how air pollutants behave and interact across city regions. This understanding helps mitigate their harmful effects and informs the public about periods of high-risk air pollution.

Given the complexity of air pollution dynamics, forecasting pollutant levels accurately presents a significant challenge. This is mainly because of the complex interactions between air pollutants and meteorological conditions, along with the non-linear and time-varying characteristics of the data. Traditional forecasting methods such as moving averages, exponential smoothing, and autoregressive models often fall short in accurately capturing these complex relationships [16, 17]. In response, artificial intelligence (AI)-based $PM_{2.5}$ models have demonstrated superior performance, particularly in handling nonlinearity and time-variant aspects of environmental data [5, 18].

However, the effectiveness of these models often varies based on factors such as geographic location, the spatiotemporal characteristics of the data, and prevailing weather conditions. Therefore, understanding the dynamics of air pollution and how different factors influence specific locations and times in the city is crucial. Gaining these insights can improve the accuracy of existing models when they are incorporated as input data.

In light of these challenges, our research introduces a unique approach using supervised clustering based on Shapley Additive exPlanations (SHAP) values, applied to a publicly available outdoor air quality dataset from HCMC. This methodology aims to go beyond traditional statistical analysis of air pollutants by identifying the specific factors that contribute to air pollution levels in different locations across the city. Our research primarily focuses on key aspects of air pollution in HCMC, including (1) identifying the key air pollutant factors and their dynamic combinations at different time intervals, (2) determining the stations or city regions most affected by these pollutants, (3) assessing the broader impact of escalated pollutant levels on other HCMC areas, and (4) evaluating the practicality and effectiveness of employing SHAP-based supervised clustering for identifying intersections among the affected stations.

In working towards these goals, our research focuses on exploring a number of key questions, all of which are essential for our analysis:

- Which air pollutant factors are most influential in HCMC, and how do their combinations change at different times?
- How can we effectively identify affected stations or regions in HCMC using a supervised clustering approach based on SHAP values?
- What is the impact of increased pollutant levels on other areas of HCMC, and how can this information be utilized to improve air quality management?
- Can the supervised clustering approach based on SHAP values be used to identify intersections between affected stations in HCMC, and how can this information be utilized for urban planning and policy formulation?

Through addressing these research questions, our study involves comprehensive experiments to validate the efficacy of our methodology and its capacity to deliver insightful observations on the spatial and temporal dynamics of air pollution in HCMC. This approach is pivotal in facilitating informed policymaking and fostering the development of targeted intervention techniques. Summarizing the primary contributions and implications of our research, the study is characterized by the adoption of a supervised clustering approach that integrates SHAP values with tree-based machine learning (ML) models. This methodology is specifically designed to dissect and understand the various air pollutant factors prevalent in HCMC. A significant aspect of our approach is the incorporation of a feature set as referenced by Rakholia et al. (2023), coupled with the application of eXplainable AI (XAI) via the SHAP framework. This combination not only allows for a deeper exploration of the roles played by different variables but also utilizes the Uniform Manifold Approximation and Projection (UMAP) technique for mapping the intersections between areas affected by air pollution. Overall, our research underlines the technical feasibility and practical benefits of using supervised clustering informed by SHAP values, aiming to enhance the understanding of air pollution's spatial and temporal dynamics in HCMC and thereby offering essential insights for strategic air quality management.

# 2 Related Work

## 2.1 Traditional Methods for Forecasting Air Quality

In the realm of air quality prediction, traditional forecasting methods such as the moving average and exponential smoothing have been prevalent. The moving average technique, which involves computing the average of data points within a specific time window, is noted for its pattern recognition and data smoothing capabilities but is less effective in capturing complex air quality changes [19]. Exponential smoothing improves upon this by assigning decreasing weights to past data points, enhancing responsiveness to recent changes. Although it can adapt to changes in the data more effectively than the moving average approach, it still has trouble capturing the complex relationships between variables [20]. Autoregressive models, employing linear regression to predict future values based on past data, can account for trends and seasonality but often struggle with the nonlinear relationships common in air pollution data [21].

Despite their widespread use, the complexity of air pollution data and the relationships between various influencing factors causes traditional forecasting methods to fall short in terms of prediction accuracy, incremental learning, and adaptability to new data [16, 17].

## 2.2 AI-Based Models for Forecasting Air Pollutants

In response to the limitations of traditional methods, AI-based techniques have emerged as a popular option for forecasting air quality. They are capable of modelling non-linear relationship and managing large dataset, making them better suited for air pollution prediction. The application of these methods across diverse locations, such as Beijing, Shanghai, Tehran, and HCMC, resulted in different prediction outcomes due to factors like spatiotemporal variability, meteorological conditions, and local pollution sources [22–30]. The following are some examples of AI-based models:

- *Random Forest*: This ensemble learning method uses multiple decision trees to improve prediction accuracy. Random Forest can handle non-linear relationships and complex interactions between factors, making them suitable for predicting air quality [24].
- *XGBoost*: An efficient gradient boosting approach that builds an ensemble of weak learners, typically decision trees, and combines them to make predictions. XGBoost is highly adaptable and can identify complex relationships between air pollutants and meteorological factors [30].
- *Neural Networks*: Multilayer Perceptron (MLP), Convolutional Neural Networks (CNN), and Long Short-Term Memory (LSTM) networks are only a few examples of neural networks that can describe complicated relationships between variables and adapt to new data. These networks have been utilized in numerous studies to forecast $PM_{2.5}$ values with high accuracy [23, 26, 29].
- *Hybrid and Multi-output Models*: A deep learning architecture for time series forecasting that consists of a stack of fully linked layers with backward and forward residual links. N-BEATS neural network-based architecture, designed for neural basis expansion analysis for interpretable time series forecasting, has been utilized to forecast

multiple air pollutants simultaneously. This approach consider temporal variations, meteorological circumstances, and interactions among pollutants for more accurate prediction [18, 23]. In addition, AI-based hourly $PM_{2.5}$ forecasting models were developed for predicting hourly $PM_{2.5}$ concentrations across six different locations in HCMC [5].

AI-based models have demonstrated their effectiveness in air quality forecasting by providing enhanced accuracy and adaptability compared to traditional approaches. They can handle complex relationships between variables and non-stationary data, producing more accurate and informative predictions [5, 31].

### 2.3 Interpreting Models with XAI – SHAP Approach

XAI has become essential in AI research, focusing on making ML models more transparent and interpretable [32]. Among the XAI techniques, the SHAP approach is a significant XAI technique that offers clear and understandable explanations of model predictions, providing model-agnostic explanations, local interpretability, and consistency [33, 34]. By employing SHAP to AI-based models, researchers and practitioners can gain valuable insights into the complex relationships between variables of the feature sets, thereby facilitating more informed decision-making processes.

### 2.4 SHAP Applications in Environmental Research

The SHAP technique has been used successfully in a variety of environmental studies where interpretability is critical for understanding the complex interactions between variables and producing practical conclusions. The following are some notable SHAP applications in environmental research:

- *$PM_{2.5}$ prediction:* Yan et al. (2021) used a spatial-temporal interpretable deep learning model, using SHAP to improve the interpretability and predictive accuracy of satellite-based $PM_{2.5}$ estimates [35].
- *Seasonal $PM_{2.5}$ concentration prediction:* Wu et al. (2022) used SHAP to provide interpretable ML models for the seasonal prediction of daily $PM_{2.5}$ concentrations in Beijing, China [36].
- *Air quality forecasting:* Lei et al. (2022) applied ML methods to forecast air quality in Macao, using SHAP to interpret the importance of different feature sets in their models [37].
- *Air pollution prediction:* Gu et al. (2022) developed a hybrid interpretable predictive ML model for air pollution prediction, using SHAP to enhance the model's transparency and interpretability [38].
- *$NO_2$ forecasting:* García and Aznarte (2020) applied SHAP to explain the importance of various factors in forecasting $NO_2$ concentrations, resulting in enhancing the interpretability of their model [39].
- *Respiratory disease prediction:* Ku et al. (2022) used SHAP to ML models for predicting the occurrence of respiratory diseases using climatic and air pollution factors, providing an depth-insights into the contribution of specific features to the predictions [40].

These applications demonstrate SHAP's effectiveness in providing deeper insights into environmental models, thereby aiding in more effective air quality management strategies.

# 3 Experiments

## 3.1 Dataset and Experimental Settings

For our evaluation, we utilized the HealthyAir dataset, a publicly available outdoor air quality dataset containing 52,549 records from the Air Quality Monitoring Network in HCMC, Vietnam. This dataset covers the period from mid–February 2021 to mid–June 2022 and includes data from six air pollution monitoring stations strategically located across HCMC to capture data from varied environments such as traffic, urban background, residential areas, industrial districts, and densely populated regions [41].

The dataset encompasses hourly concentrations of various air pollutants including particulate matter ($PM_{2.5}$), Total Suspended Particles (TSP), Sulfur Dioxide ($SO_2$), Ozone ($O_3$), Nitrogen Dioxide ($NO_2$) and Carbon Monoxide (CO) (measured in $\mu g/m^3$), as well as two meteorological parameters, namely Temperature (°C) and Humidity (%). The selected monitoring stations in HCMC for our study are:

- *Urban background*: Industry + Traffic + Residential – Vietnam National University in Ho Chi Minh City, Linh Trung Ward, Thu Duc City, HCMC (10.86994333, 106.7960143)
- *Residential* – 49 Thanh Da Street, Ward 27, Binh Thanh District, HCMC (10.81584553, 106.7174282)
- *Traffic* – 268 Nguyen Dinh Chieu Street, Ward 6, District 3, HCMC (10.77636612, 106.6878094)
- *Traffic + Residential* – MM18 Truong Son Street, Ward 14, District 10, HCMC (10.78047163, 106.6594579)

The dataset underwent preprocessing steps including the conversion of pollutant measurements from "ppm" and "ppb" to $\mu g/m^3$, transformation of data to an hourly format, and the treatment of negative values as missing data [5, 18].

For analyzing air quality dynamics at specific times, we categorized input variables for pairs of air pollutants and selected target time points as follows:

- $NO_2$: with CO, $O_3$, $SO_2$, Humidity, and Temperature.
- $O_3$: with $NO_2$, and Temperature.
- *Time points*: 7 AM, 9 AM, 1 PM, 5 PM, and 7 PM.

Taking into account the regular patterns of daily human activities and the common traffic congestion in HCMC, we have pinpointed specific times as key for analyzing the fluctuations in air quality during the day at various monitoring stations. These selected time points align with the city's peak traffic hours, encompassing the morning and evening rush hours, as well as the times of afternoon commutes. During these periods, factors contributing to air pollution, such as increased solar radiation, vehicle emissions, and heightened human activities, are typically more pronounced. By concentrating our analysis on these key time intervals, we aimed to deepen our understanding of how these variables collectively impact air quality in different areas of the city, thereby providing a more nuanced view of the environmental challenges faced by HCMC [42–44].

### 3.2 Constructing and Assessing ML Classification Models

In our experiments, we opted for cutting-edge tree-based ML techniques, including decision tree [45], random forest [46], gradient-boosting decision tree (GBDT) [47], histogram – based gradient – boosting classification tree (HistGBDT) [48], and light gradient – boosting machine (LightGBM, version 3.3.3) [49]. These methods were specifically chosen for their proven effectiveness in sophisticated classification tasks within the realm of environmental data analysis.

Our experimental setup involved several critical steps. Initially, we employed the '*train_test_split*' method to divide the dataset into distinct training and testing sets. This separation was done ensuring a 30% allocation for testing, with a set random state of 42 to facilitate reproducibility of results. To maintain a balanced representation of classes in both training and testing sets, stratification was applied, and this step was carried out using Python 3.9.1 with the *sklearn.model_selection* module from scikit-learn version 1.1.1.

For the classifiers, identifying optimal parameters and their values is crucial for model development. Due to the time complexity of various tree-based algorithms, we employed the random search algorithm for parameter tuning to find their optimal values. We experimented with different configurations, such as those for the Random Forest classifier, including setting 100 estimators, no maximum depth, a minimum sample split of 2, and using the '*Gini*' criterion, all with the same random state of 42. We conducted a thorough performance evaluation of these ML classifiers, using four key metrics: accuracy, precision, recall, and *F1* – score. This comprehensive approach allowed for a detailed assessment of each model's ability to classify accurately using the air quality data provided.

All experiments were conducted on a GPU server (2× NVIDIA Ampere A100 PCIe, 250 W, 40 GB Passive; 2× Intel Xeon Gold 6252 2.1G, 24C/48T, 10.4GT/s, 35.75 M Cache, Turbo, HT (150 W) DDR4-2933; 12× 32 GB RDIMM, 3200 MT/s, Dual Rank).

### 3.3 Evaluating Feature Significance

In our analysis, we evaluated the significance of different features in the ML models tailored for each target time series. This assessment was conducted using permutation feature importance scores within the optimal classifier framework. Permutation feature importance is a technique that gauges the impact on model performance when the values of a particular feature are shuffled randomly, thereby disrupting the original feature-target relationship [50]. However, this method may present certain limitations, such as susceptibility to multicollinearity and challenges in capturing complex interactions among features. To mitigate these issues and gain a more nuanced understanding of feature significance, we integrated the SHAP TreeExplainer (version 0.41.0), a tool designed for multi-classification tasks. This approach provided a balanced perspective on feature importance, weighing both model interpretability and computational efficiency [51].

### 3.4 SHAP-Based Dimensionality Reduction

Dimensionality reduction plays a key role in the development of ML models, as it aims to reduce computation and training times, thereby improving the model's efficiency. In our study, we also investigated the benefits of using SHAP values for dimensionality reduction. This method is especially effective in streamlining complex datasets while preserving crucial information. We conducted supervised clustering using mean SHAP values derived from the feature set for each target time series, as outlined in previous research [18]. By employing tree-based ML models, we classified target locations based on a carefully selected set of features, deliberately excluding $PM_{2.5}$ and TSP to focus on specific pollutants. Additionally, we utilized the UMAP technique, a powerful tool for visualizing high-dimensional data in a more comprehensible, low-dimensional space. This application of UMAP allowed us to visually explore and understand the relationships and intersections between various areas affected by different levels and types of air pollution, thus providing valuable insights into the spatial distribution of air quality factors [52].

## 4 Ablation Studies

### 4.1 Hourly Fluctuations of Air Pollutant Levels Across Different Monitoring Stations

We analyzed the performance of five tree-based ML models at four specific time times of day for predicting $O_3$ air pollution levels, using $NO_2$ and Temperature as input features (Table 1). These models are employed to classify monitoring stations into four categories: *Urban Background*, *Residential*, *Traffic*, and *Traffic plus Residential* categories. In the context of air pollution, failing to identify actual cases (false negatives) can lead to an underestimation of the impact of pollutants, potentially resulting in inadequate policy or intervention measures. Thus, recall is a particularly important metric in our study, ensuring the model's accuracy in identifying stations affected by air pollutants. The Random Forest model was most effective at most time points (7 AM, 1 PM, 5 PM, and 7 PM), while the LightGBM model performed best at 9 AM.

Additionally, we evaluated the performance of these models for $NO_2$ air pollution prediction, using CO, $O_3$, $SO_2$, Humidity, and Temperature as inputs at targeted time points (7 AM, 9 AM, 1 PM, and 5 PM), as outlined in [44]. Models like LightGBM, HistGBDT, and Random Forest consistently showed high performance across different times, particularly in recall, reducing false negatives. The Decision Tree model, however, yielded lower scores. Notably, all tree-based ML models performed well at 9 AM and 5 PM, with the Random Forest model excelling at both times in accuracy, precision, recall, and *F1*-scores. Therefore, the performance of all models was typically better at 5 PM compared to 9 AM, except for the HistGBDT model. These findings demonstrate the models' effectiveness in classifying monitoring stations based on the provided input variables and time points, effectively detecting areas heavily impacted by air pollution.

Overall, tree-based models seem to have better performance in predicting $NO_2$ levels as compared to $O_3$ concentrations, as evidenced by higher accuracy scores for the $NO_2$ scenario. For the $O_3$ predictions, the Random Forest model achieved the highest accuracy at four out of the five time points, while the LightGBM and HistGBDT were optimal at one time point each. In the $NO_2$ scenario, LightGBM had the highest accuracy in two time points, with Random Forest and HistGBDT each excelling at two different time points. Hence, among the models, Random Forest emerges as the top performer for $O_3$ predictions, while LightGBM and HistGBDT show consistent effectiveness for $NO_2$.

**Table 1.** Performance comparison of tree-based machine learning models in classifying *Urban background*, *Residential*, *Traffic*, and *Traffic plus Residential* monitoring stations for $O_3$ air pollution levels using $NO_2$ and Temperature as input features at targeted time points (7 AM, 9 AM, 1 PM, and 5 PM).

| | | *Percentage Split* | | | |
|---|---|---|---|---|---|
| *Time* | *Model* | *Accuracy* | *Precision* | *Recall* | *F1-score* |
| *07:00* | GBDT | 84.680 | 83.874 | 84.681 | 83.974 |
| | LightGBM | 84.681 | 83.981 | 84.681 | 84.082 |
| | HistGBDT | 84.255 | 83.413 | 84.255 | 83.529 |
| | Decision Tree | 84.255 | 83.518 | 84.255 | 83.642 |
| | Random Forest | 87.234 | 86.876 | 87.234 | 86.384 |
| *09:00* | GBDT | 68.421 | 67.785 | 68.421 | 66.871 |
| | LightGBM | 75.657 | 75.012 | 75.658 | 74.752 |
| | HistGBDT | 75.657 | 74.951 | 75.658 | 74.456 |
| | Decision Tree | 75.000 | 75.492 | 75.000 | 74.790 |
| | Random Forest | 75.000 | 74.196 | 75.000 | 73.361 |
| *13:00* | GBDT | 67.702 | 66.902 | 67.702 | 64.481 |
| | LightGBM | 69.565 | 71.188 | 69.565 | 67.699 |
| | HistGBDT | 69.565 | 71.298 | 69.565 | 67.207 |
| | Decision Tree | 67.702 | 66.564 | 67.702 | 66.405 |
| | Random Forest | 71.429 | 75.410 | 71.429 | 69.066 |
| *17:00* | GBDT | 75.839 | 76.790 | 75.839 | 74.416 |
| | LightGBM | 76.511 | 76.343 | 76.510 | 74.505 |
| | HistGBDT | 77.181 | 77.095 | 77.181 | 75.756 |
| | Decision Tree | 73.154 | 72.408 | 73.154 | 72.523 |
| | Random Forest | 79.865 | 81.502 | 79.866 | 78.426 |
| *19:00* | GBDT | 87.288 | 86.875 | 87.288 | 86.601 |
| | LightGBM | 85.169 | 83.102 | 85.169 | 83.058 |
| | HistGBDT | 84.322 | 82.007 | 84.322 | 82.421 |
| | Decision Tree | 82.203 | 80.543 | 82.203 | 81.178 |
| | Random Forest | 88.136 | 87.880 | 88.136 | 86.515 |

### 4.2 Assessing Critical Factors and Ranking Their Impact on Air Pollution Concentrations

We utilized model-agnostic permutation importance and feature importance ranking, based on the mean SHAP TreeExplainer values, to assess the significance of air pollutant concentration feature sets in our trained ML models at specific time points. In this context, SHAP values act as a latent representation of the air quality dataset, highlighting key factors for understanding spatial and temporal variations.

For example, we analyzed the global feature importance ranking from the Random Forest classifier for $O_3$ air pollution levels at 7 AM (Fig. 1A). This analysis shows that factors like Temperature has a greater impact than $NO_2$, as evident from the decrease in model performance when feature values are randomly permuted. However, due to limitations in permutation feature importance, such as multicollinearity and inability to assess interactions between factors, we explored the relative feature importance. This approach combines both global and local scores, utilizing SHAP explanations to offer a more detailed perspective on the relative importance for each area class assignment. Figure 1B displays the mean absolute SHAP values from $O_3$ levels with $NO_2$ and Temperature, indicating their average impact on model output magnitude. This reveals that $NO_2$ is a key predictor for Traffic monitoring stations, while Temperature is more indicative of Urban stations during morning commute.

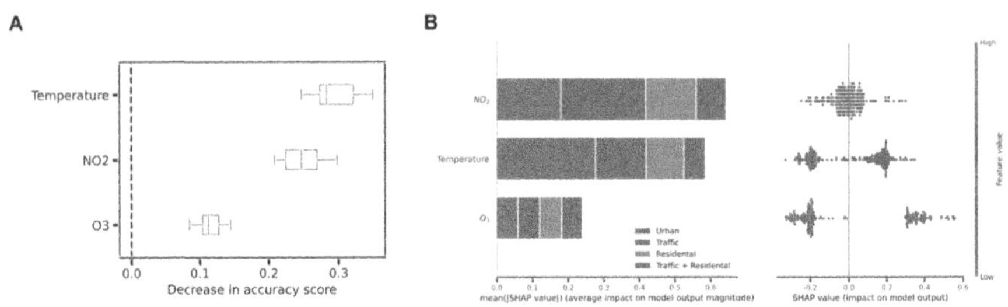


**Fig. 1.** Assessing $O_3$ air pollution features at the 7 AM with Random Forest classifier and SHAP explanations. (A) Permutation feature importance – Highlights key factors based on model performance reduction when features are shuffled. (B) *Left*: Global Feature Importance – Showcases overall significance of each feature via SHAP values. *Right*: Local Feature Influence – Details the impact and direction of each variable on individual pollution levels.

Additionally, we conducted a similar analysis for $NO_2$ air pollution levels at 5 PM using the Random Forest classifier (chosen for its optimal performance) to determine global feature importance (Fig. 2A) and relative importance using SHAP explanations (Fig. 2B). These results highlight the significance of factors like CO and Temperature in influencing air pollution levels.

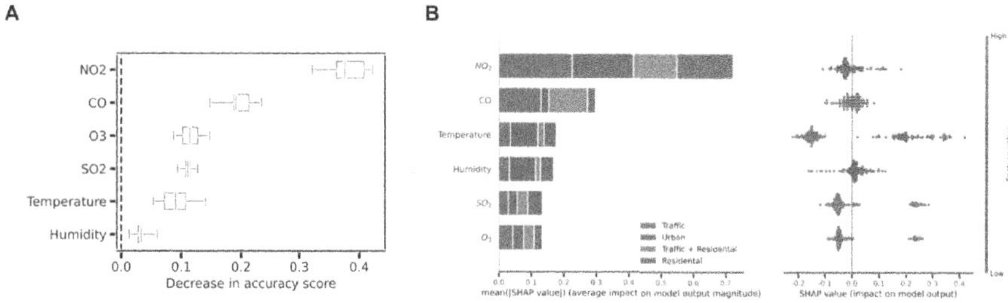


**Fig. 2.** Feature importance analysis for $NO_2$ levels at 5 PM with Random Forest and SHAP. (A) Permutation Importance – Identifies major factors affecting air pollution. (B) *Left*: Global Importance – Assessed through SHAP values, highlighting overall feature significance. *Right*: Local Importance – Provides insights into the impact of each variable on individual pollution levels.

## 4.3 Assessing the Viability of Supervised Clustering with SHAP Values

In our experiments, we faced challenges in distinguishing stations based on $NO_2$ air pollution levels at specific targeted time points when visualized in a two-dimensional space using UMAP (Fig. 3A). To address this issue, we adopted a supervised clustering approach, wherein we transformed raw data into SHAP values derived from tree-based machine learning models. This transformation helped enhance the characterization of

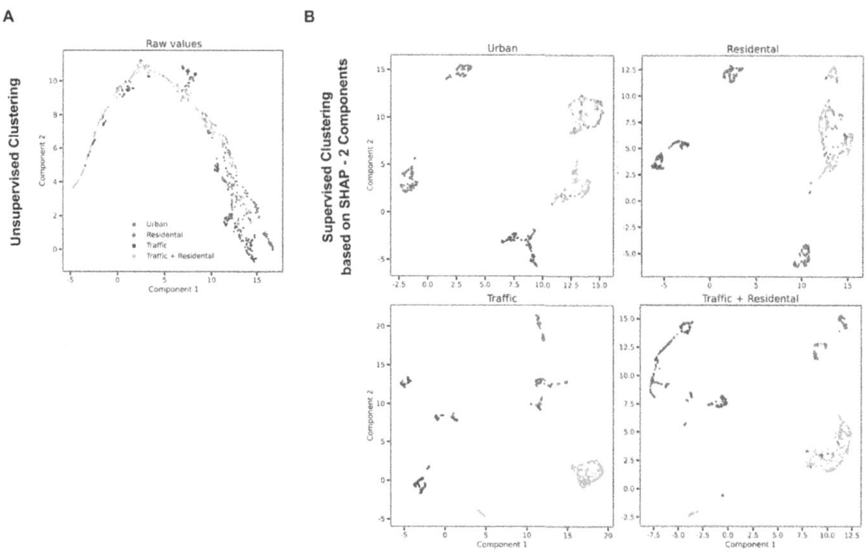


**Fig. 3.** UMAP visualization and SHAP-based supervised clustering of air quality monitoring stations for $NO_2$ air pollution levels at the 5 PM targeted time point. (A) Unsupervised UMAP projection of stations from the air quality dataset, illustrating the challenge of distinguishing stations based on raw data alone. (B) Application of a supervised clustering approach using SHAP values obtained from tree-based ML models, showcasing enhanced station characterization with respect to air pollutant attributes.

stations within the context of various air pollutants. Leveraging the XAI SHAP approach, we gained insights into the mechanisms underlying the contribution of these variables to specific area assignments. Furthermore, we examined the overlaps between affected areas through the application of the UMAP technique (Fig. 3B; right panels). Our investigation into the spatial and temporal dynamics of air pollution variables in HCMC suggests that using SHAP embedding plots for interference mapping between monitoring stations has the potential to improve classification accuracy in specific city regions. Additionally, we assessed the feasibility of supervised clustering for predicting $O_3$ air pollution levels at 7 AM targeted time point, as described in [44]. This analysis allowed us to observe how increased pollutant levels in our targeted classification area affected other regions.

## 5 Conclusion

In this study, we utilized a supervised clustering approach that relies on mean SHAP values to assess the influence of diverse air pollutant factors in HCMC, Vietnam. Our analysis incorporated a feature set sourced from Rakholia et al. (2023) within tree-based machine learning models and leveraged the XAI SHAP method in conjunction with the UMAP technique. This allowed us to gain insights into the contributions of variables and the intersections between affected areas. The benefits of our proposed methodology include:

- *Enhanced classification performance*: Improved accuracy and precision in categorizing air pollution levels.
- *Interpretability*: SHAP values enable a deeper understanding and explanation of model predictions.
- *Visualization*: The combination of SHAP and UMAP techniques provides an effective visualization of the relationships between variables and their impacts on air quality.
- *Adaptability*: The methodology can be readily applied to other datasets, locations, and environmental challenges.

However, there are certain limitations to our proposed approach:

- *Computational complexity*: Calculating SHAP values can be computationally intensive, particularly for large datasets and complex models.
- *Sensitivity to hyperparameters*: The performance of the methodology may be influenced by the choice of hyperparameters in the ML models and clustering techniques.
- *Inability to capture complex interactions*: The methodology may not fully capture complex interactions among air pollution factors, especially in the presence of multicollinearity.

Despite these limitations, our methodology holds the potential to offer valuable insights into the spatial and temporal dynamics of air pollution variables. Future research efforts should focus on addressing these limitations to enhance classification accuracy and interpretability of extensive air pollution datasets. This, in turn, can aid policymakers and other stakeholders in their endeavours to mitigate air pollution in HCMC.

**Acknowledgements.** This work is part of the MSCA Career-FIT PLUS fellowship, funded by the Enterprise Ireland and the European Commission (Fellowship Ref. Number: MF20200157). It has received funding from the European Union's Horizon 2020 Research and Innovation programme under the Marie Skodowska-Curie Grant Agreement. In addition, The HealthyAIR project had established air quality monitoring stations, funded by the Irish Research Council and the Department of Foreign Affairs in Ireland through the COALESCE programme (Better World Awards 2020). The project was a collaboration between CeADAR, Ireland's Centre for Applied Artificial Intelligence based in University College Dublin (UCD), Ireland, and Vietnam National University (VNU) in Ho Chi Minh City through the Institute for Environment and Resources and the School of Economics and Law.

## References

1. Mills, N.L., Donaldson, K., Hadoke, P.W., Boon, N.A., MacNee, W., Cassee, F.R., et al.: Adverse cardiovascular effects of air pollution. Nat. Clin. Pract. Cardiovasc. Med. **6**(1), 36–44 (2009)
2. Xing, Y.F., Xu, Y.H., Shi, M.H., Lian, Y.X.: The impact of $PM_{2.5}$ on the human respiratory system. J. Thorac. Dis. **8**(1), E69–E74 (2016)
3. Kurt, O.K., Zhang, J., Pinkerton, K.E.: Pulmonary health effects of air pollution. Curr. Opin. Pulm. Med. **22**(2), 138–143 (2016)
4. Mannucci, P.M., Franchini, M.: Health effects of ambient air pollution in developing countries. Int. J. Environ. Res. Publ. Health **14**(9), 1048 (2017)
5. Rakholia, R., Le, Q., Vu, K., Ho, B.Q., Carbajo, R.S.: AI-based air quality PM2.5 forecasting models for developing countries: a case study of Ho Chi Minh City, Vietnam. Urban Climate **46**, 101315 (2022)
6. Perez Velasco, R., Jarosinska, D.: Update of the WHO global air quality guidelines: systematic reviews - An introduction. Environ. Int. **170**, 107556 (2022)
7. Lelieveld, J., Evans, J.S., Fnais, M., Giannadaki, D., Pozzer, A.: The contribution of outdoor air pollution sources to premature mortality on a global scale. Nature **525**, 367–371 (2015)
8. WHO. >60,000 deaths in Vietnam each year linked to air pollution (2018). https://www.who.int/vietnam/news/detail/02-05-2018-more-than-60-000-deaths-in-viet-nam-each-year-linked-to-air-pollution
9. Amann, M., Klimont, Z., An Ha, T., Rafaj, P., Kiesewetter, G., Gomez Sanabria, A., et al.: Future air quality in Ha Noi and Northern Vietnam (2019)
10. Fan, P., Ouyang, Z., Nguyen, D.D., Nguyen, T.T.H., Park, H., Chen, J.: Urbanization, economic development, environmental and social changes in transitional economies: Vietnam after Doimoi. Landsc. Urban Plan. **187**, 145–155 (2019)
11. Manisalidis, I., Stavropoulou, E., Stavropoulos, A., Bezirtzoglou, E.: Environmental and health impacts of air pollution: a review. Front. Publ. Health **8**, 14 (2020)
12. EPA. Nitrogen Dioxide (NO2) Pollution (2022). https://www.epa.gov/no2-pollution/basic-information-about-no2
13. EPA. Sulfur Dioxide (SO2) Pollution (2022). https://www.epa.gov/so2-pollution/sulfur-dioxide-basics
14. Lee, Y.G., Lee, P.H., Choi, S.M., An, M.H., Jang, A.S.: Effects of air pollutants on airway diseases. Int. J. Environ. Res. Publ. Health **18**(18), 9905 (2021)
15. EPA. Carbon Monoxide (CO) Pollution in Outdoor Air (2022). https://www.epa.gov/co-pollution/basic-information-about-carbon-monoxide-co-outdoor-air-pollution

16. Kulkarni, G.E., Muley, A.A., Deshmukh, N.K., Bhalchandra, P.U.: Autoregressive integrated moving average time series model for forecasting air pollution in Nanded city, Maharashtra, India. Model. Earth Syst. Environ. **4**, 1435–1444 (2018)
17. Xu, Z., Dun, M., Wu, L.: Prediction of air quality based on hybrid grey double exponential smoothing model. Complexity **2020**, 1–13 (2020)
18. Rakholia, R., Le, Q., Ho, B.Q., Vu, K., Carbajo, R.S.: Multi-output machine learning model for regional air pollution forecasting in Ho Chi Minh City. Vietnam. Environ. Int. **173**, 107848 (2023)
19. Chatfield, C., Xing, H.: The Analysis of Time Series: An Introduction with R. CRC Press (2019)
20. Hyndman, R.J., Athanasopoulos, G.: Forecasting: Principles and Practice. OTexts (2018)
21. Box, G.E., Jenkins, G.M., Reinsel, G.C., Ljung, G.M.: Time Series Analysis: Forecasting and Control. Wiley (2015)
22. Minh, V.T.T., Tin, T.T., Hien, T.T.: PM2.5 forecast system by using machine learning and WRF model, a case study: Ho Chi Minh City, Vietnam. Aerosol. Air Qual. Res. **21**, 210108 (2021)
23. Pak, U., et al.: Deep learning-based PM2.5 prediction considering the spatiotemporal correlations: a case study of Beijing, China. Sci. Total Environ. **699**, 133561 (2020)
24. Zamani Joharestani, M., Cao, C., Ni, X., Bashir, B., Talebiesfandarani, S.: PM2.5 prediction based on random forest, XGBoost, and deep learning using multisource remote sensing data. Atmosphere **10**, 373 (2019)
25. Zhang, L., et al.: Trend analysis and forecast of PM2.5 in Fuzhou, China using the ARIMA model. Ecol. Indic. **95**, 702–710 (2018)
26. Karimian, H., et al.: Evaluation of different machine learning approaches to forecasting PM2.5 mass concentrations. Aerosol Air Qual. Res. **19**, 1400–1410 (2019)
27. Ma, J., Yu, Z., Qu, Y., Xu, J., Cao, Y.: Application of the XGBoost machine learning method in PM2.5 prediction: a case study of Shanghai. Aerosol Air Qual. Res. **20**, 128–138 (2020)
28. Xiao, F., Yang, M., Fan, H., Fan, G., Al-Qaness, M.A.: An improved deep learning model for predicting daily PM2.5 concentration. Sci Rep-Uk. **10**, 20988 (2020)
29. Li, T., Hua, M., Wu, X.: A hybrid CNN-LSTM model for forecasting particulate matter (PM2.5). IEEE Access **8**, 26933–26940 (2020)
30. Zhong, J., Zhang, X., Gui, K., Wang, Y., Che, H., Shen, X., et al.: Robust prediction of hourly PM2.5 from meteorological data using LightGBM. Natl. Sci. Rev. **8**, nwaa307 (2021)
31. Aydin, A.D., Cavdar, S.C.: Two different points of view through artificial intelligence and vector autoregressive models for ex post and ex ante forecasting. Comput. Intell. Neurosci. **2015**, 88 (2015)
32. Das, A., Rad, P.: Opportunities and challenges in explainable artificial intelligence (XAI): a survey. arXiv preprint arXiv:2006.11371 (2020)
33. Lundberg, S.M., Lee, S.I.: A unified approach to interpreting model predictions. Adv. Neur. In. **30** (2017)
34. Lundberg, S.M., Erion, G., Chen, H., DeGrave, A., Prutkin, J.M., Nair, B., et al.: From local explanations to global understanding with explainable AI for trees. Nat. Mach. Intell. **2**, 56–67 (2020)
35. Yan, X., Zang, Z., Jiang, Y., Shi, W., Guo, Y., Li, D., Zhao, C., Husi, L.: A spatial-temporal interpretable deep learning model for improving interpretability and predictive accuracy of satellite-based PM2.5. Environ. Pollut. **273**, 116459 (2021)
36. Wu, Y., Lin, S., Shi, K., Ye, Z., Fang, Y.: Seasonal prediction of daily PM2.5 concentrations with interpretable machine learning: a case study of Beijing, China. Environ. Sci. Pollut. Res. **29**, 45821–45836 (2022)
37. Lei, T.M., Siu, S.W., Monjardino, J., Mendes, L., Ferreira, F.: Using machine learning methods to forecast air quality: a case study in Macao. Atmosphere **13**, 1412 (2022)

38. Gu, Y., Li, B., Meng, Q.: Hybrid interpretable predictive machine learning model for air pollution prediction. Neurocomputing **468**, 123–136 (2022)
39. García, M.V., Aznarte, J.L.: Shapley additive explanations for $NO_2$ forecasting. Ecol. Inform. **56**, 101039 (2020)
40. Ku, Y., Kwon, S.B., Yoon, J.-H., Mun, S.-K., Chang, M.: Machine learning models for predicting the occurrence of respiratory diseases using climatic and air-pollution factors. Clin. Exp. Otorhinolaryngol. **15**, 168–176 (2022)
41. Rakholia, R., Le, Q., Vu, K.H.N., Ho, B.Q., Carbajo, R.S.: Outdoor air quality data for spatiotemporal analysis and air quality modelling in Ho Chi Minh City, Vietnam: a part of HealthyAir Project. Data Brief **46**, 108774 (2023)
42. Ho, B.Q., et al.: Study loading capacties of air pollutant emissions for developing countries: a case of Ho Chi Minh City. Vietnam. Sci Rep-Uk. **10**, 5827 (2020)
43. Zhang, K., Batterman, S.: Air pollution and health risks due to vehicle traffic. Sci. Total. Environ. **450**, 307–316 (2013)
44. Goktas, P., Rakholia, R., Carbajo, R.S.: Investigating air pollution dynamics in Ho Chi Minh City: a spatiotemporal study leveraging XAI-SHAP clustering methodology. In: Nowaczyk, S., et al. (eds.) ECAI 2023 International Workshops. CCIS, vol. 1948, pp. 201–207. Springer, Cham (2024). https://doi.org/10.1007/978-3-031-50485-3_20
45. Breiman, L., Friedman, J.H., Olshen, R.A., Stone, C.J.: Classification and Regression Trees (2017)
46. Breiman, L.: Random forests. Mach. Learn. **45**, 5–32 (2001)
47. Friedman, J.H.: Greedy function approximation: a gradient boosting machine. Ann. Stat. **29**(5), 1189–1232 (2001)
48. Scikit-learn. Histogram-based gradient boosting classification tree. https://scikit-learn.org/stable/modules/generated/sklearn.ensemble.HistGradientBoostingClassifier.html
49. Ke, G., et al.: Lightgbm: a highly efficient gradient boosting decision tree. Adv. Neural Inf. Process Syst. **30** (2017)
50. Molnar, C.: Interpretable machine learning: a guide for making black box models explainable. Lenpub (2020)
51. Lundberg, S.M., Lee, S.-I.: A unified approach to interpreting model predictions. Adv. Neural Inf. Process. Syst. **30** (2017)
52. McInnes, L., Healy, J., Melville, J.: UMAP: uniform manifold approximation and projection for dimension reduction. arXiv preprint arXiv:1802.03426 (2018)

# Crowdsourcing as a Tool for Smart City Within Sustainable Development

Lukasz Przysucha(✉) and Adam Sulich

Faculty of Business Management, Wroclaw University of Economics and Business, Komandorska 118/120, 53-345 Wroclaw, Poland
lukasz.przysucha@ue.wroc.pl

**Abstract.** Increasingly, more individuals are opting to reside in urban areas, a trend that is driving city administrators to develop innovative strategies for effective urban resource management. The Smart City (SC) concept, increasingly adopted in various global metropolises, significantly enhances residents' quality of life, safety, social participation, and operational efficiency of urban areas, aligning with the crucial paradigm of Sustainable Development (SD). A key initiative underpinning the SC model is crowdsourcing, a method whereby urban administrations gather knowledge and feedback from their citizens. This approach, increasingly focused on SD aspects, is gaining prominence due to the current climate challenges and rapid dynamics of urban development.

This paper presents findings from an examination of scientific literature indexed in the Scopus database, using keywords: 'crowdsourcing', 'smart cities', and 'sustainable development'. Employing Classical Literature Review (CLR) and Systematic Literature Review (SLR) methodologies, supplemented by bibliometric analysis with VOSviewer software, this study conducts an in-depth investigation of keywords and research themes closely linked to the development of crowdsourcing within the SC framework, specifically in the context of SD. The results are presented in the form of bibliometric maps and tables, highlighting identified keywords.

SCs integrate science and technology to enhance urban life, addressing contemporary challenges by transforming urban areas into intelligent, efficient, and sustainable spaces. Crowdsourcing plays a pivotal role in this transformation, enabling community involvement in urban planning and decision-making. This study on crowdsourcing as a tool for SC initiatives within SD reveals numerous practical and theoretical implications and opens avenues for future research.

**Keywords:** Crowdsourcing · Smart City · Sustainable Development

## 1 Introduction

Recent global trends indicate an accelerated migration from rural to urban areas, with projections suggesting that urban populations will constitute about 70% of the global population by 2050, a stark increase from 30% in 1950 [1, 2]. This demographic transformation has heightened interest in the Smart City (SC) concept, which emphasizes


Published by Springer Nature Switzerland AG 2024
E. Mercier-Laurent et al. (Eds.): AI4KMES 2023, IFIP AICT 693, pp. 204–219, 2024.
https://doi.org/10.1007/978-3-031-61069-1_15

the integration of science and technology to enhance accessibility and mobility in urban environments [3, 4]. SC is 'connecting the physical infrastructure, the IT infrastructure, the social infrastructure, and the business infrastructure to leverage the collective intelligence of the city' [5]. Other definition of SC is 'a city well performing in a forward-looking way in economy, people, governance, mobility, environment, and living, built on the smart combination of endowments and activities of self-decisive, independent and aware citizens' [6]. There are three main dimensions of a SC: technology, people, and institutions. These dimensions include the integration of infrastructures and technology-mediated services, social learning to strengthen human infrastructure, and governance aimed at institutional improvement and enhanced citizen engagement [7].

As technological advancements and urbanization progress, SCs are increasingly recognized for their transformative impact on living spaces and the interaction between individuals and their environment [8, 9]. The evolution of SCs as a fundamental aspect of modern urban life involves leveraging technology to boost efficiency, improve residents' quality of life, and pursue Sustainable Development (SD) [10, 11]. Addressing modern urbanism challenges [4], SC projects transform urban areas into intelligent, efficient [12], and sustainable spaces [13, 14], with crowdsourcing playing a pivotal role [15, 16]. This approach encompasses idea generation, data collection, and community involvement in decision-making processes, thereby facilitating a more inclusive and responsive urban development [17]. Crowdsourcing in this research is defined as dynamic and multifaceted phenomenon that emerged in 2006 [18], characterized by its ability to harness the collective intelligence, skills, and input of a wide audience or 'crowd' through digital platforms. It represents a strategic approach to solving problems, generating innovative ideas, or achieving specific tasks by tapping into the diverse potential of the crowd. This approach has found applications across various sectors including online banking, media, postal services, and higher education, demonstrating its versatility in creating value and uncovering new business opportunities. Crowdsourcing operates as a modern form of externalization, evolving into numerous forms such as crowdfunding and crowd control, and is utilized by organizations to access untapped resources, engage with communities, and foster collaborative development [18].

This paper aims to present the findings from an examination of scientific literature indexed in the Scopus database, employing the keywords: 'crowdsourcing', 'smart cities', and 'sustainable development'. Employing Classical Literature Review (CLR) and Systematic Literature Review (SLR) methodologies, supplemented by bibliometric analysis via VOSviewer software [19], this study offers a comprehensive examination of the development of crowdsourcing within the SC framework, particularly in the context of SD [11, 20].

The study helps to bridge existing knowledge gaps by scrutinizing the role of crowdsourcing within SCs to bolster urban SD. This involves exploring how crowdsourcing in SC initiatives not only facilitates data collection but also empowers residents to contribute to urban innovation and planning [21]. Such community engagement in data gathering, urban planning, strategy [22], and environmental monitoring enables SCs to align more closely with the genuine needs of their inhabitants, thereby positively influencing urban SD [14]. Crowdsourcing proves essential in driving SD, enabling community participation in decision-making, identifying environmental issues, and fostering innovative solutions. Crowdsourcing platforms empower community members to report pollution, oversee air quality, and propose upgrades to urban infrastructure, contributing to ecological balance [23]. Moreover, it enhances urban resource management, reducing greenhouse gas emissions and promoting sustainable mobility [14, 24]. Crowdsourcing also supports renewable energy development [25], identifying locations for wind farms or solar panels, thus expediting the transition to a more sustainable energy paradigm [26, 27].

This study follows a traditional structure. It begins with the Introduction section and is followed by the Materials and Methods section, which details the research procedures and their limitations. The Results section presents the data analyzed using SLR method. The study concludes with the Discussion and Conclusions sections, where CLR method was applied. These sections highlight the theoretical and practical managerial implications of the study, important for policy makers, business owners, researchers, and the general public. The final Conclusions section also explores potential avenues for future research.

## 2 Materials and Methods

The study adopts the SLR method with targeted queries (Table 1), utilizing the Scopus database to source scientific literature [19]. Scopus is a bibliographic database containing an organized collection of various published documents, including journal articles, conference proceedings, books, and patents. These resources are utilized by scientists as references for scientific literature [28]. The research focused on publications within Scopus, selected for its esteemed reputation and the high quality of its indexed material [29]. Table 1 shows the query syntaxes, but it does not specify the years. Query 1 resulted in 126 documents, with the oldest one from 2013. Query 2 had 25 publications, and the oldest was from 2015. The topic of crowdsourcing as a tool for SC within SD in Query 2 is also included in the wider results of Query 1. Therefore, the subsequent part of the article focuses on analyzing the results from Query 2. Although the formulated queries have syntax compatible with the Scopus database, there are differences between them (Table 1).

**Table 1.** Queries syntaxes used for the Scopus scientific database exploration

| No. | Query Syntax | No. of Results |
|---|---|---|
| Query 1 | (TITLE-ABS-KEY ("crowdsourcing")) AND ("smart cities") AND ("sustainable development") | 126 |
| Query 2 | (TITLE-ABS-KEY ("crowdsourcing") AND TITLE-ABS-KEY ("smart cities") AND TITLE-ABS-KEY ("sustainable development")) | 25 |

Source: Authors elaboration based on Scopus data.

This study is based on bibliographic metadata gathered from the Scopus database, which can be analyzed using visualization tools such as VOSviewer version 1.16.19.

This software enables the performance of keyword co-occurrence analysis. This method has gained popularity due to its ability to provide not just numerical data, but also an elegant graphical representation of co-occurring keywords. In the bibliometric map, co-occurring keywords are depicted as nodes within a network. The co-occurrence analysis of keywords also emphasizes the publications, which are represented as edges. These edges suggest a link through the use of specific keywords. Therefore, graphically presented results in the form of networks reveal patterns of influence, diffusion, and conceptual development within the analyzed query results [28]. The VOSviewer software allows researchers to define the research gaps covered by published articles and indicate the directions of scientific development [19].

The results from the queries listed in Table 1 were downloaded as.csv files for each query. During the export process, all available fields pertaining to the publications were selected [28]. For Scopus exports, these fields included citation information, bibliographic information, abstracts, keywords, funding details, and other relevant information. This data was then utilized by VOSviewer software to generate bibliometric maps. The selection of the number of keyword co-occurrences dictates the clarity and detail of the resulting graphical representation and bibliometric analysis [30, 31].

In this study, the focus was on the analysis of Query 2 results, as they include the results of Query 1 as a subset. For each bibliometric map, a minimum of two co-occurring keywords was required. In the procedure, all keywords were selected using the full counting method. VOSviewer automatically implements a clustering algorithm to group co-occurring keywords into clusters of closely related nodes. Each node within a subnetwork is assigned to a single cluster. The number of clusters is influenced by the resolution parameter; a higher value results in a greater number of clusters. VOSviewer uses color coding to denote cluster assignments [29].

In the VOSviewer software, the configuration settings for the visualization parameters were meticulously adjusted to optimize the clarity of the bibliometric maps. Within the 'Analysis' panel on the software's left sidebar, the 'Normalization' option for the 'Layout' was set to a value of 2, while the 'Repulsion' parameter was assigned a value of -2. To further enhance the legibility of the visual data, the character length for labels displayed within the visualizations was standardized to 30. These methodical adjustments were essential for augmenting the readability of the bibliometric maps, specifically Fig. 1, which illustrates the network visualization, and Fig. 2, which provides the overlay visualization. The careful calibration of these parameters was integral to the presentation of the data, ensuring that the maps are both interpretable and visually coherent, thereby aiding in the comprehensive analysis of the depicted research networks.

However, VOSviewer's primary limitation is that it does not label clusters or specify the common themes of the keywords within them, leaving room for the researcher's interpretation and introducing an element of subjectivity into the analysis. Despite this, keyword co-occurrence analysis and the resulting maps offer valuable insights into the intellectual structure of a research field. Pattern recognition is enhanced by VOSviewer's ability to generate a keyword list through text mining of titles, abstracts, and keywords from the dataset's publications [32]. Bibliometric maps and the results of the co-occurrence analysis facilitated an iterative analysis to identify similarities, patterns, and differences between the results of the two queries (referenced in Table 1). Discrepancies in individual observations were addressed and resolved in weekly conferences to achieve interrater consensus. The interpretation of these results lays the groundwork for the subsequent section of this article.

## 3 Results

This section presents the results of the Systematic Literature Review (SLR) method applied to explorations performed in the Scopus scientific literature database. Table 1 displays the outcomes of the search procedure in Scopus, using queries that, despite employing similar keywords, yielded varying numerical results. Separate datasets obtained from each query were analyzed in depth using VOSviewer software to examine the relationship between the results of Query 1 and Query 2. The analysis revealed that the results of Query 2 are a subset of those from Query 1, and this group also includes the most cited works. The primary difference between the queries stems from the fact that Query 2 is a filtering query operating on subsets. These initial findings suggest that each time SLR method should explore the subject using at least two similar queries with varied syntaxes.

Bibliometric maps convey three key features: the size of the nodes, the connections between them, and the co-occurring keywords. The maps created in this study allow for the visualization of the intellectual structure of the investigated domain. Figure 1 is a network visualization of keyword co-occurrence highlighting the interconnectedness of Smart Cities, Sustainable Development, and Crowdsourcing themes.

Figure 1 presents a multicolored, networked bibliometric map generated by VOSviewer, depicting the interconnectedness of various research topics. Central to the map is the theme of 'sustainable development', which is connected to a range of other topics such as 'smart cities', 'urban planning', 'crowdsourcing', and 'environmental sustainability'. These key subjects are further linked to more specific areas of study, including 'internet of things', 'data analytics', 'citizen participation', and 'environmental technology'. Each cluster of topics is distinguished by different colors, indicating the thematic groupings within the larger research landscape. The visualization illustrates the density and complexity of the relationships between keywords, with lines indicating the co-occurrences and nodes representing the indexed keywords. Some of the notable clusters are characterized by themes related to technology integration in urban spaces, such as 'internet of everything (IoE)' and 'intelligent systems', and others focus on aspects of community and quality of life, such as 'community engagement' and 'life qualities'. The overall structure of the map reveals the multidisciplinary nature of SD research, highlighting the interplay between technology, community, and environmental considerations in the academic discourse.

Figure 1, as illustrated in Table 1, is derived from 25 publications identified through Query 3. The bibliometric map was generated using VOSviewer software. The analysis involved examining co-occurrences among indexed keywords using the full counting method. A minimum threshold of two co-occurrences was set for keywords. Out of a total of 336 indexed keywords, 36 met this threshold. The five clusters that were automatically identified are color-coded and displayed in both Fig. 1 and Table 2.

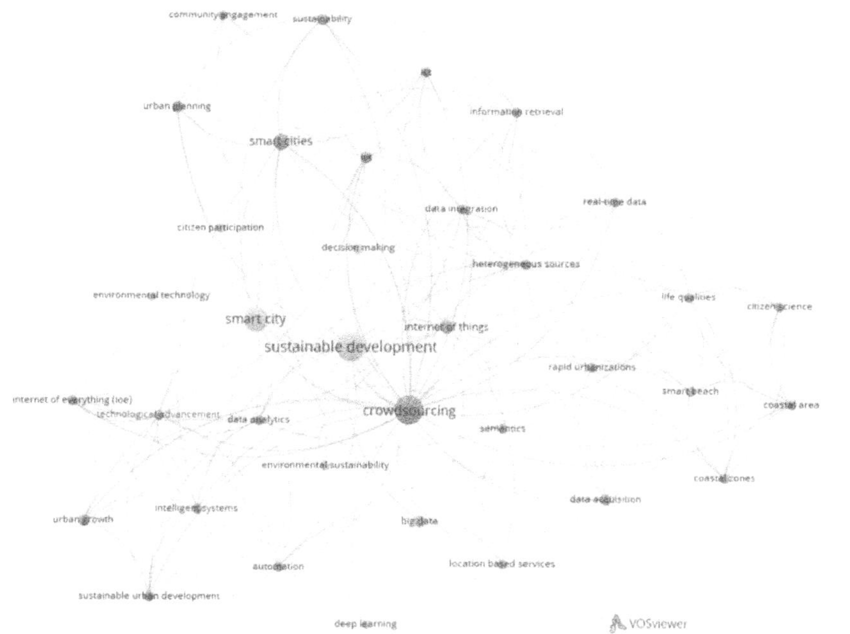


**Fig. 1.** Bibliometric map of keywords co-occurrences results from Scopus based on original Query 2. Source: Authors elaboration.

In Fig. 1 and Table 2, the color-coded clusters represent thematic concentrations within the broader research landscape, each delineating a distinct area of focus.

The red cluster encapsulates themes that intersect with technological applications within urban contexts. It emphasizes the incorporation of information and communication technologies (ICT) in fostering community engagement and the convergence of data from heterogeneous sources. Within this cluster, the fields of smart cities and sustainability are prominent, highlighting the critical role of urban planning in achieving sustainable outcomes through the integration of Internet of Things (IoT) and information retrieval strategies.

The green cluster pivots around environmental and social dimensions of coastal regions, underscoring the importance of citizen science and data acquisition in understanding and managing coastal areas. This cluster reflects concerns about the quality of life and the challenges posed by rapid urbanization, addressing the necessity for real-time data to inform SD strategies in coastal zones, including innovative concepts such as 'smart beach' initiatives.

In the blue cluster, the focus is on the deployment of automation and crowdsourcing within urban growth and development, showcasing the application of data analytics and intelligent systems. This cluster reveals a discourse on sustainable urban development that is heavily reliant on technological advancement, particularly the 'Internet of Everything (IoE)', which integrates various components of an urban ecosystem into a coherent whole.

**Table 2.** Keywords gathered in colored clusters identified in the research

| Cluster | Color | Keyword | Links | Total Link Strength | Occurrences |
|---|---|---|---|---|---|
| 1 | red | community engagement | 7 | 7 | 2 |
| | | data integration | 13 | 14 | 2 |
| | | heterogeneous sources | 13 | 14 | 2 |
| | | ict | 13 | 15 | 2 |
| | | information retrieval | 12 | 13 | 2 |
| | | iot | 15 | 17 | 3 |
| | | smart cities | 17 | 29 | 6 |
| | | sustainability | 8 | 15 | 3 |
| | | urban planning | 8 | 14 | 3 |
| 2 | green | citizen science | 9 | 15 | 2 |
| | | coastal area | 9 | 15 | 2 |
| | | coastal zones | 9 | 15 | 2 |
| | | data acquisition | 12 | 15 | 3 |
| | | life qualities | 9 | 15 | 2 |
| | | rapid urbanizations | 12 | 13 | 2 |
| | | real-time data | 15 | 16 | 2 |
| | | smart beach | 9 | 15 | 2 |
| 3 | blue | automation | 13 | 14 | 2 |
| | | crowdsourcing | 32 | 74 | 17 |
| | | data analytics | 13 | 14 | 2 |
| | | intelligent systems | 11 | 13 | 2 |
| | | internet of everything (ioe) | 11 | 15 | 2 |
| | | sustainable urban development | 9 | 11 | 2 |
| | | technological advancement | 11 | 15 | 2 |
| | | urban growth | 9 | 14 | 3 |
| 4 | yellow | citizen participation | 8 | 9 | 2 |
| | | decision making | 14 | 17 | 3 |

*(continued)*

**Table 2.** *(continued)*

| Cluster | Color | Keyword | Links | Total Link Strength | Occurrences |
|---|---|---|---|---|---|
| | | deep learning | 4 | 6 | 2 |
| | | environmental sustainability | 8 | 10 | 2 |
| | | environmental technology | 10 | 12 | 2 |
| | | smart city | 25 | 54 | 13 |
| | | sustainable development | 35 | 86 | 18 |
| 5 | purple | big data | 10 | 14 | 3 |
| | | internet of things | 19 | 25 | 4 |
| | | location based services | 7 | 10 | 2 |
| | | semantics | 9 | 10 | 2 |

Source: Authors elaboration based on Fig. 1 in VOSviewer software

The yellow cluster is oriented towards the engagement of citizens in the SD of urban spaces. It brings to light the integral role of public participation in environmental decision-making processes, leveraging technologies such as deep learning to enhance environmental sustainability. This cluster also indicates a significant interest in how environmental technologies can be harmonized with the concept of a 'smart city' to propel the agenda of SD.

Finally, the purple cluster addresses the data-centric aspects of urban environments and the role of technology in managing them. It concentrates on the analysis of big data and the utility of the Internet of Things (IoT), emphasizing the importance of location-based services and the semantic interpretation of vast data sets. The inclusion of these topics suggests a scholarly focus on the ways in which data-driven insights can inform and transform urban living spaces.

These clusters demonstrate the multifaceted nature of SD research, highlighting the integration of technology, community engagement, environmental stewardship, and data-centric approaches in addressing the complexities of modern urbanization.

Figure 2 provides a visual depiction of keyword co-occurrence analysis from Scopus, derived from original Query 2. This dynamic bibliometric network map utilizes gradations of color to illustrate the temporal progression of research themes related to Smart Cities, Crowdsourcing, and SD over the period 2018–2022. Developed using VOSviewer, the map's color variations represent the chronological development of these research topics. In the Fig. 2, there is a discernible shift towards emphasizing environmental and social dimensions, indicating an evolving research direction focused on these critical areas.

Central to this visualization is 'sustainable development', a pivotal term that interlinks various research domains, underscoring its essential role in the discourse. Adjacent

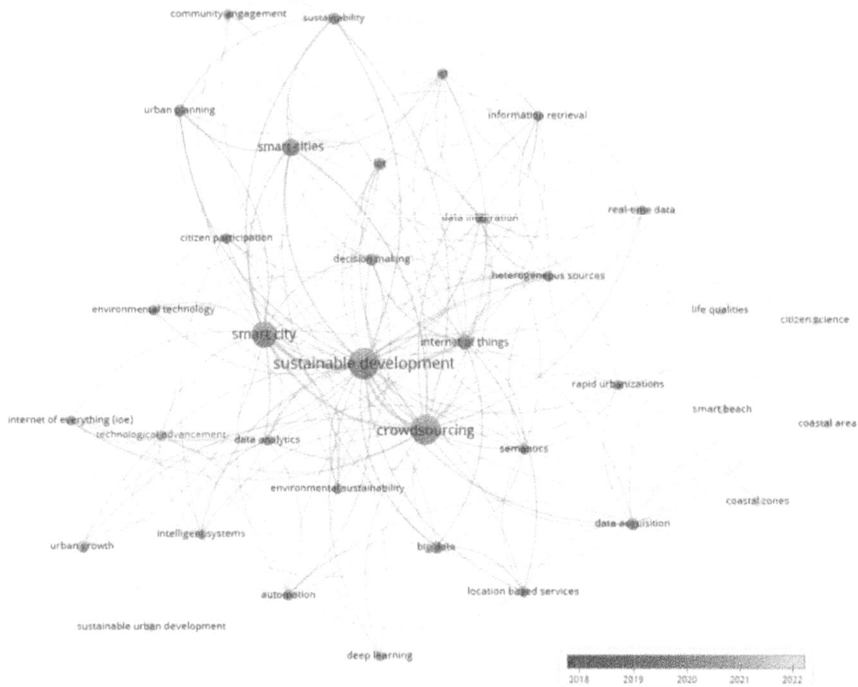


**Fig. 2.** Evolving trends in Smart City, Crowdsourcing and Sustainable Development research. Source: Authors elaboration.

to this core are terms such as 'smart city', 'crowdsourcing', and 'environmental sustainability'. These terms are depicted in distinct shades, reflecting their prominence and continuity in scholarly discussions in scientific literature. The lines connecting these terms signify their co-occurrences within the literature, thereby forming a complex network of interconnected keywords and themes.

The color coding of the nodes offers insights into the temporal relevance of these academic topics. Darker colors suggest a topic's established or emerging importance in recent scholarly discourse, while lighter colors indicate topics gaining prominence in the most recent timeline, signaling shifts in research focus. For example, 'smart city' is depicted in a medium dark blue, highlighting its sustained presence in the field, whereas emerging topics like 'smart beach', 'citizen science', 'internet of things' (IoT), and 'coastal zones' are presented in yellow, denoting their increasing scholarly interest.

Additionally, the visualization accentuates the significance of 'citizen participation' and 'decision making' in contemporary research, with their lighter shades pointing towards a trend in research prioritizing inclusive governance and community involvement in urban development. Other themes, such as 'urban planning', 'community engagement', and 'automation', are also indicated as yellow nodes, signifying their status as both established and evolving areas of scientific inquiry.

More than a mere depiction of the thematic landscape of SC research, this network map narrates the evolution of the academic field. The gradual shift in color from the periphery to the center indicates the emergence and integration of new research topics, like 'smart beach' and 'coastal zones,' which are gaining attention due to the challenges posed by rapid urbanization and the pursuit of sustainable solutions.

In summary, this bibliometric network map serves as a visual representation of the dynamic and interconnected nature of SC research. It reflects the field's commitment to sustainability principles and its adaptability to technological advancements and societal changes, thereby providing a comprehensive overview of the evolving landscape of SC research.

## 4 Discussion

The topics of Smart City, Crowdsourcing, and Sustainable Development, evidenced by diverse keywords in publications, reflect various scholarly interests and the integration of academia with business and politics, extending topic coverage to include urban management. Demographic changes and urban migration further contribute to this diversity, with cities facing challenges like aging populations and rural influx, focusing on accessibility, mobility, urban development, new residential zones, and sustainable growth.

Table 3 lists the top ten influential articles shaping the bibliometric map in Fig. 1, aligning research within thematic clusters of sustainable urban development using the CLR method. Key themes include technology and crowdsourcing in urban planning, demonstrated by the most cited paper by Li [33], which discusses the evolution of geospatial information science in the big data era, highlighting advancements in global information technology, IoT, and cloud computing. Other notable works address SC data efficiency [34], propose fog-cloud hybrid architectures for energy efficiency [35], and present frameworks for SC development [36]. The role of public-private partnerships [37], the integration of autonomous vehicles [38], and the use of crowdsourced data for environmental assessment [39] are also explored. Community-based sustainable initiatives [40] and the smart allocation of residential areas [41] emphasize the importance of crowdsourcing in sustainable urban development, as does the role of citizen participation in urban planning [42].

Crowdsourcing's critical role in SD involves community decision-making and identifying environmental issues [43]. It contributes to ecological balance, managing urban resources, and enhancing sustainable mobility [44]. Crowdsourcing also supports the development of renewable energy and sustainable projects in European cities, generating ideas for educational campaigns and ecological events with community involvement [45].

The formulated queries explored the Scopus scientific database, which contains reputable peer-reviewed publications that collectively constitute the analyzed data set. The period proposed in the results of the systematic review is a consequence of the indexing of the concept in the Scopus database [46].

**Table 3.** Top 10 most cited articles influencing the clusters presented in bibliometric map in Fig. 1.

| Cluster connection | Authors; Year | Research area | Citations |
|---|---|---|---|
| Red Cluster Technological applications in urban contexts, integration of IoT and information retrieval | Li [33]; 2016 | Geospatial Information Science and Big Data | 105 |
| | Abdur Rahman et al. [35]; 2018 | Energy Efficiency and IoT in Urban Environments | 50 |
| | Kuru and Ansell [36]; 2020 | Smart City Development Frameworks | 42 |
| | Papadopoulou and Hatzichristos [41]; 2020 | Residential Area Planning in Smart Cities | 5 |
| Green Cluster Citizen science in coastal regions and environmental data acquisition | Kim et al. [39]; 2019 | Environmental Assessment via Crowdsourced Data | 13 |
| Blue Cluster Deployment of automation and crowdsourcing in urban growth, including data analytics | Milenkovic et al. [37]; 2017 | Public-Private Partnerships in Urban Technology | 23 |
| | Kuru and Khan [38] 2021 | Autonomous Vehicles and Urban Mobility | 21 |
| Yellow Cluster Citizen engagement in sustainable urban development, leveraging technology | Ceccarini et al. [40]; 2020 | Community-Based Sustainable Initiatives | 9 |
| | Murphy et al. [42]; 2016 | Citizen Participation in Urban Planning | 5 |
| Purple Cluster Data-centric aspects of urban environments, focus on big data and IoT | Sta [34]; 2017 | Smart City Data Efficiency | 70 |

Source: Authors elaboration based on Query 2.

## 5 Conclusions

Crowdsourcing proves to be a formidable tool in SD, particularly within SC initiatives. By tapping into community intelligence and engagement, it addresses environmental challenges and enriches urban life, guiding us towards a more sustainable future. The analysis of scientific publications in this study showcases the growing synergy of crowdsourcing, technology, and SD within SC contexts. It illustrates crowdsourcing's role in ecological balance and resource management, and its importance in facilitating community participation in decision-making processes [47]. This multifaceted approach is essential in addressing the varied needs of expanding urban populations, highlighting the potential and complexity of integrating technology with community involvement in SC planning [43].

The study identified key thematic clusters: the application of technology in urban contexts, citizen science in coastal areas, the integration of automation and crowdsourcing in urban development, citizen engagement in SC development, and data-centric approaches in urban environments [48]. These clusters underscore the varied nature of SD research, blending technology, community engagement, and environmental stewardship.

The integration of technology and crowdsourcing within SCs is key to addressing a range of urban management challenges [46]. Significant research in this field points to advancements in geospatial information science, SC data efficiency, and frameworks for SC development, emphasizing crowdsourcing's crucial role in promoting sustainable urban living.

In SC initiatives centered on SD, crowdsourcing is a standout component. It not only elevates urban living quality but also promotes community involvement in tackling environmental issues. This study highlights the collaboration between crowdsourcing, technology, and SD in SCs, underscoring its significance in efficient urban resource management and community engagement. Future research could delve into the evolving trends in crowdsourcing applications and their influence on the sustainability of SCs. In terms of practical implications, the findings of this study can significantly influence urban policy and planning. Urban planners and policymakers can utilize the insights to design and implement SC projects that are more inclusive and sustainable, leveraging crowdsourcing for effective urban development strategies. The importance of community engagement highlighted in the research suggests that cities should use digital platforms for involving residents in decision-making, thereby improving the relevance and effectiveness of urban projects [49]. Additionally, the role of technology in facilitating crowdsourcing is underscored, guiding technology developers and city administrations in creating more user-friendly and accessible platforms. The study also has implications for environmental management, as it provides valuable insights for environmental agencies and organizations on how crowdsourcing can aid in environmental monitoring and sustainability initiatives within urban settings [50].

Theoretically, the research contributes to the expansion of the SC conceptual framework by integrating crowdsourcing, broadening the scope of SC literature. It reinforces theories related to community participation and engagement, demonstrating their practical application in urban development and sustainability [51]. Moreover, the research adopts an interdisciplinary approach, bridging the gap between technology, urban planning, and community engagement, and offering a more holistic theoretical framework for understanding SCs.

For future research, there are several promising directions. Longitudinal studies assessing the long-term impacts of crowdsourcing on urban development and sustainability would be valuable. Comparative research across different cities or countries could provide insights into how cultural and political contexts influence the effectiveness of crowdsourcing in SC initiatives. Investigating the barriers to technology adoption in crowdsourcing and exploring ways to overcome these challenges is another potential area for future research. Additionally, future studies might explore how crowdsourcing influences urban governance structures and decision-making processes. Lastly, a focus on the direct impact of crowdsourcing initiatives on urban environmental sustainability could yield important findings.

## References

1. Duvernoy, I., Soulard, C.-T.: Smart Agriculture, grassroots initiatives and urban food governance: case studies in two metropolitan areas in Southern France (2021). https://doi.org/10.4324/9780429354670-11
2. United Nations Department of Economic and Social Affairs: World Urbanization Prospects. The 2018 Revision (2018)
3. Przysucha, Ł.: Effective Management of Information Processes with CMS in Smart City. The concept of crowdsourcing. In: Mercier-Laurent, E. (ed.) Artificial Intelligence for Knowledge Management, 6th IFIP WG 12.6 International Workshop, AI4KM 2018 Held at IJCAI 2018 Stockholm, Sweden, July 15, 2018 Revised and Extended Selected Papers. pp. 65–76 (2020). https://doi.org/10.1007/978-3-030-52903-1_6
4. Mercier-Laurent, E.: Can artificial intelligence effectively support sustainable development? IFIP Adv. Inf. Commun. Technol. **614**, 144–159 (2021). https://doi.org/10.1007/978-3-030-80847-1_10
5. Harrison, C., et al.: Foundations for Smarter Cities. IBM J. Res. Dev. **54**, 1–16 (2010). https://doi.org/10.1147/JRD.2010.2048257
6. Giffinger, R., Fertner, C., Kramar, H., Kalasek, R., Milanović, N., Meijers, E.: Smart cities - Ranking of European medium-sized cities (2007)
7. Nam, T., Pardo, T.A.: Conceptualizing smart city with dimensions of technology, peoaple and institutions: digital government innovation in challenging times. In: the Proceedings of the 12th Annual International Digital Government Research Conference: Digital Government Innovation in Challenging Times. pp. 282–291. University of Maryland, Maryland, USA (2011)
8. Yu, H., Raychoudhury, V., Saha, S., Edinger, J., Smith, R.O., Gani, M.O.: Automated surface classification system using vibration patterns - a case study with wheelchairs. IEEE Trans. Artif. Intell. **4**, 884–895 (2023). https://doi.org/10.1109/TAI.2022.3190828
9. Trzaska, R., Sulich, A., Organa, M., Niemczyk, J., Jasiński, B.: Digitalization business strategies in energy sector: solving problems with uncertainty under industry 4.0 Conditions. Energies. **14**, 1–21 (2021). https://doi.org/10.3390/en14237997
10. Torres, S., Lalanne, F., Del Canto, G., Morales, F., Bustos-Jimenez, J., Reyes, P.: BeCity: Sensing and sensibility on urban cycling for smarter cities. In: Proceedings - International Conference of the Chilean Computer Science Society, SCCC. IEEE Computer Society (2016). https://doi.org/10.1109/SCCC.2015.7416587
11. Przysucha, Ł.: The concept of crowdsourcing in knowledge management in smart cities. In: Owoc, M.L. and Pondel, M. (eds.) Artificial Intelligence for Knowledge Management, 7th IFIP WG 12.6 International Workshop, AI4KM 2019, Held at IJCAI 2019, Macao, China, August 11, 2019, Revised Selected Papers, pp. 17–26 (2021). https://doi.org/10.1007/978-3-030-85001-2_2
12. Korczak, J., Pondel, M., Sroka, W.: An approach to customer community discovery. In: Ganzha, M., Maciaszek, L., Paprzycki, M. (eds.) Proceedings of the 2019 Federated Conference on Computer Science and Information Systems, FedCSIS 2019, pp. 675–683. Institute of Electrical and Electronics Engineers Inc. (2019). https://doi.org/10.15439/2019F308

13. Vahdat-Nejad, H., Tamadon, T., Salmani, F., Kiani-Zadegan, Z., Abbasi, S., Seyyedi, F.-S.: A survey on crowdsourcing applications in smart cities. Stud. Comput. Intell. **1061**, 239–253 (2022). https://doi.org/10.1007/978-3-031-14748-7_14
14. Shemyakina, T.Y., Astafieva, O.E., Gorelova, O.A.: Scenarios of smart cities creation as a trend of sustainable development. Lect. Notes Networks Syst. **155**, 3 (2021). https://doi.org/10.1007/978-3-030-59126-7_1
15. Kozar, ŁJ., Sulich, A.: Green Jobs: bibliometric review. Int. J. Environ. Res. Public Health **20**, 2886 (2023). https://doi.org/10.3390/ijerph20042886
16. Kolobova, S.: Renovation of Moscow as a subprogram of creation of a creative city. In: D.B., S. (ed.) IOP Conference Series: Materials Science and Engineering. Institute of Physics Publishing (2020). https://doi.org/10.1088/1757-899X/753/6/062003
17. Sliwa, P., Krzos, G., Pondel, M.: Dynamic modelling of inter-organizational networks using the domain knowledge and big data analytics. In: 26th Americas Conference on Information Systems, AMCIS 2020. Association for Information Systems (2020)
18. Lebraty, J.-F., Lobre-Lebraty, K.: Crowdsourcing: one step beyond. Wiley (2013). https://doi.org/10.1002/9781118760765
19. Zema, T., Sulich, A.: Models of electricity price forecasting: bibliometric research. Energies **15**, 5642 (2022). https://doi.org/10.3390/en15155642
20. Owoc, M., Andres, F., Weichbroth, P., Flisikowski, K., Żuralski, K.: Toward tracking knowledge evolution. IFIP Adv. Inf. Commun. Technol. **518**, 48–56 (2017)
21. Owoc, M.L., Weichbroth, P.: A note on knowledge management education: towards implementing active learning methods. IFIP Adv. Inf. Commun. Technol. 588 IFIP, 124–140 (2020). https://doi.org/10.1007/978-3-030-52903-1_10
22. Stanczyk-Hugiet, E., Piorkowska, K., Ider, M.: Theoretical and methodological perspective of the research on strategic groups and performance in a retail sector [Strateginių grupių ir veiklos rezultatų mažmeninės prekybos sektoriuje tyrimo teorinė ir metodologinė perspektyva]. Transform. Bus. Econ. **20**, 925–938 (2021)
23. Przysucha, Ł.: Implementation of crowdsourcing as an integral element of communication engineering in the Smart City concept. RISTI - Rev. Iber. Sist. e Tecnol. Inf., 97–108 (2020)
24. Grzesiak, S.S., Sulich, A.: Electromobility: logistics and business ecosystem perspectives review. Energies 16, (2023). https://doi.org/10.3390/en16217249
25. Dall-Orsoletta, A., Romero, F., Ferreira, P.: Open and collaborative innovation for the energy transition: an exploratory study. Technol. Soc. 69, (2022). https://doi.org/10.1016/j.techsoc.2022.101955
26. Sulich, A., Sołoducho-Pelc, L.: Changes in energy sector strategies: a literature review. Energies **15**, 7068 (2022). https://doi.org/10.3390/en15197068
27. Owoc, M., Hauke, K., Weichbroth, P.: Knowledge-grid modelling for academic purposes. IFIP Adv. Inf. Commun. Technol. **497**, 1–14 (2016). https://doi.org/10.1007/978-3-319-55970-4_1
28. Sulich, A., Zema, T.: Green energy transition in Germany: a bibliometric study. Forum Sci. Oeconomia. **11**, 175–195 (2023). https://doi.org/10.23762/FSO_VOL11_NO2_9
29. Baas, J., Schotten, M., Plume, A., Côté, G., Karimi, R.: Scopus as a curated, high-quality bibliometric data source for academic research in quantitative science studies. Quant. Sci. Stud. **1**, 377–386 (2020). https://doi.org/10.1162/qss_a_00019
30. Fortunato, S., et al.: Science of science. Science **80**, 359 (2018). https://doi.org/10.1126/science.aao0185
31. van Eck, N.J., Waltman, L.: Software survey: VOSviewer, a computer program for bibliometric mapping. Scientometrics **84**, 523–538 (2010). https://doi.org/10.1007/s11192-009-0146-3

32. Donthu, N., Kumar, S., Mukherjee, D., Pandey, N., Lim, W.M.: How to conduct a bibliometric analysis: an overview and guidelines. J. Bus. Res. **133**, 285–296 (2021). https://doi.org/10.1016/j.jbusres.2021.04.070
33. Li, D.: Towards geo-spatial information science in big data era. Cehui Xuebao/Acta Geod. Cartogr. Sin. **45**, 379–384 (2016). https://doi.org/10.11947/j.AGCS.2016.20160057
34. Sta, H.: Ben: quality and the efficiency of data in "Smart-Cities." Futur. Gener. Comput. Syst. **74**, 409–416 (2017). https://doi.org/10.1016/j.future.2016.12.021
35. Rahman, M.A., Hossain, M.S., Hassanain, E., Muhammad, G.: Semantic multimedia fog computing and IoT environment: sustainability perspective. IEEE Commun. Mag. **56**, 80–87 (2018). https://doi.org/10.1109/MCOM.2018.1700907
36. Kuru, K., Ansell, D.: TCitySmartF: a comprehensive systematic framework for transforming cities into smart cities. IEEE Access. **8**, 18615–18644 (2020). https://doi.org/10.1109/ACCESS.2020.2967777
37. Milenkovic, M., Rasic, M., Vojkovic, G.: Using public private partnership models in smart cities - Proposal for Croatia. In: Cicin-Sain, M. et al. (ed.) 2017 40th International Convention on Information and Communication Technology, Electronics and Microelectronics, MIPRO 2017 – Proceedings, pp. 1412–1417. Institute of Electrical and Electronics Engineers Inc. (2017). https://doi.org/10.23919/MIPRO.2017.7973643
38. Kuru, K., Khan, W.: A framework for the synergistic integration of fully autonomous ground vehicles with smart city. IEEE Access. **9**, 923–948 (2021). https://doi.org/10.1109/ACCESS.2020.3046999
39. Kim, J., Yadav, M., Ahn, C.R., Chaspari, T.: Saliency detection analysis of pedestrians' physiological responses to assess adverse built environment features. In: Cho, T., et al. (ed.) Computing in Civil Engineering 2019, pp. 90–97. American Society of Civil Engineers, Reston, VA (2019). https://doi.org/10.1061/9780784482445.012
40. Ceccarini, C., Delnevo, G., Prandi, C.: FruGar: exploiting deep learning and crowdsourcing for frugal gardening. In: Frugalthings 2020 - Proceedings of the 2020 1st Workshop on Experiences with the Design and Implementation of Frugal Smart Objects, pp. 7–11. Association for Computing Machinery, Inc. (2020). https://doi.org/10.1145/3410670.3410862
41. Papadopoulou, C.-A., Hatzichristos, T.: Allocation of residential areas in smart insular communities: the case of Mykonos. Greece. Int. J. E-Planning Res. **9**, 40–60 (2020). https://doi.org/10.4018/IJEPR.2020100103
42. Murphy, A., Dahlhaus, P., Thompson, H.: Historic urban landscapes and visualising Ballarat: citizen participation for sustainable urban planning and design. In: Both, A., et al. (ed.) CEUR Workshop Proceedings, pp. 41–46. CEUR-WS (2016)
43. Lebraty, J.-F., Lobre, K.: Value creation and crowdsourcing: the two paths; [Création de valeur par le crowdsourcing: Deux voies possibles]. In: 14th International Conference of the Association Information and Management 2009, AIM 2009 (2009)
44. Mercier-Laurent, E.: Artificial intelligence and sustainability the use of AI in sustainability initiatives. In: T.X., B. (ed.) Proceedings of the Annual Hawaii International Conference on System Sciences, pp. 5190–5191. IEEE Computer Society (2020)
45. Biercewicz, K., Sulich, A., Sołoducho-Pelc, L.: The improvements propositions for players' engagement and sustainable behaviors in managerial games. Procedia Comput. Sci. **207**, 1509–1518 (2022). https://doi.org/10.1016/j.procs.2022.09.208
46. Renaud, A., Walsh, I., Kalika, M.: Is SAM still alive? A bibliometric and interpretive mapping of the strategic alignment research field. J. Strateg. Inf. Syst. **25**, 75–103 (2016). https://doi.org/10.1016/j.jsis.2016.01.002
47. Owoc, M., Pondel, M.: Selection of free software useful in business intelligence. Teaching methodology perspective. IFIP Adv. Inf. Commun. Technol. **518**, 93–105 (2018). https://doi.org/10.1007/978-3-319-92928-6_6

48. Kozar, Ł: The financial sector and sustainable development - a review of selected environmental practices implemented in financial institutions operating in Poland between 2016 and 2020. Finans. i Prawo Finans. **1**, 143–157 (2022)
49. Kozar, L.J.: Self-employment and sustainable development-using the ICT solutions for greening economic activity. Procedia Comput. Sci. **225**, 468–475 (2023). https://doi.org/10.1016/j.procs.2023.10.031
50. Verdejo, D.P., Mercier-Laurent, E.: Video intelligence as a component of a global security system. IFIP Adv. Inf. Commun. Technol. **571**, 132–145 (2019). https://doi.org/10.1007/978-3-030-29904-0_10
51. Mercier-Laurent, E., Monsone, C.R.: Ecosystems of industry 4.0 - Combining technology and human power. In: 11th International Conference on Management of Digital EcoSystems, MEDES 2019. pp. 115–119 (2019). https://doi.org/10.1145/3297662.3365793

# Model of Relationship Between Circular Economy and Industry 5.0

Adam Sulich(✉)

Wrocław University of Economics and Business, ul. Komandorska 118/120,
53-345 Wrocław, Poland
adam.sulich@ue.wroc.pl

**Abstract.** This research examines the interaction between Industry 5.0's role in developed European nations and their efforts to achieve a Circular Economy (CE). Both concepts are innovative socially, sustainable ecologically, and viable economically. Specifically, the study focuses on the European Union (EU), exploring how CE initiatives are integrated within its member states using various representational variables. The primary goal of this research is to develop an econometric model that elucidates the impact of CE activities on the advancement toward Industry 5.0, potentially indicating a significant shift in the approach to technology and the environment. Within the EU context, the study delves into the complexities of CE, utilizing selected indicators and data from Eurostat. Methodologically, the research employs both the taxonomic method and regression analysis. It also highlights the importance of Industry 5.0 in incorporating Sustainable Development (SD) principles across various sectors, thus underlining its key role in driving broader economic transformation through technological innovation. The study posits that the path of economic development is influenced by strategic management where the outcomes of Industry 5.0, in concert with CE principles, play a pivotal role in promoting green jobs, bolstered by eco-innovation and green patents.

**Keywords:** Green Economy · Industrial Revolution · Green Jobs · Sustainability

## 1 Introduction

Discussions regarding the impact of human actions on the natural environment and the need for its protection emerged in Europe at the beginning of the 20th century [1]. Climate change is an extremely complex problem involving quite all disciplines [2]. The concept of Sustainable Development (SD) [3], aimed at addressing this issue, can be traced back to Antoine de Saint-Exupéry's 1939 publication 'Terre des hommes' ('Wind, Sand and Stars') and is further explored in his later work 'The Little Prince'[2, 4]. These works emphasize the importance of preserving the environment for future generations [4, 5]. Concepts evolving the state of the environment alongside technological progress [6, 7] gained significance with the acceleration of economic development [8, 9]. On the other hand, not only in European Union countries but also globally, economic progress and


Published by Springer Nature Switzerland AG 2024
E. Mercier-Laurent et al. (Eds.): AI4KMES 2023, IFIP AICT 693, pp. 220–236, 2024.
https://doi.org/10.1007/978-3-031-61069-1_16

SD have often been at odds, historically marked by the exploitation of natural resources and consequential environmental degradation [10, 11]. Despite the implementation of ecological initiatives at various levels, from corporate to international, efforts to combat pollution and emissions have largely been reactive and insufficient in the face of widespread environmental challenges [12, 13]. The increasing impact of human activities on the environment, termed anthropogenic pressure, is a growing concern [14]. Therefore, instead of denying the negative impact of humans on the natural environment, there is a need to appropriately redirect these actions and systematize them according to the concepts of SD and their implementation in the form of a Circular Economy (CE).

However, there is a notable gap in the existing literature [15], specifically in integrating taxonomic linear ordering with linear regression and statistical analysis of the CE and Industry 5.0. This paper identifies these methodological shortcomings and the challenge of accurately reflecting economic shifts influenced by ecological concerns and technological progress. This study aims to fill these gaps through a comprehensive analysis and discourse.

This research examines the interaction between Industry 5.0 and the CE within the European Union (EU), proposing an econometric model to understand this relationship. Establishing the CE is acknowledged as a critical factor in promoting pro-ecological strategies and integrating sustainable, green practices. These practices, aimed at reducing the environmental impact of organizational operations and products [16], are increasingly shaped by green jobs, technological innovations and patents focused on environmental preservation [17, 18].

The structure of this paper is as follows: After this introduction, the first section presents a literature review. The second section details the variables used in the analysis. The third section describes the methods employed, followed by the presentation of results and their discussion. The conclusion offers final remarks, managerial implications, and directions for future research.

## 2 Theoretical Background

This paper's theoretical framework is grounded in two main areas, the CE and the emerging concept of Industry 5.0. These frameworks are essential for understanding how technological innovation can be aligned with ecological sustainability. In this section, the interaction between CE and Industry 5.0 is explored, providing a basis for the selection of variables and the analyses conducted in the subsequent chapters of this study.

Sustainable development is defined as 'development that meets the needs of the present generation without compromising the ability of future generations to meet their own needs' [19, 20]. It goes beyond merely reducing human impact, encompassing proactive measures for environmental conservation, such as habitat restoration, species revitalization, and natural resource management [21, 22]. These elements of environmental management are increasingly relevant in the context of Industry 5.0, which represents a synergistic blend of human and technological efforts in ecological stewardship [23, 24].

The concept and definitions of the CE have evolved significantly in recent decades, mirroring a paradigm shift in both organizational and societal values [25]. Initially, CE was primarily reactive, with a focus on adhering to regulations and rectifying environmental harm [26, 27]. However, it has progressively adopted a proactive and forward-thinking stance. This evolution marks a broader acceptance of sustainable practices [28] as fundamental, extending beyond mere compliance with regulatory mandates to form an integral part of ethical corporate strategy and operations management [29].

CE transcends basic regulatory adherence, championing the comprehensive integration of environmental considerations into the strategic nucleus of organizational decision-making [30, 31]. This holistic approach affects various operational dimensions, encompassing everything from supply chain management and product design to corporate governance and customer engagement strategies [2, 32]. Such an approach enables organizations to anticipate and address environmental challenges proactively, potentially securing a competitive advantage and enhancing their reputation [33, 34].

The modern ethos of CE is further strengthened by the tenets of SD, offering a framework for striking a balance between economic growth, environmental protection, and social welfare [35]. These principles advocate for a future where economic development occurs without sacrificing ecological integrity or social equity [36]. As a result, CE is increasingly recognized as a catalyst for innovation, driving research and development towards more sustainable technologies and products [37]. This shift encourages organizations to critically assess and improve their production processes, energy usage, and overall business models in pursuit of greater sustainability [38].

Additionally, CE's influence extends into the area of marketing strategies, reflecting a trend toward sustainability in branding and communication efforts [39]. This change is indicative of evolving consumer preferences and an escalating demand for transparency and corporate accountability in environmental governance [40, 41]. Consequently, organizations are not only revamping their internal operations but also redefining their engagement with markets and communities [42], aligning their practices with the objectives of SD [43].

As the urgency of environmental challenges intensifies and stakeholder expectations rise, CE is emerging as an essential discipline [44]. It is poised to offer innovative solutions and guide industries toward a path of sustainable and equitable progress. This evolving role of CE is pivotal in shaping future business models and economic policies, emphasizing the need for a seamless integration of environmental responsibility into the fabric of organizational and societal practices. The growing prominence of CE indicates a transformative era in business and environmental stewardship [45], where the pursuit of profit is harmoniously aligned with the principles of ecological and social responsibility.

The evolution of industrial development, has been characterized by significant technological advancements and a progressive shift towards the CE [2]. This trajectory is essential for understanding the current dynamics of major business trends [9].

Originating in the 18th century, the first industrial revolution signified a transition from manual craftsmanship to mechanized production, primarily powered by water and steam. This era marked the beginning of significant environmental impacts, leading to initial stages of ecological consciousness and response, laying the groundwork for early CE principles.

At the close of the 19th century, the second industrial revolution ushered in an era of mass production and electricity. This period saw a substantial increase in industrial pollution and resource consumption, bringing environmental issues into sharper focus and underscoring the need for sustainable practices in line with CE.

Following World War II, Industry 3.0 was defined by advancements in automation, computing, industrial robotics, and electronics. These developments introduced new environmental challenges, necessitating a more nuanced approach to CE, focusing on sustainable production and resource efficiency.

The onset of the 21st century marked the beginning of the fourth industrial revolution (Industry 4.0), characterized by cyber-physical systems, the Internet of Things (IoT), and a surge in digitization [9]. This era demanded more sophisticated CE approaches, emphasizing the life cycle of technologies and the reduction of their environmental footprints [46].

The current phase is Industry 5.0, it prioritizes personalization, sustainability, and human-machine collaboration. It seeks to embed human-centric values and environmental stewardship within industrial processes. Industry 5.0 aligns closely with CE, advocating for the sustainable use of resources and the incorporation of green technologies into manufacturing [47].

The progression through these industrial phases has greatly influenced the evolution and transformation of CE. With the emergence of Industry 5.0, CE faces new challenges and opportunities, highlighting the imperative for innovative, sustainable, and socially responsible practices [18].

Figure 1 presents a visual depiction of this technological evolution. Industry 1.0 was initiated with the invention of the steam engine, facilitating production at a factory scale. Industry 2.0 transitioned to the use of electricity for mass production. Industry 3.0 introduced computers and data processing, improving production efficiency and automation.

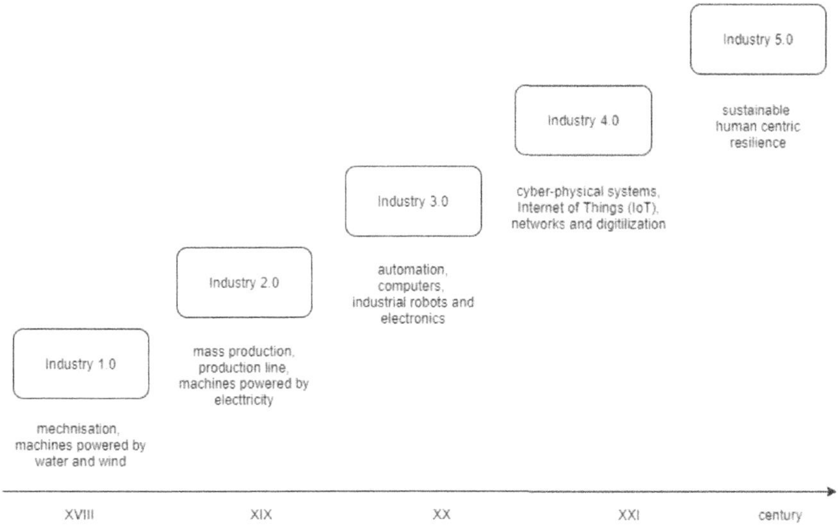


**Fig. 1.** Technological progress stages. Source: own elaboration based on [48].

Finally, Industry 4.0, synonymous with the development of advanced technologies, integrated systems and networks, fostering a synergy between human and digital machine interactions.

Figure 1 illustrates the technological evolution across the industrial stages, from the mechanization of Industry 1.0 to the digitization and system integration of Industry 4.0.

The intersection of the CE and Industry 5.0 represents a pivotal shift in industrial development, where environmental sustainability becomes integral to technological innovation [19]. This synergy is critical for effectively addressing the challenges of anthropogenic impact and climate change [23]. Integrating CE principles into Industry 5.0 enables businesses to achieve a balance between advancing technological capabilities and upholding environmental responsibility [45, 49]. This paper proposes that such integration is essential for the SD of both the economy and the environment.

This exploration of selected CE variables can demonstrate the effective integration of CE and Industry 5.0. This conceptual framework parallels the five stages of the industrial revolution. It facilitates an understanding of the relationship between the CE and Industry 4.0, leading to the transition to Industry 5.0. In this phase, the importance of CE is highlighted, advocating for the emulation of natural cycles and the incorporation of sustainable practices in all aspects of product and service development, aiming to improve durability and longevity.

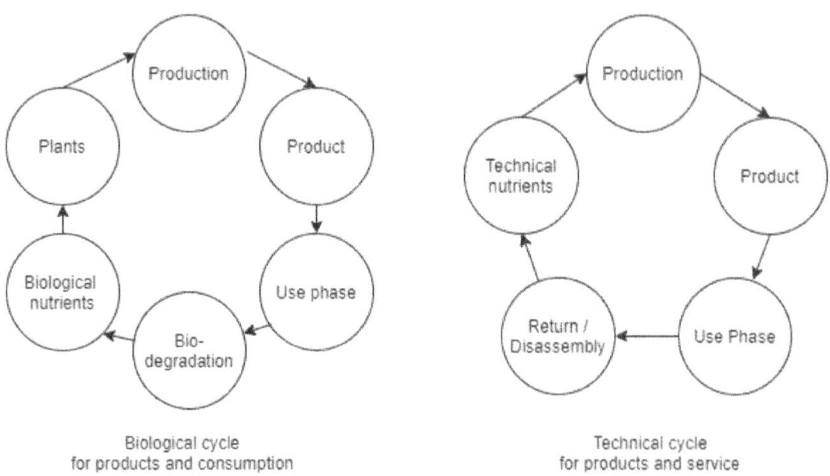


**Fig. 2.** Circular models of compared cycles. Source: own elaboration based on [50].

Figure 2 compares the biological and technical cycles involved in product and service consumption. The biological cycle showcases the natural process of production, use, and biodegradation. In contrast, the technical cycle illustrates the lifecycle of products and services, emphasizing the need for recycling and disassembly. Industry 5.0 seeks to enhance these cycles' efficiency and sustainability by incorporating recycling and reuse processes, augmenting the CE. The primary challenge is that the recycling methods developed to date consume significant resources and energy, and can also generate pollution [51].

The circular economy model, illustrated by the biological and technical cycles in Fig. 2, is a central component of Industry 5.0 and CE highlighting the shift towards a system that is restorative and regenerative by design [43].

## 3 Materials and Methods

In assessing Industry 5.0 in the context of Circular Economy (CE) and eco-friendly strategies of nations, local authorities, and corporations, the taxonometric reference method and its variants are often employed [52, 53]. This method determines a synthetic variable based on normalized data inputs, known as the information capacity indicator method [54]. It involves selecting a set of explanatory variables from a matrix to maximize integral information capacity [54]. It selects a combination of explanatory variables from a matrix, aiming for the highest integral information capacity [55]. This technique enables the measurement and comparison of variables of different sizes and dimensions through data standardization. The goal is to compare the level of Industry 5.0 development on an international scale, especially in establishing a circular economy within the European Union [56]. The Eurostat-defined indicators and their respective units are outlined in Table 1, with variables in the calculations represented as x with a subscript ($x_i$), comprising a total of 12 variables.

For the calculations in this study, secondary data from 2019, collected by Eurostat [56], were utilized, ensuring data comparability and reliability. Each EU-28 country's raw source data are included in the appendices (Table A). The selection of the taxonomic method, specifically the zero unitarization method [57], was driven by the aim to develop an econometric model of the Industry 5.0 and CE relationships. Furthermore, using the standard method facilitates the verification of results when comparing countries with similar development profiles as described in the literature [44]. Due to the presence of variables in the independent feature set that cannot be directly aggregated, normalization formulas were employed. The zero unitarization method was chosen for standardizing the process based on the interval of a normalized variable [53]. Variables positively affecting the phenomenon are termed stimulants, while their counterparts are referred to as de-stimulants. Indicators were chosen for standardization based on specific formulas 1 and 2.

$$\text{for stimulants: } z_{ij} = \frac{x_{ij} - \min(x_{ij})_i}{\max(x_{ij})_i - min(x_{ij})_i} \tag{1}$$

$$\text{for de - stimulants: } z_{ij} = \frac{max(x_{ij})_i - x_{ij}}{\max(x_{ij})_i - min(x_{ij})_i} \tag{2}$$

where:

$z_{ij}$– is the normalized value of the *j*-th variable in the *i*-th country;
$x_{ij}$– is the initial value of the *j*-th variable in the *i*-th country.

**Table 1.** Circular economy indicators based on the Eurostat database

| Green Growth area | Measured characteristic | Symbol |
|---|---|---|
| Production and consumption | Generation of municipal waste per capita [kg/person] | $x_1$ |
| | Generation of waste excluding major mineral wastes per GDP unit [kg/thousand euro] | $x_2$ |
| | Generation of waste excluding major mineral wastes per domestic material consumption [%] | $x_3$ |
| Waste management | The recycling rate of municipal waste [%] | $x_4$ |
| | The recycling rate of all waste excluding major mineral waste [%] | $x_5$ |
| | The recycling rate of e-waste [%] | $x_6$ |
| | Recycling of biowaste [kg/person] | $x_7$ |
| | The recovery rate of construction and demolition waste [%] | $x_8$ |
| Secondary raw materials | Circular material use rate [%] | $x_9$ |
| | Trade in recyclable raw materials [tones $\cdot$ $10^{-3}$] | $x_{10}$ |
| Competitiveness and innovation | Private investments, jobs, and gross value added related to circular economy sectors [bn. Euro $10^{-3}$] | $x_{11}$ |
| | Patents related to recycling and secondary raw materials [number] | $x_{12}$ |

Source: Own study based on [56]

Diagnostic features, once normalized as described, assume values within the interval [0; 1]. Values closer to unity indicate a more favorable condition regarding the feature under investigation, while values nearer to zero suggest a less favorable situation. Subsequently, these normalized values form the foundation for calculating the median and standard deviation for each country analyzed. The median values are computed using a specific formula:

$$\text{for even number of observations}: \ Me_i = \frac{Z\left(\frac{m}{2}\right)_i + Z\left(\frac{m}{2}+1\right)_i}{2} \tag{3}$$

$$\text{for odd number of observations}: Me_i = Z\left(\frac{m}{2}+1\right)_i \tag{4}$$

where:

$z_{i(j)}$– is the $j$-th statistical ordinal for the vector $(Z_{i1}, Z_{i2}, \ldots, Z_{im})$, i = 1, 2, ..., n; j = 1,2, ..., m.In turn, the standard deviation was calculated according to the following equation:

$$S_{di} = \sqrt{\frac{1}{m}\sum_{j=1}^{m}(z_{ij} - \overline{z})} \tag{5}$$

Based on the median and standard deviation, an aggregate measure $w_i$ of the CE towards the Industry 5.0 was calculated for each country, based on:

$$w_i = M_{ei}(1 - S_{di});\ w_i < 1 \tag{6}$$

Values of the measure close to one signify a higher level of industrial greening in a specific EU member state, correlating with a higher ranking. The aggregate measure favors countries with higher median values of features that describe them and those with smaller variations in feature values, as indicated by standard deviation [58]. The chosen evaluation procedure for the CE enables a multidimensional comparative analysis [52], facilitating the comparison of EU member states and providing a basis for classifying them into uniform groups, as shown in Table 2.

**Table 2.** Green Growth Indicators aggregate measure comparative analysis

| Group | Mathematical characteristic | Meaning |
|---|---|---|
| I | $w_i \geq \overline{w} + S$ | high level |
| II | $\overline{w} + S > w_i \geq \overline{w}$ | medium-high level |
| III | $\overline{w} \geq w_i \geq \overline{w} - S$ | medium-low level |
| IV | $w_i < \overline{w} - S$ | low level |

Where $\overline{w}$ is the mean value of the synthetic measure; S is the standard deviation of the synthetic measure.

According to the $w_i$ values the EU countries were assigned to one of the groups concerning their level of evaluating the CE based on the technological progress.

The evaluation of the CE level in the 28 EU countries was conducted using 12 variables (Table 1), and the findings are presented in Table 3. The analysis identifies countries that demonstrate high-level CE toward the Industry 5.0, highlighting those with optimal conditions for sustainable development at the international level.

## 4 Model of the CE and Industry 5.0 Relationship

Monitoring the development level of the Circular Economy (CE) in the European Union is a crucial aspect of evaluating Industry 5.0. To this end, an econometric model depicting the relationship between Industry 5.0 and CE was proposed, utilizing secondary data

**Table 3.** Groups of the EU countries with a similar level of CE achieved

| Group | Countries |
|---|---|
| I | Finland, Denmark, Sweden, Germany, Austria, Estonia, Latvia, United Kingdom, |
| II | Luxembourg, The Netherlands, Lithuania, Belgium, France, Czechia, Slovakia, Slovenia, Ireland |
| III | Poland, Hungary, Malta, Cyprus, Italy, Spain, Portugal, Greece |
| IV | Romania, Bulgaria, Croatia |

Source: Authors' calculations

gathered by Eurostat in 2019. The model's variables were consistent with those used in the proposal. These determinants serve as fundamental tools for both diagnosing and observing the development of CE and Industry 5.0 across various socio-economic sectors. The model was developed using the regression method in the Statistica® software. The dependent variable chosen was the number of patents related to recycling and recyclable materials (x12, as indicated in Table 1). The selection of this particular variable is based on the significant influence of technology on environmental protection, which can be, among other metrics, gauged by the number of patents. This mathematical model primarily serves as a descriptive tool for the data.

The study covered 28 European Union countries due to 12 indicators as their features (Table 1). Raw data presented in Table A in the appendix section. The methods of regression and correlation were used to create the regression model. Correlation is the study of the strength of the relationship between variables, and regression determines the shape of this relationship. Eurostat found that circular economy indicators also correspond to the concept of the GE [56]. Moreover, there is a cause-and-effect relationship between the indicators, variables [52]. The study of the relationships between many independent variables ($x_1$-$x_{11}$) and one dependent variable ($x_{12}$) is called multiple regression.

Table 6 shows the results of the regression procedure for the variable number of patents related to recycling and secondary raw materials. The computer programme used the full number of countries (cases) under consideration $N = 28$. The basic measure of the theoretical and experimental curve fitting is the coefficient of determination $R^2 \approx 0.88$ (equal to the square of the correlation coefficient $R \approx 0.88$). The closer the absolute value $| R |$ is to 1, the correlation is stronger.

The table above shows that the number of patents ($x_{12}$) is influenced by the variables marked in bold ($x_{10}$). The highest computer level of significance of $p$ coefficients is shown by variable $x_{10}$, therefore this index was included in the linear equation (a value lower than 0.05 proves the significance of the coefficients and is marked by the Statistica® programme in bold). Corrected $R^2 \approx 0.5982$ is the coefficient of determination for small trials. $F(12.15) \approx 4.35$ is the value of the F statistic, while $p < 0.00044$ is the computer significance level for the F-test. The standard error of estimation $\approx 0.185$ denoted by the symbol $u_i$ in the equation, in form:

$$y_i = a_i x + a_0 + u_i \quad (7)$$

**Table 4.** Dependent Regression Summary - Number of Patents

| N = 28 | b* | Std. Err b* | b | Std. Err b | t(15) | p |
|---|---|---|---|---|---|---|
| Intercept | | | 9,85358 | 39,40932 | 0,25003 | 0,805955 |
| x1 | −0,02396 | 0,179326 | −0,00367 | 0,02745 | −0,13361 | 0,895489 |
| x2 | 0,83166 | 0,241834 | 0,13312 | 0,03871 | 3,43896 | 0,003654 |
| x3 | −1,15224 | 0,297816 | −3,34653 | 0,86497 | −3,86895 | 0,001514 |
| x4 | 0,33587 | 0,251141 | 0,36087 | 0,26983 | 1,33736 | 0,201032 |
| x5 | 0,21358 | 0,179599 | 0,19962 | 0,16786 | 1,18922 | 0,252838 |
| x6 | 0,02814 | 0,210937 | 0,06793 | 0,50921 | 0,13341 | 0,895644 |
| x7 | −0,22880 | 0,153723 | −0,32462 | 0,21810 | −1,48842 | 0,157362 |
| x8 | −0,30414 | 0,270217 | −0,13541 | 0,12031 | −1,12555 | 0,278043 |
| x9 | −0,07820 | 0,179469 | −0,12157 | 0,27901 | −0,43574 | 0,669233 |
| x10 | 0,82916 | 0,268304 | 2,86924 | 0,92845 | 3,09036 | **0,007463** |
| x11 | 0,44654 | 0,155048 | 0,00002 | 0,00001 | 2,88002 | 0,011449 |
| x12 | 0,43033 | 0,171987 | 0,00103 | 0,00041 | 2,50213 | 0,024403 |

Model details: R = 0,88137228; R^2 = 0,87681709; Corrected $R^2$ = 0,59827077; F(12,15) = 4,3508 p < 0,00044 Std Err. Estim.: 0,185.

**Table 5.** Summary of the statistics obtained results

| Statistic feature | Value |
|---|---|
| R multiple | 0,881372279 |
| MultipleR2 | 0,776817095 |
| CorrectedR2 | 0,59827077 |
| F(12,15) | 4,35078738 |
| *p* | 0,00044596 |
| Error std. Estimation | 0,18548170 |

The predicted values of the $x_{10}$ variable differ from the empirical values by an average of 0.185% (error standard estimation value). In Eq. 7, the coefficients $a_1$ and $a_0$ are listed in column b of Table 4, while column b* contains standardized regression coefficients. The relationship of the number of patents related to recycling and secondary raw materials ($x_{12}$) depends on $x_{10}$ - the share of recycled materials in the demand for raw materials. The regression equation has the form:

$$x_{12} = 0,553 \cdot x_{10} - 0,065 \pm 0,66349 \quad (8)$$

This means that the growing share of recycled materials means that the number of patents related to recycling and secondary raw materials is increasing by 0.553(%). This model explains about 60% of the variability in the number of patents (Table 5).

Then, the obtained results were verified using the Statistica® programme, in which a residual normality plot was prepared (Fig. 3) is the result of the verification procedure for the obtained regression model (Table 6).

**Table 6.** Summary of test values verifying the obtained equation

| Characteristics | Durbin-Watson | Serial correlation |
|---|---|---|
| Values | 1,642365 | 0,176710 |

Source: Authors calculations

In Table 6 values of Durbin-Watson and serial correlation, statistics prove that there is no residuals autocorrelation.

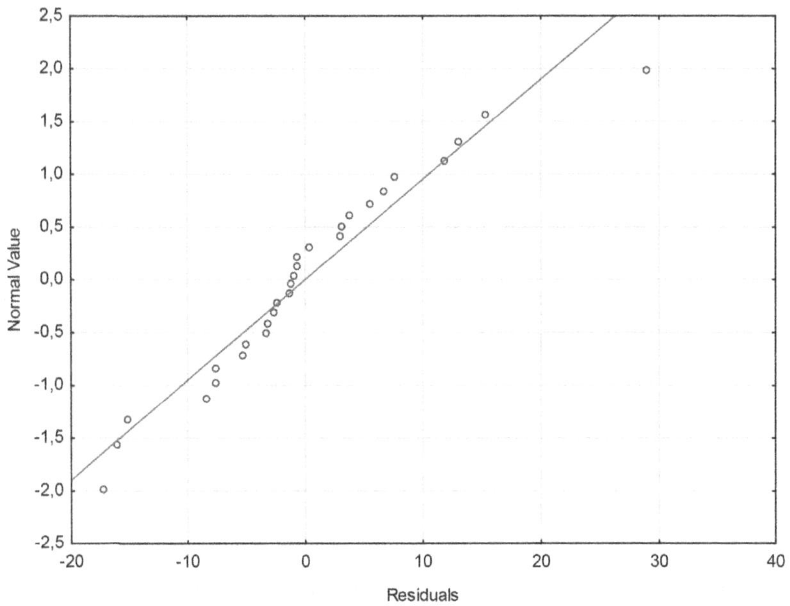


**Fig. 3.** Residual distribution normality plot. Source: own study results

The proposed econometric model of the Industry 5.0 and CE relationship is measured by the number of trade in recyclable raw materials. There also patents related to recycling and secondary raw materials assumes that the share of recycled materials in the demand for raw materials has the greatest impact on their quantity.

## 5 Conclusions

From the preceding discussion and findings, several conclusions can be drawn. First, integrating the Industry 5.0 with the CE is likely to foster SD and, consequently, an environmentally sustainable economy [59]. Second, the concept of Industry 5.0, widely applied in industry, research, and education, significantly influences our perception of the natural environment. More crucially, the changes instigated by the CE extend well beyond the industrial sector, influencing the entire economy [60]. These transformational processes are characterized by convergence, incorporating all the aforementioned concepts, and may be aptly termed the Industry 5.0.

Industrial civilization, and by extension the Industry 5.0, must be closely aligned with an CE geared towards. This connection is particularly prominent in the area of recycling and the patenting of secondary raw materials [61]. The models of biological and technical cycles exemplify this relationship.

The 21st century's most groundbreaking advancements are occurring not only due to technological innovation but also through the evolving concept of the CE. This specifically addresses the challenge of integrating environmental protection with economic development. This paper posits that the answer lies in the area of patents and the development of environmental technologies, which are driving changes in the labor market through eco-innovations and the emergence of green jobs [62].

Conversely, these premises pave the way for new research opportunities in green jobs [17] and eco-innovations [63], which often lead to patents. It is crucial to establish a clear connection between the labor market and the natural environment [64]. Furthermore, GM strives to reduce natural resource consumption, minimize waste, lower greenhouse gas emissions, and crucially, eradicate social inequalities. The increasing number of patents in recycling, the use of secondary raw materials, and the rising demand for ecological products and services exemplify the growing impact of the Industry 5.0 on CE. Accompanied by advancements in environmental technologies (Industry 5.0) the shift towards CE the is becoming more observable and measurable.

**Acknowledgments.** The article is financed by the National Science Centre in Poland under the programme "Business Ecosystem of the Environmental Goods and Services Sector in Poland" implemented in 2020–2022 project number 2019/33/N/HS4/02957 total funding amount 120 900,00 PLN.

The author expresses gratitude to dr. Hab. inż Małgorzata Rutkowska, from the Faculty of Management at Wrocław University of Science and Technology, for her valuable consultations and discussions related to this paper.

## Appendix

**Table A.** Indicators of the Green Industrial Revolution for individual European Union countries in 2019 - non-standardized values.

| Country symbol | $x_1$ | $x_2$ | $x_3$ | $x_4$ | $x_5$ | $x_6$ | $x_7$ | $x_8$ | $x_9$ | $x_{10}$ | $x_{11}$ | $x_{12}$ |
|---|---|---|---|---|---|---|---|---|---|---|---|---|
| BE | 412 | 97 | 26,1 | 53,5 | 78 | 81,5 | 33,8 | 80 | 95 | 18,3 | 289,5 | 2,8 |
| BG | 419 | 418 | 13,3 | 29,4 | 27 | 64,1 | 96,5 | 43 | 90 | 3,1 | 88,1 | 0,5 |
| CZ | 316 | 74 | 7,8 | 29,7 | 60 | 74,3 | 37,9 | 13 | 92 | 6,9 | 3,3 | : |
| DK | 781 | 35 | 7,2 | 45,6 | 61 | 73,9 | 43 | 138 | 90 | 8,4 | 116,3 | 2,3 |
| DE | 632 | 55 | 12 | 66,7 | : | 69,3 | 33,9 | 114 | : | 11,4 | 1621,2 | 28,6 |
| EE | 359 | 657 | 35,1 | 28,3 | 10 | 59 | 33,3 | 13 | 7 | 11,4 | 4,1 | : |
| IE | : | 35 | 8 | : | 41 | 67,5 | 46,1 | : | 96 | 1,9 | 40,2 | : |
| GR | 488 | 78 | 11,5 | 15,8 | : | 60,3 | 32,7 | 12 | 88 | 2 | 222,0 | 0,6 |
| ES | 456 | 62 | 17,2 | 30 | 46 | 68,4 | 35,6 | 53 | 79 | 7,5 | 2319,9 | 11,0 |
| FR | 516 | 46 | 13,4 | 40,7 | 54 | 65,5 | 32,2 | 93 | 71 | 18,7 | 643,5 | 21,3 |
| HR | 393 | 75 | 8,2 | 18 | 52 | 60,1 | 58,3 | 7 | 76 | 4,3 | 70,7 | 0,6 |
| IT | 486 | 69 | 22,5 | 44,3 | 68 | 66,8 | 32,1 | 86 | 98 | 16,6 | 683,9 | 17,8 |
| CY | 638 | 38 | 5,4 | 17,9 | 31 | 59,8 | 27 | 30 | 57 | 2,4 | 0,2 | 0,1 |
| LV | 404 | 97 | 9,1 | 28,7 | : | 53,9 | 23,1 | 24 | 98 | 5,4 | 29,2 | 0,2 |
| LT | 448 | 102 | 7,8 | 33,1 | 68 | 59,8 | 45,9 | 46 | 97 | 4,1 | 35,2 | 0,4 |
| LU | 607 | 32 | 11,4 | 47,4 | 64 | 67,9 | 42,5 | 111 | 100 | 9,6 | 23,5 | : |
| HU | 377 | 98 | 9,2 | 32,2 | 43 | 50,1 | 50,7 | 23 | 99 | 5,8 | 41,3 | 0,9 |
| MT | 606 | 63 | 9,3 | 6,7 | 43 | 37,1 | 13,1 | 0 | 100 | 7 | 0,1 | : |
| NE | 523 | 64 | 25,6 | 51,8 | 72 | 71,7 | 39,3 | 143 | 100 | 25,8 | 1049,9 | 5,2 |
| AT | 560 | 52 | 10 | 56,9 | 66 | 67,1 | 40,7 | 175 | 88 | 10,9 | 224,8 | 3,5 |
| PL | 286 | 183 | 11,8 | 32,5 | 56 | 57,6 | 33,1 | 17 | 91 | 11,6 | 236,0 | 4,7 |
| PT | 460 | 67 | 7,7 | 29,8 | 52 | 57,1 | 42,7 | 72 | 97 | 2,1 | 653,7 | 1,4 |
| RO | 247 | 140 | 4,7 | 13,2 | 30 | 55,9 | 22,5 | 18 | 85 | 1,7 | 27,1 | 1,1 |
| SL | 449 | 79 | 11,4 | 54,1 | 80 | 67 | 47,7 | 34 | 98 | 8,4 | 110,3 | 0,5 |
| SK | 329 | 100 | 11,8 | 14,9 | 44 | 64,3 | 40,3 | 24 | 54 | 5 | 9,0 | 0,6 |
| FL | 500 | 74 | 8,2 | 40,6 | 37 | 60,9 | 43,2 | 62 | 87 | 6,5 | 17,4 | 2,0 |
| SE | 451 | 50 | 9,2 | 47,5 | 49 | 71,8 | 51,6 | 70 | 61 | 6,8 | 674,3 | 4,1 |
| UK | 483 | 57 | 21,3 | 43,3 | 58 | 60,6 | 36,6 | 78 | 96 | 16,2 | 83,1 | 31,0 |

Source: own study based on secondary data [56].

Symbol: means no data. Country symbols by ISO 3166–1 alfa-2.

## References


1. Wiek, A., Iwaniec, D.: Quality criteria for visions and visioning in sustainability science. Sustain. Sci. **9**, 497–512 (2014). https://doi.org/10.1007/s11625-013-0208-6
2. Mercier-Laurent, E.: Climate change – can AI help understanding and more effective facing of various interrelated impacts? In: Gülgün Kayakutlu, M., Kayalica, Ö. (eds.) Decision Making Using AI in Energy and Sustainability: Methods and Models for Policy and Practice, pp. 3–19. Springer International Publishing, Cham (2023). https://doi.org/10.1007/978-3-031-38387-8_1
3. Koutsi, D., Stratigea, A.: Shipwrecks' underwater mysteries - identifying commonalities out of globally-distributed knowledge. Heritage **4**, 3949–3969 (2021). https://doi.org/10.3390/heritage4040217
4. Guéno, J.-P.: La Terre en héritage. Antoine de Saint Exupéry: Sauver la planète du Petit Prince (2011)
5. Matta, N., Carrillo, T.R., Mercier-Laurent, E., Boulanger, D.: Special issue: knowledge engineering and management applied to sustainability and innovation. Artif. Intell. Eng. Des. Anal. Manuf. AIEDAM. **33**, 114–116 (2019). https://doi.org/10.1017/S0890060419000167
6. Bird-David, N.: Us, relatives: Scaling and plural life in a forager world. University of California Press (2017)
7. Rani, S., et al.: Threats and corrective measures for IoT security with observance of cybercrime: a survey. Wirel. Commun. Mob. Comput. 2021 (2021). https://doi.org/10.1155/2021/5579148
8. Scapini, T., et al.: Future of biorefineries from a circular economy perspective. Nova Science Publishers, Inc. (2023)
9. Rutkowska, M., Sulich, A.: Green Jobs on the background of Industry 4.0. In: Procedia Computer Science (2020). https://doi.org/10.1016/j.procs.2020.09.132
10. Mercier-Laurent, E.: Knowledge management & risk management. In: Ganzha, M., Paprzycki, M., and Maciaszek, L. (eds.) Proceedings of the 2016 Federated Conference on Computer Science and Information Systems, FedCSIS 2016, pp. 1369–1373. Institute of Electrical and Electronics Engineers Inc. (2016). https://doi.org/10.15439/2016F555
11. Maj, J.: Organizational culture and leadership as facilitators of creativity and innovation: insights from the ICT sector in Poland in a post-COVID-19 reality. J. Econ. Manag. **45**, 182–215 (2023). https://doi.org/10.22367/jem.2023.45.09
12. Mercier-Laurent, E.: Artificial intelligence for successful kflow. IFIP Adv. Inf. Commun. Technol. **497**, 149–165 (2016). https://doi.org/10.1007/978-3-319-55970-4_9
13. Mercier-Laurent, E.: From data programming to intelligent knowledge processors: how computers can improve the global KM flow. Cut. IT J. **17**, 32–39 (2004)
14. Santos, C., Mehrsai, A., Barros, A.C., Araújo, M., Ares, E.: Towards Industry 4.0: an overview of European strategic roadmaps. Procedia Manuf. **13**, 972–979 (2017). https://doi.org/10.1016/j.promfg.2017.09.093
15. Philippopoulos-Mihalopoulos, A.: Absent environments: theorising environmental law and the city. Routledge-Cavendish Taylor & Francis Group (2007). https://doi.org/10.4324/9780203945308
16. Kozak, A.: Application of ICT in the co-production of social services. J. Econ. Manag. **45**, 441–467 (2023). https://doi.org/10.22367/jem.2023.45.17
17. Sulich, A., Zema, T.: Green jobs, a new measure of public management and sustainable development. Eur. J. Environ. Sci. **8**, 69–75 (2018). https://doi.org/10.14712/23361964.2018.10
18. Chaparro-Banegas, N., Mas-Tur, A., Roig-Tierno, N.: Driving research on eco-innovation systems: crossing the boundaries of innovation systems. Int. J. Innov. Stud. **7**, 218–229 (2023). https://doi.org/10.1016/j.ijis.2023.04.004

19. Chen, J., Yin, X., Mei, L.: Holistic innovation: an emerging innovation paradigm. Int. J. Innov. Stud. **2**, 1–13 (2018). https://doi.org/10.1016/j.ijis.2018.02.001
20. Andersson, A., Hatakka, M.: ICT4D and the sustainable development goals: a road well-traveled. Inf. Technol. Dev. **29**, 1–8 (2023). https://doi.org/10.1080/02681102.2023.2166279
21. Kayakutlu, G., Mercier-Laurent, E.: Intelligence in Energy. Elsevier (2016)
22. Przysucha, Ł.: Effective management of information processes with CMS in smart city. The concept of crowdsourcing. In: Mercier-Laurent, E. (ed.) Artificial Intelligence for Knowledge Management. 6th IFIP WG 12.6 International Workshop, AI4KM 2018 Held at IJCAI 2018 Stockholm, Sweden, July 15, 2018 Revised and Extended Selected Papers. pp. 65–76 (2020). https://doi.org/10.1007/978-3-030-52903-1_6
23. Mejía-Moncayo, C., Kenné, J.-P., Hof, L.A.: On the development of a smart architecture for a sustainable manufacturing-remanufacturing system: a literature review approach. Comput. Ind. Eng. 180 (2023). https://doi.org/10.1016/j.cie.2023.109282
24. Voulgaridis, K., Lagkas, T., Angelopoulos, C.M., Nikoletseas, S.E.: IoT and digital circular economy: principles, applications, and challenges. Comput. Netw. 219 (2022). https://doi.org/10.1016/j.comnet.2022.109456
25. Alshwayat, D., Elrehail, H., Shehadeh, E., Alsalhi, N., Shamout, M.D., Rehman, S.U.: An exploratory examination of the barriers to innovation and change as perceived by senior management. Int. J. Innov. Stud. **7**, 159–170 (2023). https://doi.org/10.1016/j.ijis.2022.12.005
26. Moller, D.P.F., Vakilzadian, H., Haas, R.E.: From Industry 4.0 towards Industry 5.0. In: IEEE International Conference on Electro Information Technology, pp. 61–68. IEEE Computer Society (2022). https://doi.org/10.1109/eIT53891.2022.9813831
27. Sulich, A., Sołoducho-Pelc, L.: The circular economy and the green jobs creation. Environ. Sci. Pollut. Res. **29**, 14231–14247 (2022). https://doi.org/10.1007/s11356-021-16562-y
28. Sulich, A., Sołoducho-Pelc, L.: Changes in energy sector strategies: a literature review. Energies **15**, 7068 (2022). https://doi.org/10.3390/en15197068
29. Kolk, A.: Environmental Issues and the MNE. Res. Glob. Strateg. Manag. **11**, 147–162 (2005). https://doi.org/10.1016/S1064-4857(05)11009-2
30. Duran, C.A., Fernandez-Campusano, C., Carrasco, R., Vargas, M., Navarrete, A.: Boosting the decision-making in smart ports by using blockchain. IEEE Access. **9**, 128055–128068 (2021). https://doi.org/10.1109/ACCESS.2021.3112899
31. Kozina, A., Zema, T., Sulich, A.: Between deep learning and alternative costs: bibliometric analysis. Procedia Comput. Sci. **207**, 1842–1849 (2022). https://doi.org/10.1016/j.procs.2022.09.242
32. Sulich, A., Sołoducho-Pelc, L., Ferasso, M.: Management styles and decision-making: pro-ecological strategy approach. Sustainable 13 (2021). https://doi.org/10.3390/su13041604
33. Macalik, J.: Alpha Wolves are local business leaders important for the region brand? Case study of Wroclaw agglomeration. Zesz. Nauk. Politech. Śląskiej. Organ. i Zarządzanie, pp. 457–467 (2023). https://doi.org/10.29119/1641-3466.2023.173.30
34. Bai, O., Wei, J., Yang, X., Chen, R.: (Rongxin): Third-party relational governance and collaborative innovation performance: the role of IPR protection. Int. J. Innov. Stud. **4**, 1–15 (2020). https://doi.org/10.1016/j.ijis.2020.02.002
35. Tang, Z., Zhang, X.: Public welfare crowdfunding decision-making of environmental non-profit organizations based on social responsibility. Environ. Sci. Pollut. Res. (2023). https://doi.org/10.1007/s11356-023-29114-3
36. Turner, C., Oyekan, J., Garn, W., Duggan, C., Abdou, K.: Industry 5.0 and the circular economy: utilizing LCA with intelligent products. Sustainable 14 (2022). https://doi.org/10.3390/su142214847

37. Dhayal, K.S., Giri, A.K., Kumar, A., Samadhiya, A., Agrawal, S., Agrawal, R.: Can green finance facilitate Industry 5.0 transition to achieve sustainability? A systematic review with future research directions. Environ. Sci. Pollut. Res. **30**, 102158–102180 (2023). https://doi.org/10.1007/s11356-023-29539-w
38. Mercier-Laurent, E.: What technology for efficient support of sustainable development? In: Paprzycki, M., Maciaszek, L., Ganzha, M., and Maciaszek, L. (eds.) Proceedings of the 2015 Federated Conference on Computer Science and Information Systems, FedCSIS 2015, pp. 1651–1654. Institute of Electrical and Electronics Engineers Inc. (2015). https://doi.org/10.15439/2015F010
39. Macalik, J., Sulich, A.: External employer branding of sustainable organizations. In: Skvarciany, V. (ed.) International Scientific Conference Contemporary Issues In Business, Management and Economics Engineering'2019, pp. 239–250. Vilnius Gediminas Technical University (2019). https://doi.org/10.3846/cibmee.2019.054
40. Grossi, G., Meijer, A., Sargiacomo, M.: A public management perspective on smart cities: 'Urban auditing' for management, governance and accountability. Public Manag. Rev. **22**, 633–647 (2020). https://doi.org/10.1080/14719037.2020.1733056
41. Sulich, A., Zema, T.: Green energy transition in Germany: a bibliometric study. Forum Sci. Oeconomia. **11**, 175–195 (2023). https://doi.org/10.23762/FSO_VOL11_NO2_9
42. Zylfijaj, K., Nikoloski, D.: The impact of access to finance and institutional barriers on SMEs' performance: difference between the formal and informal sector. Int. J. Entrep. Small Bus. **43**, 479–501 (2021). https://doi.org/10.1504/IJESB.2021.117343
43. Siakas, D., Lampropoulos, G., Rahanu, H., Georgiadou, E., Siakas, K.: Emerging Technologies Enabling the Transition Toward a Sustainable and Circular Economy: The 4R Sustainability Framework. Commun. Comput. Inf. Sci. 1891 CCIS, 166 – 181 (2023). https://doi.org/10.1007/978-3-031-42310-9_12
44. Atif, S.: Analysing the alignment between circular economy and industry 4.0 nexus with industry 5.0 era: an integrative systematic literature review. Sustain. Dev. 31, 2155–2175 (2023). https://doi.org/10.1002/sd.2542
45. Berglund, E.Z., et al.: Smart Infrastructure: a vision for the role of the civil engineering profession in smart cities. J. Infrastruct. Syst. 26, (2020). https://doi.org/10.1061/(ASCE)IS.1943-555X.0000549
46. Hadi, A., Cheung, F., Adjei, S., Dulaimi, A.: Evaluation of lean off-site construction literature through the lens of industry 4.0 and 5.0. J. Constr. Eng. Manag. 149, (2023). https://doi.org/10.1061/JCEMD4.COENG-13622
47. Ruiz-de-la-Torre-Acha, A., Guevara-Ramirez, W., Río-Belver, R.M., Borregan-Alvarado, J.: Industry 5.0. The road to sustainability. In: Borgianni, Y., Matt, D.T., Molinaro, M., Orzes, G. (eds.) Towards a Smart, Resilient and Sustainable Industry: Proceedings of the 2nd International Symposium on Industrial Engineering and Automation ISIEA 2023, pp. 247–257. Springer Nature Switzerland, Cham (2023). https://doi.org/10.1007/978-3-031-38274-1_21
48. Roblek, V., Thorpe, O., Bach, M.P., Jerman, A., Meško, M.: The fourth industrial revolution and the sustainability practices: a comparative automated content analysis approach of theory and practice. Sustainability **12**(20), 8497 (2020). https://doi.org/10.3390/su12208497
49. Macalik, J.: Start-Up leaders in the media – results of qualitative content analysis of online press news. In: Soliman, K.S. (ed.) Education Excellence and Innovation Management: A 2025 Vision to Sustain Economic Development during Global Challenges, pp. 6529–6537. International Business Information Management Association (IBIMA) (2020)
50. EPEA: The Cradle to Cradle design framework. https://epea.com/en/about-us/cradle-to-cradle#:~:text=Cradle to Cradle® describes,longer exist%2C only useful nutrients
51. Haddad, R., Mercier-Laurent, E.: Integrated system for students' evaluation using KM approach. IFIP Adv. Inf. Commun. Technol. 588 IFIP, 14 – 24 (2020). https://doi.org/10.1007/978-3-030-52903-1_2

52. Kasztelan, A., Sulich, A.: Green transformation of the polish economy. Emerald Group Publishing Ltd. (2023). https://doi.org/10.1108/978-1-83753-654-220231004
53. Molenaar, S., Schiphorst, L., Doyran, M., Salah, A.A., Dalpiaz, F., Brinkkemper, S.: Reference method for the development of domain action recognition classifiers: the case of medical consultations. Lect. Notes Bus. Inf. Process. 387 LNBIP, 375–391 (2020). https://doi.org/10.1007/978-3-030-49418-6_26
54. Malinowski, M., Smoluk-Sikorska, J.: Spatial relations between the standards of living and the financial capacity of polish district-level local government. Sustain. **12**, 1–27 (2020). https://doi.org/10.3390/su12051825
55. Sulich, A., Grudziński, A.: The analysis of strategy types of the renewable energy sector. In: Kapounek, S., and Vránová, H., (eds.) Enterprise and Competitive Environment: 22nd Annual International Conference, p. 59. Mendel University in Brno, Brno, Czech Republic (2019)
56. Eurostat: Tables on EU policy - Circular Economy. https://ec.europa.eu/eurostat/web/circular-economy/indicators/main-tables
57. Sulich, A., Rutkowska, M., Popławski, Ł: Green jobs, definitional issues, and the employment of young people: an analysis of three European Union Countries. J. Environ. Manag. **262**, 1–6 (2020). https://doi.org/10.1016/j.jenvman.2020.110314
58. Kasztelan, A.: Green competitiveness of the EU Countries. In: Kovářová, E., Melecký, L., Staníčková, M. (eds.) Proceedings of the 3rd International Conference on European Integration 2016, pp. 415–424. VŠB - Technical University of Ostrava, Ostrava (2016)
59. Trzaska, R., Sulich, A., Organa, M., Niemczyk, J., Jasiński, B.: Digitalization business strategies in energy sector: solving problems with uncertainty under industry 4.0 conditions. Energies. **14**, 1–21 (2021). https://doi.org/10.3390/en14237997
60. Kozar, ŁJ., Sulich, A.: Energy sector's green transformation towards sustainable development: a review and future directions. Sustainability. **15**, 11628 (2023). https://doi.org/10.3390/su151511628
61. Zema, T., Kozina, A., Sulich, A., Römer, I., Schieck, M.: Deep learning and forecasting in practice: an alternative costs case. Procedia Comput. Sci. **207**, 2958–2967 (2022). https://doi.org/10.1016/j.procs.2022.09.354
62. Kozar, ŁJ., Sulich, A.: Green jobs in the energy sector. Energies **16**, 3171 (2023). https://doi.org/10.3390/en16073171
63. Kozar, ŁJ., Matusiak, R., Paduszyńska, M., Sulich, A.: Green jobs in the EU renewable energy sector: quantile regression approach. Energies **15**, 6578 (2022). https://doi.org/10.3390/en15186578
64. Sołoducho-Pelc, L., Sulich, A.: Between sustainable and temporary competitive advantages in the unstable business environment. Sustainability. **12**, 1–16 (2020). https://doi.org/10.3390/su12218832

# Reduction of Carbon Dioxide Emissions of IT Hardware

Kamil Hudaszek[1(✉)], Iwona Chomiak-Orsa[1], and Saeed Abdullah M. AL-Dobai[2]

[1] Wroclaw University of Economics, Komandorska 118/120, Wroclaw, Poland
kamil.hudaszek95@gmail.com, iwona.chomiak@ue.wroc.pl

[2] Sana'a University, Sana'a, Yemen

**Abstract.** Every software needs hardware to be run on. Nowadays we encounter urgent need to mitigate the adverse effects of climate change. It prompted a paradigm shift towards the development of low carbon dioxide (CO2) emission hardware infrastructure. This scientific paper presents a thorough analysis of the current state of low CO2 emission hardware infrastructure, highlighting its significance in achieving sustainable and environmentally friendly technological advancements. The paper begins by highlighting the global greenhouse gas emissions and their significance in changing the climate. It emphasizes the crucial role of hardware infrastructure in this context, as the energy consumption and carbon footprint of data centers, communication networks, and other hardware-intensive systems continue to rise. Next, in the paper have been analyzed various strategies and technologies that have been developed to reduce CO2 emissions during computations. These include energy efficient designs, advanced cooling techniques, renewable energy integration, audits and controls, and optimization algorithms such modern AI tools. The advantages and limitations of each approach are discussed, with a focus on their potential for widespread adoption and scalability.

The paper concludes by outlining the future prospects and challenges associated with low CO2 emission hardware infrastructure. It emphasizes the need for continued research and innovation to overcome existing barriers and accelerate the adoption of environmentally friendly hardware systems on a global scale.

The research methods used in the article are literature analysis and analysis of commercial research reports.

**Keywords:** green computing · sustainability · climate change · AI

## 1 Introduction

The escalating issue of climate change and its profound consequences have propelled the need for sustainable practices across various industries. One sector that has garnered significant attention in recent years is the technology industry, particularly in terms of energy consumption and carbon emissions. Economic development based only on economic calculation and the criterion of profitability has led to the devastation of natural


Published by Springer Nature Switzerland AG 2024
E. Mercier-Laurent et al. (Eds.): AI4KMES 2023, IFIP AICT 693, pp. 237–251, 2024.
https://doi.org/10.1007/978-3-031-61069-1_17

resources and an imbalance in the biological balance of the entire planet [1]. This article focuses on the environmental impact and greenhouse gas emissions associated with different types of hardware architecture, specifically the comparison between in-house data centers and cloud computing infrastructure.

The continuous release of greenhouse gases into the atmosphere has resulted in a troubling rise in global temperatures, causing numerous adverse effects on our planet.

Amidst these risks, it becomes crucial to prioritize sustainability and energy efficiency across all sectors, including the technology industry. This article delves into the analysis of minimizing carbon emissions resulting from running algorithmic trading software, with a particular focus on the hardware aspect. IT systems consist of both software and hardware components, and optimizing both is essential for achieving energy efficiency.

The choice of hardware plays a vital role in carbon dioxide emissions. Innovative hardware solutions, such as energy-efficient processors, memory systems, and cooling mechanisms, contribute to a significant reduction in the carbon footprint of algorithmic trading software.

The analysis presented in this article aims to provide insights into how the selection and optimization of hardware components can contribute to minimizing carbon emissions in algorithmic trading software. By adopting energy-efficient hardware and incorporating sustainable practices throughout the software development lifecycle, the financial industry can play its part in mitigating climate change while meeting the demands of a rapidly evolving market [1].

Furthermore, this article highlights the efforts made by cloud service providers in their pursuit of sustainable practices. Cloud computing providers actively tailor hardware to specific requirements, focusing on providing leaner and more sustainable solutions. They optimize data center cooling systems to maintain temperatures at safe levels while ensuring energy efficiency. Regular energy audits and comprehensive control measures help monitor and optimize energy consumption.

The research methods used in the article are literature analysis and analysis of commercial research reports. In the first stage, a study of the scientific literature was performed. In the second stage, gray literature studies were analyzed, which included commercial reports and industry literature studies.

## 2 Theoretical Background

### 2.1 Sustainable Development

Global energy-related CO2 emissions grew by 0.9%, or 321 Mt, in 2022, reaching a new high of over 36.8 Gt. These emissions have significant consequences that could be irreversible for over 1000 years [2]. The continuous release of greenhouse gases into the atmosphere has led to an alarming rise in global temperatures. According to the Intergovernmental Panel on Climate Change (IPCC), human activities have already caused approximately 1.0 °C of global warming, contributing to the increasing frequency and intensity of extreme weather events worldwide [3, 4].

If the current rate of emissions continues unchecked, the projected rise in global temperatures could reach 1.5 °C between 2030 and 2052 [5]. This temperature increase would have profound impacts on our planet. Rising mean temperatures would not only affect land and ocean regions but also disrupt delicate ecosystems and ecological balance. The consequences would extend beyond temperature changes, leading to more frequent heatwaves and scorching temperatures in inhabited areas. Additionally, the altered climate patterns would result in increased heavy precipitation in some regions, leading to a higher risk of floods and water-related disasters. Conversely, other areas may experience prolonged periods of drought, further exacerbating water scarcity issues.

Moreover, the impacts of global warming go beyond immediate weather events. Rising sea levels, triggered by the melting of polar ice caps and thermal expansion of water, pose significant threats to coastal communities and low-lying regions. The resulting inundation can lead to the displacement of populations, loss of valuable habitats, and increased vulnerability to storm surges and coastal erosion. Furthermore, as the oceans absorb a significant portion of the excess CO2, they become more acidic, leading to adverse effects on marine ecosystems and marine life, including coral reefs, shellfish, and other sensitive organisms [6, 7].

Given these risks and the urgent need to address climate change, every decision and action taken now becomes critical. It is essential to prioritize sustainability and energy efficiency in all sectors, including the technology industry. In 2013 data centers were accountable for 1–2% of global electricity use [8–11]. In this paper, the author delves into the analysis of minimizing carbon emissions resulting from running algorithmic trading software. While software development plays a crucial role in energy efficiency, the focus of this study lies in the hardware aspect.

IT systems encompass both software and hardware components, and optimizing both is crucial for energy efficiency. One fundamental consideration is the choice of programming language for software development. Different programming languages have varying performance characteristics and task execution times, which directly impact energy consumption. For example, a web application that calculates Fibonacci's sequence written in Node.js demonstrates superior performance compared to one developed in Python. On average, generating 30 elements in the sequence took only 16.993 ms in Node.js, while the same task took 354.307 ms in Python, nearly 21 times longer [12]. The choice of programming language can significantly influence energy consumption and carbon emissions [13, 14].

While the choice of functions within a selected programming language also plays a role in energy efficiency, this paper primarily focuses on analyzing the choice of hardware and its implications on carbon dioxide emissions. As technology advances, hardware optimization becomes increasingly vital. This includes the design of energy-efficient processors, memory systems, and cooling mechanisms. By employing innovative hardware solutions, such as low-power processors, intelligent power management systems, and efficient cooling techniques, the carbon footprint of algorithmic trading software can be significantly reduced.

The analysis presented in this paper aims to provide insights into how the selection and optimization of hardware components can contribute to minimizing carbon emissions in algorithmic trading software. By adopting energy-efficient hardware, incorporating sustainable practices throughout the software development lifecycle and modern AI tools utilization, the financial industry can play its part in mitigating climate change while still meeting the demands of a rapidly evolving market. Where AI might be used not only for energy consumption management itself, but also by different tools and processes optimization.

## 3 Research Methodology

### 3.1 Research Tools

The considerations presented in the article were developed as a result of the use of such research tools as a review of scientific literature, analysis of industry reports, and analysis of reports on the sustainable development of major solution providers. The scope of application of the mentioned research tools was as follows:

- A classic literature review using the snowball method. Selected publications from google Scholar were analyzed. The authors used the following search criteria:

  - query:

    - "Data center energy consumption",
    - "Green data center",
    - "Data center cooling methods",
    - "Energy consumption, software optimization".

  - period: 2015–2023, publications with highest number of citations.

- secondary research analysis of industry reports – was to understand the potential solutions to use. Reports on ICT impact on the environment in English have been analyzed for period 2016–2023,
- secondary research analysis of reports on sustainable development – was to understand the reasons for the differences in the effects of applying individual solutions.

### 3.2 Research Procedure

The research procedure involves conducting literature research and analyzing selected industry studies enabling a comparison of available solutions and an indication of their impact on the environment. The steps of the procedure are presented in Fig. 1.

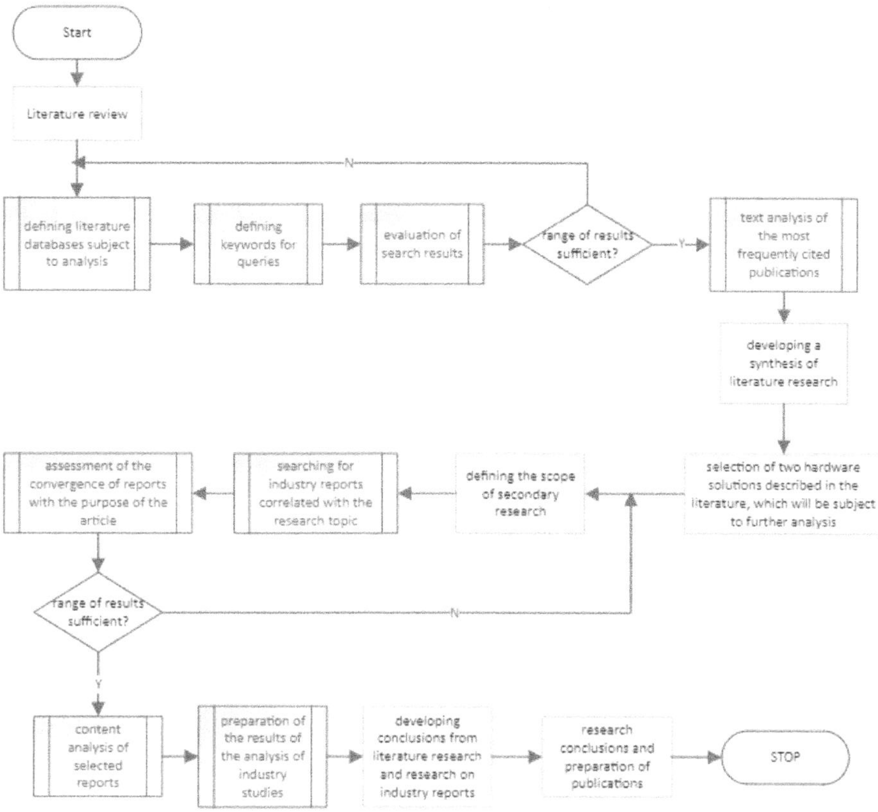


**Fig. 1.** The steps of the procedure. Source: own elaboration

# 4 Empirical Results and Discussion

## 4.1 Results

In this article, the author delves into a comprehensive comparison between two distinct types of hardware architecture:

- in-house data centers,
- cloud computing infrastructure.

The primary focus of this analysis lies in assessing the environmental impact and greenhouse gas emissions associated with these two approaches.

To shed light on the environmental implications, a study conducted by *451 Research*, an esteemed information technology research and advisory company, in 2019, scrutinized the reduction in greenhouse gas emissions achieved by transitioning from premises data centers to Amazon Web Services (AWS). The study encompassed 302 companies across 13 diverse industries, featuring annual revenues ranging from $10 million to $1 billion. Employing a carbon efficiency model, which integrated survey data, information from

Amazon Web Services, and third-party industry data, the research yielded noteworthy results, showcasing a remarkable 87.93% decrease in carbon emissions. These emissions reductions were attributed to several factors: around 61 percentage points resulted from the implementation of more efficient servers and enhanced server utilization, approximately 11 percentage points were linked to the employment of advanced and greener data center facilities, while an additional 17 percentage points stemmed from the reduced electricity consumption and the adoption of renewable energy sources. Consequently, the findings emphasized that Amazon Web Services demonstrated 2.5 times greater energy efficiency compared to the median performance of the analyzed American companies [15]. The remarkable efficiency can be primarily attributed to the optimal utilization of available resources and the adoption of cutting-edge server technologies. Furthermore, the research highlighted that the efficiency of data center facilities associated with cloud computing was 3.6 times higher due to the implementation of free cooling methods and the establishment of a leaner electrical infrastructure, which resulted in reduced power distribution losses. Notably, the research firm concluded that even if the analysis was confined to the top 10% most efficient companies, a significant reduction of 72% in carbon emissions would still be observed.

In addition to the aforementioned study, an insightful paper titled 'Cloud Libraries: A Novel Application of Cloud Computing' authored by Faiz Abidi and Hasan Jamal Abidi published a compelling comparison of carbon emissions derived from utilizing three Microsoft applications: Microsoft Exchange, Microsoft SharePoint, and Microsoft Dynamics CRM. The investigation revealed that the migration from on-premises solutions to Microsoft Cloud yielded an astounding reduction of up to 90% in carbon emissions [16]. To further solidify these findings, Microsoft published the 'Microsoft Cloud Carbon Studies,' which showcased energy efficiency improvements ranging from 22% to 93% upon migrating to their cloud platform. These energy savings extend beyond the ecological benefits, as they also translate into substantial financial advantages. According to the Carbon Disclosure Project, prominent US companies that embrace cloud computing have the potential to save an impressive $12.3 billion in energy costs and concurrently curtail $CO_2$ emissions by a staggering 85.7 million tons on an annual basis [17].

Supporting the case for cloud-based solutions, a research publication by the Lawrence Berkeley National Laboratory in 2014 unveiled a remarkable finding. The research suggested that the migration of every office worker in the United States to cloudbased solutions could potentially reduce hardware energy consumption by a remarkable 87%. This equates to an astounding 326 petajoules, which, at that time, would have been sufficient to power the bustling metropolis of Los Angeles.

Undoubtedly, the most notable disparity between on-premises solutions and cloud architecture lies in the primary operational focus of cloud service providers—their data centers. These data centers are meticulously designed and optimized to deliver unparalleled operational efficiency, maximize resource utilization, and minimize environmental impact. By prioritizing energy efficiency, employing advanced monitoring systems, and adhering to stringent modeling methods, cloud service providers constantly strive to develop and maintain sustainable solutions.

Cloud computing providers spend a significant amount of money on electricity. This is why they feel strong financial motivation to optimize such expenses. For instance, AWS designs chips by itself, they claim that their Elastic Compute Cloud (EC2) service that runs on AWS-designed Graviton 3 general-purpose processor uses up to 60% less energy than non-Graviton EC2 instances. Every provider actively tailors hardware to the specific requirements to provide leaner and more sustainable solutions.

We will delve into details of cooling technology and its optimization due to its significance from the energy consumption perspective. To achieve the highest safe level of hardware heat, while ensuring energy efficiency, data center operators employ advanced monitoring systems and modeling. Additionally, they conduct regular energy audits and implement comprehensive control measures to monitor and optimize energy consumption [18].

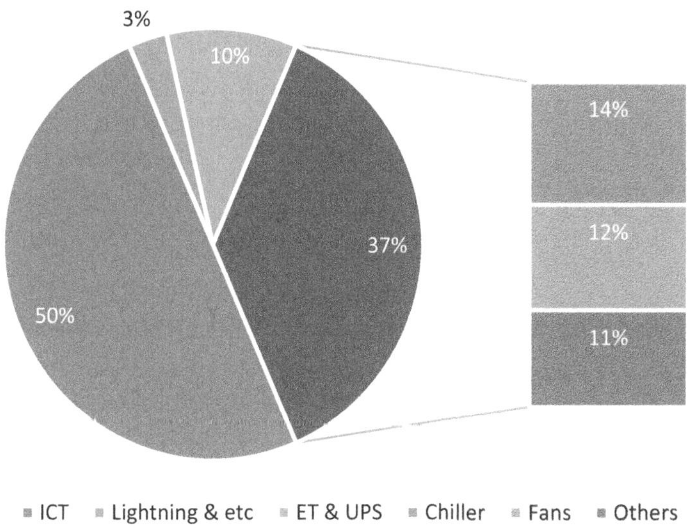


**Fig. 2.** The power consumption breakdown in data centers. *Source:* Q. Zhang, Z. Meng, X. Hong et al., A survey on data center cooling systems: Technology, power consumption modeling and control strategy optimization, Journal of Systems Architecture (2021)

The efficient removal of heat by the cooling system remains a significant challenge in the maintenance of data centers. In general, a standard cooling system consists of a Mechanical Refrigeration Sub-System (MRSS) and a Terminal Cooling Sub-System (TCSS). The MRSS, typically composed of equipment such as chillers, pumps, and cooling towers, provides a cold supply to handle the heat removed in the TCSS. It transfers heat from the indoor environment to the outdoor environment via the MRSS, with primary solutions being air-cooling, liquid-cooling, and free-cooling techniques. During the operation of a data center, the cooling system constitutes approximately 37% of the total power consumption. What is shown in Fig. 1, the primary power consumers in the cooling system are the fans of the computer room air conditioner (CRAC) and the chiller (Figs. 2 and 3).

To minimize power consumption, adaptive control strategies leveraging various algorithms have been suggested to adjust set-points based on real-time conditions such as workloads and operational temperatures. Two main paradigms for obtaining optimal control strategies are Model-Predictive Control (MPC), which relies on system dynamics modeling of cooling equipment, and reinforcement learning control (RLC), which analyzes system feedbacks for decision-making. Given the increasing workloads of data centers, research on the operation management of the cooling system should not only concentrate on the cooling techniques themselves but also take into account control strategies aligned with the characteristics of the scenarios and users.

The most common solution employed in extensive data centers is air-cooling technology. Its primary benefits include straightforward maintenance and reasonable operational costs [19].

**Table 1.** Air cooling summary

| Level | Subtype | Advantages | Main Challenges |
|---|---|---|---|
| Room level | Raised floor design | Easy for implentation and maintenance | Low heat dissipitation efficiency and air intermixing |
| Row level | Inter-row Cooling | Flexible distribution of cold air | Spatial confinement |
| | Overhead Cooling | Higher space utilization efficiency | High possibility of cold air bypass |
| Rack level | Internal Enclosure | Relativeley highest power density | High installation cost |

*Source:* Q. Zhang, Z. Meng, X. Hong et al., A survey on data center cooling systems: Technology, power consumption modeling and control strategy optimization, Journal of Systems Architecture (2021)

Depending on the equipment densities within data centers, the applications of air-cooling technology can be further categorized into various branches, each designed to enhance power consumption efficiency at specific cooling terminal levels. Among these branches, the most advanced implementation is chip-oriented cooling. Nevertheless, optimizations carried out within the rack, such as server-level or chip-level schemes, may not be feasible for certain data centers due to substantial increases in implementation and maintenance expenditures. Therefore, the methods outlined below include room-level, row-level, and rack-level air-cooling technology, with their respective advantages and challenges summarized in Table 1.

Air cooling stands out as the predominant method for cooling in data centers. Nonetheless, its efficiency is compromised due to the limited density and heat dissipation capabilities of air. Conversely, liquid cooling emerges as one of the most efficient methods, resulting in overall energy savings when compared to air-cooling systems. Depending on how the liquid coolant interacts with the heat source, liquid-cooling methods can be broadly categorized into indirect and direct liquid-cooling methods.

Analogous to air-cooling methods, discussions on liquid-cooling methods can revolve around the Mechanical Refrigeration Sub-System and Terminal Cooling Sub-System.

Indirect liquid-cooling involves a heat dissipation method where heat sources and liquid coolants come into contact indirectly. Instead of using air-cooling radiators, this process relies on evaporators or alternative liquid-cooling radiators. In typical representations of indirect liquid-cooling systems, there exists a coolant distributor. It facilitates a loop connecting the cooling source and the heat source. Essentially, liquid from an external cooling source enters the cooling distributor, travels to the heat sources, and then comes back before being expelled. Most often, the cooling factor is directed to processors with the highest heat dissipation, while the other heat sources utilize air-cooling.

From the sustainability perspective very interesting is free cooling technique. By utilizing a naturally occurring cold sources, free cooling has the potential to significantly decrease the overall energy consumption of data centers. As outlined in references, free cooling might be broadly categorized into air-side, waterside, and heat pipe-based systems. This classification aligns with the conventional technologies. To clearly outline optimization strategies, we categorize free cooling technologies into three key aspects: natural cold sources, cooling carriers, and heat transfer mechanisms.

Data centers utilizing free cooling systems are typically situated in areas where there is access to cold air or water. Beyond these direct sources of cold, various forms of energy, such as solar energy, waste heat generated by data centers, motion energy from seawater, and other heat sources, can be gathered to serve as a power supply for mechanical units like chillers, pumps, cooling towers with CRACs, and heat exchangers. Cooling carriers are substances designed for the direct exchange of heat with heat exchangers or the equipment within the data center. Natural cold resources may not directly engage in the heat transfer process with internal heat sources. For instance, certain water-side free cooling systems extract cold water from auxiliary air-cooled or cooling tower systems, which are employed to cool the water circulating to internal CRACs operating in economizer mode. Air cooling systems are integrated with dry coolers to facilitate direct heat exchange between chilled water from the data center and the surrounding cold air. Cooling carriers can be adaptably combined with various unstable natural cold sources to create unified cooling resources for efficient and indirect heat transfer schemes.

Depending on whether the cold sources physically interact with the internal heat sources of the data center, the heat transfer mechanisms can be categorized into direct and indirect classifications.

Direct air-side free cooling drains the cold fresh air source directly into the da-ta center through the air circulation system. The energy saving effect of this scheme depends directly on the short-term and real-time indoor and outdoor temperature difference, as well as the climate environment at the data center location. Contaminants or high humidity air can increase potential risks of equipment aging and damage. Therefore, higher requirements for environ-mental conditions lead to the restriction on the data center site choices and additional costs for dehumidification and filtration sub-systems.

By implementing indirect free cooling techniques and economizers, data center facilities are effectively protected from the unpredictable impact of environmental conditions. Heat exchangers now play a crucial role in managing the heat transfer process between internal and external heat sources. The influences and risks associated with extreme weather and polluted air are minimized, resulting in increased stability and an extended service life for IT systems.

In the context of air-side free cooling, wheel heat exchangers, like the Kyoto wheels system, achieve simultaneous heat and humidity exchange through rotating wheels. While heat wheels can deliver high cooling efficiency, their effectiveness relies on having an efficient and sufficient exchange surface to meet the cooling requirements for data centers. It's important to note that the physical exchange of heat and humidity on wheels may pose potential risks of internal air contamination (Tables 2, 3 and 4).

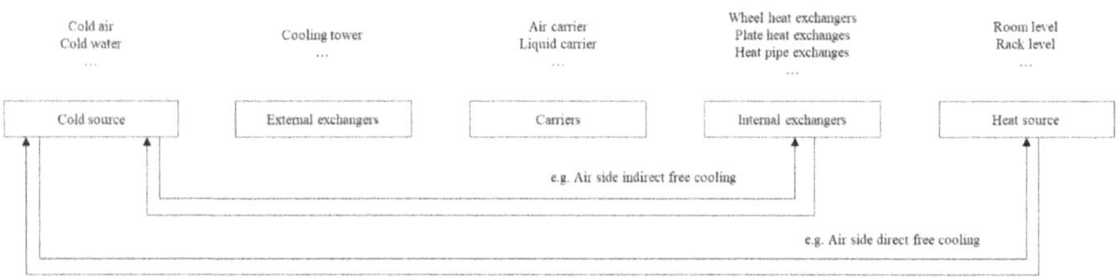


**Fig. 3.** Free Cooling Paradigm and Examples. *Source:* Q. Zhang, Z. Meng, X. Hong et al., A survey on data center cooling systems: Technology, power consumption modeling and control strategy optimization, Journal of Systems Architecture (2021)

Plate heat exchangers come into play when bypassing chillers becomes feasible due to the outside ambient temperature reaching predetermined thresholds. These exchangers effectively isolate outdoor and indoor air from each other, making them suitable for environments with polluted air. However, the deployment of plate heat exchangers is constrained by maintenance costs and operating temperature limits.

Evaporative free cooling systems employ direct or indirect evaporative strategies to transfer heat from hot air to condensate water. Particularly suitable for dry climates, they efficiently extend the operation periods of free cooling. The evaporation process's precision is challenging to model and control due to various factors, including ambient humidity and temperature, air flow velocity, humidity, and contact surface form. Consequently, unstable cooling performance can result.

Heat pipes, with competitive thermal conductivity, are well-suited for exploiting natural cold sources. Heat pipe-based free cooling systems are commonly categorized into three types: independent system, integrated system, and cold storage system. Temperature fluctuations during heat exchange with cold sources can impact heat pipe exchangers. Therefore, effective monitoring of the cooling effects of heat pipe-based economizers and auxiliary cooling systems is essential for maintaining stable cooling performance.

By utilizing natural cold sources and adapting measures to local conditions, free cooling technologies have the potential to significantly reduce energy consumption in data centers. However, challenges arise from the instability of environmental factors such as temperature and humidity changes, as well as air pollution. In summary, achieving both efficient heat transfer with natural cold sources and sustainable cooling performance under complex and volatile ambient conditions remains a top technical concern for free cooling technologies.

**Table 2.** Summary of Free Cooling Heat Transfer Mechanisms

| Mechanism | Subtype | Advantages | Main Challenges |
|---|---|---|---|
| Direct free cooling | - | Natural cold source comprehesively blend with internal heat source with low investment costs | Direct contact brings potential damages to facilities |
| Indirect free cooling | Wheel heat exchangers | Shield internal space from external unstable cold sources while keeping high heat transfer efficiency | High maintenance cost. Contamination on centralized wheels can lead to performance degradation |
| | Plate heat exchangers | Isolation from internal and external enviroment with scalable heat transfer capacity | Limited operating temperature and pressure use |
| | Evaporative heat exchangers | Isolation from internal and external enviroment and expansion on free cooling operating time | Relies on enviromental charactestic like temperature and humidity |
| | Heat pipe exchangers | High heat transfer efficiency without external disturbance | Backup and complementary cooling technologies and devices are needed for failures |

*Source:* Q. Zhang, Z. Meng, X. Hong et al., A survey on data center cooling systems: Technology, power consumption modeling and control strategy optimization, Journal of Systems Architecture (2021)

Besides innovative cooling systems, optimization methods also contribute in decreasing costs and carbon footprint of computing. Gartner analysts predict that the early adoption of AI will be a key factor separating data centers of the future from those destined to be dinosaurs of the past [20]. Power consumption modeling involves using measurable variables as inputs to estimate the power consumption of cooling equipment. As shown in Fig. 1, the chiller and the fans of the Computer Room Air Conditioner (CRAC) are the primary power consumers in the cooling system, and therefore, their power consumption models will be discussed here. Depending on the modeling method, power consumption models can be broadly categorized into mechanism-based methods and data-driven methods. Mechanism-based methods entail constructing explicit relations between the input variables and power consumption based on domain knowledge. This approach is more suitable for modeling relatively simple processes. In contrast, data-driven methods establish gray-box or black-box models, utilizing readily measurable environmental variables as inputs. These methods leverage historical data analysis to better capture the

**Table 3.** Practice for Adopting Different Cooling Strategies

| Technology | Advantage | Suitable Scenarios |
|---|---|---|
| Air cooling | Easy for maintanance and acceptable operation cost | Data centers with underfloor space and relatively low heat load |
| Liquid cooling | Higher efficiency on thermal conduction with enviromental impact | Liquid cooling should be utilized in scenarios with large heat load, where the air cooling cannot meet cooling demand |
| Free cooling | Lower overall energy consumption by leveraging natural cold sources | Data center is located where are ambient conditions, such temperature, humidity and air quality are appropriate and can produce sustainable cold sources for cooling |

*Source:* Q. Zhang, Z. Meng, X. Hong et al., A survey on data center cooling systems: Technology, power consumption modeling and control strategy optimization, Journal of Systems Architecture (2021)

**Table 4.** Summary of Power Modeling Methods and Optimization Methods for Cooling Equipment Operation

| Type | Methods | Advantages | Main Challenges |
|---|---|---|---|
| Power modelling method | Mechanism-based methods | Interpretable models based on priori knowledge | Hard to model complex operation process |
| | Data-driven methods | More powerful models that can handle complex process | Hard to solve the problems of overfitting and data paucity |
| Optimization Algorithm | Model Predictive Control | Achieve optimal step by step control actions through optimization methods under safe boundary conditions | Hard to model physical dynamics and computationally intensive |
| | Reinforcement Learning | More real-time and dynamic than traditional control models | Slow convergence and faults on early stages |
| | Deep Reinforcement Learning | More capable of extracting features with deep learning modules | Requirments of a large amount of operational data which is difficult to collect in real system |

*Source:* Q. Zhang, Z. Meng, X. Hong et al., A survey on data center cooling systems: Technology, power consumption modeling and control strategy optimization, Journal of Systems Architecture (2021)

complex nonlinear relations between inputs and the target, making them more powerful for handling sophisticated equipment such as the chiller.

Optimization and lowering energy consumption is definitely key point of data centers agenda during the way to become fully sustainable, but technological progress and further economy development make further overall energy consumption increase inevitable. This is why conventional energy sources replacement is a must. Efforts by major cloud service providers allow purchases of green power. Google Cloud Platform is already carbon neutral and plans to be carbon-free by 2030. AWS and Microsoft Azure aim to fully operate on renewable energy sources by 2025 [21, 22].

## 5 Conclusion

The considerations contained in the article result from the literature research conducted, which allowed the authors to formulate research questions. In order to verify them, the authors examined industry reports and business studies. IT systems design matters from the perspective of emitting greenhouse gases. Every architect should keep in mind the environmental cost of creating the system from the very beginning of the creation process to reduce emissions from computing and storage by optimizing both software and hardware.

The biggest cloud computing providers are in the corporate efficiency race which entails innovation and technology development. With surgical precision, they cut the energy consumption of data centers to lower their costs by creating their computer equipment tailored for specific needs and appropriately selected cooling techniques, optimized with modern AI tools. The study outlines the components of a standard cooling system, comprising the Mechanical Refrigeration Sub-System (MRSS) and the Terminal Cooling Sub-System (TCSS). Air-cooling technology, despite its prevalence in extensive data centers, faces challenges due to limited density and heat dissipation capabilities. In contrast, liquid cooling emerges as an efficient alternative, offering overall energy savings. The exploration of free cooling techniques, categorized into air-side, water-side, and heat pipe-based systems, underscores their potential to significantly reduce data center energy consumption. These techniques leverage natural cold sources, cooling carriers, and various heat transfer mechanisms. However, challenges arise from the unpredictability of environmental conditions, including temperature and humidity fluctuations and air pollution. Adaptive control strategies, such as Model-Predictive Control (MPC) and reinforcement learning control (RLC), are proposed to minimize power consumption by adjusting set-points based on real-time conditions. The research emphasizes that optimization efforts should not only focus on cooling techniques but also align with the specific characteristics of scenarios and users. The paper discusses the diverse applications of air-cooling technology based on equipment densities, with room-level, row-level, and rack-level implementations. It highlights the challenges associated with advanced optimizations like chip-oriented cooling at the rack level, considering potential increases in implementation and maintenance expenditures. Furthermore, the study delves into power consumption modeling, particularly for the primary power consumers - the chiller and fans of the Computer Room Air Conditioner (CRAC). Mechanism-based and data-driven methods are explored, emphasizing the importance of accurate modeling for efficient energy management. In essence, the research underscores the need for a holistic approach to cooling system optimization in data centers, considering not only the technological aspects but also control strategies, environmental conditions, and power consumption modeling. The findings contribute to the ongoing efforts to enhance the sustainability and efficiency of data center cooling systems amid increasing workloads and evolving technological landscapes. Additionally service providers due to the effect of scale, perform large green energy purchases.

## References

1. Chomiak-Orsa, I., Greńczuk, A., Łuczak, K., Piwoni-Krzeszowska, E.: AI in accelerating the creation of renewable energy sources. Bibliometric Analysis. Artif. Intell. ECAI 2023 Int. Workshops, Kraków (2023)
2. Goede, R.: Sustainable business intelligence systems: modelling for the future. Syst. Res. Behav. Sci. **20**(10), 685–695 (2021)
3. Solomona, S., Plattnerb, G.-K., Knuttic, R., Friedlingsteind, P.: Irreversible climate change due to carbon dioxide emissions. The National Academy of Sciences of the USA, pp. 1704–1709 (2009)
4. Peters, R.L.: Effects of global warming on forests. For. Ecol. Manage. **35**, 13–33 (1990)
5. Rosenthal, D.H., Gruenspecht, H.K., Moran, E.A.: Effects of global warming on energy use for space heating and cooling in the United States. J. IAEE's Energy Econ. Educ. Found. **16**, 77–96 (1995)
6. Taalas, P., Msuya, J.: Global Warming of 1.5°C, Intergovernmental panel on climate change. Office for Climate Education (2019)
7. Adla, K., Dejan, K., Neira, D., Dragana, Š.: Integrated approach to 21st century challenges to health. One Health, 281–327 (2022)
8. Feagin, R.A., Sherman, D.J., Grant, W.E.: Coastal erosion, global sea-level rise, and the loss of sand dune plant habitats. Front. Ecol. Environ. **3**(7), 359–364 (2005)
9. Masanet, E., et al.: The energy efficiency potential of cloud-based software. A U.S. Case Study, p. 1 (2013)
10. Shehabi, A., et al.: United States Data Center Energy Usage Report. Ernest Orlando Lawrence Berkley National Laboratory (2016)
11. Steve, E.: Environmentally Sustainable ICT: a critical topic for is research?. In: PACIS 2007 Proceedings (2007)
12. Steve, E., Binney, D.: Environmentally Sustainable ICT: developing corporate capabilities and an industry-relevant is re-search agenda. In: PACIS 2008 Proceedings (2008)
13. Lei, K., Ma, Y., Tan, Z.: Performance comparison and evaluation of web development technologies in PHP, Python and Node.js. In: IEEE 17th International Conference on Computational Science and Engineering (2014)
14. Pereira, R., et al.: Ranking programming languages by energy efficiency. Sci. Comput. Programm. 205 (2021)
15. Ahmad, T., Chen, H., Shah, W.A.: Effective bulk energy consumption control and management for power utilities using artificial intelligence techniques under conventional and renewable energy resources. Int. J. Electrical Power Energy Syst., 109 (2019)
16. Bizo, D.: The carbon reduction opportunity of moving to amazon web services. Research 451 (2019)
17. Abidi, F., Abidi, H.J.: Cloud Libraries: a novel application of cloud computing. Int. J. Cloud Comput. Serv. Sci. **1**, 79–83 (2012)
18. International Energy Agency, CO2 Emissions in 2022, International Energy Agency (2022)

19. Farooqi, A.M.: Comparative analysis of green cloud computing. Int. J. Adv. Res. Comput. Sci. 8 (2017)
20. Zhang, Q., et al.: A survey on data center cooling systems: technology, power consumption modeling and control strategy optimization. J. Syst. Archit. (2021)
21. Siemens, How Artificial Intelligence is Cooling Data Center Operations (2021)
22. Microsoft, The carbon benefits of cloud computing, A study on the Microsoft Cloud in partnership with WSP, Microsoft (2020)
23. Cloud Google. https://www.cloud.google.com/sustainability

# Author Index





Published by Springer Nature Switzerland AG 2024
E. Mercier-Laurent et al. (Eds.): AI4KMES 2023, IFIP AICT 693, pp. 253–254, 2024.
https://doi.org/10.1007/978-3-031-61069-1

The manufacturer's authorised representative in the EU is Springer Nature Customer Service Centre GmbH, Europaplatz 3, 69115 Heidelberg, Germany. If you have any concerns regarding our products, please contact ProductSafety@springernature.com

Printed and bound by CPI Group (UK) Ltd, Croydon, CR0 4YY
30/09/2026
02225494-0013